In Township Tonight!

South Africa's Black City Music and Theatre

David Coplan

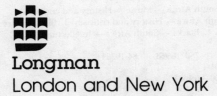

Longman
London and New York

Longman Group Limited
Longman House,
Burnt Mill, Harlow, Essex, UK
and associated companies, branches and representatives
throughout the World.
Published in the United States of America
by Longman Inc., New York.

First published 1985

Produced by Longman Group (FE) Ltd
Printed in Hong Kong

British Library Cataloguing in Publication Data

Coplan, David
    In township tonight!: South Africa's black city music and theatre.
    1. Blacks in the performing arts — South Africa
    790.2'092'2   PN1590.B53

    ISBN 0-582-64401-1
    ISBN 0-582-64400-3 Pbk

Library of Congress Cataloging in Publication Data

Coplan, David B. (David Bellin)
    In township tonight!

    Includes index.
    1. Blacks — South Africa — Music — History and criticism.
2. Music — South Africa — History and criticism. 3. Black theatre
— South Africa. 4. Blacks — South Africa — Intellectual life. I.
Title.
ML350.C6 1982   780'.89968   84-19385
ISBN 0-582-64401-1
ISBN 0-582-64400-3 (pbk.)

To my *abafundisi*: Alan P. Merriam

David K. Rycroft

Wilson 'Kingforce' Silgee

Acknowledgements

MY gratitude goes first, among the many who have given assistance and encouragement, to my teacher, adviser, and friend, Professor Alan P. Merriam, who died in a tragic plane crash on 14 March 1980. I wish to express my appreciation also to my friends and co-sponsors at the International Library of African Music in Grahamstown, South Africa, Gei Zantzinger and Andrew Tracy, for their unfailing support in difficult circumstances. David Rycroft of the School of Oriental and African Studies, University of London, offered great inspiration and made many useful comments; and Timothy Couzens, Charles van Onselen, and Jonathan Clegg of the University of Witwatersrand encouraged and guided me in the field. I owe an equal debt to my research assistants, Wilson 'King Force' Silgee, and Eugene Skeef, the importance of whose faith in me and belief in my work matched that of their untiring attention to the tasks at hand. My appreciation also extends to all my friends and informants in Southern Africa and in exile abroad whose world I have tried to interpret faithfully here. Finally, I would like to thank Thayer Warshaw for his editorial comments on the manuscript, and Elizabeth Getliffe, librarian during 1976–7 at Johannesburg's Africana Library, a helper and a special friend.

The Publishers are grateful to the following for providing photographs:

Africana Museum, Johannesburg for plate nos 7, 8, 9, 10, 27 and 39; Barnaby's Picture Library for nos 1, 3 and 4; Camera Press for no. 28; David Coplan for nos 11, 12, 13, 14, 15, 16, 17, 18, 19, 20, 21, 22, 24, 25, 30, 33, 34 and 38; Jak Kilby for nos 36 and 37; Popperfoto for nos 5, 6 and 26; David Redfern for nos 36 and 35; South African Museum for no. 2; Val Wilmer/Format for no. 31; Val Wilmer/Louis Moholo for no. 23.

The Publishers would also like to thank The Morija Sesuto Book Depot, Lesotho for permission to reproduce 'Meloli le Lithallere tsa Africa (U ea Kae)' by J. P. Mohapeloa and 'Chabana sa Khomo' and The Lovedale Press for 'Si lu Sapo or i Land Act' and 'Influenza (1918)' both by R. T. Caluza but regret that they have been unable to contact the copyright holders of 'Lion Killer' by Aaron Jake Lerole and would be most grateful for any information enabling them to do so.

The cover photograph of Dudu Pukwana was provided by Val Wilmer/Format.

Contents

A note on terminology

VERNACULAR, colloquial, official and analytical terms play a major role in this study, and must be carefully defined. The first group of terms includes labels for sociocultural categories and 'population groups', as they are known in South Africa. Such terms have no necessary objective value. They are used here as they are used, with some variation, by South Africans of all categories themselves. 'African', for example, refers only to native speakers of Bantu languages who are of reputedly complete African Negro ancestry. There is, then, no such thing as an African of European, Asian, or Eurafrican ancestry. Racially based, negative terms such as 'Native', 'Bantu', and 'Kaffir' are never used to refer to Africans descriptively, but appear only in quotations and historical context. 'Khoisan' refers to indigenes of so-called 'Hottentot' (Khoi-khoi) and 'Bushman' (San) origins. The term 'Coloured' (so-called) refers to persons of mixed ancestry.

The South African Malay, descendants of East Indian and Malabari slaves imported during the seventeenth and eighteenth centuries by the Dutch East India Company, constitute a separate Islamic East Indian segment within the Coloured community. The term 'Malay' refers only to them, while so-called 'Coloured' may refer to any person of mixed racial heritage. 'Black' indicates a person or thing either African or Coloured viewed as a single category. This is the common black usage of the term in South Africa, as opposed to the official white terminology, which prefers to use black as a synonym for African and never for Coloured. 'Other than European' (colloquially, 'Non-European') refers to South Africans who are not of complete European ancestry. 'White' indicates persons of exclusive European ancestry. The term 'European', a synonym for white in South African usage, appears only rarely to avoid confusion between South African whites and present or past natives of Europe.

A second set of terms is employed in the analysis of African society, and they refer to levels of socio-economic status and quality of urbanisation. Thus the 'elite' are the highest African urban social stratum, specifically those who were entitled to carry an exemption certificate instead of an ordinary pass before the 1950s. Elite Africans are in general those educated at mission schools and employed in the professions and other skilled occupations. Since no urban African group could conceivably be labelled 'upper-class', 'elite' is used interchangeably with 'middle-class' and 'petty bourgeois', terms corresponding to the values, education, and occupations they may share with white middle-class counterparts.

'Working-class' designates unskilled or semi-skilled persons or spouses of persons ordinarily employed within the formal, white-controlled economic sector. 'Lower-class', as distinct from 'working-class', refers to members of the lowest economic and social stratum of black society, who may be unemployed or occupied in the non-official, informal sectors of the economy, and whose urban status is not recognized by white authorities. 'Proletarian' refers to those who have lost access to land, livestock, capital, or other material means of production, and are compelled to make a living either by selling their labour in the commercial economy, providing services to those who do, or by forms of parasitism such as crime. Hence this term includes working-class and lower-class people taken together. 'Migrant' applies first of all to persons leaving rural areas to work in industrial areas. In a more specific sense it refers to urban workers who return after a period, or habitually, to homes in the countryside.

A third group of terms aids in the analysis of cultural products and processes. They function primarily in the classification of performance styles and patterns of development, and their applications may overlap. 'Urban music', for example, includes any style developed in a city and in response to urban residence, being *of* the city and not merely *in* it. 'Traditional', an appallingly imprecise but nonetheless indispensable term, refers to performances, held anywhere, of forms created in a rural area with no perceptible Western influence; or on occasion to forms perceived (by members of the culture) as entirely indigenous. 'Neo-traditional' music is traditional in idiom and style but transformed by urban context or by changes in performance rules and occasions, or performed on Western instruments. 'Syncretic' is the acculturative blending of performance materials and practices from two or more cultural traditions, producing qualitatively new forms. 'Modern' refers to syncretic styles of the twentieth century.

A fourth and final class encompasses vernacular and colloquial terms from South African languages, including Zulu, Xhosa, Sotho, Tswana, Afrikaans, and English. Examples include words used by virtually all South Africans, such as 'shebeen' (Gaelic: 'little shop') meaning an illegal liquor bar in a private residence, as well as terms confined to one language group only, such as *maskanda* (Afrikaans: 'musikant') a Zulu term for neo-traditional African music played on Western instruments. Many of these terms are given brief definition in the text, and for reference there is a glossary on page 264.

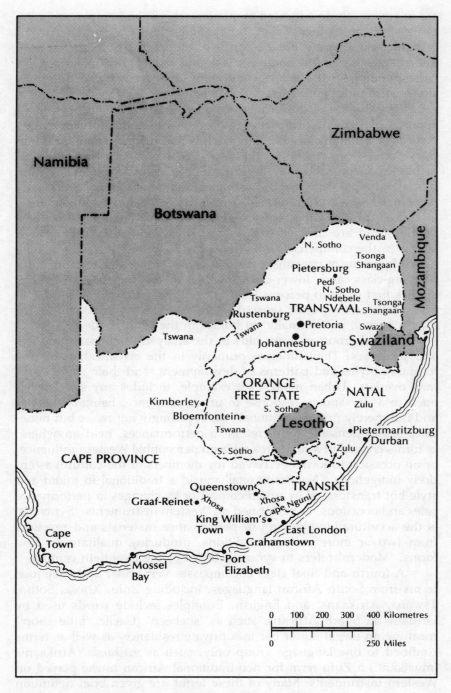

South Africa: provinces, major cities and ethnic groups

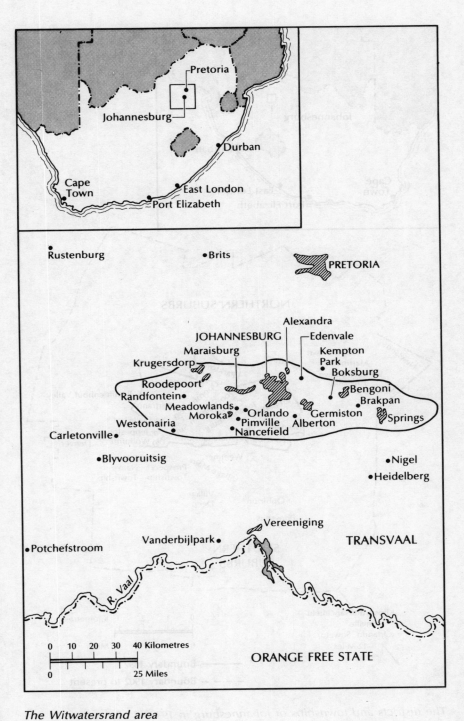

The Witwatersrand area

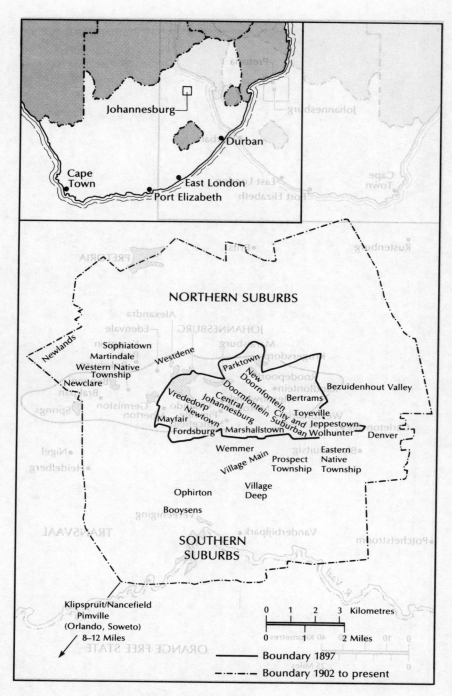

NORTHERN SUBURBS

Newlands

Sophiatown
Martindale
Western Native
Township
Newclare

Westdene

Parktown
New
Doornfontein
Doornfontein
Vrededorp Central
Johannesburg
Newtown
Mayfair
Fordsburg Marshallstown

Bertrams

Bezuidenhout Valley

Toyeville
City and Jeppestown
Suburban Wolhunter
Denver

Wemmer
Village Main

Prospect
Township

Eastern
Native
Township

Ophirton

Village
Deep

Booysens

SOUTHERN
SUBURBS

Klipspruit/Nancefield
Pimville
(Orlando, Soweto)
8–12 Miles

| 0 | 1 | 2 | 3 | Kilometres |

0   2 Miles

—————— Boundary 1897

— · — · — Boundary 1902 to present

The districts and townships of Johannesburg in 1930

Johannesburg

Durban

Cape
Town

East London

Port Elizabeth

1 Introduction

IN the context of an increasingly violent social conflict in South Africa, readers may well question the appropriateness of an account of African performing arts and artists in the cities of that country. Weighed against *apartheid*, the contribution of musicians, composers, dancers, dramatists, comedians, actors, and impresarios to the quality of life in the black community may appear trivial, if not in fact a diversion of energy from the central task of self-liberation. Two years of living in the homes, churches, schools, taverns, mine compounds, servants' quarters, concert halls, recording studios, and streets of black South Africa, and in Botswana, Lesotho, and London, however, convinced me that performing artists have given the struggle for black self-determination an indispensable cultural vitality. Since the time of clergymen-composers Tiyo Soga and John Knox Bokwe more than a century ago, black nationalists have combined political, spiritual, and cultural leadership, and recognised the importance of this aspect of black identity. This book, then, is both a record of and a small contribution to the efforts of black South Africans to gain control of their national culture and to use it to regain control of their individual and national lives.

My own involvement with South Africa began in 1975, when I undertook a short survey of black performance activity in Johannesburg at the request of Gei Zantzinger and Andrew Tracey of the International Library of African Music. I spent my time among musicians, talent scouts, producers, theatrical directors and actors, journalists, managers, social workers, educators, *shebeen* (tavern) patrons, students, and eccentric hangers-on like myself. Trying to assemble the outlines of stylistic interconnection and variety, I found myself drawn deeper into the complex world humming beneath the surface of the

1

everyday recreations of urban Africans. Perhaps the only significant result of this first experience was a commitment to comprehend some of its richness through further study. A thorough exploration would not only provide a record of the culture history of black South Africans and inform the world outside of the dimensions of their achievements. It would also increase the understanding of black social experience and class formation; how and why they came to the cities, and how they created new institutions, communities, and cultural forms in the struggle for urban survival.

The achievements of urban Africans must be viewed, of course, in relation to the obstacles they have faced. Culture is not simply a broadly shared system of knowledge and its products. It is also the voice of a community, and urban black South Africans were eager, like people elsewhere, to have their voices heard. An oppressed people, they wanted their complex humanity acknowledged, their hard-won successes admired, their failings understood. Their active contribution to this work, which went far beyond mere cooperation, carried with it the responsibility to tell their story as faithfully and perceptively as possible.

When I returned to Johannesburg on 17 June 1976, its African ghettoes of Soweto (Southwest Townships) had exploded in rage and fire. Violent political protests that eventually claimed hundreds of lives in townships throughout South Africa had broken out, immediately over an issue of cultural autonomy: the resistance of schoolchildren to instruction in Afrikaans, the parochial language of the oppressor. Regular visits to the townships were difficult, and all outdoor gatherings there, including performance events, were temporarily forbidden. Despite these obtacles, I was reluctant to abandon my project or to leave South Africa at such a time. African friends argued that going home would be both wasteful and cowardly: things, they said, were just getting interesting.

For the next year I moved about Johannesburg and other cities, observing and participating in performances and other family and community events, attending rehearsals, recording sessions, plays, clubs, and concerts, interviewing past and present members of the performance community, digging into archival materials in four languages with the help of my research associates; trying to place contemporary black performance culture in the context of the historical processes and social forces that had shaped it. My collection of hundreds of commercial, library, and field recordings representing musical styles from the 1930s to the present was of enormous value, particularly when interpreted by Africans or compared with each other and with live performances. My field recordings included not only current urban music but also historical styles recreated by older musicians. They also contained stylistic transformations so popular among performers in the rural areas where older styles have remained alive.

Involvement in performance occasions helped me to understand the application of cultural principles of performance and composition. My appearances as a percussionist with Malombo, an internationally travelled and respected musical group from Pretoria, gave me invaluable insight into relationships among performers, other participants, audiences, and performances. Together they composed the social world that is the immediate arena of artistic development.

Broadly, this narrative is about black experience over the course of South African industrialization, cultural change in a racial caste system, and how the forms and processes of change have been embodied in performance culture. I have tried to integrate external and internal factors guiding performance creativity, and to treat the interrelationship of social and cultural forces in a manner both empirical and humanistic. Studies of popular culture provide an important means of understanding the experience, attitudes, and reactions of the mass of otherwise inarticulate people, those who vitally affect the course of urban development but who do not read or write about it.[1] So this book provides a unique perspective on cultural patterns associated with the changing forms of a particular community.[2] Moreover it tells a story of resistance and achievement that is inherently worth recounting.

The study of Africa's urban art forms is certainly in its infancy, though in South Africa their beginnings can be traced back more than three centuries. Lack of interest in these forms may be explained by the widespread perception that they are not authentically African, but rather the diluted, bastardised, commercial stepchildren of Western cultural colonisation. This perception is mistaken on two counts. First, much of the Western popular music so influential in Africa has grown luxuriantly in the Americas from African roots. Among urban black South Africans, the sustained appeal of black American performance styles derives also from the comparable experience of the two peoples under white domination. Hence it follows that modern urban forms are African because Africans have chosen to play them. They have composed and selected performance materials from diverse sources to express, celebrate, and comment upon their experience, needs, and aspirations in a world of insecurity and change.

Urban performing arts therefore represent not the disintegration but the creation of a culture: part of a search for autonomy in an environment in which black people have little control over anything except a culturally guided sense of collective humanity and individual self. Performance expression, like other cultural forms, does not derive solely from the minds of creative individuals. It emerges as an aspect of social action and resonates with emotion and meaning

3

among members of communities in the context of social institutions. If black South Africans have retained some vitality and autonomy in their culture, it is only because in their segregated neighbourhoods they have managed to build new structures for social order and survival. Careful attention must then be given to the role performing arts have played in urban black social dynamics as well as culture change, and the effects of this involvement on performance itself. The impossibility of separating performance from social action helps in understanding how successive forms of expression arise out of South African history.

The concept of style gives material reality to the structure of this process. So the exploration of the role of performing arts in cultural identity centres on the organisation of expressive features into styles, labelled and recognised by their participants. The style of a performance is itself an index of meaning, established collectively over time by artists and their audiences.[3] As a category of performance, a style represents a distinctive system of meaningful forms or method of treating characteristic elements, organised around the expressive purposes and outlook of its practitioners. Dance scholar Anya Royce has defined style simply as 'the whole complex of features that people rely on to mark their identity . . . . composed of symbols, forms, and underlying value orientations'.[4] A given performance need not fall within just one stylistic category; nor do practitioners necessarily agree on the elements that belong to a style, or to which performance a particular stylistic label applies. Styles provide a foundation, a vocabulary of forms, activities, and occasions which constitute and express social and cultural processes. Participants may apply a range of meanings to stylistic metaphors, yet there is a core of association and feeling that unites form and meaning in a shared identity. This unity in variation promotes cultural patterning and social organisation in developing urban communities. People attracted to specific performances need agree only on the appropriateness of the action, not on its meaning.[5]

The social history of urban black performing arts is therefore an account of the development and relationships of styles. The phrase 'performing arts' may in turn require explanation. I use it because it best reflects the nature of black expression in South Africa, which cannot be divided realistically into Western categories of music, dance, or drama. These categories are not only foreign to Africa: they fail to recognise the close integration of song, lyric, tone, rhythm, movement, rhetoric, and drama in African performance. I use the term 'performance culture' as well, to represent a crucial conjunction between performance and everything that immediately supports it – a social crossroads of performers, participants, styles, categories, materials, and occasions of performance. What we are looking at is

4

a whole complex of different resources, experiences, motivations, and actions belonging to the full range of people involved in performance.

This book is organised both by social class and history, because modern developments in black performing arts are directly related to the long-term process of class formation in South Africa. As historical conflicts and communities of interest emerged and changed the relationships and destinies of people, performance culture became an instrument of identity, competition, and self-transformation. The contact and unequal assimilation of various groups into South Africa's colonial political economy is therefore a powerful and unavoidable underlying theme. In Chapter 2 we first explore the roots of a distinctively South African performance culture in the early relations of Europeans, slaves, and Khoisan peoples in the Western Cape. Rapidly, however, we trek to nineteenth century Kimberley, where Africans were exposed to performance traditions from all over the subcontinent and the world beyond. Some brought their rural culture to life in the diamond camps. Others, mission school-educated, became a black elite and adopted European and Afro-American culture to their social needs. A third group of people, a proletarian majority among the permanent black townsmen, lived by their wits in the shadows and shanties of the mushrooming locations, creating hybrid styles of cultural survival that permanently shaped black music and drama.

Kimberley set the pattern for black city culture and social life as well, and in Chapter 3 we see the dramatic development of these patterns in the industrial and human explosion that was early Johannesburg. There the creation of new communities was both helped by and reflected in the emergence of new performance styles. Professional black performers, itinerant artistic entrepreneurs of the mining camps, shantytowns, and railway depots of industrialising South Africa began to take their place as permanent residents of the growing urban locations. Cultural resources flowed into the Golden City from all over Southern Africa and abroad. Mission graduates and migrant workers blended them together and brought new urban influences into the changing performance culture of the countryside.

By the 1920s and 30s, the churches, schools, clubs, drinking houses, parties, and dance halls of the black locations were producing a new generation of performance professionals. Versatile musicians absorbed almost everything, played for almost everyone, and gave birth to an authentically South African jazz. Singers, dancers, and comic actors drew on American vaudeville to create the beginnings of a new popular musical theatre on the African variety stage. Class formation in a segregated society, with its associated symbols of status and cultural identity, made the relationships between performers and audiences, styles and occasions increasingly complex. Chapters 4 and

5 attempt to sort out the lines of opposition and interconnection in the black city culture of the interwar period by dealing in turn with working-class and middle-class performance.

Chapter 6 brings it all together with the story of legendary Sophiatown, the leading centre of black South African cultural and political life during the 1940s and 50s. More than any other community, Sophiatown embodied the aspirations of black urbanites while supplying the conditions for their achievement. Its destruction epitomised the nature of *apartheid* and remains one of the darkest chapters in South Africa's modern social history. Chapters 7 and 8 bring us up to date with accounts of the new music and theatre of the past two decades; tied up, of course with the rapid growth of government townships like Soweto, repressive legislation, and black political awareness. The interface between black performance culture and consciousness in South Africa today is complex and often ambiguous. Not every important artist, viewpoint, or stylistic trend could be covered; but key personalities and movements are placed within their social context in a way that enables outsiders to get a feel for them and black South Africans to recognise them. The emergence of a new black theatre in the townships is especially significant. Its creative vitality suggests that qualities of performance are as important as social authenticity and ideological content in effective cultural communication. This theatre demonstrates that it is not simply the power of the tale but the fresh and artful nature of the telling that turns performance into transformation.

What unites all the personalities, materials, styles, audiences, ideas, and aims at work in this theatre is that the best of it is popular in the best sense – arising out of the community it serves and organic to the lives and concerns of those of all races who produce and support it. Furthermore, it provides a critical interpretation of political conditions that can be heard in no other popular forum in South Africa. In giving the expression of common concerns such emotional force, this theatre gives a voice to the voiceless and a sense of psychic community to the alienated. Together its art and its urgency give black South African theatre energy and potency, and make it a force to be reckoned with in South Africa's continuing political crisis.

This book is a tribute to the cultural and spiritual vitality of black South Africans, who humanised a wasteland of oppression and neglect, and produced a rich expression of both the conditions and aspirations of their lives. To begin to understand the creative development of their performing arts, we must start with the founders of urban black society in South Africa's industrial revolution – the first who came to *éDiamani*, Kimberley, the City of Diamonds; and to *éGoli*, Johannesburg, the City of Gold.

Notes

1 Terence O. Ranger, *Dance and Society in East Africa*, London, 1975, p. 3.
2 Clifford Geertz, *The Social History of an Indonesian Town*, Cambridge, Mass., 1965, p. 2.
3 Michael Etherton, *The Development of African Drama*, New York, 1982, p. 36.
4 Anya P. Royce, *The Anthropology of Dance*, Bloomington, Indiana, 1977, p. 157.
5 James Fernandez, 'The mission of metaphor in expressive culture', *Current Anthropology*, 15, 2, (1974), p. 132.

2 City life and performing arts in nineteenth century South Africa

THE first local centre to influence the development of urban African performing arts had few Africans until 1830, 178 years after its founding. This was Cape Town, supply station for the ships of the Dutch East India Company, and eventually the 'Mother City' of South Africa. When the Dutch arrived in 1652, they found only the pastoral Khoi-khoi, known by them as 'Hottentots'. Colonists from Holland, Germany and France attempted to lure or coerce as many Khoi-khoi as possible into their service. These nomads had no previous experience of regulated manual labour, however, and they resisted the harsh system of virtual serfdom imposed by the Europeans.

The failure to turn the Khoi-khoi into a reliable subject labour force had two immediate social consequences. First, there sprang up an urban Khoi-khoi underclass, composed of 'servants' and *strandlopers* (beachcombers), who earned money by various informal means. Second, the Company imported slaves from Java, Malaya, the Malabar Coast of India, Madagascar, West Africa, and Mozambique. Working together on farms or as tradesmen's apprentices in the Cape, Khoi-khoi and immigrant slaves interbred and soon formed a single category in the minds of the colonists.[1] Mixing with whites as well, this diverse subject population formed the basis of the so-called Coloured community, which over the past three centuries has, among other things, made important contributions to South African musical styles.

One of the first such contributions was in the form of the *ramkie*[2], a three- or four-stringed plucked guitar brought to South Africa by Malabar slaves (see plate 1). The *ramkie* rapidly became a favourite with Cape Khoi-khoi, who played on it the first blendings of Khoi and European folk melodies. Other instruments included a Khoi-khoi

A Mosotho playing the 'Mamokhorong', or single stringed violin, fashioned on the European model

drum (*khais*; Dutch, *rommelpot*) and an imitation of the European bugle made of kelp and called the 'sea-weed trumpet'. All three accompanied slave-Khoi dances modelled after those of the Europeans.[3]

European folk instruments and their local imitations spread rapidly to Khoi-khoi on European farms throughout the Western and Central Cape. Very popular was an adaptation of the violin, the *t'guthe*, whose strings were adjusted 'to the intervals peculiar to the Hottentots',[4] and which accompanied both neo-traditional and syncretic styles of dance and song. Rural Dutch (Boer) folk musicians participated in these musical innovations by sharing with their Griqua (Eastern Cape Coloured) neighbours the *velviool*, made by stretching a steenbok skin over a wooden frame.[5] Such instruments were used to transmit Euro-Khoi music to Bantu speaking Africans. Burchell[6] recalls the skill of his Nama Khoi-khoi servant, Gert, in playing versions of European country dances upon the *velviool*, and how quickly the Bathlapin (Tswana), among whom they were travelling, learned to reproduce its tunes in vocal chorus. A number of other local African instruments fashioned on European models such as the Sotho *mamokhorong*, a one-string violin, or the *igqongwe*, a Zulu ramkie, have developed along very different musical lines from the originals. Playing techniques for performing traditional and syncretic styles on them have become standardized, and several types described in nineteenth-century accounts are still in use.[7]

Music was among the most highly valued trades practised by slave artisans in early Cape Town. Some slaves 'sold for a higher price than others and if a good cook or musician, the seller was sure of an enhanced value.'[8] Almost all country estates kept slaves who played in orchestras with as many as thirty musicians.[9] The Dutch governor possessed his own slave orchestra as early as 1676, and most of the music at public functions was performed by slaves. At weekends the colonists visited Cape Town's taverns to hear 'violins, flutes, hautboys, trumpets, harps and other instruments' played by slaves whose owners had bought them especially for their musical skills.[10] The Malay brought musical skills to South Africa, contributing the romantic *liederen* (ballads) they had learned from Dutch colonials, as well as the indigenous music of the East Indies.

The Malay adopted Afrikaans, the local variant of the Dutch *handelstaal* (trade language), as their own, and Kirby remarks that:

> Along with their language they have also lost their music and have adopted the simple strains which they heard from the lips of their masters, clothing them in an idiom, both vocal and instrumental, which is characteristic of themselves and which they have returned to the white-man in the form of folksong and simple dance measures, now regarded as typical of South Africa.[11]

The word 'lost' must be qualified since the vocal idiom of the South African Malay still contains accentuated ornamental cadences of several notes sung to one syllable of text (melisma) and other features directly traceable to traditional Malay music.

During the eighteenth century, sailors, soldiers, and travellers of many nations joined the resident population in bringing a stimulating flow of creative influences and cash to Cape Town's popular performance culture. As a result, a class of semi-professional musicians who were able to earn considerable sums for both themselves and their masters and employers emerged among the Coloured slaves and freemen. Europeans of doubtful qualification were often hired to teach instrumental performance to slaves, 'though neither master nor pupils knew a single note, playing instead entirely by ear'.[12] Slave bands on rural farms rarely had any formal instruction.

Performing in settings ranging from country dances and official balls to the racially mixed seaside taverns and dancehall canteens, Coloured musicians took the lead in creating a popular Western Cape performance culture. This culture developed over a period of about 250 years during which segregation of the races was customary and class-oriented rather than legal. Based on Afrikaans, it was common to whites as well as Coloureds. Both the 'picnic songs' of the Cape Afrikaners and the *ghommaliedjies* ('drum songs') of the Malay, for example, appear to have developed simultaneously and are 'in spirit so similar and intertwined that it would be unreasonable to designate any particular one as specifically of Malay or of Afrikaans origin'.[13]

Even before their takeover of the Cape in 1806, the British began to contribute to local performance culture. English country dances became popular with whites at the Cape as early as the 1730s, and slaves enjoyed performing them at 'Rainbow Balls' modelled on the social occasions of the wealthier masters. An early visitor noted that the slave women at these affairs displayed 'much taste and even elegance in their dress, nor are their dances wild, irregular, or unaccompanied with proper music'.[14] Charles Bell attended a European dance at the Castle in Cape Town in 1834, where music was provided by black men dressed in British uniforms and playing Western instruments.[15] Military marching bands also made a strong impression, and Coloured bands paraded in the streets during the traditional New Year's festivities as early as 1823. This aspect of British influence led to the development of two traditions of Coloured social dancing. The first was the relatively high status dress ball or 'social'. The second was a more popular Anglo-Afrikaans style of 'square dancing', distantly related in form to that which developed from British sources in America, and which remains popular in Coloured communities today.

Itinerant Cape Coloured musicians brought their Western Cape performance styles to towns in other parts of the country in the second half of the nineteenth century. The major centre of cultural contact between Coloureds and Africans was Kimberley, where both groups participated in the beginnings of South Africa's industrial revolution. The conditions of black settlement greatly influenced the performance culture that arose there.

In 1867, great quantities of diamonds were discovered at Kimberley, located on the Orange Free State border of the Griqualand West reserve in the Northern Cape. Within months a city of tents arose, housing the thousands of diggers eager to scratch a quick fortune from the famous 'yellow ground'. They found not only that luck but a plentiful supply of manual labour was required.

Africans hemmed in on diminished tribal lands by the Europeans, or unsettled by the aftermath of the Zulu quest for empire, responded to this call in numbers that eventually reached 25 000 mineworkers.[16] Cattle disease, land scarcity, and colonial taxation intensified the economic motivation of the migrants. Most important was the desire for European goods, especially the guns with which African leaders were preparing for decisive struggles with the white colonisers.[17] An American mining engineer, Gardner Williams, recalled the situation in the 1870s:

> Then the white camps were lively, humming social resorts abounding with good food and tempting drink, where black men were welcome and well protected . . . some of this swarm could be persuaded to remain at the mines for a year or more and work quite steadily but most drifted away as soon as they were able to get their coveted guns and powder pouches.[18]

On the edge of the European encampment 'were scattered the huts of wood and dirty canvas or mud-plastered stones, where the native Blacks huddled together'.[19] Most of these were Tswana, Northern and Southern Sotho, and Portuguese East Africans. They performed traditional music and dance in their leisure hours and avoided the rowdy canteens of the mining camp. As British financial interests moved in and Kimberley began to take on the appearance of a permanent town, cultural exchange among these peoples from all over the world intensified.

Africans had already begun to experience urban life in the towns of the Cape and Natal. But the size, diversity, and rapid expansion of Kimberley, along with the labour conditions of mining in the late nineteenth century, set a pattern for African urbanisation. The Africans in Kimberley either did not have or soon lost any intention of returning home. Their desire to establish themselves permanently in Kimberley came into direct conflict with the aggressive racial prejudice of white colonists and with a segregationist policy based on the notion of South African towns as white preserves. For African workers in early Kimberley, the absorption of some aspects of Western culture was part of a struggle for urban status.

From the early 1870s, Kimberley was divided into two administrative sections: the Crown Estate, under direct control of the colonial government, and the London Estate, owned by a private corporation. The Crown Estate was controlled and nearly all Africans lived either on their employer's property or in official, segregated locations such as those near the suburb of Beaconsfield. The London Estate owners, however, resisted the 'proclamation' of black locations and rented to anyone willing to pay the inflated prices. Fortune seekers of all races crowded into its high-crime areas, such as Newsome, where everyone from African squatters and poor whites, to Chinese, Malays, and African salaried and civil service employees lived openly together, though the great majority of residents were black (see plate 6).

Here the Coloured 'Cape Boys', exempted at first from the pass restrictions suffered by Africans and Khoisan people, formed well-organised and powerful gangs who made certain areas off limits to the colonial police. White employers continually complained about desertion and the shortage of African labour. Two-thirds of all Africans who arrived for work in the years before the establishment of controlled labour compounds in 1887 deserted within a week of entering employment.[20] Deserters, estimated at 8 000 by 1877, were absorbed into the London Estate, where they often made a livelihood from horse-trading and from stolen diamonds. Illicit diamond-buying rapidly produced a flourishing counter-economy in Kimberley; by the 1880s it was reputed to involve fully fifty per cent of the city's residents.[21] African shop assistants worked for themselves as well as for whites in the illegal diamond traffic, and the cooperative involvement of people of all races in the trade gave thousands of blacks both economic opportunity and mobility since they could easily betray their white employers to the police if they chose.[22]

Although few black men brought wives to the diamond fields, the camps attracted thousands of African, Coloured, and Khoisan women. Providing home-brewed beer, liquor, and sexual and housekeeping services to men of all races, they also participated in illicit diamond-buying – activities that only reinforced the unhealthy social conditions at the fields.

Entertainment was much sought after among members of this disorganised community. African evangelist Gwayi Tyamzashe recalled Kimberley in 1874:

> On my first arrival at the New Rush I observed that nearly every evening was devoted to private and public amusements . . . The evenings resounded with the noise of the concert, the circus, and all sorts of dances from one end of the camp to the other. The life then of both Coloured [non-Europeans] and Whites was so rough that I thought the place only good for those who were resolved to sell their souls for silver, gold, and precious stones, or for those who were determined to barter their lives for the pleasures of a time.[23]

In Kimberley, Africans were exposed to a wide variety of new musical influences. Many of the young white diggers held musical evenings frequented by black workers where the whites played guitar, concertina, banjo, cornet, violin, and even piano.[24] Others came to the fields with Khoisan servants who improvised new dance tunes on home-made violins.[25] American prospectors brought their 'honky-tonk' (early ragtime) piano styles to the canteens, and

> Even American Negroes arrived in the dust-tortured village in the veld, the advance guard of a fairly substantial number now living at the Cape; and the simple-minded black from the kraal was immensely impressed by the sophisticated dress of his brother from the far side of the Atlantic.[26]

But among these varied strains it was the Coloureds, arriving from

13

the Cape with traditions of professional musicianship extending back more than two hundred years, who most strongly influenced early African urban music and dance.

In Kimberley, Coloured artisans, drivers, and servants played their blend of Khoi-khoi, Malay, European, and American popular music on the violin or guitar for anyone who promised them a coin. Xhosa choral composer Ben Tyamzashe first heard the violin played by Malays in Kimberley, and recalled 'exuberant music and vibrant rhythms emanating from gambling dens, saloons and dance halls', as well as Malay singing from the mosques of the city during the 1890s.[27]

It was here also that Coloured guitarists perfected the Cape style called *tickey draai* (Afrikaans: 'turn on a tickey', a threepence), played for a dance in which one couple swings at the centre of the ring while the other dancers clap hands to a rapid rhythm, based on the Afrikaans *vastrap* (faststep) folk dance. Coloured performers brought *tickey draai* playing and dancing to other towns in the Eastern Cape, Free State, and Transvaal, where it attained great popularity among Africans. Although they rarely socialised as equals, diggers and labourers of all races enjoyed Cape Afrikaans folk tunes such as 'Jannie met die Hoepel Been' (bandy-legged Jannie).

The majority of professional Coloured musicians, all of whom were men, belonged to a broader social category known as *oorlams*. The meanings of this term reveal a good deal about the place of black performers on the fringes of colonial society and their role in promoting cultural exchange. During the early years of Dutch settlement at the Cape, the term *oorlams* first referred to hard-drinking, veteran sailors of the Dutch navy and merchant fleet who raised havoc in the local taverns. Later it came to be applied to the tough, experienced Dutch colonials brought from the East Indies, as distinct from their more sober, *baar* (raw, naive) counterparts fresh from Holland.[28] Soon, the term came to refer to Khoisan who had learned Dutch and acquired a worldly knowledge of the ways of Europeans. A fondness for drink and clever manipulation of those in authority became closely associated with Khoisan *oorlams*, and the Nama Khoi-khoi used it as a name for themselves, reputedly because they delighted in their own shrewdness and joked that many drinks make a person clever. The connotation of cunning was reinforced among Dutch farmers, who found that *oorlamse* Khoisan were more useful but also more disingenuous household servants than *baar kaffirs* (raw, tribal Africans).

By the nineteenth century, many Afrikaans farmers had an African *'oorlamse kaffir'* or *'oorlamse jong'* (African old hand, well trained 'boy') as a foreman or personal retainer. The notion of *'oorlamse skepsel'* (clever rascal) remained among these farmers, who had to rely upon such men to mediate in their relations with their African labourers or to carry out personal business despite the conviction that no black person could ever be entirely trusted. Among Africans, *oorlams* came to refer to those who had become 'Westernised' through Afrikaans and work experience in Afrikaner farms and towns, rather than through involvement with English-speaking mission schools.

The first association of this term with musical activity stems from the role of Khoi-khoi and Coloured musicians in the annual Christmas festivities of eighteenth-century Cape Town, the *'oorlams* time', when many merchantmen were in port. Later, players of the *oorlamsramkie* earned themselves an unflattering reputation in upcountry districts:

> Of the *ramkie*, the Bloemhof men stated that it belonged to those Hottentots who had lost their own language and had adopted Dutch, and this is indirectly confirmed by the Griqualand Korana [Hottentots] for they also disown it and call it the instrument of the *ondervelders* [lowlanders].[29]

In Kimberley, Coloured *oorlams* musicians acted as cultural brokers by working musical influences into new styles and performing for diverse audiences. These entertainers belonged neither to the settled, highly structured rural Coloured communities of the Koranna or Griqua, nor to the church-oriented, wage-earning, Westernised middle class.

Among these performers were a number of African men, particularly Cape or Natal Nguni (Mfengu, Xhosa, Zulu, Bhaca) from Cape Town or the towns of the Eastern Cape and Natal. Familiar with, or quick to learn, *tickey draai* and other Coloured styles, they created new variants by blending in traditional African melodies. As distinct from the highly Westernised African graduates of Cape mission schools, they were called 'dressed people' (Xhosa: *abantu abayi esontweni*)[30] implying a superficial adoption of European culture, a limited command of Afrikaans or English, lack of interest in Christianity, and an individualised, opportunistic social outlook. Like their Coloured fellows, they favoured the portable trade-store concertina, guitar, and violin, and displayed a flair for keyboard instruments. The music of these proletarians became one of the most important sources of Coloured and Afrikaans influence on the development of African popular music.

The 'dressed people', also called *abaphakathi* ('those in the middle'), occupied an insecure position between mission school Africans and non-Christian traditionalists in African society as a whole. Their ranks were swelled by migrants who elected to abandon their rural-traditional communities for permanent urbanisation. The *abaphakathi* and *oorlams* formed the core of an emerging urban black proletariat that formed the majority of Kimberley's total population by the 1880s.[31]

Residence at Kimberley or an expedient contact with a mission station was often sufficient to disengage Africans from the traditional-rural community. They became acquainted with the value of the material trappings of European life but did not fully adopt the social and moral patterns and restraints of their adopted culture. In particular, they had to contend with the whites' resentment and fear of Africans who tried to stake their own diamond claims and who spoke English and wore trousers. Advancing segregation was defended on the grounds that blacks were primitive and barbarous. In reality, their continuing Westernisation was perceived as a threat to whites, who pushed Africans to the towns and then resisted African urbanisation. As one astonished English visitor to Kimberley in the 1880s recounted, 'We are told that here, at Johannesburg, or at Barberton the Natives actually dress for dinner! What *is* the world coming to?'[32]

Neither mission school nor traditional Africans liked the proletarian opportunists, who appeared unrestrained by any recognised code of morality, social behaviour, or cultural values, European or African. Traditionalists called them *Makgomocha* (Tswana), or *Amakumsha/Amakurumsha* (Zulu-Xhosa), meaning literally 'speakers of European languages', but implying deceivers, cheats, or turn-coats who used their command of European speech and manners to exploit those less Westernised than themselves.[33] African mission school graduates regarded them as immoral, combining the worst of African and European social traits. They shuddered to think that whites rarely differentiated between themselves and these 'impostors', but regarded all Africans in European clothing as criminals. When the racist letter writer 'T.O'C.' complained in the press that 'Obviously full-blooded Kaffirs, recognisable as such despite the glories of stand-up collars and evil-odoured manillas' were allowed to attend brigade band concerts and other public entertainments, 'A Native' answered that faults attributed to the 'innocent Kaffir' were really 'the evil doing of the Kaapenaar' (lower-class Coloured or African from the Cape).[34]

Even so, it was African proletarians who had the greatest opportunities for social contact with Coloureds and whites. Many were important cultural innovators, including urban popular musicians. The background, behaviour and social role of these musicians contributed to their deviant image among many Africans. This image has been responsible for the continuing insecure status of professional performers, despite public appreciation of their talents. Nineteenth-century Kimberley not only spawned an urban proletariat with its own performance styles; it also transformed the music and dance of migrant workers, with consequences for urban as well as rural performance culture.

The rural migrants' experience in Kimberley expanded their awareness of the larger world in which they were being forced to participate. The challenges and hardships they faced deeply affected their self-images and concepts of manhood, changes reflected in their verbal art. The Sotho, for example, traditionally express social identity through recitative musical poetry. On the more than two-hundred mile journeys by foot to Kimberley or during leisure hours on the mines, Sotho miners adapted elements of these forms into a new vehicle for the expression of their experience and its personal significance.

The primary formal inspiration for this genre, called *sefela* (pl. *lifela*) is *lithoko* or praise poetry. In Southern Africa, praise poems are a traditional medium of socialised competition, and may involve criticism as well as eulogy. Praise poems are a communicative dimension of influence and power, and a record of personal prestige which persists even after death.[35] Traditionally, young men developed skills in verbal composition and dramatic performance by reciting their own praises at post-initiation ceremonies. These *lithoko tsa makoloane* (young men's praises) consist of imaginary representations of the challenges of adult life. They expressed both images of a new identity and the capacity to meet cultural expectations.[36]

As mature men, Sotho could compose *lithoko* which apostrophised not only their chiefs, but the genealogy, community, regiment, character, travels, exploits, and bravery of ordinary persons, including themselves.

In composing *lifela*, migrant *likheleke* ('eloquent persons') have developed the potential of forms such as *lithoko* for interpreting and ordering their relationships to family, community, work, and fellow workers. *Lifela* help to resolve the contradictions between village and mine as domains of experience, relating self-image to social values in the total environment. As mining replaced the challenges of earlier times, migrants sought poetic self-definition as modern heroes, men who descend into the sweltering darkness of the earth to test their strength against backbreaking labour, deafening machines, and the chance of injury or death.

Banna ke bana merafong	Men, these are the mines
joale ho ea theo'etsoe	now we have gone underground
joale ke betsa joale ka sephoqo	now I throw like a fool
batho ba ne ba laecha ba Mokhachane	people, we are really loading those of Mokhachane,
ba ne ba laecha mpa libenya	they were loading and their
lihempe li nqamathela'mele	stomachs glistening,
tsa e ja ngoana Mosoetsi	with shirts gripping their bodies, even into Mosoetsi's child

Lifela clearly help to release work-related stress. The sense of elated pride in the ability to do 'men's work' is evident in these wry self-praises. Pleased as they are to be alive at the end of a working day, *lifela* composers also express the insecurity and emotional suffering of men who toil for a pittance in the face of death, far from home and subject to the harsh authority of a white supervisor:

... *Basotho bana le ba bonang
    mona
ke batho be phelang ke bothata
Limaeneng koana le ha uka
Etsa malebaleba ua sebetsa
ka thata. Uke ke ua bona
leburu le tseha le ka mpa.
la sheba morao la tseha
ha le khutla lese le loana*

... These Basotho that you see are the people who live in difficulties. In the mines where they work, though they toil hard to please the Boer, I mean trying everything in their power, Even if they do the impossible I swear you'll never see the Boer smile. The best he can do is look in the opposite direction, and laugh at you When he faces you again, He is declaring war, and fighting you.[37]

The role of these compositions in expressing their deepest feelings, tempered by the ironic manner of delivery, is recognised by the miners in their choice of the term *sefela*. *Sefela* can mean simply 'a song' in Sesotho, but the word has strong emotional connotations. In other contexts, it specifically refers to Christian hymns by virtue of their emotional value for African converts.

With the institutionalisation of migrant labour as the principal means by which young men earn the money for *bohali*[38] (bridewealth), cattle, and other necessities, a period of service at the mines has largely come to replace initiation as the rite of passage into male adulthood for the Sotho.[39] Young men earn the respect of potential wives by 'facing the whiteman's machines', and the adventure and manly comradeship of a year in the mines and locations are almost as important in establishing a sense of adulthood as the earnings they bring back home.[40]

Contract labour is often compared with military campaigning, since it involves discipline, the hardships of barracks life, uncertainty, violence, and danger in hostile territory.[41] Young men praise their genealogies and villages, assert their toughness and courage, and formulate their concepts of ideal personality in *lifela* recitations during their hours of leisure from the mines. Back at home, they entertain and instruct their younger brothers in the nature of manhood and the art of *sefela* through poetic accounts of their exploits. In this way, many youngsters learn *lifela* before they go to the mines. The transmission of memorable stanzas from one generation of migrants to the next has preserved some texts and they have become part of the general corpus of Sotho verbal art.

Young migrants face an acute problem of social identification. They make a virtue of the necessity of going to the mines, but the migratory labour system and the external forces which control it rob them of autonomy. Despite the hardships, it is only after years of labour that they can think of acquiring the land, cattle, or other capital assets that bring status and security at home. Sometimes called *likoata* (sing. *koata*; from Eng., 'squatter': 'rude, uncivilized, decultured') in Lesotho, they bring the rough speech and behaviour of the mines and urban areas to their home towns and rural villages. Unable to identify with their place of work, they may feel alienated as well from the women and elders who spend their earnings but do not share their experience. Even at home, they may feel most comfortable in the company of their fellow migrants and the female *matekatse* whose occupation is to entertain them.

Many young migrants take a rebellious pride in the name *koata*, and employ *sefela* as a means of self-realisation, status achievement, and social commentary within a system of values they themselves have partly formulated. One poet, for example, used the common theme of praise for his village as an opportunity to criticise contemporary morals:

Le ntse mpotsa ke haile kae	You keep asking me where I live.
ke haile ha Mojela Makoateng	I live at Mojela's place, Makoateng
koana moo sebe se tsoang ka lerato	where sin is committed through love.[42]

Others focus on their obstreperous behaviour as infants, a sign of the future strength and toughness required of a mineworker. The naming of the poet as an infant, an act of deep significance in Sotho tradition, is also a frequent theme. Naming emphasises the importance of both the composer's birth and his later success as a miner for his family and community. Similarly, *sefela* verses express a miner's sense of himself as a troublesome spirit, unconstrained by the norms of polite Sotho society:

Ke qoti ea khomo ke tena batho	I am a stomach of a cow,
Ke nyokola mahleu a maobane	I disgust people
Ke ka joala ba maoba ke hlasitse	I am sour beer of yesterday;
	I am like beer of yesterday,
	I am sour.[43]

The young migrant's independence of mind and freedom from social constraint is commonly expressed through the theme of elopement, yet the theme through which composers most often assert their unique character and status is that of poetic excellence itself. Ultimately, the aesthetic values of *sefela* are the measure of a performer's prestige among his peers. *Sefela* is a competitive art, and today prizes are still awarded for imaginativeness, evocative metaphor, and originality in *sefela* contests on the mines. As in *lithoko*, *lifela* require twelve or thirteen syllables to a metrical line, and a smooth rhythmic flow in delivery. All this is directed towards realising oneself through the cultural interpretation of experience: the facts of life and history, the nature of being, events, and things.[44] Many *lifela* recount, in the context of the mines, the envy and fear other composers feel towards the poetic reputation of the performer:

Mehlolo eo ke ne keng e etsa	The miracles that I once did.
ke se ke leba Matlatsane koana	I then went to Matlatsane
ke fihla ka har'a kompone	(Klerksdorp)
ke fumana banna ba likheleke	I came into the compound
batho ba tsejoang ka ho bua	I found men who are good poets
banna bana joale ka ho ntseba	people known for their talk.
ba late ntona ea kompone.	These men because they knew me,
'Morena tseba re tlilo u joetsa	they went to the *induna* of the
moshanyana enoa ke Lethetsa oa	compound.
~ *Malimatle*	'Chief, know we have come to tell
Hae ha habo ke Koro-Koro koana	you,
motho enoa o se ke be ea mothola	this boy is Lethetsa of Malimatle
o ka mo thola mona re tla tsamea	His home is at Koro-Koro yonder.
kompone re ka e tlola holimo'	This person you should not hire.
hore u tlo u utloe ba ea ntsenya	If you can hire him we'll go,
ba re 'Oa beta, oa utsoa, o mobe	the compound we can jump over.'
oa loea	To show that they slandered me,
o rata le basali ba lintona. . .'	they said, 'He rapes, he steals, he
	is a witch,
	he loves the wives of the *indunas* . . .'[45]

Finally, the primary goal of *sefela*, and of migrancy itself in a sense, is self-transformation; heroic redefinition as a person capable of coping with the alien industrial world of the mine in the service of traditional social values:

'O hlonametseng Lethetsa oa	'Why are you sad Lethetsa of
Malimatle?'	Malimatle?'
'Ke se leba har'a naha Kopanong,	'I am going into the wilderness of
koana moo ho pheloang ka ho	the Republic [South Africa],
sekoloa.'	there where people live through
A re 'O isoa keng melekong	hard work.'
koana?'	She said, 'What makes you go to
Ka re, 'Ba heno ngoanana ba	the devilish place?'
ntena	I said, 'Your relatives disgust me,
ba batla likhomo bohaling ba hau.'	girl,

20

Ke moo a roakang batsoali ba hae,   they want cattle for your *bohali*
'Tlohela ho ea makhooeng koana,   (bridewealth).'
Bontate ba hlanya ke maketse.'   She then insulted her parents,
Ka thola feela Mokoena ka   'Don't go to the mine yonder,
  tsamaea.   My fathers are mad, I am
Ke tlohile hae e le bosiu,   surprised.'
ha likhoho li lla oe   I, Mokoena, kept quiet and left.
le hona ho lla khoho tse pele.   I left home at night
Tsa bobeli li lla ke le tseleng.
Tsa boraro ke feta Phutiatsana.
Ka kena Maseru toropong koana,   When the cocks were crowing
ha tsatsi le re chapha lithabeng.   Further crowing the first cocks.
B. A. Maseru, Mejametalana.   The second ones crew while I was
Banna, ka eiti khomo li hanngoe,   on the way.
Thene ka isoa ngakeng.   The third ones when I was passing
E ne e le Mokose thaka tsa me.   Phuthiatsana.
A beha tsepe sebubeng mona,   I entered Maseru at the town
ke heme habeli a khotsofale.   yonder,
Oloraete! ngoana Malimatle   when the sun touched the
Ha ho molato, moshanyana oeso;   mountains.
tsamaea o li chofe makhooeng   B. A. Maseru; Mejametalana.[46]
  koana.   Men, at 7 in the morning I was
Masimphane ke monna oa sebetsa.   hired.
  Then at 8 cows were milked.
  At 9 schools were in
  At 10, poor me, I was taken to the
  doctor.
  It was 'Mokose', my companions.
  He put a metal on the chest here,
  I breathed twice, he was satisfied.
  'All right! the child of Malimatle
  there is nothing, my brother;
  go and drive them at the mines
  yonder.'
  Masimphane is a man, he works.[47]

Sotho *sefela* is a good example of how shared interpretations as well as specific conditions of labour define a situation such as migrancy through a set of values and collective images. *Lifela* are created from traditional resources in the crucible of migrant labour. They reveal how people struggling to deal with social and economic coercion will carve out a sphere of personal autonomy within which they may truly act. The reinterpretation of new challenges through the reworking of existing cultural models is essential to social survival. Autonomy is also partly psychological and cultural. It requires the positive reassertion of one's own human value, through forms like *sefela*, in opposition to identity as a mere labour unit within South Africa's political economy.

The De Beers conglomerate under Cecil Rhodes completed its takeover of Kimberley diamond operations in 1887. It housed Africans according to a harsh system of 'closed compounds'; overcrowded, unhealthy, and dilapidated labour camps designed to control workers' movements and reduce the illicit diamond and liquor trades.[48] Further restrictions regulated the coming and going of African contract workers as the basis of the migrant labour system, and the distinction between migrant and townsman became fundamental to the structure of urban African society. Performance styles like *sefela* both expressed and created class consciousness and psychic resistance to such controls, which materialised in the African strikes against low wages and poor compound rules and conditions in 1890.[49] In August 1892, migrant workers struck again on the gold mines of the East Rand, and eight died in the hail of police bullets that constituted the management's response.

The Africans working in the mines, brickyards, coalfields, and municipal services of Kimberley, all of whom lived under the closed compound system during the 1890s,[50] spent their Sundays in traditional group dancing. Sometimes they played traditional instruments including Pedi (Northern Sotho) or Bamalete (Tswana) *dinaka* (*dithlaka*) reed-pipe ensembles, and the Southern Sotho *lesiba* (a respirated, strung quill) which accompanied the singing in the *mokorotlo* and *mohobelo* choral dances.

The acknowledged leaders in early mine dancing were the Chopi from Mozambique, who based their vigorous, complex dances on the music of *timbila* (wooden xylophone) ensembles (see plate 2). Though only a few instruments were available at first, these ensembles eventually included between twenty and thirty players on xylophones of three sizes. They produced a rhythmically organised set of melodically independent parts (polyphony) accompanying the vocal alternation of soloist and chorus and supporting and directing the synchronised movements of the dancers.[51]

Apart from the fairly traditional Sunday afternoon dancing, music and dance among migrants was highly personal and stylistically varied. Influenced by Coloured-Khoi, white, or African musicians, Southern Sotho miners, for example, played the guitar or 'German' (Czech) concertina in place of traditional solo instruments as accompaniment to the individualised singing and dancing of their friends. Nevertheless, in preference to *Vat Jou Goed en Trek, Ferreira* ('Take Your Travel Gear, Ferreira'), and other Afrikaans dance tunes, they played music constructed according to traditional Sotho principles.[52]

Here we must review the principles fundamental to traditional musics of Southern Africa as they are performed today and use them as a baseline in the analysis of urban stylistic change. Ethnohistorical evidence shows stylistic and textual continuity in traditional music;

1 *A young Kavango musician playing a three-stringed* ramkie

2 *Chopi musicians playing the* timbila *(wooden xylophone). Chopi mime dances were based on the music of* timbila *ensembles*

3 *An Ovahimba man playing a mouth harp. The sound is resonated by his mouth*

4 *San father with his son plays the* gvashi, *a popular stringed instrument*

its fundamental principles have not changed and have continued to operate uniformly in examples recorded over the past half-century. This persistence suggests their existence before that time. These principles apply equally to the structure of vocal and instrumental performance and, with some variation, to all the indigenous African musical cultures of the region.

Unlike Central and West Africa, communal music in the South was basically vocal, without drumming or other instrumental accompaniment, though solo performance often involved instruments, with or without voice. Communal vocal music always involved dancing or gestures or work movements by the singers themselves. There were at least two voice parts in antiphonal, leader-and-chorus relationship to each other, and the parts frequently overlapped, producing polyphony. An essential feature was that the two basic parts never entered or ended simultaneously. Additional counter-melodies were often added, and the leading part was frequently varied through extemporisation.[53] With single-stringed mouth-resonated instruments such as the Sotho *lesiba* and *setolotolo*,[54] vocal melody could be simulated through the selective resonation of harmonics (see plate 3). On gourd-resonated musical bows such as the Zulu *ugubhu*,[55] vocal chorus parts could be simulated, against which the player could sing an antiphonal leader's part, and choral music was often composed in this way.[56]

So interrelated are instrumental and vocal traditions that it is uncertain which is more basic to traditional musical development. Kirby,[57] a musical evolutionist, argued nearly half a century ago that pentatonic multipart structures in traditional South African choral music derived from the harmonics of stretched strings in instrumental playing. Today, however, most ethnomusicologists would agree with Rycroft[58] that the use of instruments among the Zulu and other peoples is an indirect extension of the principles of vocal music. Sotho migrants produced neo-traditional music with the concertina, guitar, and voice through the polyphonic movement of parallel fourths and fifths within the structure of the Western 'three chord' (tonic-dominant-subdominant) system. Retired miners can recall this music, called *focho* (disorder) being played in Johannesburg as early as the decades preceding the First World War. The guitar and concertina, along with the autoharp, harmonica, and violin, were available in compound stores and rural trade stores even long before that. These instruments became popular with Africans in part because they could achieve 'an expression of indigenous principles which in some can be more effectively realised through these new media than could be done on the traditional instruments they have replaced'.[59] The Sotho for example, have favoured the concertina because it allows the performer to play two or three voice parts fully and at far greater volume than is possible with traditional instruments, while at the same time allowing the players or the dancers to sing their own accompanying melodies. The sound of the concertina has a dense texture that resembles the broad sonority of a Sotho male voice chorus. It also enabled players to set the ostinato to a lively African or Coloured-Afrikaans urban dance rhythm. Furthermore, it was uniquely suited to self-accompaniment on the long journeys by foot or train to and from the mines since it did not involve use of the mouth or lungs and could even be played beneath a blanket to generate warmth while travelling in cold weather. In the city, traditional instruments had a strongly negative image and were quickly abandoned.

Many miners carried Western folk instruments back to the countryside as a prestigious emblem of urban experience. Migrants enjoyed performing their new dances and instrumental music while at home, an urban influence on rural performance culture.

These trade-store instruments achieved such wide distribution among non-Christian Africans by the early 1900s that they came to be considered fully traditional, part of the 'tribal' or 'heathen' musical heritage.[60] Consequently, urban African Christians began to avoid them. Their passion was choral music, along with keyboard and brass instruments when these were available.

Students of African traditional music often find that melodic lines and polyrhythms are less clearly articulated and tonal contrasts less subtle in the Sotho concertina than in the more delicate sounds of the lesiba or setolotolo. While this is true, the identification of Western instruments with urban culture and status and the flexibility of these instruments both for creating and performing syncretic styles and for providing lively music for city dances made their adoption inevitable. Furthermore, Sotho musicians are highly conscious of the contrasting properties of various instruments; they insist that their favourite instrument today, the piano-accordion (Sotho: koriana), allows for greater melodic and tonal variety and solo improvisation than does the concertina. Xhosa-speaking Mpondo miners were present in large numbers in Kimberley, where they adapted their young men's initiation dances (amakhwenkwe) to the space and time restrictions of compound recreation as organised by the management. Like the Sotho, they developed an affinity for the concertina. New concertina dances integrated rhythms and steps developed by migrants in urban areas into a framework of traditional dances and spread throughout the Cape African reserves.[61] With few indigenous instrumental traditions of their own, Cape migrants were most strongly influenced by the music that their 'dressed' fellow-Xhosa were making in the city's canteens and dance halls. Mpondo players depended more on European and Cape Coloured folk rhythms and melodies than the Sotho, although the latter were by no means immune to Afrikaans vastrap rhythms, Cape Melodies, and the 'three chord vamp' which have since become characteristic of syncretic African music in South Africa.

Both fully urban and migrant performers transformed and combined traditional and foreign musical materials in response to changed conditions and expressive needs. Western instruments provided new means and possibilities for the elaboration of traditional music principles. The new instruments also offered a medium for the creation of new musical forms and practices as part of the process of developing urban African cultural models through performance.

During the later 1900s, Cape Nguni (Xhosa and Mfengu) musicians predominated not only in the urban dance halls but also in the mission schools, where they led the development of African hymnody, secular choral music, and Westernised social dancing. Because of the nearness of the Xhosa-speaking chiefdoms to the expanding European settlement of the Cape, these peoples experienced military defeat, missionisation, and wage labour beginning in the early 1800s. In addition, cosmopolitan Cape Town and the growing towns of the Eastern Cape gave Xhosa speakers a head start in the process of Westernisation that eventually affected all black South Africans to some degree. Many Cape Africans who travelled to the diamond and gold fields already possessed an acculturated background which enabled them to assume a special position of leadership among urbanising Africans. For this class of Africans, mission life and Christian education greatly influenced their adjustment to city life. The social background of early Cape Nguni immigrants to Kimberley and Johannesburg illustrates the impact of European missionisation on African performance culture. Believing that the wholesale conversion of entire clans and nations was necessary to stamp out 'heathen' customs and ideas, missionaries were dismayed to discover that Christianity had little appeal for people firmly located in strong traditional communities.[62] Forced to accept such individual converts as they could find, evangelists came to view the destruction of African institutions, especially in the Cape, Transkei, and Natal, as necessary to their success. The irony of this attitude was not lost on some missionaries; the Rev. Barret reported in 1871 that among Africans, 'the only people inclined to be Christians are those who despair of their own nation ever becoming anything by itself'.[63]

By this time, mission communities were well established throughout the southern Cape and Transkei, swollen by members of homeless Nguni-speaking clans pushed into Xhosa country by Zulu expansionism during the 1820s and 1830s. Chief among these were the Mfengu or 'Fingos' who initially took refuge among Ama-Gcaleka and other powerful Xhosa clans. The missionaries' offer of free land and cattle attracted many refugees into communities that became a buffer for the Europeans in their struggle against the powerful Xhosa chiefs.[64] A group of Mfengu workers founded the African Community in Cape Town when the colonial government settled them there in 1830.[65]

Missionary efforts in the Cape and the Transkei concentrated on education. The intention was to produce African teachers and evangelists who would serve the expanding mission field and also teach 'useful arts' of printing and building. This training of disciples would then actively spread the gospel along with European cultural values. Joined by solitary wandering blacks from other areas and a variety of outcasts from local Xhosa communities, the Mfengu converts paid for their economic and social security with compulsory participation in an alien way of life, isolated from the surrounding traditional communities. Establishing their own courts, mission churches penalized participation in 'revolting' traditional communal dances, beer drinks, feasts, and 'other customs inconsistent with Christianity',[66] which were their only means of maintaining social contact and reciprocal obligations with non-Christian kinsmen. Expulsion from the stations for such participation was frequent, and some who could not accept the restrictions left voluntarily.

Those who remained soon found out that their sacrifices were not without rewards. Africans taken from the ranks of refugees, the disinherited, and marginals of various kinds could rise to leadership, positions of considerable influence in Christian communities. The relationship of mission stations to the colonial administration led to further changes in the role of the African Christians in the Cape society as a whole. In addition to material gains, collaboration with the colonial power led them to adopt Western ideas. With the help of missionaries and white employers, the converts became the core of an emerging class of prosperous small-scale farmers.

The missionary ideal was to reconstruct African society in ways that would secure it to the British colonial economy,[67] an ideal shared by the British Governor, George Grey, during the 1850s and 1860s. The development of Kimberley led to the accelerated growth of already prosperous centres in the Cape Midlands, such as Queenstown and Kingwilliamstown. Located close to newly established 'native reserves', these towns involved thousands of Africans in the money economy of transport riding, small trades, railway construction, and wool and leather industries. Between 1870 and 1890, independent African Christian farmers became an influential, economically significant social group. African society in the Cape was already beginning to develop patterns of social stratification based on a degree of Westernisation.[68]

These patterns, which have retained much of their original outline over the past century, derive from the socio-economic consequences of Cape Nguni missionisation, which made mission stations islands of acculturation in a traditional sea, and led to the opposition of 'red' (traditional) and 'school' (Western educated) categories of Xhosa speakers in the towns of the Eastern Cape.[69] As sources of social disruption and change, as well as of new wealth and technological change, mission stations presented a challenge to the already weakened traditional Xhosa society. Non-Christians feared church communities as 'the abode of witches', an impression reinforced by the frequency with which people accused of witchcraft fled to them for refuge.[70] Yet, with their power and their resources diminishing, traditional authorities were losing followers to the missionaries, who appeared willing to help Africans cope successfully with new social realities.

Increasingly insecure Cape Africans had to choose between the reduced but familiar parameters of traditional society and the expanding but uncertain opportunities of nineteenth-century colonialism. Neither option proved very rewarding. Traditional Xhosa who had lost much of their land to the whites were often forced to supplement the subsistence economy with temporary wage labour. Westernising Africans found that once the military threat to white settlements from traditional chiefdoms was gone, only the missionaries retained any interest in helping to create an African middle class. The colonists preferred tractable 'red' Xhosas and denied 'mission boys' the opportunities for which they had become prepared. White farmers and businessmen considered themselves entitled to African labour and felt threatened by Africans who worked independently in agriculture and trade. The settlers' efforts to eliminate competition and obtain labour by proletarianising Africans were greatly aided by the droughts and wars of 1877–81, and the depressed economic conditions of 1873–96. Between 1890 and 1913, the state itself intervened to further the goals of the settlers and undermine African self-sufficiency in the Cape. In response, the emerging Cape African middle class placed its hopes for increased social mobility on education rather than on economic enterprise.[71] In the sixty years following the establishment of the first Presbyterian school and mission press at Lovedale in 1824, no fewer than fourteen missionary educational institutions were founded in the Cape and Transkei to keep pace with the demand.[72] Deprived of the support of traditional society, mission Africans of the nineteenth century focused their drive for advancement on becoming 'civilised': on proving themselves worthy of equal participation with whites in the power structure of the Cape Colony. Those who chose Westernisation were immediately made aware of their social distance from whites, and for them, acculturation became part of the struggle for recognition and legal rights.

The role of performance in this struggle has influenced changes in the form of performance styles themselves. Stylistic development is strongly influenced by participants' attempts to use performances

27

to articulate their identities, aspirations and interpretations of experience. The power relations of colonial society encouraged Cape Africans to pursue acculturation actively. The role of acculturation in the drive for status led mission Africans to distance themselves socially from other Africans, and to adopt local features of European culture in line with the positive value they appeared to have.

As with neighbouring peoples, highly organised unaccompanied song is the basis of traditional Cape Nguni communal dance occasions.[73] These occasions include virtually every event of social significance in Zulu and Xhosa life, including ceremonies for newborn children, puberty and age-grade initiations, hunting, courting, ancestral sacrifices, weddings, training and preparation for battle, and funerals. Group distinctiveness and competition as well as solidarity is manifested and reinforced through dance songs at times when the gain, loss or transition of individual members are celebrated or mourned. Important structural features of Nguni songs include the staggered entry of at least two voice parts in a call-and-response relation to each other. Frequent overlapping produces an intentional polyphony, and the staggered entry and ending points of the parts remain fixed in relation to each other through numerous cyclical repetitions, which rule out complete collective cadences.[74]

Most missionaries were culturally unequipped to recognise or appreciate the subtle complexities beneath the apparent simplicities of traditional song. Moreover, their concern was to eradicate music associated with pagan dancing, beer-drinking, and ritual. They adopted nothing from indigenous culture in their African hymns except the vernacular language. As a more perceptive and sympathetic missionary put it, 'much of the early hymn-making for the Christian church in Africa was an unhappy yoking of British and American tunes to badly translated chunks of unidiomatic vernacular prose, clipped into the right number of syllables to fit a line'.[75] While part singing is common to both African and European music,

> European hymnody is constructed on a four-part basis in which a dominating melodic line. . . prescribes harmonization. This is totally at variance with the Bantu technique of harmonization in which a melody is freely embellished and intensified by adding voice parts . . . . Our major-minor concept, tonality, and modulation were equally foreign to the Bantu.[76]

The separation of African converts from the non-Christian community, combined with the discontinuities between African and European musical systems led to the compartmentalisation of African church and traditional musical idioms. Other musical and sociopolitical factors, however, worked towards breaking down this isolation and producing vibrant new traditions of syncretic choral music in Southern Africa. Among the musical factors were the elaborateness of group vocal traditions, and more especially, the established tradition of singing in parts.

Sympathetic but naively ethnocentric nineteenth-century observers commented frequently upon the importance of part structure in both traditional and Christian African choral music. Holden said of traditional vocalists that 'although they have no scientific rules by which to conduct their singing processes, yet they are not ignorant of parts'.[77] Scully was more perceptive:

> Many of the Native songs and chants are very intricate compositions, in which the different parts are adjusted to each other with ingenious nicety . . . such part songs are probably extremely old, and have reached their present development very gradually.[78]

'When they become Christian, and are taught the rules of music and singing,' Holden continued, 'their performances are of the very first order in vocal song. They have a fine ear for music, keep the most exact time, and take their parts with unvarying correctness'.[79] Scully, too, remarked, 'The mission-trained Native . . . picks up part music with strange facility.'[80]

Forbidden to perform the dances and dance songs that had been indispensable to organised social interaction in the traditional community, mission Africans channelled their desire for musical socialising into Christian congregational singing. The violation of the proper tone-tune relationship and the introduction of patterns of European accentuation that altered syllabic stress in Xhosa song was 'at first bitterly resented by thoughtful converts . . . but in time became accepted by their successors'.[81] Their education promised to raise them to the position of an African elite, so nineteenth-century converts were reluctant to voice their objections to the 'continual violence . . . done to the language in almost every celebration of Zion's songs'.[82]

Towards the end of the nineteenth century, however, a small but influential group of mission cultural leaders began to question the wisdom of abandoning the heritage they shared with all Africans in favour of a poorly integrated Westernism whose benefits were doubtful in the context of South African racialism. Typical of this leadership was the Rev. Tiyo Soga, educated at Lovedale and in Scotland; the first African to be ordained a minister of the Presbyterian church in South Africa. Though the hymns he composed in the late 1850s employed Scottish church melodies, his collections of Xhosa fables, legends, praise songs, genealogies, and customs did much to prevent oral traditions from going unrecorded.[83]

Writing with a new awareness born of Western education, Soga and his successor, the Rev. William Gqoba, began to reassess the value of the Christian way of life for Africans. In articles and lengthy poetic dialogues published in the Lovedale paper *Isigidimi sama Xhosa* (*Kaffir Express*), which he edited from 1884 to 1888, Gqoba debated the question of whether, like Esau, the Christian African had traded the birthright of his cultural heritage for a Western pottage of unattainable goals and unkept promises. Certainly conversion was not bringing skilled jobs, good wages, or social acceptance; the laws enforcing racial discrimination applied equally to Christian and traditional Africans.[84] Other writers for the paper emphasised the discrepancy between Christian teachings and white behaviour and pleaded for a new nationalistic solidarity among blacks.

By the 1880s, many mission school Africans were beginning to believe that a satisfying self-image could not be built entirely on adopted European models. They looked instead for a distinctively African concept of civilisation (see plate 7). With political, social, and economic mobility so sharply restricted, cultural attainment, including performance, became a major means of proving that a new African culture, clearly separate from the 'barbaric' and 'heathen' past, could develop. Syncretic African choral music became a vital resource in the African Christian search for cultural autonomy.

Among the many Xhosa Christians who tried their hand at musical composition in the later 1800s, John Knox Bokwe of Lovedale is by far the outstanding figure (see plate 8). Bokwe was disturbed by the way in which European hymnody destroyed not only the poetic beauty but even the intelligibility of the Xhosa language. He attempted in some of his works to combine traditional melody, proper tone-tune relationships, and Xhosa patterns of accentuation with four-part harmony and the use of diatonic triads.[85] Though this effort caused 'linguistic distortions in other directions',[86] his hymns were the first good Xhosa verse set to music.[87] Most important, Bokwe's works contained African as well as Christian musical features. A pioneer in the field of secular as well as religious African choral composition, he became the first Xhosa musician to acquire fame, as church and school choirs begged Lovedale Press for copies of his songs.

Under the influence of men such as Soga and Gqoba, Bokwe came to recognise the ministry as the most powerful platform for expressing African social aspirations. In 1892, at the age of 37, he went to Scotland for training as a Presbyterian minister. There he performed his own compositions in a series of highly successful private recitals that helped raise funds for the Church of Scotland in South Africa and aroused sympathy for the plight of African Christians in the Cape Colony. Among the original works he performed was the political hymn, 'Plea for Africa' (with music in the style of Scottish hymnody and lyrics by an unidentified 'Glasgow Lady'). Bokwe gave powerful musical support to the cultural nationalism of mission

Plea from Africa

Words by
A GLASGOW LADY

Music by
JOHN KNOX BOKWE

1. Give a thought to A - fri - ca! 'neath the burn-ing sun There are hosts of wea - ry hearts, wait - ing to be won. Ma - ny lives have passed a - way; but on swamps and sod, There are voi - ces cry - ing now, for the liv - ing God.

2. Breathe a pray'r for A - fri - ca! God the Fa-ther's love Can reach down and bless the tribes, from His heav'n a - bove. Swarth-y lips when moved by grace ev - er sweet - ly sing; Pray till A - fric's heart be made loy - al to our King.

III

Give your love to Africa! they are brothers all,
Who, by sin and slavery, long were held in thrall.
Let the white man love the black; and, when time is past,
In our Father's home above all shall meet at last.
Chorus — Tell the love of Jesus, &c.

IV

Give support to Africa! has not British gold
Been the gain of tears and blood, when the slaves were sold?
Let us send the Gospel back, since for all their need,
Those whom Jesus Christ makes free, shall be free indeed.
Chorus — Tell the love of Jesus, &c.

intellectuals, but he was not the first Xhosa musician to compose in the service of African Christianity.

In 1816 a minor Gaika Xhosa chief named Ntsikana Gaba experienced a revelation and converted to Christianity, possibly with the assistance of the Rev. J. Williams of the London Missionary Society's Kat River station. An inspired singer, dancer, diviner, and charismatic religious leader, Ntiskana became the first known 'Bantu prophet', gathering about him a strong personal following which included the father of Tiyo Soga. Ntsikana learned to read, and his followers gave up traditional dance and body decoration and were the first Cape Africans to promote literacy among their own people.[88] Ntsikana's movement involved a restructuring of traditional Xhosa religion rather than a radical break with it. His spiritual conversion reflected the need to fuse Xhosa belief with Christianity in order to construct a world view that could accommodate military defeat and colonisation by Europeans. Through the efforts of his followers, Christianity came to be viewed by many Xhosa as an African religion brought by Ntsikana, not by missionaries.[89] Before his death in 1821, Ntsikana composed hymns for the call to prayer and congregational singing, and four of these have survived despite African unfamiliarity with any form of musical notation at that time.

Transmitted orally among Xhosa Christians for half a century, Ntsikana's *Ulo Tixo Mkulu* (Thou Great God) was published in *Isigidimi* . . . in 1876. To this hymn were added three more of Ntsikana's songs, transcribed by Bokwe in 1884. He wrote them all in the simplified Curwin tonic-solfa system of notation introduced into South Africa by a London missionary, Christopher Birkett, at Fort Beaufort in 1855.[90] One of these songs is pentatonic and three are hexatonic; all voices have parallel movement, and the melodies are recognisably Xhosa.

The interest of mission Xhosa in Ntsikana's religious ideas and practices was part of their effort to measure the relative value of traditional and Western culture for a new Christian African society. Few other composers used traditional African features in their hymns, but Bokwe was inspired to write a biography of Ntsikana,[91] in which the four extant hymns can also be found.

Tonic solfa notation was rapidly becoming the basis of musical education among African choirs in the last half of the nineteenth century. This tended to enforce conformity to European hymnody. Unfortunately, tonic solfa had no way of indicating modulation or key shifts within a piece, and so cannot be used to teach written music played on Western instruments. Africans who wished to learn piano or organ had to learn staff notation from European and Coloured music masters in the educational centres of the Eastern and Central Cape and Transkei. Nevertheless, the very sketchiness of tonic-solfa

Ulo Tixo Mkulu
Thou Great God

NOTE — *Ntsikana's Great Hymn has been printed in all the Xosa-speaking collections used for Church praise. Words and Music had been traditionally handed down till committed to print as arranged by compiler of 'Amaculo ase Lovedale.'*

Ntsikana's Hymn **Arranged by John Knox Bokwe**

Key F — *Gravely*

Ulo Tixo omkulu, ngosezulwini;
Ungu Wena-wena Kaka lenyaniso.
Ungu Wena-wena Nqaba yenyaniso.
Ungu Wena-wena Hlati lenyaniso.
Ungu Wena-wen 'uhlel' enyangwaneni.

Ulo dal' ubom, wadala pezulu.

Lo Mdal' owadala wadala izulu.

Lo Menzi wenkwenkwezi noZilimela;
Yabinza inkwenkwezi, isixelela.
Lo Menzi wemfaman' uzenza ngabom?

Lateta ixilongo lisibizile.
Ulonqin' izingela imipefumlo.
Ulohlanganis' imihlamb' eyalanayo.

Ulomkokeli wasikokela tina.
Ulengub' inkul' esiyambata tina.
Ozandla Zako zinamanxeba Wena.
Onyawo Zako zinamanxeba Wena.
Ugazi Lako limrolo yinina?
Ugazi Lako lipalalele tina.
Lemali enkulu-na siyibizile?
Lomzi Wako-na-na siwubizile?

He, is the Great God, Who is in heaven
Thou art Thou, Shield of truth.
Thou art Thou, Stronghold of truth.
Thou art Thou, Thicket of truth.
Thou art Thou Who dwellest in the highest.

He, Who created life (below), created (life) above.

That Creator Who created, created heaven.

This maker of the stars, and the Pleiades.
A star flashed forth, it was telling us.
The Maker of the blind, does He not make them of purpose?

The trumpet sounded, it has called us.
As for His chase He hunteth, for souls.
He, Who amalgamates flocks rejecting each other.

He, the Leader, Who has led us
He, Whose great mantle, we do put it on.
Those hands of Thine they are wounded.
Those feet of Thine, they are wounded.
Thy blood, why is it streaming?
Thy blood, it was shed for us.
This great price, have we called for it?
This home of Thine, have we called for it?

Chimes of Ntsikana's Bell

'NTSIKANA'S BELL' — *Was chanted by the composer at dawn of day, stand-ing at his hut-door, summoning his congregation to morning prayers. As people gathered they joined in the strain adding the other vocal parts.*

Key Ab *To be sung in unison — ad libitum*

Music by John Knox Bokwe

Translated into English, the exclamation 'Sele!' being accepted as equivalent to *Ahoy!* while the chiming of *'A-hom'* is a softer imitation of *Ding-dong*. The words of 'Ntsikana's Bell' may be thus rendered:—

> Verse 1   Sele! Sele!
> Ahom, ahom, ahom!
> Come hearken, come hearken the Word of the Lord.
> Ahom, ahom, ahom, ahom, ahom.

35

Verses 2, 3 and 4

:s .,s | s :— :— | s : :s .,s | s :— :— | s : :s .s
:s .,s | s :— :— | s : :s .,s | s :— :— | s : :s .s
2. Sa-be - la - ni, sa-be - la - ni Niya-
3. Li-bi - ye - lwe langqo - nga na I -
4. Se - le! Se - le! A -
:s .,s | s :— :— | s : :s .,s | s :— :— | s : :s .s
:s .,s | s :— :— | s : :s .,s | s :— :— | s : :s .s

|m :— :m |d :— :r |s₁ :— :— |s₁ : :s .s |s :— :— |s : .s :s .s
|m :— :m |d :— :r |s₁ :— :— |s₁ : :s .s |s :— :— |s : .s :s .s
bi - zwa e - zu - lwi - ni; Zani no - nke zihlwele
zwe lo - ba - wo be - nu. Owo - li - va ngowoli
hom, a - hom, a - hom! Sabe - la - ni, sabe -
|m :— :m |d :— :r |s₁ :— :— |s₁ : :s .s |s :— :— |s : .s :s .s
|m :— :m |d :— :r |s₁ :— :— |s₁ : :s .s |s :— :— |s : .s :s .s

|s :— :— |s : :s .s |m :— :m |d :— :r |s₁ :— :— |s₁ : :d
|s :— :— |s : :s .s |m :— :m |d :— :r |s₁ :— :— |s₁ : :d
ndi - ni kunye na - ni ba - ntwa - na - na. A-
kau - la! A - hom, a - hom, a - hom! A-
la - ni Niya - bi - zwa e - zu - lwi - ni! A-
|s :— :— |s : :s .s |m :— :m |d :— :r |s₁ :— :— |s₁ : :d
|s :— :— |s : :s .s |m :— :m |d :— :r |s₁ :— :— |s₁ : :d

|l₁ :— :l₁ |f₁ :— :l₁ |m₁ :— :s₁ |r₁ : :s₁|d :— :— |— : :—
|l₁ :— :l₁ |f₁ :— :l₁ |m₁ :— :s₁ |r₁ : :s₁|s₁ :— :— |— : :—
hom, a - hom, a - hom, a - hom, a-hom!
hom, a - hom, a - hom, a - hom, a-hom!
hom, a - hom, a - hom, a - hom, a-hom!
|l₁ :— :l₁ |f₁ :— :l₁ |m₁ :— :s₁ |r₁ : :f₁|m₁ :— :— |— : :—
|l₁ :— :l₁ |f₁ :— :l₁ |m₁ :— :s₁ |r₁ : :s₁|d₁ :— :— |— : :—

gave it some flexibility. With so much room for interpretation, African melodies, part structures, and performance practices inevitably crept into African choral singing, especially in the hymns of African churches that seceded from European missions. The first independent movement was the Xhosa nationalist Nehemiah Tile's Tembu Church,[92] begun in 1884.

Converts who left the mission stations to set up Christian farm communities of their own[93] revitalised traditional musical practices as pa t of their new style of African communal life. Although European hymnals were popular with African congregations, sheet music was hard to come by. Many songs were transmitted aurally at choir concerts and competitions and rehearsed without the aid of written scores. The late Sotho composer Woodruff Buti recalled school concerts before the turn of the century that presented traditional African songs in Western choral style, along with African hymns and popular British and American songs of the day. When Christian Xhosa and Mfengu came to Kimberley and Johannesburg during the late nineteenth century, they brought with them not only European sacred and secular songs, but also materials and procedures for creating a distinctively African choral music.

The English settlers in the Cape made an enduring contribution to Cape Nguni musical culture in the form of the church organ and the small harmonium, essential pieces of colonial parlor furniture in the Victorian era. Westernised Africans, in their desire for conspicuous symbols of civilisation, often gave the harmonium priority over other European domestic 'necessities'. In Xhosa Christian homes, musical evenings took the place of traditional beer-drinks. In the childhood home of composer Ben Tyamzashe, the harmonium accompanied traditional songs sung in the diatonic scale, such as *Watsh'uhomyayi* and *Abafan' bas' Engqushwa*, as well as English songs and Xhosa hymns.[94] The tradition of keyboard and playing remains strong among Cape Africans, and in the field of jazz and popular music, Cape pianists are still regarded as the most technically skilled.

Missionaries organised Christian brass bands among nearly all the African peoples of South Africa, and the Cape Nguni may have produced some of the best trained players.[95] Independent African bands sprang up in Transvaal towns, but bands in the Cape and Transkei were almost always attached to missions where their members acquired musical literacy and a European repertoire. Brass band music among the Xhosa must be considered among the sources of pure British influence, along with hymns, Victorian 'salon' music and popular song, all of which Cape Africans brought to Kimberley and Johannesburg.

Mission Africans, mostly Cape Nguni, created an urban identity and social order in Kimberley during the last decades of the nineteenth century. Based primarily on the model of the upper level of British colonial society, African middle-class society combined nationalism with Victorian values. One of the most important contributors to this model of African Christian civilisation was the performance culture of black America, transmitted directly by visiting black American performers or indirectly by Cape Coloureds and whites.

By the later nineteenth century, Coloured performers had been drawing upon international folk and popular music for two centuries. They were greatly impressed by the music and dance styles of the black North American and West Indian sailors, adventurers[96] and minstrel troupes who displayed their talents in Cape Town.

In America, stage minstrelsy began with white performers who wore blackface make-up and caricatured the culture of slaves and free Negroes.[97] The publication of a number of minstrel songs, including Thomas Rice's classic, 'Jim Crow' (c. 1828), by the Cape Town weekly *Die Versammelar* (The Collector) helped to popularise them in the Colony. In 1848, a troupe called Joe Brown's Band of Brothers became, according to R. W. Murry, 'the first band of vocalists who gave South Africa a taste for nigger part singing'.[98] In the same year, white South Africans who had recently seen performances in London[99] of the 'refined' American company, the Ethiopian Serenaders, began a local company of the same name. In 1862, the white performers of the Harvey-Leslie Christy Minstrels, who combined lively dancing and earthy humour with concert pieces and sentimental ballads, toured South Africa to such acclaim that minstrelsy became a permanent part of the country's entertainment for the rest of the century. For many years, Malay serenaders had strolled about Cape Town in the evening singing Afrikaans lovesongs.[100] Both white and non-Malay Coloured amateur performers added to this tradition by singing 'Christy minstrel' songs in the streets during the latter half of the century.[101] The degree to which blacks were aware of or took interest in these performers is uncertain. Local white amateur minstrel troupes did spring up in towns throughout the country, and it seems that the rattling bones (Tswana: *marapo*; Zulu: *amathambo*) used as rhythm instruments by both rural and early urban Africans were taken from the minstrels.[102]

It was black American minstrels, however, who had the greatest influence on South African blacks, in particular on Coloured people and the nascent African middle class. From the mid-1870s, black American minstrelsy took a different direction from that of white blackface performers. With the international success of the Fisk Jubilee Singers, who performed spirituals in a Western classical style, black minstrel shows increasingly featured black religious music of the southern United States. The word 'jubilee', significant in the Bible as the year when slaves were to be freed (*Leviticus* 25:10), began to appear in the names of black troupes, both minstrel and non-minstrel. Those companies performing sacred concerts rather than minstrel shows, such as the Louisiana Jubilee Singers, performed minstrel favourites such as 'Carve Dat Possum' and Stephen Foster songs. James Bland, the greatest of all black minstrel song-writers, also composed many spirituals. By the 1880s, spirituals were used to open and close most black minstrel shows, and the successful Georgia Minstrels made spirituals and 'plantation' culture a fixture of nearly all forms of black stage performance.[103]

In 1887, when minstrelsy was rapidly giving way to 'coon shouters' and vaudeville in America, McAdoo's American Jubilee Singers brought black American minstrelsy to Cape Town for the first time.[104] This company toured the rest of South Africa, including Kimberley and Johannesburg, no less than four times during the 1890s. Their shows had concert party songs, Afro-American folk songs, spirituals, instrumental music, 'Grand Opera', juggling, jokes and comic sketches, solo dancing and cakewalks. Their performances appealed to whites as well as blacks, who could attend the same shows at that time, and inspired a good deal of local imitation.[105] McAdoo's company made a lasting impression on all racial groups in South Africa, and several of the company's members settled permanently in the country.

In Cape Town, thousands of working-class Coloured men formed performance clubs in the wake of McAdoo's visits. Since then, these clubs have paraded through the streets of the city every few years in the famous 'Cape Coon Carnival', dressed as blackface minstrels and singing American Negro songs and Afrikaans *moppies* (comic songs) to the accompaniment of drums, whistles, guitars, tambourines, and banjos. Highly competitive, these clubs still reflect their mixed Coloured-Afrikaans-Malay-American heritage in costume and song. Club names – Fabulous Orange Plantation Minstrels, Meadow Cottonfield Jazz Singers – illustrate how century-old images of black American entertainment styles have become a permanent part of working-class Coloured performance culture. Though the church-oriented, middle-class Coloured people would not march with the coon clubs, many enjoyed the polished concert performances of McAdoo's male quartets and soloists at Cape Town's music halls, such as the Darling Street Opera House.

Black American influence spread and deepened among black South Africans as Cape Coloured artisans, teachers, farmers, and labourers headed north and east in the wake of white settlers in the 1800s. The Coloureds brought with them their Western Cape culture and, later, new traditions of minstrel and variety entertainment. In the growing towns of the Cape, Transkei, Basutoland, Free State, and Natal, Coloured performers entertained Africans with their string bands, 'coon' vocal groups, and variety routines, usually at entertainments called 'socials'. Cape mission schools such as Lovedale and Healdtown had many Coloured as well as African students. Zonnebloem and a few other schools in Cape Town enrolled white children as well.[106] In these schools, African students began to form their own groups of 'coons'; smartly dressed vocal quartets and string bands which became a fixture of student variety concerts. Their repertoire favoured black American and English songs plus African choral compositions and arrangements of traditional tunes. Afrikaans songs and instrumental accompaniments were regarded as provincial and 'uncultured' by educated Africans, for whom the term 'coons' became synonymous with Afro-Americanized choral and variety performers in evening dress.

The same conditions of economic depression, cattle disease, drought, and legal discrimination that led struggling African commercial farmers and tradesmen to invest in schooling for their children drove many educated Xhosa and Mfengu in search of new opportunities.[107] In the last two decades of the nineteenth century, Kimberley was the 'focal point for the ambitions and aspirations of hundreds of Africans . . . who shared common ideas, values, and experiences as a result of education at the hands of Christian missionaries'.[108] Most of these people, who came from Cape schools or local institutions such as Kimberley's Lyndhurst Road Methodist School, worked as teachers, clerks, or civil servants in the colonial administration. Seeking incorporation into colonial society, they became Westernised in the hope that equality before the law, and other principles of British Imperial rule, would protect them from the oppressive racial policies advocated by local Afrikaner and British settlers.

Helping to build values and social cohesion among Kimberley's African mission graduates was a busy social life based in churches, clubs, and other associations. Organisations created a sense of class and community among middle-class Africans and gave aid and acceptance to new arrivals. Most prominent was the South Africans' Improvement Society, created to cultivate the public use of English among Africans by sponsoring readings, lectures, displays of elocution, and debates among members.[109] Tied to one another in so many ways, Kimberley's middle-class Africans often intermarried without regard to ethnic or regional background. The city became a center of cultural mixture among the core of an emerging national African elite.[110]

Music became a bond of interest and association and a means of expressing social aspiration.[111] Concerts by mission-trained performers were highlights of elite African social life. Almost every school prizegiving, organisation meeting, or other occasion included musical entertainment. Music was a potent force in the shaping of African middle-class identity, and it featured a blend of African, Afro-American, and European influences. Apart from church hymns, Westernised African choral songs, and English secular choir pieces, the most important musical influence was McAdoo's American Jubilee Singers.

Among those who resigned from the troupe to reside in Kimberley was the black American pianist Will P. Thompson. With a leading civil servant, Isaiah Bud-Mbelle, he organised and performed in several amateur minstrel companies composed of local middle-class Coloureds and Africans. One of these companies, the Diamond Minstrels, performed 'the comic songs and "wheezes" of Bones and Tambo, Stephen Foster songs, and "The Laughing Coon",' accompanied by piano, banjo, and other instruments, in honour of Queen Victoria's Diamond Jubilee.[112] Another informal group, the Balmoral Amateur Minstrels, included local white performers in addition to Thompson, Africans, and Coloureds.[113]

Ordinary performances by educated Africans already featured minstrel material. A concert in Kimberley in July 1892 offered James Bland's 'Oh Dem Golden Slippers!' along with English songs, dramatic sketches, an 'acting dance', and a comic musical comment on the growing division between permanently urbanised and migrant Africans, 'The Crackpot in the City'.[114] The most prestigious and enduring musical organisation was the Philharmonic Society, which involved Thompson as pianist, Bud-Mbelle as musical director, and a number of members who had won medals for singing at the Kimberley Exhibition in 1892. At their debut in March 1897, they performed a mixed choral programme that reveals their desire for a cultural identity that was at once 'civilised' (British), internationally black, and African. Their reportoire included:[115]

> uTixo Mkulu (Ntsikana)
> Kaffir Wedding Song (Bokwe)
> Matabili War Song
> Africa's Tears (William Kawa)
> Bushman Chorus – *Qar Qa Ba Sonxha*
> Bells Bells Bells
> Close the Shutters, Willie's Dead
> Part songs
> A mixed quartet
> Pickin' on de Harp (Bland)
> God Save the Queen

The American Negro companies also created a sense of commercial possibility for African performers. Modelling their company on McAdoo's, two white South Africans, Jason Balmer and Lillian Clark, organised an 'African Native Choir' from students at Kimberley and Lovedale which toured Britain early in 1892.[116] The quality of performance was apparently extremely high, but personal quarrels and financial disagreements between the white promoters and African performers broke up the company with considerable financial loss to everyone concerned.

Although James Stuart, headmaster of Lovedale, had described the choir as 'a heartless swindle, perpetrated at the blackman's expense'[117] Balmer had no difficulty in 1893 in recruiting a number of original and new members for a tour of Britain that was eventually

41

extended to Canada and the United States.[118] Financial and personal problems again interfered, but audiences were delighted. The group drew attention to the cultural achievements and educational ambitions of black South African Christians and sympathy for the performers. When the choir became destitute in the American Midwest, the black American Methodist Episcopal Church (AME) offered educational opportunities, and eight members eventually earned Bachelor degrees at Wilberforce and Lincoln Universities.[119]

The African Native Choir, the first international venture involving black South African performing artists, set an unfortunate precedent of financial and interpersonal difficulties during overseas tours that continues to plague their successors today. Nevertheless, the tour was both culturally and politically significant: it brought black South Africans into direct contact with concepts of education and racial progress held by blacks in the United States, and it increased the influence of black America on the early urban African culture of South Africa. Among the most important independent sources of this influence was the black American missionary effort in South Africa. A major initial impulse resulted from the contact between the African Methodist Episcopal Church and independent African clergymen, established by native choir member Charlotte Manye during and after her tour to the United States.

The history of black American missions in South Africa began with two Xhosa ministers, Mangena Makone and James Dwane. They had seceded from the Wesleyan Methodists in 1894 over the exclusion of black clergy from the decision-making councils of their white colleagues. Influenced by letters from Charlotte Manye in America, they sought affiliation with the African Methodist Episcopal Church. In 1898, the Church's leader, Bishop H. M. Turner, visited South Africa, where he ordained 65 local ministers to serve a membership already approaching 10 000. Dissatisfied with his status of 'assistant bishop', Dwane travelled to the United States in 1899, where he requested autonomy for the South African Methodist Episcopal Church, but without success. He returned to South Africa in 1900 and founded the 'Order of Ethiopia'. Both the AME and Dwane's church were important in the subsequent growth of what was known as the 'Ethiopianist Movement' in South Africa.[120]

This movement addressed the problems and needs, both political and spiritual, of black Christians as opposed to white. It grew rapidly by absorbing disaffected members of European missionary churches in many of the towns. Whites were quick to accuse the 'Ethiopian preachers' of anti-white racialism, subversion, and responsibility for the political unrest among Africans in Natal that culminated in the Bambata Rebellion of 1906.[121] While these charges cannot be proved, the AME's philosophy of African spiritual and material

42

self-reliance, and even the very existence of a large, well-organised all-black church with transatlantic ties, appeared 'subversive' to South African whites. Most fundamentally, the AME was the church of the educated African townspeople, whose broadened horizons led them to a strong identification with the struggles of the 'American Negro'.[122]

In 1897, the AME Church established Wilberforce Institute, the 'South African Tuskeegee', at Evaton near Johannesburg. There African students were exposed to spirituals, nationalist conceptions of black solidarity[123] and the strategies for racial progress proposed by the black American leader Booker T. Washington. Influenced by the ideals of men such as Washington and his American-educated South African counterpart John Dube, mission-school Africans felt a deep sense of frustration when confronted with the social and economic circumstances of African life in Kimberley and Johannesburg at the turn of the century.

In 1886, not long after diamond operations had stabilised at Kimberley under Cecil Rhodes' monopoly, the largest gold discovery in recorded history occurred on the Witwatersrand in the southern Transvaal. Once again, African labourers from rural-traditional communities as far north as Lake Tanganyika streamed in for work. White fortune-seekers, mining personnel, and financiers from all over the world joined the rush. The Europeans needed skilled artisans, literate Bantu-speaking submanagerial personnel, and domestic servants.

New opportunities for African teachers and clergy also attracted those educated at Christian mission schools from as far away as Cape Town and Nyasaland to Johannesburg, the new city of the Rand. While it had been intended that they would use their education to lead their traditional countrymen to civilisation, the mission-educated African found little call for their skills in rural areas.[124] Most initially chose to teach, but low wages and social isolation led to frequent moves. Many came to the cities in search of an income adequate to a 'respectable' Westernised African way of life.[125]

Christianity, Westernisation, and urbanisation were thus closely interrelated for 'school' Africans, who formed a relatively large portion of the African community in early Johannesburg. The Transvaal Census of 1904 reports that 25 per cent of the city's permanent African population of 24 348 was fully literate, much more than the national percentage for Africans. Their numbers, prestige, and knowledge of the dominant European culture made those who could boast a mission school education leaders of the Johannesburg African community.

Yet life in the 'Golden City' fell dismally short of their expectations. Although they were among those entitled to bring their families to town, segregation often forced them to live in conditions of

Nkosi Sikelel' i Africa

Enoch Sontonga

1. Nkosi, sikelel' i Afrika
   Malupakam' upoado lwayo;
   Yiva imitandazo yetu
   Usisikelele.

   Lord, bless Africa
   May her horn rise high up;
   Hear Thou our prayers
   And bless us.

Chorus: Yihla Moya, yihla Moya,
   Yihla Moya Oyingcwele.

   Descend, O Spirit
   Descend, O Holy Spirit.

2. Sikelela iNkosi zetu
   Zimkumule umDali wazo;
   Zimoyike zezimhlouele,
   Azisikelele.

   Bless our chiefs;
   May they remember their Creator,
   Fear Him and revere Him,
   That He May bless them.

44

Key Bb   Enoch Sontonga

3. Sikelel' amadol' esizwe,   Bless the public men
    Sikelela kwa nomlisela   Bless also the youth
    Ulitwal' ilizwe ngomonde,   That they may carry the land with
    Uwusikilele.   patience
                                          And that Thou mayst bless them.

4. Sikelel' amakosikazi   Bless the wives
    Nawo onk' amanenekazi   And also all young women
    Pakamisa wonk' umtinjana   Lift up all the young girls
    Uwusikelele.   And bless them.

5. Sikelela abafundisi   Bless the ministers
    Bemvaba zonke zelilizwe;   Of all the churches of this land;
    Ubatwese ngoMoya Wako   Endue them with Thy Spirit
    Ubasikelele.   And bless them.

6. Sikelel' ulimo nemfuyo;   Bless agriculture and stock raising;
    Gzota zonk' indlala nezifo;   Banish all famine and diseases;
    Zalisa ilizwe ngempilo   Fill the land with good health
    Ulisikelele.   And bless it.

7. Sikelel' amalinga etu   Bless our efforts
    Awomanyana nokuzaka,   Of union and self-uplift,
    Awemfundo nemvisiswano   Of education and mutual under-
    Uwasikelele.   standing
                                          And bless them.

8. Nkosi sikelel' i Afrika   Lord, bless Africa;
    Cima bonk' ubugwenza bayo   Blot out all its wickedness
    Neziggito, nezono zayo   And its transgressions and sins,
    Uyisikelele.   And bless it.

degradation, squalor and disease far worse than anything imagined in the days before the whites brought the 'blessings of civilisation'. The very people who sold them clothes and sent them to school condemned them for dressing 'foolishly' (above their station) and for competing with whites for skilled employment. Even the missions expected them to accept perpetual childhood rather than Christian brotherhood, especially in the directing of church affairs.[126] Their traditional fellows regarded them as traitors and tools of the Europeans, and local whites cried, 'Education spoils the Kaffir'.[127]

Their suffering is reflected in the 'melancholy strain' of *Nkosi Sikelel' iAfrika* (God Bless Africa), a song composed by the Xhosa teacher Enoch Sontonga at Johannesburg's Nancefield location in 1897, and first performed in 1899. The song was sung at Native day schools and widely popularised by the touring choir of Ohlange Institute.[128] It made a strong initial impression at the inaugural meeting of the South African Native National Congress in 1912, and in 1925 it was officially adopted as the anthem of the African National Congress.[129] Subsequently, the Xhosa 'national poet', S. E. Mqayi, wrote seven additional verses. Translations have appeared in many African languages, and a number of Southern African countries have adopted the song as their national anthem. *Nkosi Sikelel' iAfrika* has come to symbolise more than any other piece of expressive culture the struggle for African unity and liberation in South Africa.

To some extent, African Christians had contributed to their sad situation. Many had applauded the destruction of traditional political structures and the abandonment of traditional culture. They had thought that conversion and Westernisation would bring them power over their own people and acceptance into the mainstream of political and economic life.[130] The reality of African life in Johannesburg was for them a bitter disillusionment (see plate 5).

Most of the European missions followed their rural converts to the Rand (as the goldfields were called) and opened churches for African Christian townspeople during the 1890s.[131] Others, however, such as Albert Baker's South African Compounds and Interior Mission, were attracted to the mine compounds, where there were 'more than 100 000 of the young manhood of all the tribes of South Africa gathered in groups of from three to five thousand, and all accessible to the Gospel'.[132]

Some missions made good use of music in their evangelising efforts. Methodists formed a band of African preachers who 'made their entrance singing, shouting, and moving to the rhythm of their song and went around the compound inviting men to their service. Attracted to this animated group, the miners followed and stayed to hear what they had to say'.[133] A greater musical influence was the Salvation Army which began working among Africans in 1890, using

46

brass bands, tambourines, and singing brigades in both the city streets and mine compounds.[134] A visitor to Johannesburg in 1893 recalled that on Sunday afternoons in the Fordsburg location, 'the Salvation Army and other religious bodies held services for the Natives, who regularly gathered in large numbers. The wonderful singing was quite a feature of these meetings'.[135]

For the gold miners, conditions were similar to those experienced at Kimberley, though they did not live under a rigid, 'closed' compound system. Compounds did become gradually more like labour prison camps after 1903, as part of an effort to control desertion, organisation, and resistance among the miners; but from 1887 to the First World War there was relative freedom of movement regulated by a 'pass' system. The trading interests who sold food and goods to the workers succeeded in keeping the compounds from ever being entirely closed.[136]

Until after the First World War, the manpower requirements of gold mining on the Rand greatly exceeded the supply. Mining companies were reluctant to compete for African labour by the logical but less profitable means of higher wages. They argued that more money only 'spoiled' the workers, leading them to loaf or to return to their homes when economic necessity was not strong enough to keep them on the job.

The companies' solution to the shortage was to import more than half the underground labour force from Mozambique. These Portuguese East Africans were indentured on rigid contracts for periods of service averaging eighteen months. Unfamiliar with the urban environment, and far from their homes, they were more compliant with the harsh discipline of the mines and more likely to spend their earnings locally than workers from South Africa. These foreigners were willing to work for roughly half the £3 or £4 per month paid to local miners in the mid-1890s.[137]

The Mozambiquans suffered terribly and often died from the combined effects of exhausting labour and winter cold.[138] Despite their numbers, only a few drifted into the shanty towns and slum locations surrounding the mines to become members of the Rand's permanent workforce. The companies were under pressure from the colonial government to recruit locally and they disliked the constant need to train short-term recruits. Efficiency suffered from the perpetual inexperience of the workers.

As a result, mine management did nothing to discourage more experienced, urbanised workers from building shanty towns all along the gold reef. Taking an active hand, the mine owners recommended to the Industrial Commission in 1897 that the Transvaal Government create large 'family locations' for mineworkers, but the idea was flatly rejected. Following the Boer War, the British Transvaal administration began to knock down the unauthorised mine locations. The companies then built their own single men's barracks for underground miners and provided family housing locations for some clerks and surface workers only.[139]

Although they soon met the fate suffered by all African settlements near white residential areas, the workers' shanty towns constituted Johannesburg' first African communities. In these 'unauthorised' and unsupervised shanties long-term patterns of urban African working-class social organisation, the liquor trade, prostitution, and organised criminal groups first became established.[140] Along with the racially mixed slums – Newclare, Brickfields, Ferreira's Camp, Malay Camp-Vrededorp, and Fordsburg – on the city's fringes, and the servants' quarters in Europeans' backyards, they sheltered the nucleus of what was to be Subsaharan Africa's largest permanent African urban population. One account[141] lists the African mine workforce at 97 800 in 1899. Some of these joined the 30 000 Africans employed as rickshaw-boys, drivers, domestics, artisans, teachers, and clerks in taking up permanent residence. In 1900[142] the permanent African population of the Rand was estimated at 42 000, compared with 50 000 whites. Significant numbers of South African-born miners remained in the city and became part of a stable urban proletariat.

Much has been made by whites of the tendency of Coloured people to avoid Africans socially, but this was hardly possible in the early days on the Rand. Stringent Transvaal government regulations forced Coloureds, like Africans, to carry passes and forbade them to own property in the towns.[143] In the informal mixing and legal equality of British colonial Cape Town, they had a limited franchise and British citizenship. Coloureds in Johannesburg, however, were forced to wear metal badges, as were Africans, as proof that they were employed.[144] A government committee laid out Malay Camp in Vrededorp, otherwise occupied by poor Afrikaners, as a Coloured location in 1897; but like Ferreira's Camp, it soon became a shanty town with Africans, Asians, Coloureds, and poor whites crowded in tightly together. Conditions were especially difficult for Coloureds, few of whom were single, temporary migrants; most often they arrived as family groups.

Yet for Coloureds the social advantages of living in Cape Town as opposed to Johannesburg were more apparent than real. Cape segregation may have been more by socio-economic class than by colour, but the majority of 'Cape Boys' in Johannesburg in the 1890s were 'artisans of the humblest classes',[145] who never enjoyed much social mobility in either city. Amid the racialism, overcrowding, and squalor faced by all the black people of Johannesburg, the family basis of Coloured social life helped to give the locations a growing sense of community. Coloured social recreation was an important focus of community life and important for the development of African working-class culture in the city.

The Coloureds, Xhosas, and Sothos who lived outside the mine compounds were soon joined by Zulus from Natal and the recently defeated kingdom of Zululand. Refusing to work underground, they came to dominate the relatively well-paid field of domestic service. They did this this by drawing upon the tradition in which young boys had acted as personal servants (*izindibi*) to veteran Zulu soldiers on campaign, and on their experience as 'houseboys' among the colonial British of Natal. Some stayed only a short while, but those who decided to remain permanently began to rebel against conditions in the suburban backyard shacks. Most of them insisted upon having Sundays and a few hours of every afternoon off. Others joined together to rent houses or rooms in 'slum yards' in Doornfontein, Ophirton, or Jeppe. After long hours of isolation among whites, they sought entertainment in the new locations where drinking, gambling, sex, and, of course, music and dancing were regular weekend activities.[146]

Tuning their favourite instrument, the guitar, to their traditional five and six-note scales, African domestic workers often played at location entertainments, or performed in the streets. They strummed a simple three-chord accompaniment to traditional songs or picked up the Afrikaans-influenced styles of the Cape Coloured and Xhosa. Miners who had settled in the city made rural dances a part of competitive recreation in the locations as well as on the mines. As in Kimberley, miners played trade store instruments as they strolled in the dusty streets. Their music became an important resource for developing inter-ethnic urban African styles. Social life already featured public dances; A. A. Kumalo, the noted Zulu composer who died in 1966, recalled playing his concertina for dances in Johannesburg in 1898 for a guinea per night.[147]

The 1890s also saw the birth of organised outlaw resistance in Johannesburg. Jan Note, a former Zulu domestic, organised a secret society of Zulu proletarians called the Ninevites, ostensibly to protect Africans by force 'because it is a town without law'.[148]

Beginning by administering beatings to white employers who cheated Africans out of their wages or mistreated them on the mines, they soon became a fearsome paramilitary gang (*izigebengu*) that preyed violently on blacks and whites alike. These gangs moved to Durban as part of the general flight from Johannesburg during the Boer War (1899–1902). They wore 'distinctive wide-bottomed trousers of many colours' and paraded through the streets playing music that was 'generally a strange combination of complicated Dutch, English, and Native tunes' on the mouth organ, an instrument with which they were associated.[149] Ninevite and other African 'underworld' or-

49

ganisations were a significant feature of lower-class urbanisation in early twentieth-century Johannesburg.

Entertainment provided for Johannesburg's white community must also be included among the musical influences on urbanising Africans. Very few Africans could have had access to the rowdy English music hall and comic opera performances at the Empire, Globe, Royal, and Standard theatres.[150] Yet the 118 unsegregated canteens, many located in the poorest and most racially mixed sections, featured music for drinking and dancing of the 'honky-tonk' variety already encountered in Kimberley. Also in evidence were 'continental bands consisting of any number of performers, who played very sweetly about the streets and took up hat collections'.[151] In addition, British and local military brass and fife and drum bands, such as the Wanderers Military Band, played outdoor concerts of light classical and march music at the Wanderers' Grounds and other parks as early as 1890.

The nineteenth century saw the beginning of a number of fundamental processes in the urbanisation of African performing arts in South Africa. History made available to Africans a range of performance resources under specific conditions of contact. Performance styles represented contrasting cultural models, and the relations between their bearers were the basis for reinterpreting and selecting materials in composition. Colonialism, the missions, proletarian work experience, urbanization, and racial segregation all shaped the development of new kinds of African communities. African response to these forces led to the integration of ethnic ties into a system of social categories based on class. Social life reflected efforts to create new institutions on the one hand, and to keep them flexible on the other. The continuing tension between order and disorder was essential to African adaptation.

Performance provided an important cultural dimension to adaptation and institutional change. As cultural communication, performance linked rural and urban areas and spanned all racial and social categories. Indigenous and foreign styles interpenetrated according to the needs of specific groups of Africans for new forms of expression. These needs were related to African strategies for survival and advancement within colonial society. Black performers and conditions of performance were part of the process of adaptation and so were shaped by it. To understand how different kinds of performers recombined various cultural resources to entertain their neighbours, express common. aspirations, interpret social experience, and earn a living, we must describe the quality of African life in the Johannesburg locations in the early twentieth century.

NOTES

1   Richard Elphick, *The Cape Khoi and the First Phase of South African Race Relations*, PhD thesis, University of London, 1972, p. 298.
2   P. R. Kirby, *The Musical Instruments of the Native Races of South Africa*, Johannesburg, 1965 ed., orig. 1934, p. 249.
3   *Ibid.*, pp. 14–19, 82–84, plate 71b.
4   H. Lichtenstein, quoted in *Ibid.*, p. 252.
5   *Ibid.*, p. 269.
6   W. J. Burchell, *Travels in the Interior of Southern Africa*, vol. II, London, 1822, pp. 205, 310, 421.
7   David Rycroft, 'Evidence of stylistic continuity in Zulu "town" music', in *Essays for a Humanist*, New York, 1977, p. 219–20.
8   C. G. Botha, *General History and Social Life of the Cape of Good Hope*, Cape Town, 1962, p. 296.
9   Victor de Kock, *Those in Bondage*, London, 1950, pp. 94–95.
10 *Ibid.*, p. 9.
11 P. R. Kirby, 'The use of European musical techniques by the non-European peoples of South Africa', *Journal of the International Folk Music Council*, 1959, p. 39.
12 de Kock, *Those in Bondage*, p. 94.
13 *Music*, S. A. Information Service, n.p., n.d.
14 de Kock, *Those in Bondage*, pp. 93–94.
15 Kirby, *The Musical Instruments*, p. 254.
16 M. Wilson and D. Perrot (eds.), *Outlook on a Century: South Africa, 1870–1970*, Lovedale, 1973, p. 298.
17 King Sekhukhuni of the Pedi, Letsie of the Sotho, Montshiwa of the western Tswana, and several Xhosa chiefs all encouraged their men to go to the Diamond Fields and return with guns and ammunition in preparation for armed conflict with settler and colonial forces.
18 Gardner Williams, *The Diamond Mines of South Africa*, New York, 1902, p. 189.
19 *Ibid.*, p. 219.
20 Rob Turrell, 'Kimberley: labour and compounds, 1871–1888', in S. Marks and R. Rathbone (eds.), *Industrialisation and Social Change in South Africa*, London, 1982.
21 W. T. E., *IDB or the Adventures of Solomon Davis*, London, 1887, p. 217.
22 Turrell, 'Kimberley: labour and compounds'.
23 Wilson and Perrot, *Outlook on a Century*, p. 19.
24 John Angove, *In the Early Days: Pioneer Life on the South African Diamond Fields*, Kimberley, 1910, p. 196.
25 Kirby, *The Musical Instruments*, p. 248.
26 Eric Rosenthal, *The Stars and Stripes in Africa*, London, 1938, p. 170.
27 Dierdre Hansen, *The Life and Work of Benjamin Tyamzashe, a Contemporary Xhosa Composer*, Grahamstown, 1968, pp. 16, 6.
28 de Kock, *Those in Bondage*, p. 89.
29 J. Englebrecht, *The Koranna*, Cape Town, 1936, p. 170.
30 P. Mayer (ed.), *Black Villagers in an Industrial Society*, Cape Town, 1980, p. 67.

31 Turrell, 'Kimberley: labour and compounds'.

32 Kenneth Bellairs, *A Trip to Johannesburg and Back: the Witwatersrand Gold Fields*, London, 1889, p. 22.

33 S. M. Guma, *The Form, Content, and Technique of Traditional Literature in Southern Sotho*, Pretoria, 1967, p. 140. S. M. Molema, *The Bantu Past and Present*, Edinburgh, 1920, p. 319.

34 *Diamond Fields Advertizer*, 14 March 1896.

35 Ruth Finnegan, *Oral Literature in Africa*, London, 1970, pp. 141–2.

36 Charles Adams, *Ethnography of Basotho Evaluative Behavior in the Cognitive Domain Lipapadi (Games)*, unpub. PhD thesis, Indiana, 1974, pp. 120, 136.

37 Palisa Sebilo, *What Do the Miners Say?* B.A. Honours thesis, Lesotho, 1976, pp. 2–3.

38 Like other African societies, the Basotho seal the marriage bond, sanction the transfer of the bride's productive and reproductive capacities from her father's household to that of her husband, and legitimate the couple's children by the formal gift of cattle from the groom to the bride's father.

39 Hugh Ashton, *The Basotho*, London, 1952, p. 46f.

40 Sebilo, *What Do the Miners Say?*, p. 16.

41 Mayer, *Black Villagers*, p. 59.

42 Seeiso Mapele, *Lifela*, B.A. Honours thesis, Lesotho, 1976, p. 2.

43 *Ibid.*, p. 13.

44 Adams, *Ethnography of Basotho*, p. 137.

45 Mapele, *Lifela*, p. 37.

46 *B.A.* is the prefix attached to all license plate numbers of vehicles registered in Maseru. I am indebted to S. D. Mapele's B.A. thesis, Lesotho, 1976, for much useful information on *lifela*.

47 *Ibid*, pp. 23–25.

48 David Welsh, 'The growth of the towns', in M. Wilson and L. Thompson (eds.) *The Oxford History of South Africa*, vol. II, Oxford, 1971, p. 180.

49 Williams, *The Diamond Mines*, p. 261.

50 Ellen Hellmann, 'The Native in the towns', in I. Schapera, (ed.), *The Bantu-Speaking Tribes of South Africa*, London, 1937.

51 Kirby, *The Musical Instruments*, pp. 60–66; Hugh Tracy, *Lalela Zulu*, Johannesburg, 1948.

52 Kirby, *The Musical Instruments*, pp. 257–8.

53 David Rycroft, 'Nguni vocal polyphony', *Journal of the International Folk Music Council*, xix, (1967), pp. 88–103.

54 Kirby, *The Musical Instruments*, plate 228, p. 181f.

55 *Ibid.*, plate 55.

56 Rycroft, 'Evidence of stylistic continuity', pp. 225–228.

57 P. R. Kirby, 'The recognition and practical use of the harmonics of stretched strings by the Bantu of South Africa', *Bantu Studies*, 6 (1932), p. 35.

58 Rycroft, 'Evidence of stylistic continuity', p. 221.

59 *Ibid.*

60 David Rycroft, 'The new "town" music of Southern Africa', *Recorded Folk Music*, vol. 1, Sept./Oct. (1958), p. 54.

61 M. Hunter, *Reaction to Conquest* (London, 1936), p. 357.
62 B. B. Keller, *The Origins of Modernism and Conservatism Among Cape Nguni*, PhD, California, 1970, p. 254.
63 Colin Bundy, *African Peasants and Economic Change in South Africa, 1870–1913*, PhD, Oxford, 1976, p. 65.
64 *Ibid.*, p. 49.
65 S. Judges and C. Saunders, 'The beginnings of an African community in Cape Town', *South African Outlook*, August, (1976).
66 Keller, *The Origins of Modernism*, p 60.
67 Bundy, *African Peasants*, p. 65.
68 *Ibid*, pp. 100–6, 137.
69 Philip Mayer, *Townsmen or Tribesmen*, London and Cape Town, 1961.
70 Keller, *The Origins of Modernism*, pp. 89, 82.
71 Bundy, *African Peasants*, pp. 148–96.
72 Keller, *The Origins of Modernism*, pp. 228–9.
73 Eileen Krige, *The Social System of the Zulus*, London, 1936, pp. 340–4.
74 Rycroft, 'Nguni vocal polyphony', p. 88f.
75 Alexander Sandilands, *120 Negro Spirituals*, Lesotho, 1951, p. 3.
76 Hansen, *The Life and Work of Benjamin Tyamzashe*, p. 2.
77 W. C. Holden, *The Past and Future of the Kaffir Races*, London, 1866, p. 272
78 W. C. Scully, *By Veldt and Kopje*, 1907, p. 285.
79 Holden, *The Past and Future*, p. 273.
80 Scully, *By Veldt and Kopje*, p. 285.
81 Kirby, 'The use of European musical techniques', p. 38.
82 C. Birkett, quoted in A. M. Jones, *African Hymnody in Christian Worship*, Gwelo, 1976, p. 17.
83 J. H. Soga, *The Ama-Xhosa: Life and Customs*, Lovedale, 1931.
84 Albert Gérard, *Four African Literatures*, Berkeley, 1971, pp. 37–39.
85 J. K. Bokwe, *Amaculo ase Lovedale*, Lovedale, 1884.
86 Kirby, 'The use of European musical techniques', p. 38.
87 Gérard, *Four African Literatures*, p. 43.
88 *Ibid.*, p. 27.
89 J. B. Pieres, 'Nxele, Ntsikana, and the origins of the Xhosa religious reaction', *Journal of African History*, 20, 1 (1979), pp. 60–61
90 Jones, *African Hymnody*, p. 17.
91 J. K. Bokwe, *Ntsikana: the Story of an African Convert*, Lovedale, 1914.
92 B. Sundkler, *Bantu Prophets in South Africa*, London, 1961, orig. 1948, p. 38.
93 B. Hutchinson, 'Some social consequences of 19th century missionary activity among the South African Bantu', *Africa*, 27, 2, April (1957), p. 168.
94 Hansen, *The Life and Work of Benjamin Tyamzashe*, p. 8.
95 *Imvo Zabantsundu*, 29 November 1893.
96 Harry Dean and Sterling North, *Umbala*, London, 1929, p. 125.
97 Alain Locke, *The Negro and His Music*, New York, 1969, orig., 1936.
98 R. W. Murry, *South African Reminiscences*, Cape Town, 1894, p. 207.
99 Robert Toll, *Blacking Up*, New York, 1974, p. 37.
100 P. W. Laidler, *A Tavern of the Seas* (Cape Town, n.d.), pp. 173–4.

101 Jan Bouws, 'Minstrels, too, seem to go on forever', *Die Burger*, 12 November 1966, (G. Stone, trans.).

102 Kirby, *The Musical Instruments*, pp. 10–11.

103 Toll, *Blacking Up*, pp. 235–44.

104 John Lovell, *Black Song: the Forge and the Flame*, New York, 1972, p. 415. *Diamond Fields Advertizer*, 29 July 1895.

105 *Diamond Fields Advertizer*, 29 June 1895; 29 April 1898.

106 Welsh, 'The growth of the towns', p. 221.

107 Bundy, *African Peasants*, pp. 151–65.

108 Brian Willan, 'An African in Kimberley: Sol T. Plaatje, 1894–1898', in S S. Marks and R. Rathbone (eds.) *Industrialisation and Social Change in South Africa*, p. 249.

109 *Diamond Fields Advertizer*, 23 August, 1895.

110 Willan, 'An African in Kimberley'.

111 *Ibid.*

112 *Diamond Fields Advertizer*, 12 May 1893.

113 *Diamond Fields Advertizer*, 10 March 1896.

114 *Imvo Zabantsundu* 14 July 1892.

115 *Diamond Fields Advertizer*, 13 March 1897.

116 *Imvo Zabantsundu*, 17 March 1892.

117 James Stewart, *Lovedale, South Africa*, Edinburgh, 1894, p. 70.

118 *Diamond Fields Advertizer*, 12 May 1893.

119 R. Hunt Davis, 'The Black American educational component in African responses to colonialism in South Africa', *Journal of Southern African Studies*, 2, 1, Jan. (1978), p. 69.

120 G. B. A. Gerdener, *Recent Developments in the South African Mission Field*, Cape Town, 1958, p. 112.

121 J. D. Stewart, *A History of the Zulu Rebellion, 1906*, London, 1913, pp. 97–98.

122 *Ilanga Lase Natal*, 15 July 1904.

123 Bishop L. J. Coppin, *Observations of Persons and Things in South Africa, 1900–1904*, 1904.

124 Absolom Vilakazi, *Zulu Transformations*, Pietermaritzburg 1965, p. 139.

125 Keller, *The Origins of Modernism*, pp. 234–9.

126 *Ilanga Lase Natal*, 18 March 1904.

127 Molema, *The Bantu Past and Present*, p. 312.

128 D. D. T. Jabavu, 'The origin of *Nkosi Sikelel' iAfrika*,' *Nada* 26 (1949), pp. 56–58.

129 Gérard, *Four African Literatures*, p. 47.

130 A. C. Jordan, 'Towards an African literature (xi): the Harp of the Nation', *Africa South*, 4, 2, (1960).

131 Gerdener, *Recent Developments*.

132 Albert W. Baker, *Grace Triumphant*, Glasgow, 1939, pp. 101–2.

133 Donald Vysie, *The Wesleyan Methodist Church in the Transvaal, 1823–1902*, Grahamstown, 1969, p. 132.

134 Gerdener, *Recent Developments*, p. 49.

135 Alice Ralls, *Glory Which is Yours: A Tribute to Pioneer Ancestors*, Pietermaritzburg, 1949, p. 171.

136 Sean Moroney, 'The development of the compound as a mechanism of

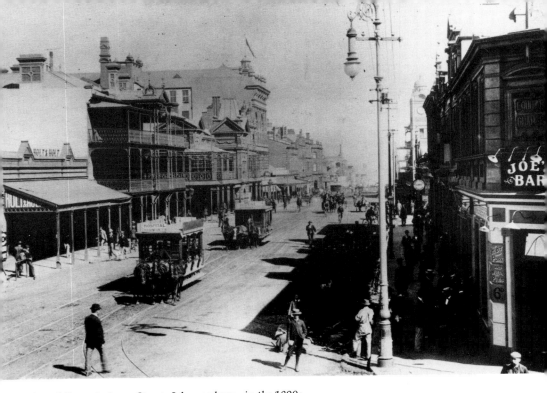

5 *A view of Commissioner Street, Johannesburg, in the 1890s*

6 *Workers at the central shaft of Kimberley diamond mine, 1886*

7 *An elite Christian wedding in the 1890s*

8 *John Knox Bokwe, a Presbyterian minister and a pioneer in secular and religious African choral music*

9 *Reuben T. Caluza, a brilliant choirmaster and the most important composer of Zulu choral music*

worker control, 1900–1912', Witwatersrand History Workshop, Johannesburg, 1978, pp. 16, 1.

137   A. H. Duminy and W. R. Guest, *Fitzpatrick*: *South African Politician; Selected Papers, 1888–1906*, Johannesburg, 1976, pp. 405, 490.

138   J. K. Macnamara, 'The development of a recruitment infrastructure: labour migration routes to the Witwatersrand gold mines and compound accommodation, 1889–1912', Witwatersrand History Workshop, Johannesburg, 1978, p. 21.

139   *Ibid.*, p. 24.

140   Sean Moroney, 'Mine married quarters: the differential stabilisation of the Witwatersrand workforce, 1900–1920', in Marks and Rathbone (eds.), *Industrialisation and Social Change*.

141   W. Bleloch, *The New South Africa*: *Its Value and Development*, London, 1902, p. 228.

142   James Bryce, *Impressions of South Africa*, New York, 1900, p. 316.

143   J. S. Marais, 'The Imposing of European Control', in I. Schapera, (ed.) *The Bantu-Speaking Tribes*, p. 275.

144   Duminy and Guest, *Fitzpatrick*.

145   *Transvaal Leader*, 30 December 1908.

146   C. van Onselen, 'The witches of suburbia: domestic service on the Witwatersrand, 1890–1914', Witwatersrand History Workshop, Johannesburg, 1978, p. 29.

147   A. A. Kumalo, Interview with David Rycroft, 1964.

148   van Onselen, 'The witches of suburbia', p. 56.

149   *Ibid.*, p. 57.

150   Hedley Chilvers, *Johannesburg: out of the Crucible*, New York, 1929, pp. 173–86.

151   Ralls, *Glory Which is Yours*, p. 177.

3 Black Johannesburg, 1900–20

AFRICANS sought work in the Witwatersrand goldfields after the end of the Boer War in 1902 primarily for economic reasons. Population pressure, rural economic collapse, taxation, and increasing involvement in the money economy intensified the need for cash. Nevertheless, the earlier experience of mine labour in Kimberley and a growing awareness of the even more inhuman conditions on the Rand kept thousands of black South Africans away. Of the more than 85 000 mineworkers listed by the Transvaal Chamber of Mines in 1904, only about 19 000 came from South Africa.[1]

In the Transvaal, black workers were at the mercy of unscrupulous recruiters, mining interests dependent on cheap labor, and a neglectful British administration that was little better than the Afrikaner government that had preceded it. It took a mortality rate of 10 per cent among miners to move the government to legislate better compound conditions in the Coloured Labourers Health Ordinance of 1905.[2]

In addition, new arrivals were unprepared for the largely unstructured proximity of so many people; and even those with experience of city life in the Cape, Natal, or Northern Transvaal found it difficult to orient themselves in the racial, ethnic, and socio-economic whirlpool of the Gold Reef. Even those who endured hardships in anticipation of returning to the relative security of rural homes suffered from severe stress due to the lack of organised community, family, and recreational life on the Rand.

The workers' need for release and redress was expressed most readily in drinking, dancing, and faction fighting. Ironically, many became part of Johannesburg's permanent urban proletariat as a result of alcoholism. Lionel Phillips recalled[3] that in early Johannesburg,

Terribly nefarious practices were rife. The drink curse was a scourge, and the government did nothing to check it or keep order over the weekends, when indescribable orgies of drunkenness occurred. The disorders were so appalling that on Sundays one hardly dared walk along the Reef. The Natives fell an easy prey to the vile stuff, and on Mondays a few had been killed and quite a considerable number were disabled in body and prostrated by the strain of the combats and the poison they had imbibed, so that work could proceed only at half speed.

The Transvaal government's Liquor Act of 1896 imposed total prohibition on Africans, but this only increased the problem. It ensured high profits for illicit sales and forbade traditional grain beers that were relatively nutritious and only mildly alcoholic. Traditional beer took several days to brew and had to be consumed in relatively large quantities for an intoxicating effect. Its production was not practical under conditions where liquor had to be made illegally. Traditional beer no longer satisfied the many workers looking for a more powerful antidote to their harsh, unfamiliar and restricted existence. Instead, the government-sponsored distillery at Pretoria and the Portuguese in Mozambique provided cheap brandy, which was mixed with beer and chemicals to produce a variety of near-lethal preparations sold in the locations or smuggled into the mine compounds. An early visitor observed that the African miners

amuse themselves at times by dancing, especially after having managed to get hold of the vile concoction representing whiskey which . . . is rapidly ruining fine races and is mainly composed of tobacco juice and 'blue stone' (sulphate of copper). The effect of this deadly mixture on even a Native's stomach and head can be imagined. Their dance is a strange, incomprehensible one, especially under the above conditions.[4]

Despite the genuine concern of some financial and civic leaders and the regular police raids on brewing operations in the locations, the liquor traffic proved uncontrollable (see plate 10). There is in fact little evidence that government or private employers ever made any serious effort to stop it. Injuries and Monday morning hangovers may have meant a significant loss in man-hours and efficiency, but as a writer for *Imvo Zabantsundu*[5] pointed out, the fondness for liquor was the main factor in keeping some Africans on the Rand long enough to become competent miners, though some might become 'staggering drunkards' as well.

The Transvaal government, for all its pious prohibitions, knew that most of the brandy distilled under government monopoly was going to Africans. Farmers found an outlet for their surplus produce at the state distillery, and government officials profited directly from the traffic through fees and bribery.[6] The mining interests themselves took a share of the huge profits from illicit liquor consumed by their own workers.[7] Moreover, drunkenness and the quarrelling that it ignited hampered African efforts to organise resistance to bad conditions on the mines. Perhaps the most extreme, if diabolically logical, extension of this policy was articulated by a white contributor to the Johannesburg *Star*.[8]

> By the force of some obscure social law . . . the African black is able . . . to accommodate himself to any known social environment . . . In South Africa, legislation as a general rule has been directed towards prohibition laws, ignoring the plain teaching of experience that *in alcohol is to be found the only influence which may be trusted to sap the fund of seemingly infinite vitality*, which will overcome civilization, if civilization does not overcome it (italics orig.).

Women played a key role in the liquor trade and in the organisation of African social life in early Johannesburg, despite their limited numbers were limited. As late as 1911, census figures showed that women comprised no more than five per cent of the African population of the Rand.[9] Traditional communities discouraged women from following the men to the notorious urban areas. Local whites, fearing the rapid growth of the urban African population and the disintegration of rural-tribal authority, hired only educated 'mission girls' as domestics and generally preferred male African 'houseboys'.[10] Service industries, however, involving the supply of beer, liquor, *dagga* (marijuana), sex, and general entertainment to blacks, provided profitable opportunities for black and even poor white women. The official figures undoubtedly omitted a significant number of females who evaded the census.

Migrants might choose merely to exist in the city, relying on groups of kin and 'homeboys' (Zulu: *amakhaya*) for aid and comfort while away from home. Those who fell permanently into the rhythm of urban life were forced to survive on their own or to create new identities, relationships, and communities where they were allowed to live. Residential and social alternatives were few for blacks, who worked for whites but were not allowed to be their neighbours or fellow citizens.

Pass laws were in effect from 1896,[11] together with a host of other restrictions. By 1910

> the natives . . . are already kept in their places with a rigour that would surprise you. One result is that they have no footing in the public life of the community outside certain menial forms of labour . . . 'The Nigger' . . . is not tolerated, except, so to speak, as a hewer of wood and a drawer of water.[12]

Central government, municipal, and private interests were in conflict over African residential policy, but the guiding principle, if there was one, seems to have been that of 'sanitation'.[13] Public services and residential planning during the 1890s in Johannesburg were the responsibility of public health authorities, whose influence remained strong within the City Council created after the Boer War. From the outset they were less concerned with providing adequate housing, sanitation, or amenities in areas occupied by non-whites than with keeping the physical and social 'infections' of these areas from the whites. Interracial contact, it was believed, would contaminate 'white civilisation' in South Africa, give non-whites social and political ambitions inconsistent with their subordinate status, and expose undesirable aspects of urban white society to blacks, who might then lose proper respect for whites.

Public health policy was intended not so much to provide genuine sanitation as to create a segregationist 'cordon sanitaire' around black residential areas. Municipal regulations, beginning in 1908, forbade whites to rent or give accommodation to blacks other than their servants, required blacks to live in municipal locations, and established a 9 p.m. curfew for Africans in the city. Because of conflicts of interest among whites, some of whom benefitted from the struggle of blacks to get unsupervised housing close to their work, the regulations could not be consistently applied. The result was inner-city residential areas accommodating a permanent African population.

While the government was busy knocking down the shanties surrounding the mines, a number of originally white areas were taken over by blacks or a racially mixed population of urban poor. After an outbreak of bubonic plague in 1904, authorities burned down Brickfields (Newtown). Africans were rehoused in Nancefield-Klipspruit, which was the major municipal location until the establishment of Western Native Township in 1918. Built next to a municipal sewage farm 12 miles from the city, lacking services and subject to white supervision, the Klipspruit location housed only 3 000 Africans by 1915. Housing shortages forced the City Council to issue permits allowing employers to house blacks in private compounds. By 1912, 10 000 such permits had been granted,[14] mostly to slumlords who filled formerly spacious backyards with mazes of corrugated iron rooms rented to blacks at exorbitant rates. The Parks and Estates Committee took note of the situation: 'in every warehouse, foundry, or factory within the centre of Johannesburg there is to be found today a native compound'.[15] These unofficial or unauthorised African living areas were known in Johannesburg as 'slumyards'.

Other areas west and south of the city centre, originally laid out by the government for poor white or Asian and Coloured occupation, soon housed hundreds of Africans as white or Indian landlords took advantage of the enormous profits to be made from slum rents and the liquor trade. Everywhere on the fringes of the city, except in the wealthy residential north, commercial real estate interests discovered that slumyards brought in a larger revenue than any other kind of investment.[16]

Public alarm over living conditions, disease, and crime in these areas provoked considerable journalistic comment.[17] While some newspapers sympathetically reported the squalor, overcrowding, and outrageous rents, others merely revealed the white fear of miscegenation and condemned the social mixing in the slums:

> These are yards like rabbit-warrens, from which lead a labyrinth of passages, the haunt of the criminal, the passless Native, the loafer. There are yards where Indians, Malays, White, Coloured, and Kafir people are herding promiscuously. There are houses, once dwellings of better class white-folk, now let out to the dregs of a mixed population. I shall not forget going upstairs in a house in Marshall Street, and finding a black man, white woman, a sheep, and a goat, all living together in the top room. Nor the yard in that choice quarter known as Malay Camp, where I found a group of young Native girls lying dead drunk in the morning after an orgie on methylated spirits and opium mixed, obtained from a Chinese store.[18]

For demographic, economic, and social reasons, African culture in Johannesburg before 1924 was a product of the slumyards and adjacent slum locations. Blocked by white residents' groups who complained of a health menace whenever a site for a new location was proposed, the City Council compounded the problem by strenuously opposing the growth of African freehold suburbs. By 1921, the African population of the three freehold areas within four miles of the city officially totalled only 2 643.[19] The slumyards, in contrast, housed at least 20 000 by 1919, and twice that number by 1927.[20] Whites in general wanted Africans to be continually available for urban labour without acquiring any of the characteristics or aspirations common to members of Western industrial societies. Housing regulations and pass laws, however, were ineffective in the face of economic and social conditions that drew people to the Rand in ever greater numbers. Specifically responsible for this townward migration was the Native Trust and Land Act of 1913, confining African land ownership to 'native reserves' covering only one-seventh of the country.

This dispossession aroused intense resentment among Africans, particularly Christians who had invested much of their new financial resources in land during the last decades of the nineteenth century.[21] Africans outside the reserves and unwilling to return had to choose between serfdom on European farms and labour in the mines or urban industries. To many, the cities seemed to offer the widest possibilities. White resistance only intensified the strain and dislocation of African urbanisation; it could not prevent it.

Internally, the diversity of the African population, combined with migrancy, insecurity, and racial oppression retarded class formation and the growth of stable social institutions and values. Though strategies of adaptation differed according to perceptions of class, there was little economic stratification; and conflicts in class interest were more apparent than real. Common residence and disabilities to some extent submerged class differences in the general struggle for survival. Police harassment and living conditions inhibited social and political association.[22] Still, Africans created genuine communities based on social co-operation, reciprocity, personal relationships, and family ties, though their structure was weak.

The conflict between African urbanisation and white resistance created an environment in which social integration and disintegration coexisted in a precarious balance. In a system that denied social identity as well as power to Africans, crime became as effective a medium of protest and self-assertion as political organisation.[23] The compounds, courts, and prisons reduced worker mobility and helped to create an African labour force with little respect for the law. Among the most influential organisations that grew out of the proletarian society of the slumyards early in the century were criminal gangs, such as the Ninevites mentioned in Chapter 2.[24]

By 1912, this gang had 1 000 members operating from numerous headquarters in the mine compounds, hostels, prisons, and slumyards. They organised burglaries, robbery, prostitution, gambling, illicit liquor and *dagga* smuggling throughout the southern Transvaal. They immobilised the black police (*nonqaai*) and physically punished both whites and blacks found abusing African workers or collaborating in the system of oppression. Other Ninevite-style organisations, which remained strong in the prisons until the mid-1930s, inspired the African labour movement with their methods.

The most significant offshoot of the Ninevites was Johannesburg's first organised group of 'juvenile delinquents'. The *Amalaita* took their name from the way in which Zulu native police pronounced 'Allrighters', a term for the Ninevites. They were mostly young Sotho who joined together to resist the pass laws.[25] Primarily children of Christian families, they imitated the Scottish military bands that played regularly in the city's parks; they drilled to commands in English and marched to the music of harmonicas and penny whistles on Sunday afternoons.[26] By 1908, their membership and activities were changing in response to the commanding social issue of the day, the 'Black Peril'.

The Black Peril controversy ostensibly centred on the rising crime rate among blacks.[27] In particular, whites feared sexual assaults on their women, so many of whom spent their days in close contact with male African domestic servants. It prompted the replacement of houseboys with cheaper and more submissive Zulu and Tswana females, available because of drought and depression in the countryside. This caused white women to fear sexual competition from female servants, so an alternative was found in the employment of young Pedi and Tswana boys from the northern Transvaal.

With no support from destitute rural families, these 'piccanins', as the new houseboys were called, struggled to stay in town and to reduce the hardships of low wages, unemployment, and Black Peril by whites. Virtually taking over the *Amalaita*, they changed the gang language from English to Sepedi. Combining European military ranking with rural Pedi patterns of organisation, particularly age-set groupings, they founded a genuine urban youth movement that included female members as well.[28] Most gangs composed their own songs, such as *Ngoma wa Amalaita*. The Scottish military bands continued to inspire the penny whistle and drum music that accompanied their parades, the boys' uniforms, and the short accordion-pleated tartan skirts called 'Scots rokkies' worn by female members.[29]

Many *Amalaita* had become young adults by the end of the First World War and formed fighting teams that battled against each other in the location streets on weekends. In the prisons, *Amalaita* organised the much-feared Scotlanders gang and challenged the dominance of the Ninevites.[30] Overall, the *Amalaita* helped to pull the isolated, suffering young domestics together in a heartless city in hard times. Gang membership provided purpose and dignity, transforming their self-image from one of menials serving white females into leaders in an urban workers' army, an autonomous organisation able to resist oppression by collective force.[31]

As a by-product, the *Amalaita* bands' introduction of the penny whistle to the locations contributed to the development of distinctive urban African musical styles. Many African brass and reed players have developed their musical skills on this simple but versatile metal flageolet, and it remains a favourite with township youngsters today. During the 1920s and 30s, youthful penny whistle bandsmen performed at many kinds of urban social occasions.

The resilient new patterns of social organisation, criminal and otherwise, were based in part on the distinction between migrants and permanent townsmen. Performing the roughest, most menial and worst-paid tasks in the mines and domestic and municipal services, the migrants were at the bottom, but to some extent outside, of the status system of urban African society. Migrancy was and still is perceived as a threat to the aspirations of townsmen. Urbanites rejected any behaviour they considered *ihlati* (Xhosa: uncivilised; provincial) and resented white unwillingness to make any social or legal distinctions between migrants and themselves.

For their part, whites tended to deny African townsmen's claims to 'civilised' (European) status. On the contrary, they preferred the 'natural dignity' (docility) of the traditional African.[32] The migrants threatened the political goals and economic security of the townsmen as well as their social identity. Migrants were less willing to participate in urban labour organisations or to campaign for African rights in the cities, and they were willing to work for lower wages and to endure poorer living conditions than were permanent residents.

Migrants isolated themselves from urban society by remaining in homeboy networks, yet the scale and diversity of the urban environment enabled them to join in town-centred activities if they chose without necessarily endangering ties to the country. In brief, migrants and their performing arts were significantly affected by urban residence whether or not they became urbanites.

To begin with, conditions in the mine compounds themselves influenced the way in which traditional male dancing was organised and performed. Looking for recreational alternatives to drinking and faction-fighting, compound managers organised regular dance competitions according to rules more appropriate to a European school or military parade ground than to the aesthetic of rural African regimental dance rivalry. For example, the Witwatersrand Native Labour Association ran annual trophy competitions for Portuguese East African miners in Johannesburg. Team dances were 'conducted in strict accordance with a carefully prepared code of rules and regulations'.[33] The white judges based their decisions on:

1   the rendering of the music;
2   the general appearance of the dancers;
3   the precision of movement of the dancers;
4   the regularity of the dancing line.

That these European aesthetic criteria bore no relation to traditional African ones did not trouble those awarding these prizes, nor did it lessen the prestige of the winners among their fellow competitors. Rivalries for land use and other resources between rural communities and clans were transplanted to the urban setting, and teams of Nyembanes, Chopis, and Shangaans from Mozambique expressed in performance competitions the inter-group tensions produced by common residence and labour in the mines. According to its translator, a Shangaan team song performed in 1928 proclaimed:

> We hear a rumour that our song-maker and leader, Nkuna,
> is getting old and cannot make any more songs.
> Sabue says this.
> Sabue has gone to Booysens now;
> they might as well have sent an owl there for all he'll teach them.
> They are shedding tears of envy in all the other compounds when they
> hear the great variety of songs we have.
> We hear heaps of songs here,
> but at No 14 Shaft they are crying out for them.[34]

Witchcraft accusations, an aspect of traditional performance rivalries, also appeared among the miners. Songs containing such accusations also displayed a recognition of new power realities:

> We are nearly being killed by all the machinations of the wizards.
> We know who they are,
> but we are afraid to mention their names, because the biggest of the lot
> is the white man who keeps the gate.

Mozambicans also became well known in the compounds for their traditions of theatrical display, which integrated music, dance, mime, acrobatics and verbal expression. Friar Joao Dos Santos visited a Bachopi royal court in 1586. His journal records that 'The King . . . has another class of kaffir who are called *marombes*, which means the same as jester, and who sang, shouted praises, told jokes, and performed acrobatics'.[35] This ancient tradition appeared in the mines. In the early 1900s, dance competitions usually featured a *marombe* in a European top hat, tail coat, shirt, and trousers worn very much awry, who performed acrobatic and mimetic turns and regaled the crowd with jokes and comic praises.

Many of these displays involved humour drawn from the immediate environment. Mine comedians performed not only satires on local European behaviour but also energetic parodies of the ordinarily highly serious practice of trance-divination, with costumes out of a 'ragshop'[36] in place of the traditional skins. Acrobatic satires by Ndaus from northern Mozambique made fun of mine personalities including the white doctor, mine captain, or shift boss.

The Xhosa, Sotho, and others from South Africa drew on equally vigorous traditions of mimetic dance, poetic expression, musical and gestural narrative[37] – all of which contributed to the development of a popular urban African theatre. In 1921, members of Johannesburg's Parks and Estates Committee visiting Western Native Township were greeted by

> A kaffir playing a sort of one-string banjo, made of a piece of hollowed bark and what looked like a paraffin [kerosene] tin. In excellent English he went through a little scene depicting a 'boy's' arrest for not having a pass, the plea being that he was an African in his own country, and did not need one. This, however, did not avail him, the magistrate's remarks being cleverly, if a little too forcibly, portrayed to the tum tum of the banjo aforesaid.[38]

Among Zulu migrants, traditional dance forms have been affected by Zulu migrants' participation in domestic, industrial, and mine labour.[39] As with the Mozambicans, the close contact of separate Zulu clans in the workers' hostels intensified the competition so vital to male dancing in traditional society.[40] As they asserted their social status and group identity, homeboy dance teams began to develop new dances with more clearly defined aesthetic requirements. City competition encouraged stylistic innovation and consensus on the quality of performances, and reputations rose or fell on the basis of achievements in the dance arena.

In Durban, workers developed new dances in traditional idiom like *isikhuze*, *is'cathulo*, *isibhaca*, *umzanzi*, and *ingoma*, and performed country dances such as *ndhlamu* in the industrial yards.[41] Commercial employers coopted workers' dance competitions, providing uniforms, colours, banners, transport, and time off for rehearsal – all to heighten the loyalty and morale of the workforce. This system of company teams and white judges and performance standards continues today, and has powerfully influenced the aesthetic of Zulu men's dancing now for more than half a century.[42] Dance teams are as much a part of the structure of 'homeboy' institutions in the hostels as burial societies, savings' clubs, and drinking clubs. Talented composers called *amagoso* become team leaders, and with their *amaphini*, or assistants, they join with the elders in the hostels in exercising authority over the homeboy group. Competitive dancing is conceived directly in terms of military metaphors. Currently, members of teams performing the popular *isishayameni* ('beaters') dance are called *amasoja* (Eng.: 'soldiers'), and compose songs called 'bullets' to fire at rival teams.[43]

Interestingly, the majority of creative innovators in competitive dance and song were not the more traditional Zulu migrants, but *amagxagxa* ('vagrants'), marginal people who, like the Xhosa *abaphakathi* ('middle ones') were neither traditional nor Christian, but somewhere in between. It was they who brought dance steps from other ethnic groups and from the urban locations into Zulu male dancing in the hostels. Similarly, they blended Zulu traditional dance music with the *Izingoma zomtshado*, the Zulu Wesleyan Methodist hymns used at both rural and urban weddings, to create some interesting syncretic dance team songs.[44] Those who found the competition too fierce devised ways to place psychic distance between themselves and the intense, winner-take-all atmosphere of the dancing ground. Out of the mix of cultural influences came a form of self-parody and dance humour called *ukukomika* (Eng.: 'comic')[45] which soon linked up with an important new style of vocal performance.

The new style first appeared during the First World War under the name *ingom'ebusuku* (Zulu: 'night music'). It has since gone through many transformations under different names and remains popular today as *isicatamiya* (Zulu: 'a stalking approach'). Informants give varying explanations of the original term. Some referred to *ingom'ebusuku* as *ikomik*. Bongi Mtethwa of Zululand University's music department says that the importance of Wesleyan Methodist hymns in African Christian musical life led to their adaptation to a range of secular contexts. One result was a light hearted form of Zulu

Christian popular song called *mbholoho*, and then the more serious and formal style of *ingom'ebusuku*.[46] Several musicians pointed out that, as its name suggests, it was performed at night, and associated with the concerts (*ikonsati*) of Westernised choirs rather than with traditional musical occasions. Mtethwa also claims that the unique *isicatamiya* dance style was influenced by the popular Charleston from America during the 1930s, and was called *ukureka* (Eng.: 'rag; ragtime').[47]

Stylistic categories are not written in stone, of course, and may vary in their meaning and usage. They reveal important distinctions in the minds of participants, and they are handy in distinguishing one form from another. Given the variety of urban experience, distinctions of style do not always operate on the same logical level or apply to the entire black community. The application and connotations of these terms are largely dependent on context. The most important aspect of *ingom'ebusuku* is the relationship between the structure and content of performance and the identity and aspirations of their participants.

The *ingom'ebusuku* male choral style became most popular with Zulu and Swazi industrial and domestic workers from the rural areas. Though they had little Western education, many had enjoyed mission school concerts in Natal. In Durban, Johannesburg, and other cities they joined social groups who had their own notions of 'modern' culture. No longer wishing to be considered rural or traditional people, they were most interested in performances that expressed their self-image as townsmen. Borrowing from the culture of the African school people, they worked vocal music drawn from traditional social, political, and military life into their own version of middle-class choir competitions.

The immediate model for *ingom'ebusuku* appears to have been the singing competitions at rural or small town weddings. In colonial times these became perhaps the most important single focus of group social interaction in Zulu society. The two extended family groups or local subclans attached to the bride and the groom competed against each other in performing well-known or newly composed songs and dances, often after weeks of rehearsal. The two subclans expressed their identity in opposition to each other most strongly in singing their *ihubo lesizwe*, a kind of anthem for the group. It commanded great respect and was accompanied by powerful pointing movements (*ukukhomba*). The Zulu do not classify these movements as dance, though they are integrated into many recognised dances.[48]

Also in the background of *ingom'ebusuku* is the competitive singing of regimental anthems (*amahubo lamabutho*),[49] accompanied by a slow, forceful, synchronised dancing equivalent in purpose to a European military drill. A. T. Bryant witnessed a first fruits ceremony in Zululand during the 1920s at which two regiments performed:

The two choirs thenceforth sang together, each its own part, with different words and different tunes, and yet all so tastefully blended together as to create perfectly harmonious, albeit exotic, music. As they sang they all danced together, assuming simultaneously, in perfect unity and much barbaric grace, identically the same poses of body and movement of limbs, shields, and sticks, as to present a combination of harmonious sound and rhythmic action most graceful at once to ear and eye. . . .[50]

Zulu and Swazi workers transferred these traditions of competitive song and movement to location hall stages. As many as thirty male choirs would compete with old or newly composed traditional songs, and prizes ranged from a goat or a bicycle to a large part of the gate receipts. *Isicatamiya* choirs still compete today in Durban and Johannesburg, where dance routines unique to each song are known as *istep*. The words of the songs are linked to the melody and the movements of the step dancing. Keeping the torso immobile helps the dancers to sing more powerfully, hence the term *isicatamiya*, a stealthy movement.[51]

Ingom'ebusuku participants at first included people of varying degrees of urbanisation and Westernisation, and the style itself could be varied accordingly. There was no strict dichotomy between migrants and townsmen or traditionalists and Christians in Johannesburg despite popular categorisation. Many migrants and urban proletarians fell into a third, intermediate category and came together in *ingom'ebusuku* competitions and other performance events. Since the Second World War social sectors and categories have hardened, and *isicatamiya* is performed almost exclusively by people who may be considered urban, but not Western, in culture.

The varied African approaches to urbanisation stemmed from differences in background, attitudes, and experience of European culture. Middle-class African culture is a good illustration of the relationship between various rural and urban strategies.

Class formation among black South Africans has been retarded by the impact of racial oppression. Middle-class and working-class identity are often more a matter of culture pattern, social aspiration, and self-perception than income or position in the relations of production. Culturally, Africans made social distinctions among themselves based on educational level and the degree to which they deliberately pursued Westernisation. Yet even here differences were more a matter of emphasis than opposition. In different ways, both middle-class and working-class Africans responded to the dehumanisation of the South African system[52] by adapting traditional social forms and principles to urban needs.

As mission school graduates left for the cities and missions built schools in the urban areas, middle-class life became increasingly town-centred.[53] During the early twentieth century, an emerging African elite culture and society established links between the rural church schools and the urban middle class. Together, rural and urban school culture influenced the aspirations and identities of all categories of urban Africans.

Perceptions of social class have gradually become more important than ethnic or regional background in structuring urban African society and in determining the membership of associations and social networks. Yet regional and ethnic identity have remained a factor in shaping social and political aspirations within various classes. The contribution of the Natal Zulu elite to early twentieth century urban culture illustrates both the relationship of class to culture and historical experience, and the importance of rural-urban ties.

Though the secretary of the American mission board observed in 1880 that the number of missions in Natal was proportionately 'greater than in any other community on the globe two or three times over',[54] evangelisation had met with little success. In Zululand itself, Zulu kings considered conversion an act of treason, classified Christian Zulu as non-Zulu, and cut them off from the traditional community. Missionary efforts there long remained at a standstill.

In neighbouring Natal, a British crown colony, missionaries were more successful, but not among members of strong traditional communities. Though landed Africans were politically fragmented, they strongly resisted conversion. Mission stations attracted instead the *oorlams* blacks: Coloureds, Khoisan, and homeless Africans of all tribes in need of land, refuge, or work. As early as 1856, the Anglican station at Ladysmith was 'notorious as the haunt of bad (i.e. dispossessed) characters representing all races'.[55]

Despite their isolation, Natal mission residents prospered from the benefits of free land and education. Recognising the value of permanent legal tenure in colonial society, African Christians sought to buy land for cash-cropping in Natal as early as 1855, often as members of Christian collectives. The best example of such a collective is Edendale, established as a Wesleyan Methodist station by W. C. Holden near Pietermaritzburg in 1847. Residents added three farms to their freeholdings by 1865 and soon became an independent religious, economic, and social community. Etherington says that 'the cooperation which the Edendale men displayed demonstrates vividly the way in which common goals, intermarriages, and the special, shared experience of mission station life welded men and women of widely varying backgrounds into one people'.[56] Ethnic divisions within such communities were further weakened through the efforts of missionaries who preached the equality of all African tribes and individuals under God.

But colonial attitudes and British policy did not favour Africans becoming substantial property owners, professionals, or economic competitors of whites. Greatly outnumbered by Africans, whites in Natal developed a strong racial consciousness. They aimed to direct African social change 'along its own lines', in contrast to the assimilationist Cape policy.[57] Created by Native Commissioner T. Shepstone, Natal Native policy in the 1870s is now widely recognised[58] as the original model for the philosophy and practice of *apartheid* in South Africa. Shepstone promoted settler interests by means of British concepts of 'indirect rule'. He used taxes and legal means to restrain African enterprise, confine African land ownership to specified rural 'locations' or reserves, and in contrast to George Grey in the Cape, attempted to reconstruct traditional political structures artificially where they had broken down.[59]

Missions in Natal established colour bars in worship and church organisation. Despite promises to train Africans for the ministry, schools such as the Adams and Inanda seminaries of the American Board (Congregationalist) never offered advancement beyond secondary education.[60]

As taxes and high rents drove Africans out of commercial farming and into transport driving and itinerant trading, the *amakholwa* ('believers') as African Christians were called, became increasingly bitter about white resistance to their advancement in every field. Yet, because British Imperial guarantees of equality before the law remained their only hope, the *amakholwa* strove to Anglicise and for the most part remained loyal to Britain through the First World War and even beyond.

As early as the 1890s, however, such loyalty was already being tempered by movements towards cultural reassertion, specifically an African (Zulu) nationalism inspired by educational, political, and religious movements in black America. For the Natal Christian elite, the Ethiopianism associated with the AME Church and other Afro-American missions represented racial progress through independent control of church affairs and the solidarity of Africans under a common religious ideology. Denied access to higher education in South Africa, graduates of mission schools enrolled in American colleges, where they gained first-hand knowledge of Afro-American political ideas. Returning home, many continued with Afro-American church work while others took steps to interpret the black American experience and relate it practically to the needs of their own people.

A leader in both the educational and political fields was Rev. John Dube, the son of a chief of the Qadi Zulu clan whose family had fled to the American Congregationalist mission at Inanda when King Mpande had him killed. Offers of land and refuge helped Christianise the Qadi as a whole,[61] and Dube emerged as a Christian leader firmly based in a cohesive local community. Dube studied at Tuskeegee and other American schools during 1887–92 and 1897–9.

In 1901, he established an independent school for liberal and industrial education modelled on Tuskeegee at Ohlange, near Inanda. Dube and other black South African Christians were attracted by the emphasis on self-help in the ideas of Tuskeegee's founder, Booker Washington, and viewed education as the key to advancement. 'Ohlange was an example of Africans adopting black American educational concepts and techniques to further African self-sufficiency, not for the purpose of ultimate incorporation into the white dominated society but for the restoration of African nationhood'.[62] Contact with Afro-America thus fostered a racial self-respect that became a basis for non-violent struggle against a society determined to crush African aspirations. Political activism on the part of Dube and others resulted in the creation of the Natal branch of the African Native National Congress in 1912 and the subsequent emergence of the Zulu cultural organisation *Inkatha Yesizwe* ('Protector of the Nation').

In Natal, African nationalism contained a strong admixture of Zulu ethnic pride. Their Christianity alienated them from the surrounding traditional communities, and they played an active role in the Natal Native Contingent in the British destruction of the Zulu state in 1879, and most of them were of Nguni clans not strictly part of the Zulu empire. Nevertheless, Natal Christians identified with the glory of the Zulu past. They referred to themselves as Zulu and attempted to create a national culture based on an adaptive blend of Zulu, Afro-American, and European elements.

The work of the most important composer of Zulu choral music, Reuben T. Caluza, can only be understood against the background of cultural nationalism (see plate 9). Raised in the Edendale-Pietermaritzburg African Christian community, Caluza began his professional career as a teacher at Ohlange in 1909. The school was already in financial trouble, and Caluza's extraordinary musical and entrepreneurial talents soon proved themselves indispensable. By 1910 his Royal Singers, a group performing hymns, Negro spirituals, ragtime, and traditional Zulu songs arranged for choral performance, were winning major student choir competitions in Natal.[63] Shortly afterwards Caluza began fund-raising tours, and his Ohlange Institute Choir became a major source of income for the school. Recognising the potential of the 'Scottish' African street bands, Caluza organized a fife and drum ensemble and took over the brass band that Dube had equipped with instruments from America. In June 1911, his penny whistlers earned the considerable sum of £8 10s marching in the streets of Ndwedwe, Natal.[64]

By 1912, Caluza's choir was touring elsewhere in the Union, popularising Sontonga's *Nkosi Sikelel' iAfrika* and other vernacular songs among African Christians. Among his many distinguished alumni was Albert Luthuli, President of the African National Congress from 1952 to 1967, who entered Ohlange in 1914. In the 1920s, before he entered politics, Luthuli was a distinguished choir conductor at Adams College, Amanzimtoti.[65]

Though he depended on his colleague Ngazana Luthuli (no relation) to notate his compositions in tonic solfa, Caluza had a remarkable talent for absorbing diverse musical influences and combining them in an original manner. The greatest foreign influence on Caluza's music apart from European and mission brass bands and choral music, was American ragtime.

The first decade of the twentieth century saw the spread of American popular culture among mission-school Africans throughout South Africa. A musical survival of minstrelsy, 'coon songs', (early ragtime from Tin Pan Alley) became available in printed albums and even on gramophone recordings. In 1902, ex-slave George Johnson's coon song, 'The Original Haw Haw Man', sold well in Central and Southern Africa. In Rhodesia, a Major Cyrill Fosset reported:

> The new box of laugh records arrived today and perfectly eased what might have been a tricky situation with the Natives. They seem to prefer these to the Reverend's piano recitals of Gilbert and Sullivan.[66]

Despite their crude, racist caricatures of Negroes, the appeal of coon songs for both American and South African blacks 'was not in what they said, but in the rhythm and swing in which they said it'.[67] At a Christmas concert in the Christian community of Groutville, Natal, in 1907, pieces performed by the local choir included 'Under the Willow', 'My Old Kentucky Home', and 'God Bless the Prince of Wales'. These alternated with the playing of gramophone recordings that included 'My Crude Sue', 'An Evening With Minstrels', and 'I'se Gwine Back to Dixie'. This last song was also performed live by the choir.[68]

School concerts and travelling choirs popularised early ragtime. As early as 1904, the Inanda Native Singers, organised by Dube, were performing coon songs like 'Who Stole My Chicken Away', 'Happy Pickaninnies, Oh!' and other turn of the century songs in English.[69] Coloured musicians also popularised American-style string bands, and groups of African schoolboys soon joined them in playing for young people's dances. One dance at New Scotland, Natal, on 3 March, 1910, featured an ensemble of two guitars, a mandolin, and a concertina.[70]

Many choirs preferred American or English tunes to traditional songs, which they associated with the 'primitive' and 'heathen' cultural past, but above all they desired modern African compositions. Works by Bokwe, Tyamzashe, and Caluza helped fill this need, and with the growth of nationalist sentiment African compositions such

71

as *uMuntu Ontsundu Makabe Munye* ('Black People Unite') became concert standards.[71]

For the first quarter of the century, *makwaya* ('choir') music other than hymns (*amaculo*) was thus divided into three distinct categories by Zulu participants: *Amagama éMusic* (British and African popular choral and light classical songs), *Amagama 'sizulu* (traditional songs arranged for choir), and *Amagama éRagtime* (American popular songs and local pieces in ragtime style).

Makwaya concerts helped to build middle-class pride and a national African culture. Admiration for black America was especially strong among early black nationalists.[72] Black racial identity and Westernisation became sources of political unity, but nationalist leaders were troubled by the need to use foreign models to create an African national culture. Such conflicts permeated the political and cultural atmosphere at the outset of Caluza's career. As a youngster, he certainly saw new urban-influenced styles of rural dancing such as *umqhumqhumbela*, *is'cathulo*, *nomchichimbwe*, and *ndhlamu* that were popular in independent African Christian communities in Natal. In the towns, ragtime companies and individual performers – with tail coats, boaters, bow ties, and canes – offered both ragtime songs and black vaudeville entertainment.[73]

Raising funds for Ohlange, Caluza created a professional stage ensemble for the paying African mass audience. Caluza was a talented organist and pianist.[74] Unlike many formally trained African choir leaders, he was eager to arrange traditional Zulu songs for *makwaya*. In achieving regional and national popularity, Caluza combined the infectious rhythm and melody of piano ragtime with socially relevant, topical Zulu lyrics, indigenous part-singing, and a mission school style of music and movement known as the 'action song' (*ukutamba*; Zulu: 'file dancing with uniform movements under the control of a conductor').[75]

The orchestration of synchronised rhythmic movement and vocal harmony in action songs at African school concerts can be traced back to indigenous performance traditions. Among the peoples of Southern Africa, military chants, folk narratives, and praise singing all co-ordinate movement, words, and music into an integrated, dramatically expressive whole. As Sotho dancers explained to Charles Adams,[76] 'the sound of a beautiful song agrees with the rhythm and steps of the feet. The beauty of the song is not its words but what is seen with the eyes'.

In the mission schools in the late nineteenth century, interpretive movement was one solution to the difficulty of getting African students to stand still while singing. White missionaries often forbade converts to perform either 'heathen' traditional dances or 'immoral' European social dances. Thus the kinds of restrictions on dancing that

72

produced the 'ring shout' among Christian black Americans may underlie the South African action song. In the 1930s, action songs were very popular with choirs in the Eastern Cape, and at concerts:

> as the night advances the girls who began with stiff gestures are swinging about the floor doing something as near a dance as the eye of teacher and parson will permit. . . .[77]

Among the Zulu, choral performance of the serious *amahubo* anthems traditionally involved movements that, with missionary blessings, could be combined with those of British school action songs and singing games, creating new patterns suited to the physical expression of Westernised African choral performance. Caluza added to these forms Afro-American stage movement taken from the minstrels and ragtime companies. This enabled him to transform the action song into a professional African musical variety tradition that smoothly integrated Zulu song, piano ragtime, and interpretive, synchronised step dancing. Caluza's performance style greatly influenced *isicatamiya*, and it may have been because of him that the term *ukureka*, 'to play ragtime music, engage in movement during music of African songs',[78] was also applied to *isicatamiya*.

The popularity of Caluza's compositions among African choirs throughout the Union was largely due to the topicality of his lyrics. Songs like *Ingoduso* warned young men about the dangers of Johannesburg, urging them to avoid drink and crime and not to abandon their families at home. 'Influenza' (see Appendix A) commemorated the 'Great Flu' of 1918 in which thousands of Africans died. *iLand Act* protested the injustice of the Land Act of 1913:

iLand Act (English translation by Fatima Dike)
We are children of Africa
We cry for our land
Zulu, Xhosa, Sotho
Zulu, Xhosa, Sotho unite
We are mad over the Land Act
A terrible law that allows sojourners
To deny us our land
Crying that we the people
Should pay to get our land back
We cry for the children of our fathers
Who roam around the world without a home
Even in the land of their forefathers

Ephraim Kuluse, a graduate of Ohlange who attended some of the Caluza choir's earliest performances, says that audiences were amazed by the different forms of music, words, and movement so

Si lu Sapo or i Land Act

Key Bb

D.C.

R.T. Caluza

(Tonic sol-fa music notation)

Land Act (English translation by Fatima Dike)

We are children of Africa
We cry for our land
Zulu, Xhosa, Sotho
Zulu, Xhosa, Sotho unite
We are mad over the Land Act
A terrible law that allows sojourners

To deny us our land
Crying that we the people
Should pay to get our land back
We cry for the children of our fathers
Who roam around the world without a home
Even in the land of their forefathers

harmoniously brought together. Achieving the integration of various modes of expression in a Westernised idiom appeared remarkable, and expanded Africans' sense of the possibilities of applying African performance principles to Western instruments and materials. Caluza orchestrated African worksongs like *Awuthi Nyikithi* for choral performance, and many original compositions, like *Umaconsana*, use call-and-response, staggered entry of parts, melodic themes carried in the bass line, lyric influence on melodic contour and rhythm, and other features of indigenous vocal music.[79]

In 1917, the Ohlange musicians began a series of Christmas concerts in Johannesburg that not only fulfilled but redefined the cultural aspirations of middle-class Africans. They had a permanent effect upon urban African concert and stage entertainments of all kinds. Journalist R. R. R. Dhlomo, writing of 'these songs which have regenerated many a soul – songs which have rekindled anew our zealous patriotic aspirations', looked forward to the publication of Caluza's works:

> When these songs are sold everywhere, when they are sung in high and low places – then, not only will Caluza triumph, but every blackman, who claims to have any welfare of his race at heart.[80]

Urban Africans needed attractive new settings for socialising and for elaborating cultural categories and a sense of personal and group identity. An important basis of coming together for a variety of groups was common taste in entertainment. Performances helped to develop social rules and relationships, and provided cultural expression of common social aspirations. Middle-class Africans organised performances for church, school, and club activities, or simply for prestige, sociability, and profit.

Gradually, urban social identity came to be realised through membership in community organisations and personal networks based on class rather than on kinship or regional origin, especially among the middle class. Churches drew their members from all ethnic groups,[81] focusing instead on education, class identity, and marriage rather than blood ties. In place of traditional social institutions, churches served as welfare associations and eased integration into the urban environment. To violate church moral and social codes was to reject the responsibilities of the community of membership, equal in significance to breaking kinship obligations in traditional society.[82]

Predictably, church organisation also helped middle-class Africans become leaders of secular voluntary associations based on Western models. Church schools in Johannesburg established African boy and girl scout troops ('pathfinders' and 'wayfarers') in 1918.[83] Youth clubs, athletic teams, cooperative societies and cultural associations proliferated. Two years earlier, a writer for *Ilanga Lase*

Natal reported the existence of more than forty clubs in Johannesburg for adult African men alone.[84]

Among the most popular recreational occasions sponsored by voluntary associations were the tea-meeting and the evening concert. The term 'tea-meeting' originated with the church-oriented social affairs of British settlers in the Eastern Cape. In the *Cape Standard* for 11 January 1866, a white observer praised an African church choir in Graaf-Rienet. Arguing that whites should not scorn African choir singing since it made Christianity more attractive, he noted that while all attending were not converts, they all enjoyed the 'tea-meeting'.

During the last third of the nineteenth century, both rural and urban church communities held tea-meetings on Saturday nights, sponsored in rotation by individual members of the church women's group (*manyano*). Liquor was not served. A novel method of raising funds was added to the entertainment through auctions.[85] People enjoyed themselves and competed for recognition by bidding for tea and cakes or to hear their friends perform specific hymns, popular songs, or variety turns. All-night tea-meetings were popular among Cape Africans at the turn of the century, taking 'the place of the European ball with the Natives',[86] and replacing the musical beer-drinks of traditional society. Tea-meetings were characteristic of early urban society, fusing economic and social activities just as traditional work-for-beer parties had done.[87]

Though no objections were raised at first, government officials and missionaries were disturbed by the expansion of 'tea-meetings' to cover a variety of African entertainments in the towns. In the 1880s, missionaries had suppressed the *intonjane* celebrations that traditionally concluded Xhosa female puberty rites despite African pleas that 'what the piano and violin are to the Englishmen, the *intonjane* dances are to us'.[88] Soon magistrates were complaining of 'brandy parties' and 'immoral night meetings' held to celebrate African marriages, or secret occasions where 'women danced half-naked before men'.[89] In 1900, the Rev. Hargreaves reported that young converts were causing trouble by 'introducing night tea-parties under the pretence of helping church funds'.[90]

In Johannesburg, many Xhosa and Mfengu school graduates from the Cape and Transkei worked for the mines as clerks (*omabhalane*). As intermediaries, the *omabhalane* had some power and prestige in the mines, and their enjoyment of tea-meetings soon spread to migrants and urban proletarians as well. Portuguese East African and Rhodesian miners, for example, held their own *itimitin* (tea-meeting) with beer, traditional instruments, guitars, concertinas and urbanised traditional dancing. Xhosa miners, mostly surface workers who regarded themselves as an elite, enjoyed imitating the Coloured and African 'coons'.

Westernised African choral music, coon groups, and ragtime helped transform the school concert and the tea-meeting into profitable evening entertainments. Though an instrumentalist might be hired for dancing afterwards, concert performers were almost all amateurs; choirs, quartets and soloists who offered part songs, dances, comic routines and variety turns. Curfew restrictions and lack of transport tended to make these entertainments all-night affairs for neighbourhood people.

Until the late 1920s these concerts were a centre of neighbourhood city social life. Community organisations created a system of links between residential areas. A sponsoring school, church or club often provided a 'featured' choir and invited their counterparts from other neighbourhoods. Profits might go to a sponsoring institution, organisation, or prominent local family; but attendance was open to urban Africans of every language group, occupation, income, and educational level.

Open admission made status competition a major feature of these occasions and worked to the sponsors' benefit. The admission fee of one shilling usually brought in far less money than the auctioning. Competitive bidding proceeded as follows: the master of ceremonies would introduce the featured group, and someone would offer a sixpence or shilling to hear a particular song. In response, another patron would offer more to hear a different piece or to bring on another set of performers altogether. Journalist H.I.E. Dhlomo recalled:

> As would be expected, this procedure led to all kinds of novel situations. For the sake of revenue the promoters encouraged it in every way possible . . . The members of the audience regarded it from different points of view. Those who loved music or were too poor to take part in the 'buying' got fed up when the thing was carried too far (although they agreed that without these oft-exciting interludes there would have been a surfeit of music and the concerts would be unbearably dull). Some regarded it as a means of making donations to the organisers (who kept a strict watch as to who contributed and who did not). Others saw in it a chance of displaying their 'wealth'. These were either 'Romeos' trying to win some 'Juliet's' hand, or Agamemnons and Ajaxes actually trying to disgrace the opposing Hectors and Parises. Still others were either secret agents trying to build up the reputation of their favourite choir, or fifth-columnists sabotaging the work of the groups they did not like. . . . The audience had to wait patiently during the long intervals occasioned by these 'battles'. . . . As the choirs sang, members of the audience went up to the stage and gave money or gifts to the performers whose voices, faces, or style of performance they admired. . . .

Buying people to sing was not confined to the performers. One was free to call upon any member of the audience to sing or make a speech.

Certain spectators liked this and considered it an honour. The shy, sensitive or untalented ones disliked it. As it was taboo to refuse to act when called upon, the latter could only save themselves from the ordeal by buying themselves off . . . At the same time young firebrands were making love in and outside the hall. But this was not easy, for the parents kept a strict watch over the movements of the young, and only the favoured ones were given chances . . .

As would be expected, now and again, fights took place inside or outside the hall. The first were the more dangerous as they often developed into a melee as men who tried to protect their loved ones invariably got themselves involved in the fight. And worse, some fool would blow out the lights, and in the darkness pandemonium reigned: the cries of women and children, men hitting out with anything within their reach, bottles and sticks whizzing in the air, and the furniture wrecked. In spite of these occasional outbursts, these concerts were more or less dignified communal affairs.. . .[91]

Amateur school and evening concerts become crucial to stylistic development in popular African performing arts. Ragtime and jazz song and dance were favourites at these occasions and soon found their way into the emerging working-class culture of the cities, which made its own contribution to the stage. Schools picked up new urban-influenced rural dances, even though missionaries forbade them. One such dance, is'cathulo ('shoe') was adopted by students in Durban; from there it spread to dock workers who produced spectacular rhythmic effects by slapping and pounding their rubber Wellington boots in performance. All this rhythm made it popular with mine and municipal labourers elsewhere, especially Johannesburg. There it became the 'gumboot' dance, divided into a series of routines and accompanied by a rhythm guitar. By 1919, gumboot had filtered back into school concerts. It soon became a standard feature of urban African variety entertainment, and a setting for satirising characters and scenes drawn from African worklife.[92]

Reuben Caluza eventually studied music in the United States during the 1930s. Long before that, he had greater popularity and influence among all classes of urban Africans than more Westernised African choir conductors such as A.J. Mtetwa of the prestigious Zulu Union Choir.[93] Caluza's success was due not only to his ability to combine African tradition with the most popular 'international' black music of the day, but also his versatility, which allowed him to appeal to a variety of audiences during the 1920s.

Caluza used penny whistle, string, and brass bands, pianos, quartets, choirs, coon troupes, and concert parties to entertain anyone with the price of admission. On one occasion his choir performed for elegantly dressed African domestic servants at the Inchcape Hall, Johannesburg. Shortly afterwards, at the working-class Nobadula Hall in Benoni (East Rand), 'shots and daggers flared during a concert partly led by R. T. Caluza'.[94] Caluza's performances influenced the development of *ingom' ebusuku* as well as school concerts.

By the mid-1920s middle-class Africans were beginning to dissociate Caluza from the ragtime music he was bringing to the lower-class audience. As ragtime became 'popular' and was adopted by the urban proletariat, African middle-class parents showed concern for the moral effect of such music on their children in the schools. A reader complained in *Umteteli wa Bantu*[95] 'that drunkards and the youth have been driven mad with Ragtime in Johannesburg and other towns'. *Ilanga* editor R. R. R. Dhlomo wanted Caluza's music 'sung in high and low places'. When the people in the low places transformed it to suit their own taste, however, he complained Rand Africans were 'so fed up with the so-called modern Ragtime and comic pieces' and the keyboard playing in the slumyard canteens, that the Christmas concert of the Caluza choir would make them feel 'like people given a taste of fresh air after a suffocating ordeal'.[96]

Clearly, the mission-educated Africans were unhappy about the way working-class acculturation was occurring amidst the poverty, overcrowding, and oppression of the slums. The self-styled *abakhulumeli* (Zulu: 'spokesmen') of the middle class regarded themselves as an elite cultural vanguard who ought to direct change among their more 'backward' brethren.[97] Africans proletarians largely ignored or resented these attitudes. In the struggle to establish their own cultural identity and patterns of city life, they adopted and modified whatever values and materials best answered their own dilemmas. As a result, beginning in the early 1920s, middle-class urban social life became increasingly separate from that of the working class.

Working-class Africans reacted against racial discrimination and their lack of influence in church affairs even more strongly than mission-educated people. Their resentment gave rise to countless independent or separatist church movements. Middle-class separatists, called 'Ethiopianists,' were in general too intent upon cultural Westernisation and incorporation within the dominant society to create a strong church-based opposition movement. The Zulu Congregational Church, for example, which was founded following a quarrel with the American Board of Missions in Natal over leadership, ordination, and property in 1896, reunited with the mother church in 1898 in response to concessions offered by the white missionaries.[98]

African proletarians took far more seriously the separatist slogan 'Africa for the Africans', popularised in South Africa by Nehemiah Tile's Tembu Church and American missionary Joseph Booth's African Christian Union.[99] Such movements became a focus for resistance to white domination following the destruction of independent traditional political authority. In the cities, separatist Christianity provided both an ideological and social foundation for working-class

African cultural and political self-assertion. Ethiopianist ideas appealed strongly to urban workers and inspired widespread labour unrest in the second decade of the twentieth century. In Natal, Ethiopianist preachers were accused of fomenting rebellion, especially the violent one led by Bambata in 1906.[100] Though there is no proof of their participation, whites denounced the AME Church and African clergy in general for sedition. In fact, the revolt drew little support from mission graduates.

The failure of Ethiopianism to bring about meaningful change for Africans led to the emergence of 'Zionism', a proletarian movement for religious and cultural rebirth. In Zionism, African 'prophets' combined aspects of traditional African and Christian ritual, belief, and organisation. Not only urban workers but large numbers of rural Africans were attracted to Christianity for the first time through Zionist churches and their programme for a new indigenous African culture.

Separatist Christianity promoted both change and continuity. It offered a new framework for supportive social relations, in defence against the size, diversity and impersonality of the wider human environment. Church membership provided a strong sense of identity and exclusiveness, outlets for leadership abilities, and a moral foundation for social cooperation.

Religious separatism also led to important innovations in performance culture and in African hymnody in particular. Afro-American missionaries were involved in these movements from the 1880s; and the musical spiritualism of black Methodist, Baptist and Pentecostal ritual greatly influenced African Zionists.[101] One example is the hymnbook of Xhosa prophet Enoch Mgijima, originally a convert of the black American Church of God and Saints of Christ.[102] His squatter community of 'Israelites' was fired upon by police in the notorious Bullhoek Massacre of 1921. Mgijima's Israelite hymns were a blend of mission hymnody and the Afro-American religious music of the Baptists.[103]

The most important figure in the early re-Africanisation of religious song in South Africa was Isaiah Shembe, a traditional *inyanga* (healer) who founded his large and powerful Nazarite sect in 1911, five years after his conversion into the African Native Baptist Church.[104] Shembe's spiritual and political philosophy has been described at length by several writers.[105] All use the famous, best-selling Nazarite hymn book *Izinlabelelo za Nazaretha* as evidence that Shembe was a self-styled Zulu Moses, Christ, and Creator all in one.

In the years following the massive dispossessions of the 1913 Land Act, Shembe gained strength from his image as redeemer of the Zulu nation. His identity as Messiah is clearly described in Hymn no. 34, which ends:

Verse: In no wise art thou least
       Among the princes of Judah
       for out of thee
       Prophets shall come forth
       Who will save
       The City of Ohlange

Chorus: So it is also today
        On the hilltops of Ohlange (holy place of the Nazarites)

Nationalistic as well as messianic, Shembe's religion was not so much an African Christianity as a revitalisation of Zulu traditional belief and practice through the infusion of Christian elements.[106] One story has it that before Shembe founded his own church, he once preached a sermon at the Harrismith Methodist Church in traditional animal skins.[107]

Although the hymnbook was only published in 1940, almost all the hymns were composed between 1910 and 1930. Composed without notation, many of the hymns were based on European models but performed in African style, transforming them into something Zulu by the use of traditional musical devices. Shembe also developed new communal dances in traditional style as a means of praising God and attracting followers, and syncretising spirituality and celebration. These were accompanied by the *isigubu*, a Zulu version of the European marching bass drum, and by hymns that 'are in their whole structure nothing but Zulu dancing songs'.[108] Many of the hymns have an African call-and-response pattern, with the prophet singing the verse and the congregation responding with the chorus.

So traditional is the Shembe movement that many Zionist churches do not consider them Christian enough to be called Zionists.[109] Singing and dancing are the corporate expression of Nazarite faith, and comprise the only form of public worship at church festivals. Reflecting Shembe's proletarian and quasi-military orientation, young men's dance groups are called *amaScotch*, and their costumes consist of boots, pith helmets, white smocks over black pleated kilts, green ties with Nazarite symbols, traditional fighting sticks, and small cowhide shields.[110]

Shembe's early hymns may be the first original Zulu compositions influenced by Christian hymnody, and in retrospect, modern Zulu song can be regarded as beginning with two nationalist composers with contrasting backgrounds, Caluza and Shembe. Equally significant for the development of urban African music was the secular use of musical styles, ensembles and occasions usually associated with European missions and independent churches in the Transvaal.

North of the Witwatersrand, warfare among African states, unending struggles with the Afrikaner settlers over land, and the whites' need for labourers and servants fostered settled African communities in towns like Pretoria and Rustenburg by the late 1860s. These communities were composed mostly of Western and Northern Sotho (Tswana, Pedi, and related groups). Their contribution to modern African performance culture grew out of their response to European intrusion, Christianity and urban life.

Fighting raged in the central and northern Transvaal from the Matabele invasion in the 1820s to the end of the Boer War in 1902. Only the intrepid German evangelists of the Hermannsburg and Berlin Lutheran churches made serious missionary efforts there in the last half of the nineteenth century. Like the British, German missionaries introduced brass bands into Africa. Even in Europe in the 1880s, 'youths of the slums were being organised into Christian "armies" and "brigades" and marching to the sound of the fife and drum band'.[111] In South Africa, missionaries thought bands would encourage 'civilisation' and social discipline as well as attract new converts. By 1895 mission stations in every province had brass bands, but the special German interest in marching brass had the greatest effect on Africans in the Transvaal.

The reasons for this emphasis are both musical and historical. As with other instrumental traditions, wind instruments in South Africa originated with the Khoi. A band of Khoi played 'four or five flutes together, in harmony' for Vasco da Gama when he landed at Mossel Bay on 2 December 1497.[112] Among Bantu-speakers, only the people of the pre-contact Transvaal – the Thonga, Venda, and much more numerous Pedi and Tswana – copied the Khoi reed-flute ensembles and adapted their performance to their own musical traditions. The Pedi, for example, patterned their *dinaka* flutes on the Venda *motaba*, taken originally from the Koranna Hottentots. The Pedi did not adopt the heptatonic scale or songs of the Venda, however, but performed their own pentatonic melodies on the flutes.[113]

In the colonial situation, Pedi and Tswana people regarded brass instruments as attractive and superior modern replacements for their reeds and drums. The traditional foundations of their interest in brass was expressed to me by retired Salvation Army bandmaster Brig. Ramhlala, who stated simply, 'To blow and beat the drum; that is our way!'[114] In contrast to the Pedi and Tswana urban communities, the large settlement (*Khaya Khulu*) of Xhosa workers in Rustenburg produced not a single known brass band or brass instrumentalist. In addition to reed-flutes, Pedi-Tswana signal horns (*phalaphala*) gave way to the bugle and the trumpet.[115]

The musical development of African brass bands in the Transvaal reflected the differing responses to missionisation by Tswana and

Pedi. The Pedi twice created powerful empires during the nineteenth century. Even after the British destroyed their state in 1879, they continued to pose a threat to white control, and resisted missionisation. Berlin missionaries stepped up their efforts after the Pedi defeat, but the area remained in turmoil. Within a decade they lost their converts to the separatist Lutheran Bapedi Church founded by the Africanised white missionary Rev. J. Winter. The Bapedi church resisted Westernisation and blended Pedi religious traditions into their practice of Christianity.

In contrast, the Tswana were divided into several chiefdoms, dispersed by war, and had little national power. They saw more advantage in the protection offered by missionaries. Though their interest in Christianity was more socio-political than religious,[116] the Tswana were among the most missionised people in South Africa. Tswana brass bands tended to be attached to European missionary institutions where many players became musically literate and mastered Western sacred and secular tunes.

Eventually, Tswana traditional communities and Zionist churches also created entertainment and cultural self-respect from the music of brass ensembles. Whites did not always share this enthusiasm. Chief Magato procured European instruments, uniforms, and instructors, only to have his performers cruelly ignored by President Paul Kruger when they attempted to play for him during their visit to Pretoria in 1885.[117] Other leaders organised reed-pipe ensembles into Western-style bands, with a Western instrument or two added for heightened effect. Petitioning for more land in the Waterberg district, Chief Hans Mosibi exhibited his 'military band' for government officials in Pretoria on 3 June 1891, 'and raised much amusement by the quaint music, which was played in excellent time on primitive reed instruments, resembling clarionettes, with bagpipe drone'.[118]

Government policy in the Afrikaner republics of the Transvaal and the Orange Free State before the Boer War virtually forbade Africans to buy land in the countryside. It did, however, allow African freehold areas and municipal locations in the towns. British administration did little to change this, and urban African communities were well established in the towns by 1910.[119] Lutheran missions, including the Salvation Army, and numerous separatist churches all had large congregations in Transvaal towns. Band performance was a major attraction for membership. A concert promoter, Thabo Job, commented:

> The only place you could get a musical education free of charge was in the Salvation Army. Also the Lutheran church. They'd teach you, even violin. Any guy in the Salvation Army knew his instrument. The Lutherans had a violin in church . . .[120]

Unlike the European missions, the separatists encouraged dancing as part of religious ceremonial. They developed special steps based on traditional dance and European military drill for church band parades. Brass bands and even small string orchestras rapidly became part of African social life beyond church-sponsored events in the urban locations. They played for private and public entertainments, and brought vitality to community affairs.

As the locations grew, so did the opportunities for paid performance and the number of experienced players. These new opportunities and common neighbourhood residence brought working-class Tswana and Pedi musicians together in bands outside the church. Distinctions based on musical literacy and institutional membership were not important. The career of Modikwe's Band from Rustenburg reflects the involvement of African brass bands in early location social life.[121]

Though Modikwe came from Rustenburg, he received formal training in the Salvation Army Native Band in Johannesburg. By 1911, after three years of annoying church restrictions on drinking and smoking, he took advantage of the new market for his musical skills. Returning to his home town, he recruited a mixed band of Tswana and Northern Sotho players, some of whom could read tonic solfa. By simple notational charts and by ear the band learned a varied repertoire of European and African songs. Often, a member would sing a traditional song or a new composition in traditional form to the others, who found the notes on their instruments by ear and harmonised their parts according to African rather than Western principles. Following the practice of the Zionist bands, Modikwe's men also recreated European hymn melodies and marches in the African polyphonic idiom and set them to syncopated urban African rhythms.

These bands infused European melodies and march rhythms with African rhythmic contrast, counter-melodies, and solo ornamentation. American and South African brass band music are not very similar to each other on the surface due to differences in musical culture between the black peoples of the two countries. Even so, the manner in which musical resources and different performance skills were blended indicates similarities of musical *process* between black American and black South African brass bands of the early twentieth century.

Similarities in the social conditions and functions of performance may have underlain this comparability of cultural process. Like black American bands, Modikwe's band earned considerable sums performing at weddings, funerals, public holidays, private parties, official receptions, voluntary associations, or just marching in the streets of the black neighbourhoods. The versatility of their performance was comparable with that of black American bands, whose business cards advertised music for all occasions. Both black American and black South African bands sometimes broadened their repertoire through reading, but actual performing was done by ear. This freed their music from set arrangements and allowed it to serve any number of purposes.[122]

The prestige of black American culture during that period is again reflected in black South Africans' use of the term 'ragtime' to describe the music of bands like Modikwe's although its rhythms were very different from those of its American namesake. A good deal can be learned from examining the sources of black American influence on both middle-class and working-class African culture, and from comparing social experience, European influence and cultural process among black Americans and black South Africans. Important themes in the social development of urban African performance culture can be seen more clearly in considering the contribution of popular performers to Johannesburg's *shebeen* society.

Notes

1   Transvaal Census, 1904: 406.
2   Alan Jeeves, 'The control of migrant labour on the South African gold-fields in the era of Kruger and Milner', *Journal of Southern African Studies*, 2, 1, October, (1975).
3   Lionel Phillips, *Some Reminiscences*, London, 1925, p. 127.
4   Sir Harold Tangye, *In New South Africa: Travels in the Transvaal and Rhodesia*, London, 1896, p. 95.
5   *Imvo Zabantsundu*, 5 December 1894.
6   W. Bleloch, *The New South Africa: Its Value and Development*, London, 1902, p. 232.
7   Charles van Onselen, 'Randlords and rotgut', paper presented to the I.C.S., Seminar on African History, University of London, 1975.
8   Johannesburg *Star*, quoted in *Imvo Zabantsundu*, 4 June 1891.
9   W.C. Scully, *The Ridge of White Waters*, London, 1912, p. 226.
10   William P. Taylor, *African Treasures*, London, 1931, p. 234.
11   Charles van Onselen, 'The witches of suburbia: domestic service on the Witwatersrand, 1890–1914', paper presented to the Witwatersrand History Workshop, 1978, p. 36.
12   *New Nation*, 1, 5, 1910.
13   The attitude of municipal authorities in Johannesburg in this respect was similar to that in other towns, for example, East London. See D. H. Reader, *The Black Man's Portion*, Cape Town, 1961, p. 10.
14   Andre Proctor, 'Class struggle, segregation, and the city: a history of Sophiatown, 1905–1940', in B. Bozzoli (ed.), *Labour, Townships, and Protest*, Johannesburg, 1979, p. 52.
15   Minutes of the Johannesburg City Council, January/June, 1912.
16   W.C. Scully, *The Ridge of White Waters*, p. 211.
17   *Transvaal Leader*, 1 March 1910.
18   *Ibid.*, 6 February 1915.

19   *Western Areas Survey*, 1950, p. 26.
20   *Rand Daily Mail*, 6 May 1919; Johannesburg *Star*, 12 November 1927.
21   Absolom Vilakazi, *Zulu Transformations*, Pietermaritzburg, 1965, p. 120.
22   John Rex, 'The compound, the reserve, and the urban location: the essential institutions of South African labour exploitation', *South African Labour Bulletin*, 4 (1974), p. 13.
23   Proctor, 'Class struggle', pp. 80–1.
24   Charles van Onselen, 'South Africa's lumpenproletarian army; *umkosi wa n'taba* – "The Regiment of the Hills", 1890–1920', I.C.S. Seminar on African History, University of London, 1976.
25   van Onselen, 'The witches of suburbia', p. 57.
26   *Rand Daily Mail*, 8 September 1908.
27   *Ibid.*, 9 September 1908.
28   van Onselen, 'The witches of suburbia', pp. 59–60.
29   *Rand Daily Mail*, 11 September 1908.
30   *Diamond Fields Advertizer*, 23 May 1919.
31   van Onselen, 'The witches of suburbia', p. 60.
32   W. H. Dawson, *South Africa: People, Places, and Problems*, London, 1925, pp. 153–4.
33   *Umteleli wa Bantu*, 1 October 1921.
34   University of the Witwatersrand, Africa Day Programme, 21 October 1928.
35   G. M. Theal (ed.), *Records of South Africa*, vol. VII, Cape Town, 1901, p. 202.
36   Alice Balfour, *Twelve Hundred Miles in a Waggon*, London, 1895, p. 63.
37   M. Hunter, *Reaction to Conquest*, London, 1936; Harold Scheub, *The Xhosa Ntsomi*, Oxford, 1975.
38   Johannesburg *Star*, 13 December 1921.
39   J. Clegg, *Dance and Society in Africa South of the Sahara*, B.A., (Witwatersrand, 1977), pp. 37–9; 'The music of Zulu immigrant workers in Johannesburg, a focus on concertina and guitar', *Papers Presented at the Symposium on Ethnomusicology*, I.L.A.M., Grahamstown, 1981.
40   E. Krige, *The Social System of the Zulus*, London, 1936, p. 110.
41   D. K. Rycroft, 'Stylistic evidence in Nguni song', in K. Wachsmann, (ed.), *Music and History in Africa*, Evanston, 1971, p. 216. J. Clegg, 'Towards an Understanding of African Dance: the Zulu *isishameni* style,' in *Papers Presented at the Second Symposium on Ethnomusicology*, ILAM, Grahamstown, 1982, p. 10.
42   Clegg, 'The Music of Zulu Immigrant Workers. . . .', and 'Towards an Understanding of African Dance. . . .'
43   Clegg, 'Towards an Understanding of African Dance. . . .' and P. F. Larlham, *Black Performance in South Africa*, PhD, New York, 1981, pp. 112–14.
44   Clegg, 'Towards an Understanding of African Dance. . . .', p. 11.
45   Clegg, *Dance and Society in Africa*, p. 39; and personal communication, 1977.
46   Bongi Mtethwa, 'Zulu children's songs', *Papers Presented at the Symposium on Ethnomusicology*, Rhodes, 1981, p. 24.

47   Bongi Mtethwa, *Zulu Folk Song: History, Nature, and Classroom Potential*, BA, Natal, 1979, p. 16.

48   Rycroft, 'Stylistic evidence', p. 215.

49   D. K. Rycroft, 'A royal account of music in Zulu life, with translation, annotation, and musical transcription', Bulletin of SOAS, University of London, xxxvii, 2, (1975), p. 389, n. 81.

50   A. T. Bryant, *The Zulu People as They Were Before the Whiteman Came*, Pietermaritzburg, 1949, pp. 517–8.

51   Larlham, *Black Performance in South Africa*, pp. 121–2.

52   Proctor, 'Class struggle', p. 8.

53   K. Sole, 'Class, continuity, and change in Black South African literature, 1948–1960', paper for the Witwatersrand History Workshop, Johannesburg, 1978, p. 8.

54   N. A. Etherington, *The Rise of the Kolwa in Southeast Africa: African Christian Communities in Natal, Pondoland, and Zululand*, 1835–1880, PhD, Yale, 1971, p. 7.

55   *Ibid,*, p. 234.

56   *Ibid.*, p. 244.

57   J. S. Marais, 'The imposing of European control', in I. Schapera, (ed.), *The Bantu-Speaking Tribes of South Africa*, London, 1937, p. 342.

58   Shula Marks, *Reluctant Rebellion*, Oxford, 1970.

59   Marais, 'The imposing of European control', pp. 343–4.

60   Etherington, *The Rise of the Kolwa*, pp. 86–8.

61   *Ibid.*, p. 174.

62   R. Hunt Davis, 'The black American educational component in African responses to colonialism in South Africa', *Journal of Southern African Studies*, 2, 1, (1978), p. 76.

63   *Ilanga Lase Natal*, 23 May, 1910.

64   *Ibid.*, 23 June 1911.

65   Mary Benson, *Chief Albert Luthuli of South Africa*, London, 1963, pp. 6–7.

66   Quoted in Ian Whitcolm, *After the Ball*, Baltimore, 1974, p. 98.

67   Alain Locke, *The Negro and His Music*, New York, 1969; orig., 1936, p. 59.

68   *Ilanga Lase Natal*, 24 January 1908.

69   *Ibid.*, 3 June 1904; 3 February 1905.

70   *Ibid.*, 25 March 1910.

71   *Ibid.*, 7 May 1910.

72   *Ibid.*, 2 and 3 March 1906.

73   *Ibid.*, 23 November 1906; *Tsala ea Becoana*, 21 October 1911, 4 December 1911.

74   *Ilanga Lase Natal*, 17 May 1912.

75   C. M. Doke and B. Vilakazi, *Zulu-English Dictionary*, Johannesburg, 1958.

76   Charles Adams, *Ethnography of Basotho Evaluative Behavior in the Cognitive Domain Lipapadi (Games).* PhD, Indiana, 1974, p. 241.

77   Hunter, *Reaction to Conquest*, p. 374.

78   Doke and Vilakazi, *Zulu-English Dictionary*.

79   Khabi Mngoma, 'The correlation of folk and art music among African

composers', in *Papers Presented at the Second Symposium on Ethnomusicology*, ILAM, Grahamstown, 1982, pp. 65–6.

80   *Ilanga Lase Natal*, 15 February 1924.

81   D. Welsh, 'The growth of the towns', in M. Wilson and L. Thompson, (eds.) *The Oxford History of South Africa*, Oxford, 1971, p. 218.

82   Vilakazi, *Zulu Transformations*, p. 102.

83   Ray Phillips, *The Bantu in the City*, Johannesburg, 1938, p. 103.

84   *Ilanga Lase Natal*, 18 August 1916.

85   C. J. Wychk, United Society for the Propagation of the Gospel, *EMSS*, II, Keiskammahoek, 31 December 1897.

86   W. C. Scully, *Daniel Venanda*, Cape Town, 1923, p. 62.

87   Brian Du Toit, 'Cooperative institutions and culture change in South Africa', *Journal of Asian and African Studies*, iv, (1969), p. 281.

88   G. W. Mills, *The Role of the Clergy in the Reorientation of Xhosa Society to the Plural Society in the Cape Colony, 1850–1915*, PhD, UCLA, 1975, p. 73.

89   Scully, *Daniel Venanda*, p. 81.

90   Mills, *The Role of the Clergy*, p. 75.

91   *Ilanga Lase Natal*, 20 June 1953.

92   Harry Bloom, *King Kong*, London, 1961, p. 61; *Ilanga Lase Natal*, 18 April 1919.

93   R. C. Samuelson, *Long Long Ago*, Durban, 1929, p. 208.

94   Todd Matshikiza, *Drum*, August 1957.

95   *Umteteli wa Bantu*, 12 August 1922 and 26 August 1922; trans. W. Silgee.

96   *Ilanga Lase Natal*, 5 October 1923.

97   David Coplan, 'The African musician and the Johannesburg entertainment industry, 1900–1960', *Journal of Southern African Studies*, 5, 2, (April, 1979), p. 184.

98   Rev. Alan Lea, *The Native Separatist Church Movement in South Africa*, Cape Town, 1925, p. 36.

99   *Ibid.*, pp. 23–5.

100   J. D. Stuart, *A History of the Zulu Rebellion, 1906*, London, 1913, pp. 97–8.

101   B. A. Pauw, 'The influence of Christianity', in W. D. Hammond-Tooke (ed.), *The Bantu-Speaking Peoples of Southern Africa*, London, 1974, pp. 433–5.

102   Robert Edgar, *Enoch Mgijima and the Bullhoek Massacre*, PhD, UCLA, 1977.

103   T. Matshikiza, *Chocolates for my Wife*, London, 1961, p. 27.

104   B. Sundkler, *Bantu Prophets of South Africa*, London, 1961, p. 110f.

105   *Ibid.*, p. 281f.; A. Gérard, *Four African Literatures*, Berkeley, 1971, p. 184f.

106   Gérard, *Four African Literatures*, pp. 185–90.

107   Larlham, *Black Performance in South Africa*, p. 90.

108   Sundkler, *Bantu Prophets*, p. 195.

109   B. Sundkler, *Zulu Zion*, London, 1976, p. 161.

110   Larlham, *Black Performance in South Africa*, pp. 81–93.

111   T. O. Ranger, *Dance and Society in East Africa*, London, 1975, p. 12.

112   Arthur Morelet, *Journal du Voyage de Vasco da Gama en 1497*, Lyons, 1864.

113   P. R. Kirby, *The Musical Instruments of the Native Races of South Africa*, Johannesburg, 1965, pp. 150–65.
114   Brig. S. Ramhlala, interview 25 May 1977.
115   Kirby, *The Musical Instruments*, pp. 76–7.
116   B. A Pauw, 'Patterns of Christianization Among the Tswana and Xhosa-speaking Peoples', in G. Dieterlen and M. Fortes (eds.), *African Systems of Thought*, London, 1965.
117   D. M. Wilson, *Behind the Scenes in the Transvaal*, London, 1901, pp. 91–2.
118   *Standard and Diggers News*, 4 June 1891.
119   *South African Blue Book on Native Affairs*, 1910, p. 320.
120   Thabo Job, interview, August 1978
121   Brig. S. Ramhlala, interview, 25 May 1977.
122   Ortiz Walton, *Music: Black, White, and Blue*, New York, 1972, p. 58; N. Hentoff and N. Shapiro, *Hear Me Talkin' To Ya*, New York, 1955, pp. 16, 19.

4 Working-class performance culture between the World Wars

DURING the 1920s and '30s, the dispossession of thousands of rural black families and the rapid growth of industry led to a massive expansion of urban African communities in South Africa. The 1921 census reported a growth of 14 per cent in Johannesburg's permanent African population between 1911 and 1921, but from 1921 to 1936 the increase was close to 100 per cent.[1] The official 1936 total of 229 122 did not count the '93 000 Natives in Johannesburg and on the Reef who live by their wits, sleep with their friends at night, and are not included in the census'.[2] Many of these were women, who had virtually no role in the formal economy outside domestic service. Housing and other facilities in African areas were severely strained. Whites' fears of being overwhelmed by 'detribalized Natives' intensified conflicts of interest within white society and resulted in an unstable, inconsistent and unenforceable 'Native Policy'.

Commercial and other local investment interests opposed housing Africans in the inner city, white workers feared job and wage competition, and the mining industry feared African unionisation. Together they resisted further urbanisation of African labour. Against these pressures, industrial firms and some international investors preferred a stable, dependent labour force, and slumlords used their influence to protect profits from African rentals.

The official response to African urbanisation was the (Natives) Urban Areas Act of 1923. Under consideration as early as 1912, the final bill was a good deal more restrictive than previous versions. On paper it represented a victory for those who felt that 'The Native should be allowed to enter the urban areas when he is willing to minister to the needs of the Whiteman, and should depart therefrom when he ceases so to minister'.[3]

Unable to make Africans depart and unwilling to recognise their permanence by providing for their welfare, the government made urban segregation more rigid. African freehold rights were reduced to unguaranteed leasehold, although those who already owned property in designated areas were exempted. African housing became the responsibility of employers and the municipalities, whose primary source of funds for its construction consisted of the small amount of revenue collected from Africans themselves. Resettlement was also hindered by the stipulation that Africans could be evicted from 'proclaimed' areas only after enough hostels and locations had been built to rehouse them.[4]

The lack of money and land for such locations, together with resistance from slum rental interests such as the New Doornfontein Stand Owners Association, delayed mass evictions until the mid-1930s.[5] In any case, the Urban Areas Act did nothing to retard the growth of an urban proletariat. What the Act did create was a legal basis for harassment, instability, neglect, and denial of rights. These, in turn, increased African misery and resentment. Their response varied according to social class, but they shared a common desire for economic betterment and urban residence, and for recognition as permanent townspeople. The struggle centred on the creation of a viable urban African self-image and social structure. The result was a system of relationships that drew on values and institutions taken from both the industrial environment and African communal life, and that shaped urban working class society and culture.

Living conditions for Africans near the center of Johannesburg grew steadily worse as services declined and the crowding increased. A report on slumyards from the early 1930s said that 'There are an average of 64 square feet per inhabitant, a space of 8 feet by 8 feet, for living rooms, yards, and space to hang out washing to dry'.[6] Yet Africans clung tenaciously to their slumyards and restricted freehold locations.

One reason was the relative freedom to organise their society and pattern their culture as they saw fit. Regulations requiring fences, single entrances, and entry permits for municipal locations were not enforced, but Africans lost mobility and self-direction in community affairs if they moved to Western Native Township (W.N.T.) or Nancefield. Economic considerations strengthened African attachment to the slumyards even more. Not only were the slumyards much closer to places of employment, stores, and other urban amenities, they were also centres for the preparation and sale of liquor and beer, laundering, and other informal but essential home industries.

The average wages of African male workers could not support a family in an urban area. Women helped out with work that allowed them to keep house and look after their children. These earnings were especially important in combating the efforts of local authorities to restrict urban African enterprise. Five years before the Urban Areas Act, in 1918, a Johannesburg ordinance prohibited Africans from trading 'except in a recognized location'; and ordered them to give up all the 'tea-houses, cafés, restaurants, hotels, boarding houses, butcher shops, kafir eating houses, bake houses, shops, factories for the manufacture of food and drink, theatres, bioscopes, music halls, billiard saloons, pawnbrokers, cycle dealers, and slaughterhouses' they had been running elsewhere.[7]

In traditional Southern African societies, beer is an economic and social currency as well as a nourishing food.[8] It is used to thank, reward, reconcile, ritually cleanse, honour, entertain, and generally bind people together. In the urban areas, these traditional forms of sociability remained strong among the working class. Women were obliged by custom to brew beer for their husbands regardless of legal prohibition. Women soon discovered that beer and often stronger brews could be sold at a profit to people their menfolk brought to the home or even to complete strangers. In addition, there was a large though necessarily undocumented number of single women who provided liquor, sex and other recreational services to men in order to earn a living on their own.

Between 1921 and 1951 there was a 500 per cent increase in the female population of South African cities, an indication that the black urban communities were becoming more stable and settled. But not all of these new women joined families as they are understood in Western society. The beer trade, prostitution, and other enterprises required a certain freedom of action, and women may not always have considered a husband an immediate advantage. Households of all kinds depended upon the beer trade to survive.[9] The most common arrangement was known as *vat-en-sit*, an informal living arrangement without brideprice that preserved the mobility of individuals while pooling their financial and physical resources.[10]

Their central location and lack of direct supervision made the slumyards the focus of black recreational life. Pleading for the establishment of a municipal social centre for Africans, the Rev. F.W. Bridgeman complained that 'these slum districts constitute the rendezvous for all classes of Natives, including house servants, male and female. In fact the yards have perforce become the Native pleasure resort during holiday and leisure hours'.[11] Based on the liquor trade, there developed what might be called 'shebeen society'.

Like other urban traditions including professional musicianship, the institution later known as the *shebeen* dates back to the slaves of Dutch colonial times. As early as 1667, the commander at the Cape lamented that

Some of the residents are not ashamed and do not hesitate not only to sell all kinds of strong drink to the company's slaves, and those of private individuals, but even give them a place in their houses where they can drink.[12]

The word itself seems also to have originated in Cape Town in the early twentieth century among immigrant Irish members of the city's police force.[13] These constables named the illegal non-white drinking houses *shebeens* (Gaelic: 'little shop'). Coloured and Xhosa people brought the term to the Transvaal, where female entrepreneurs developed the shebeen into a centre of urban African social life.

The liquor trade became highly competitive in the slumyards. Women who made it a full-time occupation became 'shebeen queens' – relatively wealthy, established personalities with considerable influence in neighbourhood affairs and even with the police. They quickly discovered how to attract and keep a large, regular clientele. They could vary their products to suit individual tastes, offering traditional maize and sorghum beer, noxious chemical mixtures such as *babaton*, '*skomfana*, '*shimiyane*, *skokiaan*, and *isikilimikwiki* ('kill me quick'), and commercial European liquors. Musical performance, essential to social drinking in traditional society, was another important attraction.

To stimulate business, shebeens featured regular weekend parties where enormous quantities of liquor fuelled enthusiasm for continuous music and dancing.[14] At first the entertainment was provided by the customers themselves, but by the 1920s hostesses began to hire musicians. Miners and contract workers who strolled about the locations playing African, Afro-Western, and Afrikaans folk music on guitars, concertinas, and violins were among the first to come in off the streets into the shebeens.

Zulu municipal and domestic workers crowded the slumyards, and miners joined them at weekends. Along with their friends the liquor brewers, some were able to escape regular employment with whites through their musicianship, a form of resistance to economic coercion in itself. Vilakazi[15] calls these musicians *abaqhafi*, 'cultural driftwood' tossed up by the impact of secular Western culture and the industrial environment upon Zulu society. The *abaqhafi*, made famous among the Zulu in songs by Reuben Caluza like *Ingoduso*,[16] were like the Xhosa *abaphakathi*, neither traditional, Christian, nor school-educated. They cared little for the traditions of either Zulu or European culture and held the social values of neither. A set of individuals rather than a social group, they took their dress and manner from the American 'wild West' films shown at black cinemas in the 1920s, which often featured singing, guitar-toting cowboys.

The *abaqhafi* (sing. *umqhafi*) strengthened the link between paid musicianship, shebeen society, and life on the margin of society. Their popular image is reflected in the dictionary definition of *umqhafi*, 'uncouth fellow; heavy drinker'.[17] They popularised the constantly expanding corpus of Zulu wedding, walking and courting songs in Johannesburg. Zulu guitarists and violinists often teamed up to play for shebeen dances. Their frequent rivals were Mozambican Shangaans who drew on the folk instrumental music of the colonial Portuguese and also gained a reputation as skilled street guitarists.

Increasingly, shebeen customers demanded urban 'modern' forms of cultural entertainment that expressed the quality and permanence of their city way of life. In response, a new class of semi-professional shebeen musicians arose. They came from every region, black ethnic group, and type of community in South Africa, but most had spent much of their lives in towns. Their status as professionals, as people able to support themselves solely through their playing, was threatened by laws that forced them into non-musical employment. Pass regulations recognised musicians only if they belonged to officially registered bands, which in practice meant those with white sponsorship or management. Others had to present proof of some other regular employment or lose their right to remain in the urban area.[18]

In the 1920s, these musicians assimilated elements from every available performance tradition into a single urban African musical style, called *marabi*. The development of *marabi* was strongly influenced by the social and economic conditions of working-class life. A kind of symbiotic relationship developed between musicians and entertainment sponsors, and helped create a new culture for an urbanising mass audience. Growing out of shebeen society, *marabi* was much more than just a musical style. As music it had a distinctive rhythm and a blend of African polyphonic principles, restructured within the framework of the Western 'three-chord' harmonic system. As a dance it placed few limits on variation and interpretation by individuals or couples, though the emphasis was definitely on sexuality. As a social occasion it was a convivial, neighbourhood gathering for drinking, dancing, coupling, friendship and other forms of interaction. Finally, *marabi* also meant a category of people with low social status and a reputation for immorality, identified by their regular attendance at *marabi* parties.

The origins of the word *marabi* are unclear, but its meaning provides some clues. A possible source is *ho raba raba* (Sotho: 'to fly around'), an apt description of the wildly individualistic styles of *marabi* dancers. Some Africans identify the word with Marabastad, the boisterous Pretoria location where African domestic workers lived as early as 1880.[20] Mabille and Dieterlen's Sotho dictionary[21] defines *marabi* as the plural of *lerabi*, slang for 'lawless person; gangster'. Several people agreed that whatever its origins as a term, *marabi* was a product of the Johannesburg slumyards, and could not have come out of the small, mostly Northern Sotho location of Marabastad. The logic of this argument demonstrates the social as well as musical nature of *marabi*.

Marabi music drew heavily on the syncretic forms that preceded it, many of which were developed in the city by specific ethnic groups Gradually, common social experience and class identification helped combine these forms into the common denominator of *marabi*, though *marabi* itself continued to encompass variants based on particular ethnic traditions. As a term, *marabi* reflects the ways urban Africans socially categorised their emerging culture.

Among the early contributors to *marabi* were Cape Coloured musicians, known in Johannesburg as 'crooners' or *die oorlamse mense van Vrededorp* ('the *oorlams* people of Vrededorp'). They carried with them the popular performance traditions of Cape Town and Kimberley and provided a source of Cape Afrikaans and black American influence on urban African working-class music. They played banjos, guitars, tambourines, and bones at slumyard parties or marched in 'coon carnival' parades in Vrededorp at New Year celebrations.[22].

In the shebeens, Coloured performers were best known for the *tickey draai* guitar style, an early Afro-Afrikaans dance music very popular in the towns. Quick to join the Coloureds were Xhosa musicians drawn from among the 'dressed people', many of whom had come to Johannesburg to take up the more desirable surface work on the mines. Dan Twala recalls the Xhosa:

> When they came to the mines, they came with this coon thing . . . you see they had their own way of coming together in a crowd like the coons do, marching up and down. They were the most popular people, really; their costumes were a bit brighter and they had a sense of showbiz, being performers, and all that.[23]

Many African musicians had learned to play Afrikaans styles such as *vastrap* while serving in Afrikaner households in the countryside.[24] They enjoyed playing *tickey draai*, adding African melody to Afrikaans rhythms and chord progressions. *Tickey draai* was first played on guitar but by the mid-1920s small Coloured-Xhosa string and concertina bands were also performing it for private African parties called 'socials'. This music survived long enough to be recorded and can be heard on 'Okay Dance' (Gallotone, GB 949) made around 1940 by the Vincent Steza Dance Band.

Gramophone recordings, albums printed in tonic-solfa, local white and coloured bands, and even a few American players all helped to popularise ragtime and early jazz in the Cape after the First World

War. Queenstown, for example, was known as 'Little Jazz Town' because ragtime song and dance companies such as the Darktown Negroes and 'dixieland' jazz bands such as Meekly Matshikiza's Big Four entertained whites and middle-class Africans at 'soirees'. The music of South African dixieland bands has also been preserved on record, including *Madala* and *Mkize* (Gallotone GE 942) by Gumede's Swing Band. Musically unlettered pedal organists in the shebeens were also influenced by ragtime and jazz. They mixed these imported styles with African musical elements according to the three-chord system, and many earned an independent living travelling around performing for the new urban African working class.

Typical of the versatile, itinerant musician of the 1920s was Boet Gashe, described by Matshikiza as a 'well known jazz organist' in Queenstown. Queenstown was well situated for Gashe because trains carrying miners from Johannesburg stopped there overnight. 'Full of jazz and women', the miners found both in the 'booze houses' where Gashe played music called *itswari* (soiree), consisting of 'three chords repeating themselves over for four to six hours'.[25] Admission was threepence, beer was sixpence per tin, women were friendly, and for a shilling a man could take his favourite partner to a room behind a curtain. Meanwhile,

Gashe . . . was bent over his organ in one corner, thumping the rhythm from the pedals with his feet, which were also feeding the organ with air; choking the organ with persistent chords in the left hand, and improvising for an effective melody with his right hand. He would call in the aid of a matchstick to hold down a harmonic note, usually the tonic (doh) or the dominant (soh) both of which persist in African music, and you get a delirious effect of perpetual motion . . . perpetual motion in a musty hole where a man makes friends without restraint.[26]

In Johannesburg, Xhosa folk melodies played on the keyboard in this manner were known in the shebeens as *tula n'divile*, from the words of a famous location song. Dan Twala recalls:[27]

Tula n'divile became the name of a location, Western Native Township. We who worked in town, we used to come out there for the shows, which were part of the African life, away from the white surroundings . . . You saw that from house to house, where there was drinks or parties, you could hear the piano playing *tula n'divile*. It was not as polished as *marabi*; it was really an advertisement, to say, 'Come this way!' From the Xhosas came *tula n'divile*, meaning, 'You keep quiet, you haven't heard what I've heard, I'll tell you!' Everybody was trying to be original, and come with his own little style. They want you to buy drinks at their sort of *timitin* there, and I say all right, I can sing song, and I put half a crown on the table, and I ask you to come and sing. It was . . . just to augment the funds of the people holding the party, or just to provide money for refreshments.

Musical competition and innovation were promoted by shebeen owners who were aware that attractive women, lively dancers, and paying customers followed the most popular musicians. As Gashe brilliantly demonstrated, the relatively inexpensive pedal organ was best suited for making dance music in the cramped shebeens, and *marabi* reached its height as a keyboard style. In a Doornfontein slumyard in 1933, Hellmann noted that 'one woman is the proud possessor of a secondhand organ which is, however, more valuable as an economic than a cultural asset as its melodious strains serve to attract beer customers to this room'.[28]

The situation described by Twala was not unlike that of Harlem in the 1920s where

> pianists were kept busy playing in tiny cabarets and honky-tonks of the black community and for its innumerable social affairs, particularly the 'rent parties'. In Harlem . . . the only way many Blacks could cope with . . . the excessive rents . . . was to give parties where 'guests' were invited to contribute . . . It was the job of the pianist to draw people in – into the barroom or cafe or the apartment itself – and the vitality and vigour of his playing was his drawing card.[29]

In both America and South Africa, even those few who could read music often learned and performed by ear. This practice 'seemed to stimulate rather than deter them in the production of a novel style of piano music'.[30]

Several musicians emphasised the role of Xhosa instrumentalists in linking Coloured-Afrikaans, black American and local African styles, or as jazzman Wilson Silgee put it, '*Tickey draai* plus *tula n'divile* equals *marabi*'.[31] In Johannesburg, the most famous of these innovators was Tebetjane (Sotho: 'little Xhosa'), who began his career in Vrededorp playing guitar and kazoo with the strolling groups of coloured crooners. By the end of the 1920s he had become a full-time musician and a favourite with the shebeen queens of Prospect Township. In 1932 his composition *uTebetjana ufana ne'mfene* (Tebetjana resembles a baboon) made him so famous in the slumyards and locations that his name became synonymous with the *marabi* genre.

Like the brass bandsmen, keyboard artists often became professionals, indispensable to the social and economic life of the slumyards. Shebeen musicians appealed to a broad mass of working-class people from every ethnic and regional background, whose only tie was their common experience of urban life conditioned by racial oppression. To please them, musicians had to assimilate elements from a variety of musical traditions into a flexible, characteristically urban style.

The famous Gashe moved to Johannesburg in the 1920s, where, like other Xhosa musicians, he was soon in general demand for his versatility on the keyboard. He became a 'house organist' in Newclare location, playing for the Sotho version of the *marabi* party, the *famo* dance. In *The Wanderers*[33] Mphahlele recalls that as a small boy he heard the sound of drums coming from a place where Basotho men and women were holding *famo*. The area was called *Seteketekeng* ('place of staggering'), a part of Newclare where Sotho migrants who had drifted into permanent urban residence had been settling since the turn of the century. In Lesotho, a miner may be called *koata* (English: 'squatter'; from an urban area, uncouth, a ruffian) if he returns acting and talking like a rough man of the urban streets. This term originated early in this century, and *famo* dances were associated with a particular category of *koata*, the *sebono morao* ('buttocks behind') – one who intends never to return home and thus 'shows only his ass to Lesotho'.[34]

For shebeen dancing, most Sotho migrants preferred neo-traditional styles such as *focho* ('disorder') played on the concertina and a home-made drum. Those who were urbanising, however,

> used to have pedal organs . . . even in the ordinary tribal dances, week-ends, they used to end up their dancing with some sophisticated instrument. Just to show they have developed, and making their steps a bit more citified, but singing the same songs, and only playing it on the organ, because you know how they can orchestrate it the instrumental way, but it's the same song, the same dance.[35]

House organists like Gashe took Sotho songs and turned them into *marabi*.

At the same time, urban Sotho dancing and praise singing acquired a new feature, the dancing of individual women for a male audience. According to numerous eye-witnesses, the *famo* (from *ho re famo*: 'to open nostrils; to raise garments, displaying the genitals',[36] was almost defiantly suggestive. Women made shaking and thrusting movements with their shoulders, hips and bosoms while lifting their flared skirts in an effort, perhaps, to 'show their ass to Lesotho'. The dancers wore no underwear but instead 'had painted rings around the whole area of their sex, a ring they called "stoplight"'.[37] The dancing was reportedly wild to the point of frenzy and accompanied by *marabi* played on a pedal organ. Men, dancing alongside or seated against the walls, chose the women they wanted and took them into the back for intercourse.[38]

Apart from the dance, the term *famo* refers to the lengthy recitative songs performed by the women which served a purpose parallel to the male *likoata*'s praise songs, the *lifela*. The women often addressed their *famo* songs to the men. Usually, they began with the salutation *Aoelele ngoana moshanyana!* (Hey, male child!) followed by a series of rhetorical metaphors and challenges expressing the singer's tragic fate. Often she expresses bitter feelings about specific people and situations, while praising her own character and physical attractions in blunt language.

Former or current *famo* singers are understandably reluctant to perform these spontaneous compositions for the taperecorder, but some have been preserved on record, and in Lesotho, a woman named Malitaba has become famous for her *famo* songs. The following text, *Famo Ngoanana* ('Famo, Young Girl!') was issued on Gallotone (GB 2021), probably in the early 1950s, by Manapetle Makara Koa Famong. The record attempts to recreate the structure of a live performance. Statements by the singer alternate with responses from members of her group in the twelve-syllable lines characteristic of *sefela* and other Sotho poetic forms.

Famo, Ngoanana	Famo, Young Girl!
Aoelele ngoana moshanyana!	Aoelele the manchild!
Heholimi le ka be le na le tulo	Heaven should have a place
Mor'a molimo e moholo ke mang?	Who is the eldest son of God?
Hela oa mantlha oa matsibolo Satane	Oh, the first and the first born is Satan
Mohla a qalang ha ntsoa motsana	At first he was allotted a small village
Hela na nsoa sekoti sa lihele.	(then) he was given the pit of hell
Hela ke eo ba mo tsoere ka toropong.	Oh, there he is, caught up in town.
A le thipa a le selepe sa hae,	On him are a knife and an axe,
Hela a le kobong tsa lefu a Feletse.	Oh, he is in full funeral dress.
Hela Khomo li besua ka mollo, Satane	Oh, the cattle are burned with fire, Satan
Ha li le ta la li ka u hlatsisa.	If they are raw, they make you vomit.
Nkoko poli ea se roala moqhaka.	Nkoko is a goat that wears a *moqhaka* [married woman's headband].
Bua ngoanan'a heso, famo! famo!	Speak, girl of my parents' home, famo! famo!
Ha ke etsa joalo ke etsa motho.	When I do this [movement imitating intercourse] I am making a human being.
Nkoko poli ea se roala moqhaka.	Nkoko is a goat that wears a moqhaka.
Ele mahlapa e eo u lahla	She swears and may disappoint you
Hela, u ea tholoa ke manong selemo.	Oh, so that you may be picked up by vultures at ploughing time

99

Famola bo ngoanana, iketle	Do the famo, young girl,
Thope ngoanyana	Take it easy, young girl
U tsamaile	You are travelled
U lahlehile . . .	You are lost to your people. [i.e., Why hold back?] . . .
. . . Ngoanana ose ke ua botsa lihlapi	. . .Girl, don't ask the water animals
hi-tsoa-metsing li meno a bohale. (repeat)	Water animals have sharp teeth
Bua Makhobane, ke utloa u nkhopotsa hae.	Say more, Makhobane (the soloist) I feel you remind me of my country.
Bua ngoanana heso	Say more, my home girl
U buile Makhobane	You have said (a lot) Makhobane
U bue.	Say more.
U tsamaile ngoana Mosotho	You have travelled, Sotho baby
U qerehetse eng.	Don't hold back anything.
Ke be ke hopole Mathakane.	Sometimes I long for Mathakane
Ke be ke hopole mae ea Ntutu.	I long for the daughter of my paternal aunt.
mali-matsebe-tseba oa Matikane isoa kae?	Sometimes I long for the mother of Ntutu.
Tsoane-betere mamohatlana	Mali-matsebe-tsebe of Matikane
Hela Tsoane-betere ngoana Moselane.	Matikane, where is Matsebetsebe taken to?
Morena ha u tebela matekatse,	Tsoane-betere Mamohatlana
U se ka siea Mamokhahlana.	Oh, Tsoane-betere child of Moselane,
Litsietsi hali makatse mosali.	Chief! When you get rid of prostitutes,
Hela malitsietsi mae ea Khobane.	Don't leave out Mamokhahlana.
Ke tihile pelo ngoana a Mosotho.	Troubles are no surprise to a woman,
	Oh, the woman of troubles, the mother of Khobane [the soloist].
Ke tihile pelo, ke hotse bohase.	My heart is tough, (I) the Mosotho child.
Ke hotse ke bo kakatlela bophelo.	My heart is tough, I grew up an orphan.
(Transcription and translation by Joachim Ntebele and David Coplan)	I grew up under hardships of life

The singer rhetorically upbraids her chorus of male listeners, treasured sons of Lesotho who have traded their home villages for the 'pit of hell'. 'Caught up in town', the men go about heavily armed, only to be sickened and destroyed by deceitful women. The chorus approve her stance, urging her to hold back nothing. For her own part, she affirms her sexuality, mourns the loss of her own home and family, and maintains the toughness of her heart in the face of misfortune. The entire performance, delivered in a high-pitched, forceful declamatory rhythm, turns a personal statement into an expression of existential reality for her community of listeners.

Famo may appear to be nothing more than the emotional response of demoralized African proletarians to a predatory social environment. Yet it reaffirms an underlying sense of community and a system of social values retained from rural life. Though *famo* provided a setting for the practice of illegal trades, it also permitted cathartic moral comment on common problems. The experience of Adelina, a woman who attended *famo* in Vereeniging, Kroonstad, and other towns during the 1950s, is a case in point. Asked if money were her primary motivation for attending *famo*, she replied:

> No, it was a form of entertainment. At that time I associated with people whose manners were rough, wild. When I was deeply depressed and worried, in order to express myself and feel contented, like a Christian would open a page in a bible, with me I went to the shebeen to sing these things. I had gone (to town) to visit my husband and I found him but we separated. I suffered a lot because of that. So I had to go to these places and get some joy out of life and unburden myself. Others came for similar reasons, and to share their feelings with others . . . they were just like me. . . . The men came and spent their weekends there. They were from the mines, or working in town. They were *likoata*, and even *MaRussia* would come to visit from Benoni. The men . . . carried sticks and axes; some who were well experienced even carried pistols. They had a regular musician, playing the pedal organ. . . .[39]

The *MaRussia* of whom Adelina spoke were notorious gangsters who often held their own *famo* parties at which the men, in order of their rank within the gang hierarchy, took their pick among the women. They first arose during the late 1920s as vigilantes organised by members of other ethnic groups. By the 1940s, they transformed themselves into the fierce *MaRussia* (a name possibly deriving from the Russian involvement in the Second World War), who preyed unhindered on location residents for several decades. Despite countless arrests and confrontations with community vigilantes and police, groups calling themselves 'Russians' remain active on the Rand even today.

The shebeens, with their *marabi* and *famo* parties, clearly played an important role in the struggle between the forces of order and disorder in the African locations. Adelina herself found more than solace at the *famo* dances in the locations. She learned the basics of the shebeen trade there, including the preparation of *se pa ba le masenke* ('stagger on the fences') and other noxious liquors, and for the past

101

fifteen years has made her living as a shebeen queen in the towns of South Africa.

In the 1920s and '30s, brass bands played at every kind of public social occasion in the Johannesburg locations. Unable to march or perform on street corners in the crowded inner-city slumyards, they played on Sundays in racially mixed areas such as Vrededorp and Fordsburg, and in suburban locations like Sophiatown, Alexandra, and W.N.T. Individual players sometimes earned extra money performing in slumyard shebeens, but the major role of independent brass bands in working-class African society during the 1920s and '30s was to support women's associations known as *stokfel*.[40]

The term *stokfel* appears to derive from the rotating cattle auctions or 'stockfairs' of English settlers in the Eastern Cape during the nineteenth century.[41] Cattle had been a principal form of currency in precolonial South African societies, serving, like cash, as a standard of value, a store of wealth, and a medium of exchange.[42] Cape Africans brought the *stokfel* to Johannesburg, where the word came to refer to small rotating credit associations based on African principles of social and economic cooperation. It is significant that a pattern of working-class social organisation in which traditional forms of reciprocity and redistribution were harmonised with the demands of the commercial economy should have taken its inspiration from European customs relating to the exchange of cattle.

Stokfels were and are credit rings in which each member contributes a set amount each week in anticipation of receiving the combined contributions of all the other members at regular intervals. Commonly, each member in her turn uses the lump sum she receives to finance a *stokfel* party, at which other members and guests pay admission and buy food and liquor and even musical entertainment. Profits go to the hostess of the week.

The principle of mutual assistance that underlay much economic effort in rural African communities in South Africa was the mainspring of the *stokfel* in the new urban locations.[43] The only protection against default was regular personal contact among members, limited in most cases to six women from the same neighbourhood. The scale of organisation could be expanded by cooperation between groups, involving rounds of mutual contributions by clubs and attendance at one another's functions. The '*stokfel* society' created by these club networks[44] spanned the Witwatersrand and was still vigorous in the late 1970s. In Johannesburg's African locations, Tswana rather than Xhosa people were most active in creating *stokfel* society, though it soon spread to members of all black ethnic groups.

In the traditional pastoral societies of Southern Africa, individuals and families could sponsor cooperative work parties through beer drinking. Those who helped others could expect to receive both beer and assistance in their turn. In the slumyards, social co-operation revolved around the beer trade, and was institutionalised in the *stokfel*. Women made sure to hold their *marabi* parties on different days, brewed beer and cared for the children of friends who were ill or in jail, and helped each other out by selling food or taking admission.[45]

Tswana women used the traditional principles of regimental and ward organisation in forming their *simpato* (*stokfel*) and gave their weekly parties a special character. They treated their urban neighbourhoods like the wards in traditional Tswana towns.[46] Individual *stokfel* clubs banded together on the basis of traditional regimental loyalties signified by distinctive club names such as Transvaalians or Black Lions.[47] While church-going women preferred occasions sponsored by their *manyano* Christian sisterhoods, the line between *stokfel* and *manyano* must have been rather thin in some cases. Wilson Silgee recalls that his father, a minister and band conductor in the 1920s and '30s, enjoyed performing brass band *marabi* for *stokfels* as well as hymns and marches for weddings and other Christian social occasions.[48] Certainly, the uniforms worn by *stokfel* members on parade were inspired by the black skirts and white blouses of the *manyano*.[49] Christian forms of community organization along with traditional institutions may therefore have influenced the development of *stokfel* among the urban Tswana.

On Sunday afternoons, *stokfel* members marched to the party in uniform, singing Tswana regimental and initiation songs, popular urban songs, and Christian hymns. Accompanying them would be an ensemble of from five to twelve players like Modikwe's or the Bakgatla Brass Band, dressed in blue European military coats with brass buttons. Like the *tula n'divile* organ music, the *stokfel* parade was an advertisement,[50] drawing casual passers-by along to the party in a dusty cloud of colour, music, and marching, dancing feet. The uniforms and parade music also expressed and reinforced the regimental identity of the association and its members, people united in aid of their families.

At the hostess' residence, the band usually performed briefly while the party got under way. Later a keyboard musician accompanied singing by participants and played *marabi.* A conspicuous feature was the bidding for refreshments, performers and musical items – a practice taken from the popular tea-meetings and community concerts.

Stokfel mobilised values and motivations familiar from rural society in the service of urban social and economic goals and helped to reconstruct those values on a more flexible basis.[51] Traditionally, personal prestige had been the most important incentive for productive activity beyond the necessary minimum. In the towns, social status depended upon Western education, occupation, urbanisation, and wealth.

Migrants, workers and mission school graduates were squeezed together in a depressed field of social competition from which there was no upward escape. Under these conditions, conspicuous consumption and the public display of wealth became a means of gaining prestige and status that the *stokfel* clubs were able to exploit.

Working-class women found the tea-meeting pattern of voluntary attendance financially unreliable, so they organised the stokfel according to a system of formal reciprocity. Rewards were based on the degree of a member's investment, so that if a woman contributed liberally to the club and her husband spent freely at parties, they became popular and did well when she held her own party. Such participation built prestige and a reputation for generosity, reliability and community-mindedness. Club hostesses also added music, making it more profitable and entertaining through the bidding custom. The social byplay and competition for status involved in bidding furnished more entertainment than the refreshments and music it was supposed to pay for.[52] In this way status competition helped to redistribute money within the community and to promote cooperation in behalf of planned savings. Similarly, *stokfel* regained for beer something of its traditional function by integrating its sale into a pervasive pattern of urban social organisation, recreation, and exchange.

The initial contributions and bidding were intended as much to keep up the supply of party refreshments and music as to make a profit for the sponsors. In addition to mutual aid and welfare services, economic redistribution, and socially controlled modes of self-promotion, *stokfel* advanced cultural urbanisation and the transition from a rural to an urban identity. *Stokfel marabi* parties provided a setting where musicians provided aspiring urbanites with a means of self-expression and a new working-class culture. So the communicative aspect of these occasions was just as important as their social and economic aspects.

Just as the religious *manyano* and the secular *stokfel* influenced each other, the link between self-help and entertainment blurred the distinction between *stokfel* and shebeen. After the initial rounds of bidding, a *stokfel* often turned into a *marabi* dance no different from those in shebeens. *Stokfel* members willing to risk arrest and to put up with the commotion used their experience to become successful shebeen operators. Shebeen owners even formed *stokfels* among themselves, and as Abrahams recalls:[53]

> Stokveld [was] the trade union of the women who dealt in illicit liquor. . . . often a well-known 'skokiaan queen' was sent to prison without the option of a fine. In such cases the stokveld helped with the home and children till the member came out of jail.

Stokfel and *mohodisana*, a type of credit ring that functioned without the parties, frequently expanded their functions to include those of provident and burial societies. Similarly, regular shebeen customers contributed whenever one of their number or a well-known yard resident suffered a death in the family.[54]

The liqour trade itself, with its organisational consequences, provided the economic foundations of social and cultural change. Drinking served more to circulate wealth among urban black people than to create it, although migrant workers did bring some outside revenue to urban shebeens. Yet at least this money remained within the community rather than going to white liquor distributors or the government.[55] Brewing and the relationships centred upon it represented survival for many women and their children in Johannesburg. When the central government pressed the city to monopolise the production and sale of beer in the locations in 1937, working-class Africans organised a boycott of the municipal beer-halls in support of the liquor trade and shebeen society.[56]

For African proletarians, middle-class entertainment was something of a model of city culture, and it certainly influenced the development of *marabi*. The 1920s and '30s were the era of 'concert and dance' among the urban African petty bourgeoisie. A choir or ragtime-vaudeville company performed for the first four hours of the evening, followed by four hours of dancing to the band. Though shebeens seldom afforded enough space for a concert, black promoters could hire most of the eight halls in Johannesburg available to Africans.[57]

At working-class concerts and dances, tireless pianists like Solomon 'Zuluboy' Cele accompanied singers and stage dancers from eight pm to midnight and then played for *marabi* dancing until four am. Some were *ndunduma* concerts, attended mostly by recent arrivals from the country who wanted to be 'town boys', and came to acquire some urban culture. The term *ndunduma* means 'mine dumps' in Zulu and symbolised the totality of Johannesburg's culture to people from Natal. The *ndunduma* concerts and dances were the favourite of the *udliwe i'ntaba*, people 'eaten by the hills', those who, like the Sotho *sebono morao*, left home on contract work and never returned.

During the early part of the evening, choirs dressed in long suit jackets competed in performing *ingom'ebusuku*. During the latter half, the pianist provided dance music that blended the *ingom'ebusuku* melodies into the structure of *marabi*. Caluza's impact on both the *ingom'ebusuku* choirs and the *marabi* players helped bring this blending about. Always on the lookout for popular material, Caluza himself recorded Tebetjane's *uTebetjana Ufana Ne'mfene* hit *marabi* (HMV 4284). His influence was so important that the Durban saxophonist Dalton Khanyile was moved to remark, 'the pianomen were the bridge between Caluza and *marabi* . . . *marabi* is *ndunduma*, Caluzafied'.[58]

Ndunduma marabi appealed to an audience that considered traditional music too uncivilised and rural for the town. Yet they were still unfamiliar with Western or black American musical culture, and a strong sense of Zulu identity permeated their growing awareness of themselves as working-class Africans. They wanted music that was recognisably Zulu as well as 'modern' (Westernised) enough to support their urbanising self-image.

Mission-educated critics such as H.I.E. Dhlomo referred to *ndunduma* functions as 'night clubs of the lowest order . . . attended by degenerate young elements, the newly arrived country bumpkins, and the morbidly curious'.[59] Despite this attitude, Dhlomo wrote one of the few accounts of how keyboard players were able to combine Zulu musical materials with ragtime to produce *marabi*:

> And yet what naturally talented players the ragtime and the *Ndunduma* concerts had! Vampers . . . who improvised many 'hot' original dance and singing numbers at the spur of the moment, and who play or accompany any piece after hearing the melody once, and do so on any key. . . . Like the tribal bards of old [they] created beauty they knew not and flung it back unrecorded to the elements which gave it birth.

Dhlomo's enthusiastic description reflects the role of 'aural transmission' in the development of *marabi*. *Ndunduma* concerts are a good example of how musicians interacted with their audiences in the process of cultural urbanization. We are fortunate that this transitional style was not completely 'flung back unrecorded'. An example entitled *Indunduma* survives on a piano and vocal recording by the Ngcobo Choir (Regal GR9-WEA808) in the archives of the British Broadcasting Corporation.

A full-scale musical transcription and analysis is necessary in order to demonstrate exactly how this flexible style could incorporate musical resources from so many cultures. For those readers with some knowledge of transcription, a detailed analysis of a classic *marabi*, 'Highbreaks', is provided in the Appendix, beginning on page 259. In brief, *marabi* songs reflect traditional principles as well as Western influences in their tonality, part structure, and characteristic rhythmic sense of 'perpetual motion'. As a term, *marabi* covers a variety of syncretic forms that have in common only segmental repetition – 'a predisposition for the merciless two or three chord vamp', as Rycroft put it[60] – and a characteristic rhythm derived from ragtime and traditional Nguni wedding dances. In the hands of less Westernised performers such as the Zulu guitarists, *marabi* drew more heavily upon traditional melody and part structure but displayed very little in the way of melodic or rhythmic variation.

The evidence indicates that there was little free or 'jazz' solo improvisation in *marabi*. Working-class shebeen and dance hall patrons in the *marabi* era retained the traditional Southern African preference for melodic repetition, which was in any case well suited to continuous dancing.

Marabi compositions had titles but often no recognised words, and participants were free to make up lyrics to suit the melody as they wished, helping to spread the melodies across ethnic lines. Like *Tebetjana Ufana Ne'mfene*, some of these songs became widely known. Dikobe recalls the following:[61]

U ndiyeshilani sithando-sami	You abandon me, my love
U ndishiyela Zweni lobu Khoboka	You abandon me for this nation of
Mina nawe sidibeni emarabini	the detribalized
U ndisheyelani sithando-sami	My companion, mixed-up one of
	the marabi dance
	You abandon me, my love
	(trans. David Coplan)

Other *marabi* songs achieved general distribution because of their commentary on urban experience or expression of political protest:

There comes the big van
All over the country
They call in the pick-up
There, there is the big van
'Where's your pass?'
'Where's your tax?'[62]

Marabi's multi-ethnic character was evident also in its dancing, performed alone or with a partner in any manner inspired by the infectious *marabi* rhythm. Many people drew their movements from rural dances of the period such as *ukuxhentso*, in which several people danced together but each with his or her own solo, without any common pattern.[63] Recorded evidence also indicates that *marabi* in turn influenced the music of dances back in the country. Unlike traditional dances or the gumboot and *ingoma* dances of migrant workers, *marabi* had no official steps. As Sotho *famo marabi* dancers told Adams,[64] 'Each person sings and dances the thing the way he likes . . . they are not together'.

Marabi is difficult to analyse stylistically because the term refers as much to a social situation and a cultural outlook as to a complex of musical features. During the interwar years, *marabi* served as both a setting and a symbolic expression of the birth of an urban community among the African proletariat. Though *marabi* retained traditional musical practices and elements, its ultimate form reflected the desire of largely unschooled and un-Westernised urban Africans to modernise by absorbing new cultural elements within a familiar structure. African efforts to apply this cognitive familiarity to urban recreation led to the development of a pervasive *marabi* culture. Todd Matshikiza recalled that *marabi* was more than 'the hot, highly rhythmic repetitious single-themed dance tunes of the later 20s . . . marabi is also the name of an epoch'.[65]

As the slumyards came under the shadow of removal, the focus of African community life shifted to the freehold and municipal suburban locations in the Western areas of Johannesburg. There the *shebeens* found a new home, and *marabi* became part of the variety concert and the backyard party. A *marabi* party usually took place in a square yard, bordered on all four sides by the backs of location houses, with a temporary roof of canvas sacking. Beer, food, and *marabi* dancing entertained the neighbours for as long as the weekend or the refreshments lasted. The musicians were not professionals but local residents playing battered organs, kazoos, shakers, banjos, guitars, string bass, drums, or perhaps a few instruments acquired from a brass band. They were paid in liquor or, as location slang had it, 'petrol' to keep the *marabi* machine humming. By the 1930s, some of these neighbourhood bands had become widely known. They competed with each other at location dance halls in devising new variations on such *marabi* standards as *Tamatie Saus*.

Marabi also invaded other social occasions. For weddings, young people customarily formed choirs and composed special songs in traditional idiom, much as they had at rural celebrations. Soon they too were composing songs in the *marabi* style, and an amateur choral *marabi* developed that blended more traditional wedding songs into the *marabi* repertoire. Sotho people, for example, transformed their *wa sala wena* ('We are leaving you behind'; i.e., at your husband's home) wedding songs into *marabi* played on the concertina or accordion.

Working-class Africans developed a secular urban culture of their own based upon *marabi*, which much distressed the Westernising middle class. The better educated regarded *marabi* as a threat to African community life and to the 'civilised' status on which their claims to social and political rights were based. Middle-class black children who ran off to hear the music at neighbourhood parties were sternly warned that hellfire awaited *marabi* patrons. Influential Africans in the locations did what they could to stifle *stokfel* and *marabi* parties. The minutes of the (African) Advisory Board at the new township of Orlando outside Johannesburg resolved on 14 April 1933, that

> all night entertainments be not allowed in private houses – that is entertainments that are conducted for money – by reason of disorder, rowdiness, and being a nuisance to neighbors. There are other evils noticeable in connection with these functions, which evils are not for the social welfare of the community or in the interests of good order.

Mission school Africans considered *marabi* a misguided attempt at Westernisation that combined the worst customs of Africa and Europe rather than the best. The journalist 'Musicus' pleaded

> The problem of African music must be solved by Africans. The 'marabi' dances and concerts and the terrible 'jazz' music banged and wailed out of the doors of foul-smelling so-called halls are far from representing real African taste. They create wrong impressions.[66]

Underlying this attitude was the struggle by wage-earners for social mobility in a depressed social field. Packed into locations that were strongholds of informal enterprise, they resented the 'easy money' made by shebeen operators as much as the immorality and disruption shebeens were said to cause.

Though African proletarians clearly had their own notions of what constituted 'real African taste', white and middle-class accusations of a raucous, sex-charged, sometimes violent atmosphere at the halls had some basis in fact.[67] Among other things, African youngsters acquired a taste for liquor at *marabi* dances. Many working-class people, concerned with the preservation of family life in the slumyards and locations, condemned *marabi* as vigorously as mission school people. In Dikobe's novel, *The Marabi Dance*,[68] Mrs Mabongo warns her daughter, a popular *marabi* singer, that

> Marabi is for women who don't care to live with men, and don't want to have children. When they get children they kill them at birth and go again to marabi and look like girls who have never had children.

Like the shebeens, *marabi* occasions were a focus of the continuing struggle for order in urban African society. They were in many ways centres of community life that gave working-class people some sense of social coherence. Yet they were easily disrupted by a new type of social predator, the Blue Nines. These were gangs of youths born and raised in the ethnic mixture of the Johannesburg slums. They spoke the Afrikaans-based blend of African and European languages known as *mensetaal* or *flytaal* (literally: 'people's tongue; clever language'). *Mensetaal* was the only dialect or language that many gang members could speak fluently. Blue Nines had a great love for *marabi* dances, and drummer Lefifi Tladi once described *marabi* to me as a kind of musical *mensetaal*.[69]

In contrast to the *amalaita*, who worked regularly and maintained family ties, Blue Nines typically lived entirely by robbery and were alienated from African society beyond their own gangs. Fond of liquor, marijuana, and flashy clothing, Blue Nines were feared by other Africans not only for their crime and violence but because they were essentially beyond social control. The gangs were simply another destructive force with which the urban African community had to contend.

During the 1920s and '30s, working-class Africans in Johannesburg experienced severe hardships intensified by white resistance to their urbanisation. As we have seen, the involvement of performance in the African struggle for autonomy in Johannesburg was affected by social and economic pressures, tendencies toward order and disorder, and the dynamics of class and culture. The development of class identification among urban Africans has been complicated not only by ethnic and regional differences but also by contradictions within the black community and South African society as a whole. Class differentiation in the cities has always been hindered by racial discrimination, which promoted class levelling and common interests across social boundaries. These opposing movements were clearly reflected in urban African performing arts. To understand most fully the relationship of class and culture in black music and theatre in the cities, we should take a look at the styles associated with the upper level of urban African society.

Notes

1   Native Laws (Fagan) Commission Report, Union Government 28/1948.
2   City Councillor A. Immink, quoted in E. Roux, *Time Longer Than Rope*, London, 1949, p. 278.
3   Transvaal Local Government (Stallard) Commission, 1922.
4   Andre Proctor, 'Class struggle, segregation and the city: a history of Sophiatown, 1905–1940', in B. Bozzoli, (ed.), *Labour, Townships and Protest*, Johannesburg, 1979, pp. 54–7.
5   A. W. Stadler, 'Birds in the cornfields: squatter movements in Johannesburg', in Bozzoli, *Labour, Townships and Protest*, p. 26.
6   John Burger, *The Blackman's Burden*, London, 1943, p. 87.
7   *Rand Daily Mail*, 6 May 1918.
8   E. Krige, 'The social significance of beer among the Balobedu', *Bantu Studies*, 7, 6, (1932), pp. 347–856.
9   Ellen Hellmann, *Rooiyard: a Sociological Study of an Urban Native Slumyard*, Cape Town, 1948, pp. 41–3.
10 E. Koch, 'Town and countryside in the Transvaal: capitalist penetration and popular response', paper for the Witwatersrand History Workshop, Johannesburg, 1981, p. 15.
11 Johannesburg *Star*, 21 June 1920.
12 P. W. Laidler, *A Tavern of the Oceans*, Cape Town, n.d., p. 40.
13 C. C. Saunders, 'The creation of Ndabeni: urban segregation, social control, and African resistance', paper for the Witwatersrand History Workshop, Johannesburg, 1978, p. 16.
14 Hellmann, *Rooiyard*, pp. 7–10.
15 Absolom Vilakazi, *Zulu Transformations*, Pietermaritzburg, 1965, pp. 76–7.
16 Lovedale Tonic Solfa Leaflet 2C; HMV GU1.

17   C. M. Doke, D. M. Malcolm, and J. M. Sikana, *Dictionary of the Zulu Language*, Johannesburg, 1971, p. 258.

18   M. Dikobe, *The Marabi Dance*, London, 1973, p. 81.

19   Todd Matshikiza, *Drum*, June 1957.

20   H. Junod, *Pretoria (1855–1955)*, Pretoria, 1955, p. 76.

21   A. Mabille and H. Dieterlen, *South Sotho – English Dictionary*, Morija, Lesotho, 1950, p. 319.

22   Peter Abrahams, *Tell Freedom*, New York, 1970, p. 120.

23   Dan Twala, interview 17 March 1977.

24   D. K. Rycroft, 'The new "town" music of Southern Africa', *Recorded Folk Music*, 1, Sept/Oct (1958), p. 55.

25   Todd Matshikiza, *Drum*, June 1957.

26   *Ibid.*

27   Dan Twala, interview, 17 March 1977.

28   Hellmann, *Rooiyard*, p. 10.

29   Eileen Southern, *The Music of Black Americans*, New York, 1971, pp. 404–5.

30   *Ibid.*, p. 313.

31   Wilson Silgee, interview, 16 September 1976.

32   Todd Matshikiza, *Drum*, June, 1957.

33   E. Mphahlele, *The Wanderers*, London, 1971, p. 45.

34   Joachim Ntebele, interview, 28 July 1978.

35   Dan Twala, interview, 17 March 1977.

36   Charles Adams, *Ethnography of Basotho Evaluative Behavior in the Cognitive Domain Lipapadi (Games)*, PhD, Indiana, 1974, p. 151.

37   Mphahlele, *The Wanderers*, p. 45.

38   Can Themba, *Drum*, March, 1958.

39   A. M., interview June 1978, M. K. Malefane, trans.

40   Hilda Kuper and Sara Kaplan, 'Voluntary associations in an urban township', *African Studies*, 3, December (1944).

41   Brian Dutoit, 'Cooperative institutions and culture change in South Africa', *Journal of Asian and African Studies*, iv, (1969), p. 283.

42   Basil Sansom, 'Traditional economic systems', in W. D. Hammond-Tooke, *The Bantu-Speaking Peoples of Southern Africa*, London, 1974, p. 152.

43   DuToit, 'Cooperative institutions', p. 279.

44   Kuper and Kaplan, 'Voluntary associations', pp. 179–80.

45   Hellmann, *Rooiyard*, p. 46; 'The importance of beer brewing in an urban native yard', *Bantu Studies*, 8, (1934).

46   I. Schapera, *The Tswana*, London, 1953, p. 40f.

47   Kuper and Kaplan, 'Voluntary associations', p. 180.

48   Wilson Silgee, interview, 16 September 1976.

49   Kuper and Kaplan, 'Voluntary associations', p. 183; *Bantu World*, 17 September 1932.

50   Kuper and Kaplan, 'Voluntary associations', p. 182.

51   Clifford Geertz, 'The rotating credit association: a middle rung in development', in I. Wallerstein (ed.), *Social Change: The Colonial Situation*, New York, 1966, p. 438.

52   DuToit, 'Cooperative institutions', pp. 280–281.

53   Abrahams, *Tell Freedom*, pp. 110–11.

54 Dikobe, *The Marabi Dance*, p. 7.

55 Timothy Couzens, 'The social ethos of black writing in South Africa, 1920–1950', paper presented to the I.A.S., University of the Witwatersrand, September 1976, p. 5.

56 Proctor, 'Class struggle, segregation and the city', p. 83.

57 Ray Phillips, *The Bantu in the City*, Johannesburg, 1938, p. 293.

58 Dalton Khanyile, interview, August 1978.

59 *Ilanga Lase Natal*, 20 June 1953.

60 D. K. Rycroft, 'Melodic imports and exports: a byproduct of recording in South Africa', *Bulletin of the British Institute of Recorded Sound* (1956), p. 20.

61 Dikobe, *The Marabi Dance*, p. 44.

62 Hugh Tracey, *Lalela Zulu*, Roodepoort, South Africa, 1948, p. 55.

63 M. Hunter, *Reaction to Conquest*, London, 1936, p. 325.

64 Adams, *Ethnography of Basotho*, p. 51.

65 Todd Matshikiza, *Drum*, December 1951.

66 *Umteteli wa Bantu*, 11 November 1933.

67 Johannesburg *Star*, 13 December 1928: 'Mr. E. Nathan, on behalf of Peter Nothow, a native, applied for a license for the African Hall, 45 van Beek St. . . .Sgt. Tyler . . . said that on Friday there was an entertainment at the hall. Thirty-three natives were arrested in the vicinity without passes, or being drunk, or being in possession of liquor. The performance was still going on at two a.m. on Saturday. There was no European in charge. He found Europeans dancing with natives. There were several rooms which were known liquor dens. The hall sometimes kept open till four a.m., and there had been prosecutions for dancing on Sundays. . . . The license was granted with a warning to the applicant.'

68 Dikobe, *The Marabi Dance*, p. 79.

69 Lefifi Tladi, interview, June 1975.

112

5 Elite performance culture between the World Wars

DIFFICULTIES facing the African middle class during the inter-war years were as great as those troubling other Africans. The Urban Areas Act frustrated their hopes of winning a recognised place in South African society as a whole. Outside the cities the Land Act blocked their investment in rural real estate over 87 per cent of South Africa's territory. Africans educated at church schools found themselves cut off from positions for which their education had equipped them. Rejected by the majority of whites, who considered them insubordinate and stubborn, they were likewise resented by lower-class Africans for their self-conscious superiority and imitation of whites.

By the 1920s, these people had become a 'repressed elite'[1]. They carried the pass exemption certificate issued to 'civilised Natives' which, of course, had to be shown to police on demand like an ordinary pass. Still, middle-class Africans emphasised their importance to the country's expanding industrial economy. Encouraged by missionary teaching and the liberal movement, represented by the Joint Council of Europeans and Africans, they continued to struggle for social recognition and achievement based on Western criteria. Using the schools, cultural and sports clubs, the newspaper *Umteteli wa Bantu*, the Bantu Men's Social Centre, and a variety of other institutions, white liberals intervened in slumyard culture to prevent any alliance between middle-class and working-class Africans.[2] Culture and entertainment were among the principal means by which liberals co-opted the African middle class, softening the harshness of segregation and convincing them that advancement could come through Westernisation.[3]

Though sensitive to the 'primitive' image of traditional Africans, the middle class was distinct enough not to feel directly threatened

113

by the culture of migrant workers. But they did try to place as much social distance as possible between themselves and the *marabi* culture of the slums. Since teachers and clerks often earned no more than drivers and labourers, their status had to depend on Western education and the exclusiveness it gave to the occupations for which it was needed. Those who overcame the obstacles to become professionals were at the top of the African social scale. Doctors and lawyers gained prestige not only from their calling and substantial, independent income, but also from their work as politicians, writers and cultural leaders.

Education helped them gain the ear of sympathetic whites, reduced their sense of cultural inferiority, and reinforced their claims for racial equality. It provided the tools to compete in a world run by whites and to create shared values, patterns of behaviour, and a sense of social responsibility among the national African middle class.[4] Christian schooling also served as a basis for relationships and institutions that supported the achievement of common goals. Continually reinvigorated by new graduates from around the country, they created *isidolobha*, the culture of towns,[5] based on the ideal of a cohesive Afro-European way of life.[6]

An African academic, Professor Z. K. Matthews, wrote in 1935 that the 'synthesis of Western and Native conceptions . . . is being most successfully worked in the family life of educated Natives'. He recognised the importance of education as an integrating force, but also appreciated the many traditions that had been adapted to urban life, including 'the competitive dancing and singing which has replaced the old mock fights'.[7]

Performance culture greatly contributed to the realisation of elite ideals, and the formation of a tangible collective self-image. The performing arts also reveal much about the nature of black South African society, since as Hellmann[8] discovered, 'the kaleidoscopic succession of concerts, meetings, and dances in location community halls provides a valuable index of the direction, scope, and importance of communal activities'.

The power of the white community made acculturation attractive, and churches and schools became centres of elite African cultural development. Yet despite urbanisation, traditional culture remained a resource for African adaptation under segregation. Educated Africans drew on their pre-colonial past for elements of moral community, social control, and cultural coherence, combining them with similar elements from the dominant society.

The task of creating a viable Afro-Western culture was complicated by the attitudes of local whites. Integrationist white liberals helped to shape middle-class African expectations, but as paternalistic cultural organisers and educators, they often judged African performances by Western criteria. Such judgements inhibited the development of a relevant, creative modern African aesthetic, and intensified middle-class Africans' sense of cultural inferiority.

The missionaries' condemnation of traditional culture had a permanent effect upon the consciousness of educated Africans, who continued the fruitless struggle to win social and political concessions on the basis of their attainment of 'civilisation'. Ironically, it was the white segregationists who most clearly shared the educated Africans' recognition of the potential for equality and power that lay in African Westernisation. Segregationists spoke enthusiastically of the beauty and value of African traditions. Meanwhile, they used ·government policy to rigidify the remnants of African political organization for the perpetual separation and subordination of Africans.[9]

Cultural leaders among school Africans then tried to create a 'Bantu National Music'[10] that avoided both the slavish imitation of Europe and the artificial revival of tradition. Above all, they believed that a powerful mission school performance culture was necessary as a defence against the 'debased' ragtime, *marabi*, and jazz so popular among all classes of Westernising Africans.

Efforts to create a national culture resulted in voluntary associations modelled on the South Africans' Improvement Society of Kimberley in the 1890s. Most prominent among these were the 'Gamma Sigma' clubs, begun in 1918 in Doornfontein with the help of an American missionary, Ray Phillips. By 1938 they involved 5 000 educated Africans on the Witwatersrand in lectures, discussions, and debates on social and political issues as well as concerts, dances, and other forms of recreation. The clubs created links between Africans and white liberals, and helped divide Africans along class lines. As Ray Phillips pointed out, 'whoever captures the leisure time of the people gets the people . . . a people's character is moulded by the kind of investment made of their free time'.[11]

Social work to help the less educated was also emphasised, and missionaries like the Rev. F. W. Bridgeman argued that since 'for weal and woe Johannesburg has become unwittingly the greatest educative agency among the Native people',[12] something must be done to steer their acculturation along bourgeois lines. The interest of Capital in a cooperative African workforce enabled the missionaries to mobilise the liberal white community to provide funds for 'a great cultural centre for Native life',[13] and in 1924 the Bantu Men's Social Centre was built in Eloff Street Extension, Johannesburg.

The BMSC, managed by Africans under the direction of an executive committee of both whites and blacks, did in fact become a central institution of African society in the city. It provided educational, athletic, and performance activities for all classes of Africans. Of these activities, the most prestigious, culturally representative and successful was the annual Eisteddfod.

It is uncertain when this ancient Welsh term for a bardic and choral festival was first applied to African school choir competitions in South Africa, though it was current from the early twentieth century.[14] By the 1920s African teachers had founded adult choirs in most of the towns. In 1931, the pianist and conductor Mark Radebe of Johannesburg and the composer Hamilton Masiza of Kimberley founded the South African Bantu Board of Music (SABBM) to organise provincial Eisteddfodau among teachers' choirs.

The first Eisteddfodau took place in Port Elizabeth and Johannesburg late in 1931. They had two official aims: 'to preserve and develop the individuality of Native music, and, concurrently, to encourage the finer refinements of European music'. Further, the constitution of the SABBM pledged the organisation to:

1 awaken interest in musical talent
2 promote interest in African music
3 discover how to use music for the glory of God and the amelioration of social and cultural conditions
4 establish a Bantu Academy of Music
5 research and collect Bantu folk music
6 encourage and publish Bantu composers
7 hold concerts for funds, publicity, study, and appreciation

In 1934 the Transvaal Eisteddfod became a national event, and renowned choirs and soloists poured into Johannesburg for several days of competitions at the BMSC. People from all over South Africa met there, discussed national and community issues, formed new personal and organisational links, argued over political strategy, and developed resources for an elite national culture. The Eisteddfod became a setting for middle-class African interaction and sharpened the definition and consciousness of their class identity.

Seeking to provide liquor-free recreation for the urban African work-force, white members of the executive committee arranged for an Eisteddfod programme more inclusive than African members might have wished, allowing nearly all types of Africans to compete. In addition to competitions in English and African written classical songs, folk songs, and hymns performed by choirs, there were male, female and mixed quartets, solo and band instrumentalists, institutional brass bands, and even performers on traditional African instruments. The literary section included vernacular and English recitations, written collections of African folksongs, poems, short stories, essays, dramatic pieces, and song lyrics. Dance events were open to teams of miners performing a range of ethnic styles and to Westernised urbanites doing the waltz, foxtrot, and quickstep.[16] Working-class *ingom'ebusuku* choirs and anything associated with *marabi* culture, however, were excluded.

The educated African solution to the problem of how to draw upon the resources of traditional performing arts without abandoning 'civilisation' was to 'modernise' traditional song. They performed it with classically trained choirs in four-part harmony or blended African melodic and polyphonic features into the Western choral idiom. African composers and conductors had been evolving a syncretic choral tradition since the late nineteenth century, though not in the ways approved by educators such as Hamilton Masiza and Mark Radebe. The tonic solfa system, which even today remains the basis of modern African composition, is not entirely suitable for notating African music.[17] Its indications for tempo, modulation and complex rhythms are awkward and inconvenient, and its simple harmonic scheme makes it difficult to accurately represent African melody and polyphony. Nevertheless, its very simplicity provided a structure for the re-Africanisation of modern choral music.

As early as 1917, a disgruntled contributor to *Ilanga Lase Natal*[18] complained that the standard of secular urban choirs had fallen because 'the only conductors remaining are those who fail to read music and "sing out of their heads"', misleading people into thinking that 'that proper way to sing is to shout'. What this critic is referring to is the habit of African choirmasters to lead rather than conduct their performers. As one of the most experienced Johannesburg choir teachers, Lucas Makhema, explains,[19] the four-part structure of African choral singing is based on relative, rather than absolute pitch. The conductor sings one part, usually the bass, loud enough to be heard over the combined voices of the choir members, each of whom finds his or her part in harmonic relation to the bass line and the parts of others around them. The traditional African preference for parallel movement at perfect intervals and the melodic alternation of fundamentals a whole tone apart[20] is often freely expressed in this way.

Because the tonic solfa system uses letters rather than note symbols and gives no visual indication of melodic direction, leaders find it difficult to teach melody and lyrics at the same time.[21] A common solution has been to 'shout' the melody in the manner of traditional cantors until all have found and learned their parts, and only then to use the written score to introduce the lyrics. Aural transmission was a key element in developing South African choral music and in broadening the repertoires of individual choirs.

Tonic solfa sheet music has always been scarce and expensive in South Africa. Most often, conductors acquire new material by attending Eisteddfodau and other major competitions, where they memorise or quickly sketch out in tonic solfa the most appealing selections, and then teach them without a score. Sometimes they use phonograph recordings by local choirs to transmit new pieces aurally.[22] In general, African choirs have had a lot of latitude for muscal interpretation.

All this is not to ignore the dedication of conductors who trained their choirs to perform the 'Hallelujah Chorus' from Handel's *Messiah* or local classical compositions such as Masiza's cantata, *Emnqamlezweni* ('At the Cross') in thoroughly Western fashion. Educators like Masiza and Radebe were caught between pride in their cultural nationalism and their feelings of cultural inferiority. They praised recording companies for preserving 'this folk music which is our most treasured cultural inheritance' and 'a basic idiom thoroughly competent to express our national psychology'.[23] In practice, though, when elements of African polyphony or performance practice crept in they treated it as a failure to assimilate 'civilisation' and as an example of retarded cultural development. They also viewed miners' traditional dancing as part of the government's attempt to portray Africans as primitives unworthy of equal rights. An African contributor argued in the *Bantu World*:[24]

> There is no objection to war dances, provided they are staged by the enlightened Bantu. When they are staged by the uncivilized, it is a sign of retrogression, because finding his performance so patronised, he has no inducement to progress.

In measuring African musical performance by Western aesthetic criteria, African music educators were short-sighted. They failed to recognise that cultural nationalism would only be subverted by measuring Africans by the cultural standards of the colonisers. Some[25] admitted that the paucity of musical instruction in African schools ruled out Western standards, at least temporarily. But those at the top of the social scale were unwilling to abandon the ruling standards, giving up the opportunity for cultural self-discovery and their place as cultural pace-setters for the wider community.

Despite such ambivalence, a small number of educated African composers continued in the tradition of Ntsikana and Bokwe, producing a genuinely Afro-Western *makwaya* literature based on tonic solfa. Composers came from various regions of the country, but significantly, none of the best known arose from an urban background. Benjamin Tyamzashe, Joshua P. Mohapeloa, R. T. Caluza, and others all made use of both the traditional music of their rural homes and their training in school choirs. As a group, they had a permanent influence upon the development of African choral composition in Southern Africa. Mohapeloa's career serves as a particularly good example.

Born in 1908, the late J. P. Mohapeloa grew up in rural Lesotho then British Basutoland), where he spent many musical evenings around the family organ with his devoutly Christian parents. He was a

10 *Police destroy containers of liquor in a raid on a shebeen in the 1930s*

11 *William 'Sax-o-Wills' Mbali, saxophonist and bandleader, as Queenstown Ballroom Dance Champion in the 1920s*

12 *Pianist Meekly 'Fingertips' Matshikiza with the Blue Rhythm Syncopators, Queenstown, early 1930s. William 'Sax-o-Wills' Mbali is second from left*

13 The Rhythm Kings, founded in 1935 by John Mavimbela (far right) and drummer Dan Twala (far left)

14 Ace Buya (far right) and the Modernaires, 1940s

15 The Jazz Maniacs, a Sophiatown band founded in 1935 by Solomon 'Zuluboy' Cele: Wilson 'King Force' Silgee (standing, left), saxophonist Zakes Nkosi (seated, left), saxophonist Mackay Davashe (seated, third from left)

standout at school choir competitions and became a choir leader at the age of ten. Inspired by local composers, including Joachim Sase and Woodruff Buti, he began composing songs during a youthful convalescence from tuberculosis. Mohapeloa explained to me[26] that these were either 'school songs' on the European model or attempts to transcribe and arrange in four parts the folk music of Sotho villages. Though literate in tonic solfa, he was only partly familiar with the Western harmonic principles on which it is based.

In 1935, the Morija Sesotho Book Depot (Lesotho) published his first collection of thirty-two compositions, which were an immediate success with African choirs throughout South Africa. Many of the songs, such as *U Ea Kae*, use purely traditional melodic themes, arranged according to his own concepts of Western three-chord harmony. Indigenous Southern African vocal music is, we recall, cyclical in structure, and its solo-chorus part relationships prevent the use of collective cadence. In *U Ea Kae*, therefore, Mohapeloa attached a formal concluding cadential phrase in three-chord hymnodic harmony in order to make the whole 'beautiful' in Western aesthetic terms.[27]

Work songs transformed by literate composers soon achieved a new popularity as expressions of African nationalist political consciousness and cultural identity. The recent album issued by the ANC Cultural Workers, *Amandla* (A Disc BS800718) features a rousing version of *U Ea Kae* (see Appendix B). The lyrics rendered in English say:

Gird your loins,
Let's go to Taung (the lion's place)
to Moletsane's
To witness the threshing of the wheat
The young boys take their sticks and
strike to their satisfaction

Where are you going?
How could you come unprepared
to the place of the Lion, Moletsane?
We brought our tools (we are ready)
Hom . . . Hom . . . .

Another song, *Chabana sa Khomo* (see Appendix B), is divided into three parts: the first in traditional polyphony, the second adding Western ornamentation in the solo tenor part, and the third changing to a different traditional melodic theme and rhythm, taken from a work song to accompany the scraping of a cow-hide for clothing. The title of the published collection is *Meloli le Lithallere tsa Afrika* (1935), 'African Melody in Extemporary Harmonisation', by which Mohapeloa intended to emphasise that Africans can 'harmonise' aurally, without forethought.

African and white music educators recognised that Mohapeloa's songs realised their notion of a 'Bantu national music'. They suggested that he 'improve' his abilities by undertaking formal training in Western music. In 1938 he took a scholarship to study under Professor P.R. Kirby at the University of the Witwatersrand. To earn extra money, Mohapeloa organised a touring Sotho choir called the African Traditional Choristers, and in 1939 he published a second volume of *Meloli le Lithallere tsa Afrika*.

As he absorbed the rules of Western composition, Mohapeloa tried to 'correct' his previous work accordingly; but the revisions were never as pleasing as the originals. Even so, his four years of study permanently affected his musical outlook, and he has spent the last four decades consciously attempting to 'compose something that is African without being unmusical'.[28] He was unable to make an independent living from choral music in Johannesburg without imitating Caluza, 'whose music was all ragtime, and I thought I could do something better than that'. So Mohapeloa returned to Lesotho and became a layout and proofreading specialist in tonic solfa for his Morija publisher. The job did not enable him to promote the sale of his compositions as he had hoped, but it did in time make him something of an expert in the use of tonic solfa to notate African music.

With this knowledge, Mohapeloa was able to write highly complex pieces in tonic-solfa. They combine African and Western harmonic principles, represent durational values as small as a 1/32 note, and use African compound rhythmic structures based on the simultaneous sense of duple and triple time. Unfortunately, African choirs are rarely able to perform them at sight, and he was often asked why he no longer wrote songs like those in his first collection. The third volume of *Meloli. . . .*, published in 1947, has never been as popular as the other two. In his more recent songs, many of which were published in a new volume, *Meluluetsa*, in 1976,[29] Mohapeloa has consciously attempted to fuse Western and African principles of composition. Whether these works will succeed with African choirs remains to be seen; but his continuing effort to recreate a cultural tradition, from which his audience has long been alienated, by clothing it in more acceptable Western dress illustrates the dilemma of the modern African composer.

Many African proletarians regarded the Bantu Men's Social Centre as the 'high hat club of the Whiteman's Good boys',[30] yet it strongly influenced urban African culture in general because its prestigious leaders took seriously their pledge to use performing arts to promote African unity and improve social conditions. Most events were open to everyone, and the BMSC de-emphasised ethnic identity and 'tribalism' among Johannesburg Africans.[31] Even the term 'Eisteddfod' was significant. Africans familiar with its original meaning knew these festivals had helped maintain Welsh national identity; events where 'the laws of Welsh Bards and Minstrel-councillors were recited'.[32]

Songs made popular at Eisteddfodau around the country included Tyamzashe's *Ivoti*, which urged Africans to fight the revocation of their voting rights in the Cape,[33] and Mohapeloa's *U Ea Kae*, still a symbol of African preparedness for self-defence. Perhaps most enduring has been Masiza's *Vukani Mawethu* ('Awake My People'), in which the composer scolds his people for being the 'footstool' (*isenabo*) of all nations, lacking trust in one another and the initiative to improve their situation. Banned in the 1950s, this song reappeared in public during the Soweto uprisings of 1976.

Elite African assurances that the Eisteddfodau would 'help abolish the *marabi* menace'[34] proved hollow. *Marabi* was too important to working-class life in the city, while ragtime and jazz were an even greater problem because of their popularity among the middle class itself. They served far better as musical expressions of an urban African self-image than Anglo-African classical *makwaya*.

The rapid development of the recording and cinema industries during the 1920s and '30s brought American performance culture to many countries,[35] including South Africa. The role of American blacks in popular music, dance, and variety stage entertainment had a special appeal for black South Africans. The racial disabilities of black Americans appeared similar to their own, and they followed black American progress in overcoming them. Visits by Solomon Plaatje and other black South Africans to America during this period[36] reinforced respect for black American political and cultural leaders, and induced a hunger for equal accomplishments. Mariannhill teacher S. V. H. Mdhluli argued in 1933:

> The Negroes on the other side of the Atlantic have made a gigantic progress; all the same we are making a steady advance to the same goal. . . . They have shown among other things that this much debated 'arrested development' is practically unknown among the Negroes. For our intelligence we have been relegated to the lowest rung of the ladder of progress. That wave of pessimism can be averted only by imitating the American Negroes.[37]

Like the leaders of the black American Harlem Renaissance of the 1920s[38], the African elite hoped that achievements in the artistic and intellectual fields would help to break down the colour bar.[39]

African music educators hoped that the Eisteddfodau would replace the old ragtime and coon song competitions[40] and promote the classical and Afro-American religious music performed by Roland Haynes and Paul Robeson, in preference to jazz. The association of jazz with urban working-class culture in America and its growing popularity in Johannesburg's rowdy African dance halls, troubled elite critics such as 'Musicus':

> The old jazz of the screeching jazz maniac will not torture its victims much longer . . . King Jazz is dying. His syncopating, brothel-born, war fattened, noise drunk is now in a stage of hectic decline. . . . It is, however, true that jazz is a perversion of some of the remarkable syncopating rhythms to be found in the Native music of many races. The Negroes, we are told, contributed some, but it is a libel upon our bretheren to lay the crime of jazz upon them.[41]

But apprehensions about the growth of interest in jazz at the expense of *makwaya* were well founded. The traditions of black American minstrelsy and vaudeville continued to influence African touring companies through the early decades of the twentieth century,[42] and recordings encouraged imitation of black American performers. By the 1930s, popular stage traditions of black America were already well established in that universal training ground of middle-class performers, the school concert. Many African school teachers, who had little in the way of formal musical training themselves, were more interested in the enthusiastic participation of students and the pleasure of parents than in 'Bantu national music'. Concerts featured African part-songs, Tin Pan Alley tunes, spirituals, comic songs and sketches, action songs, tap dancing (*umqhumqhumbelo*), and especially vocal quartets performing ragtime and jazz. Elite critics like R. R. R. Dhlomo were appalled:

> . . . this jazzing craze or madness has its victims in its octopus-like grasp. It emanates from the misguided teacher, who apparently thinks jazz is the most up to date music his children should be taught. . . . I once visited a certain school . . . and was treated to what was considered the latest selections in music by the school children. The words of the first song were these: 'Thine eyes – dear love speak of paradise.' Another song . . . was this: 'Tell her in the twilight,' and 'I want to be happy, etc.' These songs were sung in precisely the same way as a music comedy company renders its songs in a theatre with suggestive movements and passionate expressions which are hand in glove with jazz music. . . .[43]

Dhlomo was, of course, the same writer who had previously found so much value for African cultural nationalism in the work of Caluza, much of which is unmistakably ragtime and therefore akin to jazz. Perhaps the most respected African academic of all, Professor B. W. Vilakazi of the University of the Witwatersrand, came up against this contradiction in an article 'African Music – Where Is It?'

> There is no name in music libraries for purely Caluza music, but for lack of an apt word we call it jazz. Jazz music is somewhat inferior to the sort of music found in Caluza's compositions . . .[44]

Though rarely performed at the elite-sponsored Eisteddfodau, black American vaudeville and jazz were turning school community concerts into the cradle of professional black show business in South Africa.

During the 1920s, Johannesburg Africans could get an idea of how American show people dressed and acted from film shows at the BMSC or the Good Hope and Small St. commercial 'bioscopes'. At the latter, black musicians accompanied the silent pictures, using sheet music sent along from America.[45]

School concert groups spent much time learning to imitate recordings of British and American popular songs. Many groups stayed together after leaving school, forming what in South Africa were still known as 'minstrel companies' of four to seven vocalists and dancers backed by a pianist. Among the most popular of the early troupes were the Versatile Seven, the Mad Boys, the Africans' Own Entertainers, and the Midnight Follies. Stage costume was formal: tail-coats, white tie, striped trousers, and black shoes, or perhaps brightly coloured sashes, straw hats, white pants, and blazers. Costumes were changed two or three times a night, often to suit the demands of stage choreography. The African Darkies and Gay Arrawaras in particular were known for vigorous dancing and 'strutting songs'[46] that combined the movement of action songs, *ingom'ebusuku*, and ragtime. Most selections were ragtime and jazz in English, jazz arrangements of Afro-American spirituals (Zulu: *itshimama*), or translations of American songs sung without regard for the tonal structure of African languages.

Concerts were held at halls near the centre of town, usually from eight pm to midnight. Dancing would follow until four am, but if the show was held at a bioscope, the concert began after the film at 11 pm. Troupes were hired by independent promoters, who charged 2s 6d admission and made more money through the bidding system. They paid each performer 15s–30s per show, at a time when few Africans earned more than 80 shillings per month through regular employment. As a result, many troupes were at least semi-professional; and the most popular, like the Africans' Own Entertainers, made a living entirely from performing.

Several groups, such as Motsieloa's Hiver Hyvas, widened their audience by touring, and by 1930 almost every major town had at least one stage company of its own. Following the tradition of mixed voice choirs like those of Caluza and William Mseleku, women also joined minstrel companies. By the 1930s there were a few all-female groups, including Queenstown's Gay Glamour Girls, led by Meekly 'Fingertips' Matshikiza's sister, Jane Matshikiza.[47]

Most recordings of the period came to South Africa not from America but from England, where black American Broadway composer J. Turner Layton and lyricist Gordon Johnstone made a series of records for Columbia in 1928 and 1929. Such Layton and Johnstone favourites as 'Can't Help Lovin' Dat Man' (Col.-E 4916) became enormously popular in South Africa and were models for local minstrel singers.

Silent films popularised show dancing, and with sound films tap dancing became a virtual craze in South Africa. Jacob 'King Jeff' Disimelo of the Diamond Horseshoes and other dancers achieved national reputations among blacks by patterning themselves upon Fred Astaire and the Nicholas Brothers. The most famous troupe, the Darktown Strutters of Johannesburg, combined the songs of Layton and Johnstone with 'step dancing' and the tap inventions of leader J. J. 'Koppie' Masoleng.

Other regular features of minstrel entertainment were comedy routines and dramatic sketches, performed by the entire company or by a 'standup' specialist in comic mime like the Darktown Strutters' Ndaba 'Big Boy' Majola.[48] Many dramatic sketches presented typical scenes and characters from location life, portrayed comically or seriously. Comedy was preferred, and the reality of location conditions inspired an urban African tragicomedy on the variety stage that later contributed much to the working-class musical 'township theatre' of today.

In the mission schools, short dramatic pieces had been part of school concerts since the 1870s.[49] Unfortunately, most teachers ignored the improvisational mime and dramatic recitation of *izibongo* and *izinganekwane* (Zulu praise poetry and storytelling) just as they did traditional music and dance. These dramatic traditions had to remain latent in African school performance culture until they reappeared on the urban stage in the late 1920s.

In fairness, not all missionaries were so ethnocentric, and a few made valuable contributions to the development of modern African theatre. In 1920, Father Bernard Huss, of the Trappist Catholic school at Mariannhill (Natal), began translating English plays and sections of the Bible into Zulu. He also adapted Zulu folktales and history for staging by his students.[50] Two of his short plays were printed in *Native Teachers' Journal* in 1921; but they give little impression of the performances, which depended as much upon student improvisation as on a script.

Huss' ideas proved popular at other schools, and influenced the commercial stage. Caluza, who seems to have tried his hand at every medium, presented a 'dramatic work treating the life of a *sangoma*' (diviner)[51] as part of a tour by his choir in 1920–21. In 1927, a teacher at Amanzimtoti Institute (Natal) named Esau Mtetwa, nephew of choirmaster A. J. Mtetwa, used some of Huss' techniques in successfully bringing African dramatic forms and themes to the popular stage. His student company, Mtetwa's Lucky Stars, presented scenes from traditional life – the preparation and drinking of beer, courting practices, village gatherings, hunting, witchcraft, and divination – as well as scenes from the lives of Zulu kings. Woven into these scenes were displays of traditional dancing and traditional songs sung in the *makwaya* style by school-trained vocalists. Musical instruments included traditional strung bows in addition to the guitar and concertina. Scenes of contemporary life focused on the movement from country to town, allowing for both Westernised music and the step dances of traditional weddings, *ingom'ebusuku* choirs and school concerts.

Mtetwa's Lucky Stars became semi-professional during the 1930s, working regular day jobs in Durban and performing at workers' hostels, middle-class concerts, schools and town halls evenings and weekends. Although presented entirely in Zulu, their colourful and carefully rehearsed displays of folk culture proved as popular with white audiences as with black. Rather than imitate European drama or narrative themes, they emphasised traditional social values and cultural patterns. Scripts were generally discarded in favour of a series of standard scenes always renewed and enlivened by spontaneous improvisation in theatrics, dance, dialogue, poetry, and song.[52]

In contrast, the study of English drama by elite writers led to the creation of sterile, imitative plays bearing little relationship to African theatrical expression. As with music and dance, elite playwrights viewed folk drama as a resource for a modern literary drama. Yet early full-length plays, like G. B. Sinxo's *Imfene KaDebeza* and H. I. E. Dhlomo's *The Girl Who Killed to Save* (1935), are entirely Western in structure.[53]

Dhlomo, among the first of the African literati to write about the drama, clearly reveals the contradictions as well as the self-conscious cultural philosophy of his class. In an article in the *Bantu World*,[54] Dhlomo wrote:

> Modern drama is not a mere emotional entertainment. It is a source of ideas, a cultural and educational factor, an agency for propaganda, a social institution, and above all, it is literature. What part will the new African play in modern drama? On its physical side, he can contribute strong fast rhythm, speedy action, expressive vigorous gesture and movement, powerful dramatic speech – no small contribution when modern plays drag so tediously. . . . We want African playwrights who will dramatize and expand a philosophy of African History. We want dramatic representation of African Serfdom, Oppression, Exploitation and Metamorphosis. . . . The African dramatist has an important part to fill. . . . He can expose evil and corruption and not suffer libel as newspaper men may – and do; he can guide and preach to his people

as preachers cannot do. To do this he must be an artist before a propagandist; a philosopher before a reformer; a psychologist before a patriot; be true to his African 'self' and not be a prey to exotic crudities.

In 1932, Dhlomo and others formed the Bantu Dramatic Society at the BMSC. In the absence of playwrights of the kind described above, they presented Goldsmith's *She Stoops To Conquer* on 5 May 1933. In succeeding years they put on *Nongqause*, a historical play in Xhosa by a white missionary, Mary Waters, and Oscar Wilde's *Lady Windermere's Fan*. These productions were well received by a limited African and white audience at the BMSC, but none was self-supporting.

Elite theatre stagnated because its creators looked to Europe even when trying to develop self-consciously African forms.[55] Meanwhile, Mtetwa's Lucky Stars were becoming a favourite with both black and white audiences in a series of highly successful professional tours. Whites enjoyed the Lucky Stars for their entertaining and accessible display of exoticism within a Western format. Urban blacks, on the other hand, responded with great nostalgia for a lost, almost mythical way of life. The Lucky Stars presented dramatisations of an idealised cohesive, culturally integrated society with clearly defined values, all the more appealing to blacks for its remoteness from the insecurity, alienation, powerlessness, and exploitation of urban life.

During the late 1930s, Dhlomo worked to preserve traditional art forms by incorporating African themes and performance techniques into European drama with his play *Chaka*.[56] A ragtime violinist, he also collaborated with Caluza and choreographer A. P. Khutlang to produce a musical drama, *Moshoeshoe*, in 1939.[57] These plays were presented in English, but we have no script or record of their content at present, though Gérard[58] claims the essays Dhlomo published in 1939 are 'undoubtedly all fragments of the same work'.

The Lucky Stars' influence on minstrel companies was far more successful in introducing African values, themes and presentational style into urban theatre. A good example is a concert given by the Africans' Own Entertainers in June, 1936 at the BMSC. Along with the usual jazz vocals, tap dancing, Negro 'plantation songs' and comic sketches, they performed an 'Abakweta (Xhosa male initiation) scene, Zulu wedding demonstration, and Hlubi love tragedy'.[59] The minstrels, of course, went beyond the Lucky Stars in drawing on the folk culture of several ethnic groups.

The year 1936 was an important one in the development of black city music and theatre, as groups gathered to perform at Johannesburg's British Empire Exhibition. Migrant mine dancers, *ingom'ebusuku* groups, jazz orchestras, minstrels, and massed church choirs all appeared. The Lucky Stars made such an impression that promoter

Bertha Slosberg organised a London tour for the following year. For reasons that are unclear, the tour was a failure and the troupe disbanded in London. Some members remained there, others returned home, and the Lucky Stars disappeared as an organised company.[60]

A more important result of the Exhibition was the cultural stimulation and cross-fertilisation that it brought to professional African show business. The most polished of the minstrel companies, the Darktown Strutters, featured the comic mime Petrus Qwabe, who had come from the Lucky Stars to replace Ndaba Majola in 1934. The Merry Blackbirds, South Africa's most elite swing orchestra, received some professional coaching there from Teddy Joyce's Band, on tour from England. In 1937, elocutionist, actor, and promoter Griffiths Motsieloa, a former Kimberley teacher who had studied in London, brought the Strutters and Blackbirds together for a history-making concert party tour of towns throughout South Africa.

In much the same way that modern Black American performance culture had been introduced to small towns in the United States by touring professionals in the 1920s,[61] this tour gave many Africans in small towns their first contact with the elite of Johannesburg's black entertainment world. The Queenstown saxophonist William Mbali wrote the following account of the Strutters–Blackbirds appearance in his community on 21 April 1937:[62]

> They have a treasure in Mr. Petrus Qwabe, the 'Zulu King of Laughter and Mirth.' He brought the house down with laughter when he rendered his comedy farce 'Umfundisi' (Reverend) . . . Mr. J. J. Masoleng – South Africa's Stephen Fetchat – as he is styled, piquant, delightful and nimble, has all the snap and sparkle of a great tap-dancer. . . . Let me add as a footnote that the local orchestra will benefit through the visit of the 'Merry Blackbirds,' and will make use of whatever tips they received from these Artists.

As a result of this tour, Motsieloa expanded his variety troupe beyond the old minstrel format and renamed it the Pitch Black Follies. It was the first of the many large mixed companies which, backed by jazz orchestras, dominated African professional entertainment during the 1940s and '50s. Although the Pitch Black Follies did not present full-length plays, they did have a major effect on urban African popular musical drama. Within a dramatic or comedy sketch, they combined the cultural and historical material of the Lucky Stars with the minstrel tradition of tragi-comic scenes from urban location life. Their 'Grand Vaudeville' performance in Johannesburg in 1938 included 'Primitive Africa', 'Recitation', 'I Qaqa' (a song about a beetle), 'Xhosa poet', 'Ntsikana's Vision', 'Tribal Dance', hymns by J. K. Bokwe and Tiyo Soga, a 'Sesotho Song and Dance', a (military) 'Recruiting Sketch', a shebeen-*skokiaan* queen sketch, an Afrikaans medley, 'Die

127

Oorlams Mense van Vrededorp', and jazz song and dance.[63]

African audiences often became actively involved, shouting their reactions from their seats or moving to the stage to give money to a character with whose situation or point of view they sympathised. Their versatile repertoire was an important aspect of the Pitch Black Follies' success since they were the first African stage company performing modern Western material to appear regularly before white audiences and black.

The universal format of middle-class African entertainment between the world wars was 'concert and dance'. Not only minstrel performances, but choir competitions, institutional functions, official receptions and meetings of political and other organizations were followed by a few hours of dancing to the music of jazz orchestras. The influence of these forms on working-class styles led to the birth of an authentic South African jazz.

For a number of years after the First World War, ragtime and choral concerts remained the chief musical entertainment of middle-class Africans. They avoided the rough dance halls where pianists or rhythm trios pounded out early *marabi* for knife and liquor-toting customers.[64] In American, European and even South African cities, though, jazz had become the most popular dance music after the war. Middle-class Africans soon responded too, since jazz had not only international prestige but African roots that could be harmonised with indigenous culture.

The missionaries could not stifle the interest of Westernized Africans in recreational dancing, which had been basic to social relations in traditional life. The solution was to give up 'heathen' traditional dances and adopt the social dances of middle-class whites. This process of cultural substitution proceeded rapidly at rural mission schools and especially in the cities, where the appropriate dance music was readily available.

Elite educators were concerned about this trend, which they associated with *marabi* culture and the more frivolous aspects of European civilization. R. R. R. Dhlomo complained in 1927:

> At present all that is considered of special interest by our enlightened people is dancing week in and week out. . . . 'On with the dance' is their slogan. Why? Most of these people are fed up of jazz and because there is no other form of excitement or entertainment they resort to dancing themselves mad.[65]

Middle-class Africans were tiring of *makwaya* and other 'sit-down' concerts, despite the publication of a volume of Caluza's songs, *Amagama Ohlange Lakwa Zulu* ('Zulu Songs from Ohlange') in 1928 and other important developments in African choral music. The Euro-American 'dance craze' had struck urban South Africa. Professor Z. K.

Matthews recalled that interest in choral singing declined in schools beginning in the mid-1920s because students and teachers were too busy dancing.[66] Even the perennial favourite, Caluza, had to add a dance band to his choir to continue attracting Johannesburg audiences.

During the 1920s, the concert-and-dance pattern held for both working-class and middle-class African entertainment. Conflicting forces of class formation and social levelling caused a struggle for status that affected performance. Both classes participated together in many cultural events, and jazz dances featured 'a curious mixture of costumes and styles of dancing'.[67] Most popular was formal ballroom dancing, which became an important arena for social competition.

· The leading ballroom dancers were Africans in domestic and restaurant service. A few, particularly women, were mission school graduates; but the majority had little or no formal education at all. On the other hand, a knowledge of Western culture was of great value in domestic service, and many became highly self-educated.[68] Most lived in the white suburbs where they were forced to conform to European expectations and isolated from African community life. Their interest in ballroom dancing was part of a struggle for status through the competitive display of symbols of Westernisation, such as dress, social comportment and cultural skills such as dancing (see plate 11).

Although Zulu people had dominated domestic service since the founding of Johannesburg, the 1920s brought competition from thousands of African men arriving from Nyasaland (Malawi) and Southern Rhodesia (Zimbabwe). These well-dressed *makirimane* (Eng.: 'clean man') as the Zulu contemptuously called them, were among the most enthusiastic patrons of concerts and dances. Having come without their women, they flocked to concert parties like Caluza's, where they used outright gifts and generous bidding to win the favours of female performers. They were also expert ballroom dancers and readily found partners at the Inchcape Ritz Palais de Dance in the city and the Undermoon Hall in Sophiatown. The Inchcape management found it necessary to schedule separate nights for local and foreign male domestics, and some dance clubs made ethnic identity a qualification for membership.[69] Apart from these few concessions to economic and social competition, though, there is little evidence of 'tribalism' in ballroom dancing.

The dance clubs provided a prestigious setting also for competitive Westernisation. Dressed in elegant evening wear, members paid as much as a guinea (21 shillings) to enter dance championships. Judges were almost always white and demonstrations by professional white dancers often began the programme. The overall rejection of Africans by whites led to an emphasis on status competition over cultural achievement. Leadership in the clubs was an important source of upward mobility within African society. Cultural organisations like the Gamma Sigma clubs often became merely sponsors of ballroom dance, beauty, and 'best dressed' contests. In this context, Brandel-Syrier's claim[70] that the Communist Party took over leadership of African cultural clubs in Germiston in the 1950s, but had to focus exclusively on ballroom dancing to please the membership, attains some credibility.

Certainly cultural organising among middle-class Africans became increasingly contentious. Even the National Eisteddfod went into a lengthy decline after the resignation of Mark Radebe in the mid-1930s. Because opportunities for recognition and leadership were so restricted, arrangements for the Eisteddfod suffered from the constant self-promotion and infighting among the committee members.

The dancers needed music, and Coloured players, with their centuries-old dance orchestra traditions, were the first to form Western style dance bands. In Johannesburg, band members varied widely in background and formal training. Those without education drew upon Cape Afrikaans folk culture and the Afro-American influenced 'Coon Carnival' clubs, who paraded every New Year in Kimberley's Malay Camp, Vrededorp in Johannesburg, and other Coloured neighbourhoods.[71] For *stokfel* parties and public dances, they performed music of Cape Coloured social dances, for example, *vastrap*, *tickey draai*, set-part, *guma*, and squares. Those with more schooling and familiarity with British white society played the two-step, waltz, foxtrot, ragtime and dixieland.

Expanded professional opportunities brought these two kinds of musicians together in the early 1920s. Professionalism encouraged Coloured musicians to improve their technical skills. One such band, the Merry Mascots, featured saxophone, banjo, drums, violin and piano, and played a mixture of Coloured-Afrikaans and American dance styles for all kinds of black social occasions. With no comparable ensembles among Africans, they were regularly engaged to back up African ragtime minstrel companies and to play for the dancing that followed.

As the 'dance craze' developed, Coloured bands like Rayners Big Six and Sonny Groenewald's Jazz Revellers (successors to the Merry Mascots) learned American dance music in response to growing African demands. By the late 1920s, African pianists, brass bandsmen, and other players were finally moved to form their own small dance bands and take advantage of this new professional music market.

The first such African bands seem to have appeared simultaneously both in Johannesburg and in smaller regional towns where missionary and British colonial influence were strong. In Mafeking, Transvaal, Tswana musicians formed the elite Empire Follies dance orchestra in 1928, 'when Mafeking was dance crazy'.[72] Appearing in

Johannesburg, they challenged the monopoly of the Coloured bands and inspired the formation of middle-class bands in the city.[73] In Queenstown, African performers had for years played for whites, especially the Jewish community, with their love for black American variety entertainment. Pianist Meekly 'Fingertips' Matshikiza's Big Four were succeeded by William Mbali's Blue Rhythm Syncopators, who acquired a national reputation (see plate 12). The Eastern Cape contributed so many talented instrumentalists and vocalists to the Johannesburg African entertainment world that Xhosa became something of a *lingua franca* among its musicians.

In Johannesburg, the first professional African dance band was not an elite, 'fancy dress' ensemble but a versatile group of musical semi-literates called the Japanese Express. They played everything from *marabi* and *tickey draai* to ragtime, jazz, quickstep and foxtrot. Led by George 'Makalman' Boswell on violin, the group copied its instrumentation from the Coloured bands and included piano, drums, trombone/trumpet, and banjo/guitar. Beginning in 1929, the Japanese Express played at *marabi* halls, weddings, and functions of middle-class cultural associations such as 'The Doornfontein Ladies Civic Society' with equal success, making 'sufficient money to enable members to live decently'.[74]

By the early 1930s, middle-class African performers and promoters such as Griffiths Motsieloa wanted more literate and Westernised alternatives to the Coloured bands than the Japanese Express. Under Motsieloa's direction, his wife Emily, a pianist from Craddock (Cape), joined with J. C. P. Mavimbela, Peter Rezant and others to form the Merry Blackbirds Dance Orchestra. They were an immediate success. With the addition of Salvation Army-trained trumpeters Steve Monkoe and Enoch Matunjwa in 1934, the band became a full-scale swing ensemble modelled on Glenn Miller's orchestra. The Merry Blackbirds played only American ragtime and jazz orchestrations for white and racially mixed audiences. They also backed minstrel companies and played for the full range of social and organizational functions of middle-class African society.

Unlike the many urban musicians who hustled a living by any means, members of the Merry Blackbirds were teachers, clerks, social workers, and active in the BMSC and other middle-class institutions. Peter Rezant proudly told me[75] that in contrast to the Japanese Express, the Merry Blackbirds of the 1930s were not professional musicians but had regular daytime jobs. Good music readers, they avoided African musical influences and achieved the highest social status of any black band.

The steady growth of interest in American dance music led to the formation of numerous African jazz dance bands. Just below the Merry Blackbirds were the Rhythm Kings, begun in 1935 by the Blackbirds' John Mavimbela and drummer Dan Twala at the BMSC's Bantu Sports Club (see plate 13). According to Twala,[76] Mavimbela left the Merry Blackbirds because he didn't want to 'play only white music and all that; ballroom and high class'. The Rhythm Kings sought ways to Africanise jazz and bring it to a wider local audience, experimenting with band arrangements of the tonic solfa ragtime songs of Caluza, whose concert party they sometimes backed. They also tried songs by Mohapeloa, Tyamzashe, and other composers plus African work songs like the famous *Tshotsholoza*. Like the Blackbirds, the Rhythm Kings were helped by white bandsmen and improved their reading skills by accompanying silent films at the local cinemas.

The Rhythm Kings were soon in great demand, and began touring smaller towns along the Rand. Playing for concert-and-dance at the 'country halls', the band learned African songs from local performers, and quickly arranged them for performance at later shows. Local audiences danced and shouted their approval at finding something of their own music jumping in the latest jazz.

The most versatile and professional band was the Jazz Maniacs, founded in 1935 by Solomon 'Zuluboy' Cele, who had been a *marabi* pianist since the age of fifteen (see plate 132). Cele had ragtime and jazz experience from backing minstrel companies like the African Sonnyboys and Erie Lads. According to Matshikiza, this training had given him a desire 'to paint *marabi* tones on a broader canvas and bigger scales',[77] and to Africanise big band jazz. Cele may have learned to read music with the help of fellow band members Jacob Medumo and Wilson Silgee, or used the common method of comparing tunes already known by ear with the written score. The Maniacs began with only four members, who gradually gave up their daytime jobs as the band's engagements increased. By the 1940s, the band had thirteen players, including Zuluboy on piano, Silgee and Medumo on sax, Vy Nkosi on trombone, David Mtimkulu and Earnest Mochumi on trumpets, Victor Hamilton on guitar, Jacob Lepere on bass and several others. Like the Blackbirds and Rhythm Kings, the Maniacs benefited from their reputation for reliability and sober habits. They also became a stylistic force in South African jazz, blending American swing with *marabi* and other urban African influences.

Another important innovator was the freelance pianist Sullivan Mphahlele. Though a slow reader, Mphahlele was a truly gifted jazz improviser, well known for his mastery of the stride piano style of the American Fats Waller. He could play every popular style and helped to introduce the improvised solo to the African jazz band. Like Cele, Mphahlele personified the professional musician – deviant, gadfly, colourful personality, culture hero, misunderstood genius – an image born in the mythology of black American show business. For several years he posed as an Afro-American musician in Cape Town.

Though the various bands had definite social status, the broad demand for their services among all classes of urban Africans brought working-class and middle-class performance culture into continual contact with each other. Interest in American jazz helped to bridge the social gap between *marabi* culture and the minstrel-variety concerts at a time when urban African society was becoming increasingly diversified. Despite status competition, black American performance helped to unify urban African culture. Because it was Western but not white, it provided a model for culture change more closely related to the African heritage and better adapted to the reality of segregation.

The middle-class performance culture that developed in Johannesburg and in rural schools and small towns affected working-class choral as well as popular music. Choir concerts appealed to people who rejected *marabi* and wanted to create a cohesive, morally governed urban community based on family and neighbourhood ties. Working-class people had neither the background nor the resources to build on the mission-school model of African society. As a rule, they retained strong links to rural kin. These links were a hedge against the insecurity of urban life. They were also a source of traditional values and behaviour patterns useful in small-scale urban social organisation.[78]

By the 1930s, the *ingom'ebusuku* style of urbanising migrants was changing under the impact of city life. It still retained the competitive traditions of rural Zulu society, but increasingly assimilated them to middle-class performance culture. Caluza influenced choirs that had some Western schooling, and groups like Malcolm Zwane's Newcastle Humming bees won *ingom'ebusuku* competitions in Johannesburg by mastering a number of his songs. Composer William Mseleku's Amanzimtoti Entertainers went beyond Caluza in blending ragtime with the melodies of traditional Zulu song.[79] Solomon Linda and his Evening Birds were the most innovative of all *ingom'ebusuku* groups. Their early recordings, *Woza Lapa 'Sitandwa Sami* and *Se Hla'se Nyuka Siya* (HMV JP28) represent the most equal, integrated blend of American ragtime and Zulu traditional melody, vocal quality and part structure.

Ingom'ebusuku choirs upgraded and standardised their stage costumes with identical blazers, wide-legged, narrow-bottomed trousers known as 'Oxford bags', and sneakers. Later the most successful groups changed to suits, hats and black shoes. This approach revived *ingom'ebusuku* and spread it among a wider African audience. It appealed to African cultural nationalism, created nostalgia for a lost society, and fused urban and rural cultural values. The Zulu, with their cultural pride and closeness to rural traditions dominated *ingom'ebusuku*, but it was not theirs alone. The Nyasalanders and Rhodesians patronised Evening Birds' concerts as well as ballroom dances. Minstrel tap dancer and singer Koppie Masoleng enjoyed performing informally with *ingom'ebusuku* groups although he was a middle-class Sotho ragtimer. As Dan Twala recalls:

> The Sothos used to sing in the [*ingom'ebusuku*] choirs, Sothos who could hardly speak Zulu clearly, but they'd join; they didn't have separate nights. And the Zulu were the people who were trying very hard to sing the Sotho songs as part of their programme. But of course this was because they used to be in love with the Free State [Sotho] girls . . ..[80]

As a form of working-class choral music, *ingom'ebusuku* entered into the cultural politics of the African labour movement. The Industrial and Commercial Workers' Union (ICU) was established in 1919 in Cape Town by Clemens Kadalie, a Nyasa waiter. It soon moved its headquarters to Johannesburg and became the most powerful black labour organisation in the country. The ICU concentrated on improving agricultural and industrial working conditions, but was never officially recognised. By 1932 internal dissention and the government's repressive use of the Riotous Assemblies Act had weakened it, but it had an enduring effect on racial and class consciousness among African working people.

Meetings at the ICU hall on Market Street usually included performances by volunteer choirs. The Natal branch had a social club with its own official choir and brass band, which played an important part in protest marches.[81] At a Johannesburg meeting in 1929, Perham[82] noted that 'hymns are mixed with an agitation which is full of dangers'. Some hymns were sung as originally written, but others were given new lyrics expressing support for the ICU and its leaders. Songs of general political protest like Masiza's *Vukani Mawethu* were also popular with union choirs. Such composers as S. Mutla of Bloemfontein wrote many songs in the *ingom'ebusuku* style with lyrics promoting the ICU, and most of these choirs could be categorised as *ingom'ebusuku* ensembles. According to union organiser Solomon Crutse:

> The groups had a certain Africanism in their set-up . . . because the suffering of the African was common, and the ICU had as its goal to alleviate the suffering of the African, therefore the African music and the ICU went together.[83]

One problem for the ICU was how to bring together the middle-class leadership and working-class membership, get them to recognise their common disabilities and interests, and cooperate to achieve common goals. In an effort to help, the Merry Blackbirds and other middle-class musicians performed with ICU groups like Makatshwa's Choir. Together they expressed the need for a broader social identification among urban Africans.

The ICU's use of music also expressed the more generalised urban African drive toward full inclusion and equal recognition in modern industrial society. Hymn music in particular emphasised claims to 'civilised' status and its associated benefits. The systematic substitution of new words promoting ICU principles and goals revealed an intention to solve worldly problems by social means. They gained support by retaining something of the emotional and spiritual fervour associated with African Christian congregational song. The use of new songs in *ingom'ebusuku* style represents a significant manipulation of 'traditional' African culture for purposes of positive self-identification and unity in a modern political context. Gramophone recordings[84] of these songs helped to widen their distribution among Africans.

In the 1920s and '30s, gramophone recordings and films became important for urban African performing arts. As we have seen,[85] recordings were available from Britain even before the First World War. Some members of an African political delegation to London recorded African songs there as early as 1912.[86] Imported recordings were so popular with school choirs and minstrel companies that some educators complained that gramophones were retarding the growth of African musical literacy and promoting foreign musical styles at the expense of 'African National Culture'.[87]

Afro-American styles became well established in urban African entertainment during the inter-war period. East London's Gipsy Melody Makers popularised a Xhosa translation of 'When My Sugar Walks Down the Street'; the youthful Manhattan Brothers of Pimville location (Johannesburg) imitated the Mills Brothers; and the Merry Blackbirds played the music of Louis Armstrong, Duke Ellington, Count Basie, Louis Jordan, and Sy Oliver from written orchestrations. This form of voluntary acculturation was generated largely by the communications media rather than by direct contact between different cultures or peoples.

By the mid-1920s English recording companies sensed the potential of the African market. In 1925, Zonophone began a small series of records by educated visiting black South Africans and experimented with portable recording equipment on the Rand gold mines. Nationalist political leaders H. Selby Msimang and Sol Plaatje recorded African folk songs and hymns, including *Nkosi Sikelel' iAfrika*, and migrants performed rural folk music.[88]

Soon Pathé, HMV, Columbia, and Polydor had all established branch offices in Johannesburg, and Brunswick and Decca were selling foreign recordings through Gallo, a local representative.[89] Gramophones became an item of status among urban Africans. Companies were pleased to discover that Africans would buy everything produced for them, though humorous musical folk stories in African languages were especially popular. In 1929, the broadcaster Hugh Tracey made a pioneering field recording expedition to Mozambique and Rhodesia. The results sold well and for a time advanced the cause of field work in African music. African music educators were also pleased. Mark Radebe[90] praised the record companies for preserving the African musical heritage from total 'hybridisation', and for providing an 'eternal source of ideas and inspiration' for African classical composers.

With the success of 'Native' recordings, companies sent Africans to record in London, since there were as yet no studios as such in South Africa. In 1930, Reuben Caluza and a group of performers recorded more than 120 selections there for HMV. These were of three types: 'records specially for the "raw" Native, for the partially civilised, and for the educated Native',[91] and they included many of Caluza's own compositions. In South Africa they sold as well as the popular imported recordings by black Americans and contributed greatly to Caluza's influence on local performers. In the same year, Griffiths Motsieloa and the Shangaan choral composer Daniel Marivate each made London recordings for Decca.[92]

In 1932 Gallo set up the first recording studio in Johannesburg, and the other companies quickly followed suit. In 1935, HMV had a 'Native' catalogue of 366 discs with sales totalling 86 436.[93] With local studios, the companies took advantage of the popularity of indigenous recordings among migrant workers. Though these workers did not consider music a potential profession, competition for prestige among song composers and instrumentalists was extended to recording. A stream of migrant instrumentalists presented themselves at the studios and made one or two recordings each, more to be lionised by their peers than for the fee of a few shillings.

The studios affected the style and pattern of migrant music-making. Producers preferred instrumental accompaniment for vocal music, to add rhythm so that records could be sold as dance music. As a result, the purely vocal music of ingom'ebusuku was often recorded with a guitar accompaniment not used in live performances. Given the emphasis on individual as opposed to group competition, many migrant musicians regarded recording as a chance to build their personal reputations among a wider public audience. Zulu migrants began to interpolate self-praises between the verses of their recorded guitar songs, despite the tradition that Zulu poets ought not to praise themselves.[94] Producers may also have encouraged these innovations for the sake of novelty. In any case the temptation to depart from tradition and engage in a little self-promotion must have been strong in the social isolation of the studio.

Sotho sefela was also a form of poetic recitation that, though developed by migrants, was not associated with instrumental performance. Some informants in Lesotho were surprised when I played them recordings of Sotho musicians who played the concertina and simultaneously recited *sefela*, though such discs have been available for more than 40 years. Recording may have encouraged the combination of poetry and instrumental playing. More recently, professional shebeen accordion player Adrian Lekgopa of Hlotse, Lesotho, explained that the melody of the accordion often suggested words to his listeners and so aided extemporaneous *sefela* and *famo* composition.[95]

Companies hired some players as permanent staff. If they could think of no more tunes to record, they were given a four-bar segment of an American song to play over and over in the African manner. This practice has continued until today and has strongly affected urban African popular music directed at the migrant audience.[96]

The record companies were eager to meet the demand for music by African performers but were generally unfamiliar with the wealth and diversity of local musical styles. They drew their talent from the mines and the Johannesburg Eisteddfod during the early 1930s, and tended to rely on mission school Africans like Mark Radebe for advice about what to record. Radebe himself made a number of recordings for Columbia and created opportunities for other middle-class performers. In 1938, Griffiths Motsieloa became Gallo's first African talent scout.

These men ignored the *marabi* music of shebeen society, which they considered degraded and unworthy of preservation. *Marabi* did not appear on records until the 1940s, when it had been blended with swing by the jazz bands and worked its way into the concertina and guitar songs of the migrants. Muff Andersson[97] suggests that the emphasis on rural styles, whether traditional, migrant, or mission school, reflected the white South African view of Africans as 'temporary sojourners' in the cities. In retrospect, it appears that the record companies suffered more from ignorance of the size, sophistication, and commitment of urban African communities than from any conscious desire to advance homeland identification among them.

On the other hand, many *marabi* pianists and jazz bands thought that recordings might enable competitors to steal their music. Furthermore, studios wanted to record their best tunes for as little as ten shillings per side, though they could earn a lot more as regular shebeen or dance hall performers. Musicians preferred not to compete with themselves by making records, and most shebeen owners preferred a live musician who would play continuously for as many as eight hours to the short, fragile and comparatively expensive discs.

The growth of the South African music industry had important cultural consequences for urban African communities. By distributing imported music, the companies offered Africans a ready-made, deceptively attractive solution to the dilemma of urban cultural identity. As musical specialisation increased, musicians increased their status by turning away from indigenous popular music and acquiring the ability to reproduce imported styles.

The Jazz Maniacs made the first *marabi* jazz recording 'Izikalo Zika Z-Boy' (Better XU 9-a) in 1939. By then, however, American swing had already replaced *marabi*. The death of *marabi* was a symptom of a more pervasive attack upon the urban African community and working-class culture under the terms of the Urban Areas Act. During the 1930s, new housing and other amenities for Africans were made available, largely through profits made from Africans by the municipal beerhalls, and one after another the slumyards were torn down. The social conditions for *marabi's* vibrant life still existed in the suburban locations, but in the new municipal townships the beer trade and its associated activities were almost eliminated. The beer halls appropriated the resources of working-class culture, *vat-en-sit* was prohibited, and the system of mutual assistance temporarily fell apart. People no longer knew their neighbours, and the physically squalid but socially supportive neighbourhoods were replaced by drab, separate rows of township houses without amenities or communal spirit.[98]

The Empire Exhibition and the growth of local recording gave black performing artists an international orientation, away from the urban community culture from which they had come. Noting the success of black American performers, a writer for *Umteteli*[99] praised the Eisteddfodau, which had produced several African recording artists and might 'one day discover a talent capable of stirring the world'. African jazz bands played the songs of Duke Ellington or Glenn Miller and dreamed of leaving the locations for London. Yet the only ensemble to do so in the 1930s, Mtetwa's Lucky Stars, were chosen precisely because of their indigenous African material.

Such ironies were the result of contradictions in middle-class culture during the inter-war period. The fundamental source of these contradictions was the racial politics of South Africa. Discrimination encouraged both Westernisation and the creation of a distinctive African cultural identity as strategies for social advancement. Middle-class Africans regarded command of Western culture and disassociation from both the 'primitive' traditions of the past and the proletarian *marabi* of the present as essential to their progress. The whites' rejection of their demands on racial grounds, however, exposed the need for African unity across class as well as ethnic boundaries.

Middle-class cultural leaders attempted to resolve this dilemma by creating a model African National Culture for all classes of African townsmen. Performance activity played an important role in effecting the necessary synthesis. The social cohesiveness of the middle class helped African educators to act as cultural interpreters. Yet a nagging sense of inferiority continued to undermine their cultural nationalism. Their ambivalence is easy to understand, since it was now clear that the African elite were the victims as well as the beneficiaries of missionisation, a situation represented musically in the dilemma of composers like Mohapeloa.

African popular performers and black American styles provided the most workable solutions to the dilemmas of urban African culture. In the hands of ensembles like Caluza's Double Quartet and Solomon Linda's Evening Birds, black American popular music and dance reinvigorated both middle-class and working-class forms of choral music and stage choreography. Bands and troupes like the Japanese Express, Rhythm Kings, Merry Blackbirds, and Darktown Strutters made jazz at once an instrument of class formation and a means of cultural communication and participation among different classes. The more versatile groups, such as the Jazz Maniacs, combined African and black American sounds and laid the foundations of distinctively South African styles of jazz music and dance.

Yet the popularity of black American styles created new problems, made more difficult by the growing involvement of the commercial media in urban African performing arts. The contradiction involved in basing the expression of urban African identity on the assimilation of black American models became apparent as performers reoriented themselves towards a multi-racial and international audience beginning in the late 1930s. Performers who wished to appeal to the large African working-class audience had to draw upon indigenous performance culture. Nevertheless, the internationalism of African jazz became part of a struggle against cultural isolation and segregation and expressed the aspirations of the majority of urban Africans. The social status of professional performers therefore rose during the 1930s, a trend that continued until the 1960s.

The development of local recording meant that the African community had to compete with the white media industry for their performers. White companies could now buy African performance culture from the musicians and sell it back at a profit to the communities from which it came. In the process, African cultural autonomy was further threatened because record producers influenced the actual composition, manner of performance, and stylistic development of the music. American popular culture and the entertainment media profoundly affected urban African performing arts during succeeding decades, but the thread of indigenous, independent cultural development was never lost. All these trends are evident in the culture of what was South Africa's most vital and autonomous urban community, Sophiatown.

Notes

1   Timothy Couzens, 'The social ethos of black writing in South Africa, 1920–1950', paper presented to the I.A.S., University of the Witwatersrand, September, 1976.

2   E. Koch, 'Town and countryside in the Transvaal: capitalist penetration and popular response', paper for the Witwatersrand History Workshop, Johannesburg, 1981, p. 20.

3   Timothy Couzens, 'Moralizing leisure time: the transatlantic connection and black Johannesburg, 1918–1936', in S. Marks and R. Rathbone (eds), *Industrialisation and Social Change in South Africa*, London, 1982, pp. 314–15.

4   M. Hunter, *Reaction to Conquest*, London, 1936, p. 476.

5   Jordan Ngubane, 'South Africa's race crisis: a conflict of minds', in H. Adam (ed), *South Africa: Sociological Perspectives*, London, 1971, p. 10.

6   J. C. De Ridder, *The Personality of the Urban African in South Africa*, London, 1961, p. 168.

7   Z. K. Matthews, 'The tribal spirit among educated South Africans', *Man*, 35, 26 (1935), p. 27.

8   E. Hellmann, 'The Native and the towns', in I. Schapera (ed), *The Bantu-Speaking Tribes of South Africa*, London, 1937, p. 437.

9   Ngubane, 'South Africa's race crisis', p. 19; *Bantu World*, 27 April 1935.

10 *Umteteli wa Bantu*, 9 July 1932.

11 Ray Phillips, *The Bantu in the City*, Johannesburg, 1938, p. 38.

12 Johannesburg *Star*, 21 June 1920.

13 Phillips, *The Bantu in the City*, p. 303.

14 S. Lekhela, interview, 12 December 1978.

15 *Umteteli wa Bantu*, 6 June 1931.

16 *Ibid.*, 10 September, 1932.

17 H. Weman, *African Music and the Church in Africa* (Uppsala, 1960), p. 119.; D. K. Rycroft, 'The new 'town' music of Southern Africa', *Recorded Folk Music*, 1, Sept./Oct. (1958), p. 56.

18 *Ilanga Lase Natal*, 12 January 1917.

19 Lucas Makhema, interview, 15 April 1978.

20 P. R. Kirby, 'The recognition and practical use of the harmonics of stretched strings by the Bantu of South Africa', *Bantu Studies*, 6 (1932), pp. 45–6.

21 Weman, *African Music and the Church*, pp. 118–19.

22 *Ilanga Lase Natal*, 8 February 1929.

23 *Bantu World*, 21 October 1933.

24 *Ibid.*, 16 April 1932.

25 *Umteteli wa Bantu*, 6 June 1931.

26 J. P. Mohapeloa, interview, 2 January 1977.

27 J. P. Mohapeloa, interview, 10 July 1978.

28 Mohapeloa, interview, 2 January 1977.

29 Oxford University Press, Cape Town, 1976.

30 Phillips, *The Bantu in the City*, p. 303.

31 Hellmann, 'The Native in the towns', p. 431.

32 *Bantu World*, 15 December 1934.

33 James S. Coko, *The Reminiscences of James Scott Coko, A Grahamstown Resident*, Grahamstown, 1973, p. 188.

34 *Umteteli wa Bantu*, 11 November 1933.

35 Ian Whitcolm, *After the Ball*, Baltimore, 1974, p. 124.

36 Brian Willan, 'In aid of the most oppressed Negroes of the world: Sol T. Plaatje's visit to North America, 1920–1922', paper presented to the conference *Afro-American Interactions with South Africa*, Howard University, 28–29 March 1979.

37 S. V. H. Mdhluli, *The Development of the African*, Mariannhill, South Africa, 1933, pp. 48–9.

38 N. Huggins, *Harlem Renaissance*, New York, 1971, pp. 5, 27.

39 *Bantu World*, 25 November 1933.

40 *Ibid.*, 13 October 1934.

41 *Umteteli wa Bantu*, 11 February 1933.

42 *Ilanga Lase Natal*, 2 July 1915.

43 *Ibid.*, 5 August 1927.

44 *Ibid.*, 10 February 1933.

45 *Umteteli wa Bantu*, 20 October 1920.

46 *Bantu World*, 7 August 1948.

47 *Drum*, May 1952.

48 *Bantu World*, 16 April 1932.

49 Anthony Graham-White, *The Drama of Black Africa*, New York, 1974, p. 66.

50 *Ibid.*, pp. 64–6.

51 *Ilanga Lase Natal*, 31 December 1920.

52 Albert Gérard, *Four African Literatures*, Berkeley, 1971, pp. 195–7.

53 *Ibid.*, pp. 70–9.

54 *Bantu World*, 21 October 1933.

55 Graham-White, *The Drama of Black Africa*, p. 89.

56 Gérard, *Four African Literatures*, p. 233.

57 *Bantu World*, 6 May 1939.

58 Gérard, *Four African Literatures*, p. 233.

59 *Bantu World*, 13 June 1936.

60 Bertha Slosberg, *Pagan Tapestry*, London, 1939, pp. 193–213; Gérard, *Four African Literatures*, p. 198.

61 Huggins, *Harlem Renaissance*, pp. 63–4.

62 *Bantu World*, 8 May 1931.

63 *Ibid.*, 12 February 1938.

64 *Bantu World*, 18 June 1932; 5 January and 28 May 1935.

65 *Ilanga Lase Natal*, 5 August 1927.

66 Monica Wilson, personal communication, April 1977.

67 Margery Perham, *An African Apprenticeship*, London, 1974, p. 46.

68 C. van Onselen, 'The Witches of suburbia: domestic service on the Witwatersrand, 1890–1914', paper for the Witwatersrand History Workshop, Johannesburg, 1978.

69 Hellmann, 'The Native in the towns', p. 431f; Phillips, *The Bantu in the City*, p. 293.

70 M. Brandel-Syrier, *Reeftown Elite*, London, 1971, p. 50.

71 Peter Abrahams, *Tell Freedom*, New York, 1970, pp. 119–21.

72   *Bantu World*, 14 May 1932.
73   *Ibid.*, 16 April 1932.
74   *Ibid.*, 30 April 1932.
75   Peter Rezant, interview, 14 August 1976.
76   Dan Twala, interview, 17 March 1977.
77   Todd Matshikiza, *Drum*, July 1957.
78   E. Hellmann, *Rooiyard: a Sociological Survey of an Urban Native Slumyard*, Cape Town, 1948.
79   See *Izizwe Ezimnyama* (HMV GU 108) and *umBoshongo* (HMV GU 81) and sheet music published in 1934 by Orient Music Salon, Durban, Killie Campbell Library, Durban.
80   Dan Twala, interview, 17 March 1977.
81   Minutes of Evidence, Native Riots Commission, Durban, July 1929.
82   Perham, *An African Apprenticeship*, p. 132.
83   Solomon Crutse, interview, 26 July 1978.
84   See *Wangishaya uBaba* and *Nase Mdubane* by Makatshwa's Choir with the Merry Blackbirds, Singer GE 143.
85   *Ilanga Lase Natal*, 24 January 1908.
86   Brian Willan, personal communication, March 1979.
87   *Ilanga Lase Natal*, 11 December 1926 and 8 February 1929.
88   *Umteteli wa Bantu*, 13 June and 5 September 1925.
89   Y. Huskisson, 'Record Industry in South Africa', *Progressus*, XXV, November, Johannesburg, 1978, p. 4.
90   *Bantu World*, 21 October 1933.
91   R. T. Caluza, 'Zulu choir in London', *Southern Workman*, November (1930), pp. 521–2.
92   *Bantu World*, 21 October 1933.
93   Phillips, *The Bantu in the City*, p. 299.
94   D. K. Rycroft, quoted in Ruth Finnegan, *Oral Literature in Africa*, London, 1970, p. 144.
95   Adrian Lekgopa, interview, 30 June 1978.
96   Andrew Tracey, quoted in M. Andersson, *Music in the Mix*, Johannesburg, 1981, p. 21f.
97   Muff Andersson, *Music in the Mix*, Johannesburg, 1981, p. 39.
98   Koch, 'Town and countryside in the Transvaal', pp. 27–8.
99   *Umteteli wa Bantu*, 11 December 1932.

6 Sophiatown – culture and community, 1940–60

IN 1897, an investor named H. Tobiansky bought 237 acres of land four and a half miles west of the centre of Johannesburg. After failing to sell it to the government as a 'Coloured location', Tobiansky planned a private leasehold township for low-income whites and named it after his wife, Sophia. But Sophiatown's distance from the city, poor drainage, and proximity to the municipal sewage depository at Newlands made it difficult to attract tenants and buyers. By 1910, lots were being sold without discrimination, creating a racially mixed area that became increasingly black. The extension of unrestricted purchase to the adjacent areas of Martindale and Newclare in 1912 and the City Council's establishment in 1918 of Western Native Township (WNT) on the Newlands site further discouraged white residence. These Western Areas, as they were collectively called, soon constituted the largest suburban black residential area in South Africa.[1]

The government specifically exempted Sophiatown from the ownership restrictions of the Urban Areas Act but did not designate it a recognised location, so that municipal services did not keep pace with the expanding population. Despite the Act, Johannesburg's industries needed labour. The government did nothing to inhibit the flow of African families to the city, and the African population increased from 229 122 to 384 628 between 1936 and 1946.[2] As the slumyards were cleared, their residents fled to freehold areas. The population of Sophiatown, a freehold location, rose from 12 000 in 1928 to 28 500 in 1937, very near planned capacity. Though Sophiatown was also 'proclaimed' (marked for removal) in 1934, the government was not prepared to absorb the cost of housing its residents or the thousands swelling the permanent urban workforce.

Furthermore, Africans preferred the freehold areas. As Sophiatown grew, houses stood vacant in municipal locations like Western Native Township, and workers' hostels reported many openings. Though it shared the social and economic problems of the slumyards and municipal locations, Sophiatown offered a greater sense of permanence and self-direction. The refusal of Africans to move to the municipal locations was partly a political protest 'against the authorities trying to rob them further of the alternative life and value systems they had created for themselves in the yards'.[3]

Ownership of real estate gave Sophiatown a sense of community, with institutions and a social identity that served as a defence against the dehumanisation of the labour system. Sophiatown's autonomy was more self-perceived than actual, since it existed at the tolerance of the government, and whites in fact owned or controlled nearly 77 per cent of its total area.[4] Sophiatown's economy afforded few sources of capital accumulation. A few house owners established themselves in retail, service, real estate, trades, and even the professions; but many residents could profit only from crime and the liquor trade.

To some extent, middle-class and working-class Africans developed different organisational patterns and outlooks on city life. The performing arts reflected these differences and highlight for us three issues central to the relationship between performance culture and the urban African community:
1) cultural autonomy – the struggle between the black community and white commercial interests for the control of African culture;
2) disorder – the losing effort to establish social accountability, institutions, and settings for the creation of community in a segregated context;
3) the role of performers – their position in the social conflict and their relationship to their audience.

Sophiatown pinpoints these issues because of what it was and what it symbolised. It was an organic community that allowed a freedom of action, association, and expression available only in freehold areas. Located in South Africa's industrial and financial capital, Sophiatown set the pace, giving urban African culture its pulse, rhythm, and style during the 1940s and '50s. Noisy and dramatic, its untarred, potholed streets ran by the communal water taps and toilets and the rectangular jumble of yards walled in with brick, wood, and iron. A new synthesis of African culture sprang up here, shouting for recognition. Materially poor but intensely social; crime-ridden and violent but neighbourly and self-protective; proud, bursting with music and writing, swaggering with personality, simmering with intellectual and political militance, Sophiatown was a slum of dreams, a battleground of the heart.

Sophiatown produced leaders in many fields, and Africans in other cities looked to them for inspiration. The location became a symbol as well as a partial realisation of their aspirations. The role of performance in the social world of Sophiatown was of course conditioned by the relations between the urban African community and the white power structure.

On the whole, Sophiatown was less proletarian than the slum-yards. Opportunities for property ownership, family and neighbour-hood life, and relative freedom from government interference attracted the growing middle-class. African professionals like Dr A. B. Xuma, MD, president of the African National Congress from 1939 to 1949, built impressive houses there and made the suburb both a sym-bol and a centre of efforts to gain entrance to the dominant society. Its white, Asian, and Coloured residents and shopowners were generally accepted as members of the community. Shebeen society, primarily a working-class innovation, flourished among all of Sophiatown's varied population. Some drinking houses – Aunt Babe's, The House on Telegraph Hill, The Back of the Moon – became genuine nightclubs where the elite of the African business, sporting, entertainment, and underworlds came to talk, listen, and dance to recordings of the latest American jazz.

Other gatherings included backyard parties organised around a wedding, celebration, or spontaneous get-together. These yards were similar to the old slumyards, and houseowners rented out rows of shacks built around the edges of their own backyards. Tenant families lived in one room, cooked in the open, and shared a common tap. Here neighbourhood musicians entertained, often imitating popular foreign and local performers in the hope of one day appearing on con-cert and dance hall stages themselves.

Community life integrated traditional African reciprocity with the cash economy. The drinking patterns of the shebeen were indis-pensable not only to the *stokfels* but also to middle-class voluntary associations. Attendance was obligatory at weddings, funerals, and birth receptions, where refreshments were purchased and contri-butions collected. Westernising Africans who sought to change the pattern were not understood, and attempts to eliminate the charge for refreshments, for example, turned the parties into gate-crashing mêlées.[5]

Frequently, middle-class sponsors hired established bands and vocal groups for their parties and fund-raisers. The musicians' pro-fessional competence, behaviour, and appearance not only reflected new urban cultural ideals but helped to define them as well. Pro-fessional musicians preferred American 'international' performance styles and strained to pull the urban African public along with them. Their success in promoting orchestral jazz gave African listeners a

145

sense of connection with the world black community, and expressed modern African identity through technical brilliance and African roots.

Recordings became a widespread source of entertainment and status for urban African families. Imports were scarce during the early 1940s due to the war and an American musicians' strike. Local performers were encouraged to fill the gap with their own versions of American hits in the hope of capturing a greater share of the record market. American and British magazines and Wilfred Sentso's local publication *African Sunrise* kept African jazz enthusiasts informed about overseas musical trends and personalities. They could see and hear black performers like Lena Horne, Bill Robinson, Cab Calloway and Ethel Waters in films such as *Stormy Weather, Cabin in the Sky,* and *Black Velvet*. These productions electrified the cultural atmosphere of black Johannesburg and permanently influenced local speech, dress, and stage shows. Impressed by these films, Zuluboy Cele hired Emily Koenane as the first female vocalist to front a major African orchestra, the Jazz Maniacs. The Pitch Black Follies and Merry Blackbirds followed suit with Snowy Radebe and Marjorie Pretorius. By the end of the 1940s Sophiatown's Dolly Rathebe and Bulawayo's Dorothy Masuku were more popular than most male vocal quartets and specialised in African cover versions of American jazz favourites. African men readily adopted 'zoot suits' and American slang, and English-speaking Sophiatown residents proudly referred to their community as 'Little Harlem'.

A contributor to *Inkundla ya Bantu* (*Bantu Forum*) criticised the adoption of European culture as a movement away from an 'Africa that is ours, into an "Africa" that is of the Whiteman's making'. Arguing that 'we deny our music the opportunity to speak to the outside world in its own language', he praised not only indigenous music but Afro-American spirituals as well:

> They speak to the world in a language evolved by Africa in a foreign environment . . . they make the world understand the things we stand for . . . We want not to be Europeanised Africans but civilised Africans.[6]

Cultural politics was not the only reason why urban Africans performed American music and dance. Jazz may also have become part of South Africa's urban black music because it reproduces many performance principles of African traditional music. As John Storm Roberts puts it:

> South African music . . . tends towards rhythmic complexity of singing voices over a regular beat; its polyrhythms come from the voices, which vary their accentuation relative to the basic rhythm. This is remarkably like jazz, especially in the 1930s and 1940s music of Count Basie and others, who riffed and soloed against a rock-solid four-four beat.[7]

Studies of transatlantic cultural relations or cultural processes among black peoples have yet to provide us with an explanation of this 'remarkable' similarity. Debate over this intriguing issue, though, can still benefit from some informed speculation. While few of the slaves imported to North America originated in Southern Africa, there is a consistency in the structural principles of indigenous music throughout Subsaharan Africa,[8] and we can recognise continuities between traditional South African and African-derived music of the New World. This does not explain, of course, why American jazz and the religious and secular forms that shaped it have found more acceptance in South Africa than in any other country in Africa or the world. One reason may be the comparable socio-historical experience of the two peoples. Both black Americans and black South Africans have undergone lengthy, mostly British missionisation. Both were subordinated to developing industrial economies created and controlled by Northwestern Europeans.

In the United States, the mixing of African ethnic populations and the severe restrictions on the practice of African cultural traditions produced a syncretism that strongly emphasised vocal music and inexpensive, portable Western solo instruments. In South Africa, group vocal music was by far the most highly developed indigenous musical tradition. Mission congregational and choir singing reinforced this emphasis and it continued in urban secular performance culture. Unmissionised Africans who came into contact with whites on the large farms and in growing towns modified their traditional vocal styles, and abandoned their instruments in favour of European harmonicas, violins, and guitars (which were also favourites with unschooled black Americans). On the mission stations, Africans had to shed their traditional culture almost as completely as did black American slaves, though the proximity of traditional communities kept them in touch with the sources of indigenous culture. They scorned trade store instruments but created strong new traditions of Afro-Christian vocal music and introduced brass and keyboard instruments. Afro-American religious vocal music was directly influencing South Africans by the 1880s, a process made easier by the tonic solfa notation system used to teach black Christians in both countries.

During the early twentieth century, thousands of black people in the United States and South Africa migrated from rural areas to the expanding cities. There both groups experienced similar conditions: overcrowding, poverty, segregation, personal harassment, economic exploitation. These conditions accompanied parallel processes of class formation within American and South African black urban communities. Together, these forces set the stage for the emergence of performance styles that served comparable expressive needs.

With all the similarities there are, of course, at least as many differences. Unlike black Americans, Africans constituted the vast majority of the population and retained their own languages, cultures, and communities, enduring the peculiar 'two-world' system of migratory labour. Yet the two worlds were part of the same socio-economic system, and the similarities of experience have been reinforced by the mass distribution in South Africa of black American performance culture. This culture attracted Africans trying to adapt positively to their own urban environment, and the international recognition given black American performers made the temptation to copy them, rather than develop problematic African models, almost irresistible.

Only a few African jazz musicians of the 1940s brought anything identifiably South African to their playing of American swing. The reason was simply the identification of traditional music with the rural present and tribal past. Begun by the missionaries, this negative association grew until the 1950s, when the Afrikaner government's policy of forcing Africans to 'develop along their own lines' entrenched the attitude for the next twenty years.

Perhaps another reason was a lack of arranging skills, making the literate musicians dependent on foreign arrangements. Deep in the philosophy of African performance was also the emphasis on exact reproduction of existing forms as a means of acquiring cultural knowledge[9] coupled with traditions of solo improvisation. The reputation of African bandsmen rested equally on their ability to replicate American arrangements and to create original solos.

The urban African schools promoted black American models of cultural modernisation. As in some areas of West Africa,[10] teachers were among the most enthusiastic transmitters of American popular performance traditions. They encouraged record collecting and used their limited formal training to help student ensembles master the latest American jazz vocals. Close-harmony groups like the Boston Stars performed regularly in the schools. At semi-annual school concerts, student performers imitated the most popular local African singers, dancers and theatrical comedians, most of whom had begun their careers in the same setting. Promoters and professional entertainers searched for talent at these concerts, and many young prizewinners went directly to the professional stage.

All this is not to ignore the importance of school choir music, which was valued as a high-status cultural activity and as a source of prestige. The Transvaal African Teachers' Association and other organisations ran major competitions, and choir singing was by far the most popular performance idiom among urban Africans. This popularity can be traced back to the choral music-making and dancing involved in social competition between groups in traditional society.

Many professional performers retained close links with their communities, and performed in support of local associations including sports clubs, which sponsored social functions, concerts, and dances. Ernest Mohlomi's teacher-student vocal group, LoSix, top-selling recording artists, regularly appeared in behalf of Eastern Native Township's Eastern Brothers Football Club, to which they all belonged. Despite criticism from those who thought school concerts should emphasise 'classical' music,[11] parents were delighted with their children's ability to sing and tap dance in the manner of popular American performers. For school Africans, there was a clear association of Afro-American performance culture with urban cultural autonomy, and even the Eisteddfodau were not immune. The winners of the 1940 Transvaal Eisteddfod promptly formed an 'African Minstrels' troupe, aimed at developing African talent, staging 'all-African shows by Africans', and 'elevating the standard of music and stage performances'. The troupe proposed to specialise in 'African numbers composed by Africans, exclusive novelty numbers, musical comedies, old classical jazz songs, all-round minstrel choruses, . . . and vaudeville reviews'.[12]

The schools continued to train young performers and disseminate new forms integrating music, dance, and drama. In addition to close harmony quartets and song and dance routines, many schools sponsored student theatrical productions. The Jan Hofmeyr School of Social Work offered teacher training courses in theatrical direction and introduced drama into African youth clubs sponsored by the City Council. Despite the efforts of the BMSC's Bantu Dramatic society, only a tiny Westernised elite were interested in written 'literary' drama during the 1940s. Most urban Africans held the traditional preference for verbal expression linked to music, dance, and dramatic action.[13]

The cultural diversity that produced first minstrelsy and later vaudeville in New York[14] also accounted in part for the continued development of concert-and-dance variety entertainment in black Johannesburg. Urban schools were ethnically mixed, and so were the performance ensembles they organised. From their ranks came a number of professional variety companies backed by professional dance bands. Concerts included American songs and stage dancing, along with improvised sketches satirising local personalities and situations. These short dramatic pieces drew on traditions of mimetic characterisation in African storytelling. Many had explicit cultural politics, like the Pitch Black Follies concert *Africa* in 1940 that featured 14 items based on 'humorous impersonifications', followed by dramatisation of 'the march of progress amongst Africans', and ending with the moral 'unity in diversity of Bantudom'.[15]

Along with the Manhattan Brothers, Gay Gaieties, and Synco Fans, the Follies were among the most widely recognised stage companies. The founder and manager of the Synco Fans, Wilfred Sentso, tried to keep all phases of performance production in African hands. Sentso founded a performance school in the mid-1930s which by 1938 had produced the Synco Fans variety troupe, backed by the Synco Beats band. Over the next twenty-three years, some of black Johannesburg's most talented performers, including bandleader, composer and saxophonist Mackay Davashe, were associated with one or another of Sentso's many ensembles. Sentso himself was the first African to compose and publish a foxtrot, 'Synco Cap Fascination', in 1939. The Synco Fans reached their height in 1947, when Sentso leased the Grand Theatre, Vrededorp, for an entire week of variety shows. After that, both internal and external forces began to transform the professional lives of performers from the city's African community.

As long as they played within the African community, the performers' approximation of black American models seemed good enough. Inevitably, though, they began not only to compete more actively with imported recordings for the African market, but also to struggle against their isolation and restricted opportunities by seeking a wider national and international audience. Comparison with their American counterparts and the choice of an imported cultural solution to problems of modernisation became serious issues. They revealed contradictions that have troubled urban Africans ever since.

The Second World War dramatically increased an 'international' consciousness among urban African performers. The military hired a number of the best African jazz bands to perform for black units of the Allied forces, and their shows also attracted many whites. Wilson Silgee led a group drawn mostly from the Jazz Maniacs, and their reception among the armed forces audience was so enthusiastic that he acquired a permanent new stage name, 'King Force'. The Pitch Black Follies and Merry Blackbirds starred in a Liberty Cavalcade for black American sailors in Cape Town in 1944. Blackbirds' leader Peter Rezant commented:

> To play for them was thrilling. They appreciated the music, understood it and whirled merrily, bringing out what Harlem, Chicago . . . have created and given the world in the form of rug cutting.[16]

In 1943, a company of African variety performers formed the Jabulani Concert Party. While entertaining allied troops in North Africa, they met American musicians, including members of the Glenn Miller Orchestra.

A white officer, Lieutenant Ike Brooks, put together a large variety company from the South African Native Military Corps that pioneered black entertainment for mass white audiences. Like most other white entertainment entrepreneurs at that time, Brooks seems to have been unaware of the professionalism of African performers.

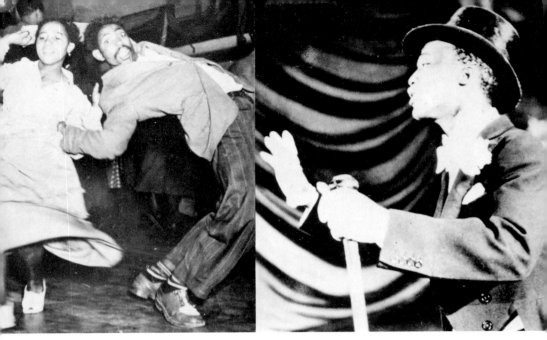

16 *'Jive' Dancers in Johannesburg, early 1950s*

17 *Skip Phahlane sings 'September in the Rain' in the successful* Zonk *show, 1949*

18 *The Band in Blue from the show* Zonk

19 *Pinocchio Mokgaleng, Modern Jazz Club founder, with Dolly Rathebe, the popular singing star*

20 *Boyce Gwele, pianist with Mackay Davashe's famous Shantytown Sextet*

21 *Committee of the Johannesburg Bantu Music Festival in the early 1950s: front row, left to right, Dale Quaker, Khabi Mngoma, Lukas Makhema, (?), Peter Rezant, Marcus Roe; back row, far left, David Rycroft, far right, J.R. Rathebe*

22 *Members of the Sophiatown Modern Jazz Club, early 1950s*

23 *Louis Moholo (aged 18) on drums, with the Chordettes, Cape Town*

24 *Advertisement for 'Jazz at the Odin', a series of jazz jam sessions held at the Odin Cinema, Sophiatown*

25 *'Jazz at the Odin'; left to right: Kippie Moeketsi, Skip Phahlane, Ntemi Piliso, (?), Mackay Davashe, Elijah Nkonyane*

His company included veteran horn players Elliot 'Bob' Twala and David Platter of the Swing Revellers, dancers Richard 'Schoolboy' Majola of the United Bantu Artists and Simon Sekgapane of the Darktown Strutters, and some members of the Jabulani Concert Party. Brooks insists that he and other whites trained the entire ensemble of African 'raw talent' from scratch, however.[17] Called *Zonk*, the company left the army following the War and made a series of professional tours of South Africa.

The *Zonk* show was enormously successful with both black and white urban audiences. It drew on stage entertainment traditions that had been developing, unknown to Brooks, from the days of the community 'bidding' concerts of the 1920s. The show included such American items as 'September in the Rain', vernacular translations of 'Copper-Coloured Girl', and original African jazz compositions by pianist Sam Maile – all backed by a fully literate jazz orchestra (see plates 17 and 18). School-boy Majola was spectacular in *is'cathulo*; miners' gumboot dancing. He also teamed with saxophonist Skip Phahlane to create 'Dockyard Dancing', a knockdown fight portrayed entirely through acrobatic tap dancing. Though all the performers were permanent urbanites, the influence of Mtetwa's Lucky Stars on African variety was clear in the musical-dramatic scenes of traditional village life and Zulu soldiers preparing for battle.

To his amazement, Brooks discovered that most of his performers were equally talented as musicians, dancers, and comic actors; Majola could even tap dance while playing the trumpet. The white press reviewed *Zonk* very favourably, demonstrating the potential of professional African performers to command a wider, possibly even international audience. Some thoughtful Africans worried, however; H. I. E. Dhlomo commented:

> After seeing the Nu-Zonk revue many Europeans were amazed at so much latent African talent . . . On the African side there have been some heart searchings: Why do we neglect our talent? Why cannot we combine into strong companies? Why cannot we organise and efficiently manage ourselves? Why must there always be a European behind us?.[18]

Though Sentso and Griffiths Motsieloa continued to organise and manage African stage companies, South African conditions favoured white producers like Brooks. They could command greater organisational and financial resources and stand between performers and the mass of segregationist legal restrictions that inhibited interracial contact and independent African enterprise. After the *Zonk* company disbanded the members returned to performing more or less exclusively for the African township audience. The company can still be seen in the film version of *Zonk* produced by Brooks in the late 1940s and still in his private possession.

While African stage variety concerts and jazz ('jive') dances continued to attract working-class as well as middle-class patrons, the majority of urban Africans were less Westernised than their school-trained entertainers. The continuing *marabi* audience admired American jazz and clothing styles as symbols of international urban black culture. But they still demanded music that was recognisably their own and expressed the ethnic variety of location society and culture.

For working-class Africans, Sophiatown represented a struggle for things more basic than inclusion in the wider society; a fight for survival amid high rents, poverty, overcrowding, wage slavery, victimisation, and police harassment. Patterns of working-class life that had evolved in the inner city slumyards were more fully developed and integrated into the new social environment of Sophiatown.

Living conditions were little better in Sophiatown, but there Africans had their own regular streets and neighbourhoods rather than the haphazard industrial backyards of the city fringes. The communal water taps, toilets and showerhouses of Sophiatown, though insanitary and inadequate, are remembered today as casual meeting places where the better-off and educated mixed with their humbler neighbours.[19]

Though subject to intense pressures, family life, friendship networks and neighbourhood recreation became social defences against a hostile city. In contrast to the slumyards' transience and lack of social co-operation, Africans in Sophiatown developed a strong community identity. Entertainment played its part, and 'more than anything else it was the backyard shebeens and dance parties that gave expression to this new proletarian identity'.[20] Anyone in search of a party had only to follow the sounds of musical uproar to the crowds of people dancing in the backyards or the street.

By the 1940s, the latest popular working-class dance music combined African melody and rhythm with the rhythms of American swing, jitterbug and even Latin American rumba and conga. Developed by black South African bandsmen, the new style was called *tsaba-tsaba*. It is played in duple time, and its rhythm has several distinctive African/Afro-American features, including rushed second and fourth beats, the freedom to accent any of the four beats, and a polyrhythmic sense of two beats against three. Although some Africans asserted that *tsaba-tsaba* developed from *marabi*, the rhythms of the two styles are quite distinct, and they seem to be related more through social function and category than content.

Tsaba-tsaba was the dance for working-class Africans at a time when American jitterbug, locally known as 'jive', and large dance orchestras dominated the dance halls (see plate 16). Dance competitions were as gymnastic as the displays at Harlem's Roseland Ballroom. In contrast to *marabi*, *tsaba-tsaba* called for recognised movements:

> A male and a female danced towards each other, shaking the knees in what is sometimes described as a 'rubber-legged' style; pelvic movement was also emphasised in addition to footwork. Just before the couple made contact a shout of the word 'Tsaba!' was given and they danced backwards to their starting points.[21]

To some extent, standardising the steps of urban dances reflected the growing crystallisation of African social structure in the Western Areas. Former residents generally agreed that the new music had originated with the migrants at all night parties in Newclare, just south of Sophiatown. The rhythm of *tsaba-tsaba* does appear identical with the neo-traditional *focho* style of Sotho migrants. By the Second World War, neighbourhood Sophiatown bands like Chico's and professional musicians like Zuluboy Cele had combined the *focho* rhythm with melodies from various local and foreign sources to create *tsaba-tsaba* dance music.

Simultaneously, Ace Buya's Modernaires and other jazz vocal groups were shifting from vernacular translations of American songs to compositions of their own based on *tsaba-tsaba* (see plate 14). Their purpose was not only to please the working-class audience but also to develop 'music of African origin [that] would find its place side by side with imported dance music'.[22] Buya, the Woody Woodpeckers' Victor Ndlazilwana, and other singers recorded worksongs of urban Xhosa migrants and arranged traditional songs for close-harmony jazz. A number of bands and stage troupes were hired to perform on the mines, where fruitful stylistic exchange took place between urban musicians and a more rural-oriented audience. The LoSix, who lived among miners in Eastern Native Township, blended costumes, melodies, rhythms, and dance steps from the mines into their stage shows and jazz recordings, often juxtaposing traditional music and jazz within the same song. Todd Matshikiza reviewed LoSix's popular *Tikoloshe* (Gallotone GB 2041):

> It is a good, modern harmonised music with words that catch on from the very start. Then suddenly you are forced to stop plumb dead in the middle of the chorus because a witchdoctor's drum and solemn prophecies in true style . . . change the entire modern number into a delightful, humorous, eloquent piece of traditional work.[23]

Tsaba-tsaba was associated with proletarians and the rough social atmosphere of the occasions where it was most often played. Middle-class musicians and jazz fans, despite their developing cultural awareness, were ambivalent towards it. The literate professionals who specialised in American swing generally considered themselves superior to the *tsaba-tsaba* audience that provided their most regular source of income. The musicians invented the phrase '*Ke tsaba tsaba*', to refer to a women of inferior character or morals.

Walter M. B. Nhlapo, a musical journalist and talent scout for Gallo records, disagreed. He urged performers and audiences of his own class to understand that it was the ongoing process of creative syncretism rather than the imitation of American performers that held the key to the development of an authentic and internationally recognised urban music and dance:

> Everybody spoke of Tsaba Tsaba. . . . There were no radios to broadcast it all over; but everybody sang it. There were no printed copies of it, but some dance bands played it; it had the spirit of Africa in it. . . . Regardless of torrents of scathing abuse, it swept the country. . . . In bioscopes we've seen Harlem dance the Big Apple, the Shag, and Africa's creation, La Conga . . . and these dances have not been recipients of abuse as Tsaba-Tsaba. . . . Europeans measure our development and progress not by our imitative powers but by originality. . . . A friend or not it (Tsaba) is an indispensable part of our musical and dance culture.[24]

Nhlapo viewed class division as an obstacle to African creativity, and wondered why *tsaba-tsaba* and other township styles could not be 'polished and given to the world as the La Conga from Africa?'.[25] His suggestion was prophetic. In 1947, August Musururgwa composed his classic *tsaba* dance tune, *Skokiaan* (Gallo GB11 52.T). It became an international success, topping the American Hit Parade as 'Happy Africa' in 1954, and was published as sheet music in 17 countries.[26]

Other indigenous African working-class forms eventually gained international audiences as well. As townward migration increased, many Zulu and Swazi migrants decided to remain permanently in the city or at least to participate in urban society. They expressed their new urban identity in *ingom'ebusuku* competitions.[27] During the 1940s, the competing groups were known as 'bombing' choirs, because their choral shouts were intended to sound like wartime aircraft shown in cinema newsreels.[28] Bombing was an urban but non-Western form, and examples survive on recordings of the period. Weekend choir competitions played a role in the urbanisation of participants, but they competed only to impress each other and not middle-class townsmen, so the effect was to intensify traditional patterns of male group rivalry.[29] Adding fuel was the African beer sold at *Kwamagaba Ngejubane* ('Sip and Fly'), located across from the Polly Street Education Centre where performances took place.

No African was allowed to adjudicate for fear he might be related to someone in a choir or otherwise be biased. The solution was to accost a white man coming from a tavern, sober or not, and offer him two pounds to decide the contest, a practice which continues in choral competitions today. No one could talk to the judge. At four am he called out a number, and the choir to which it had been assigned was the undisputed winner.[30] Rather than risk fierce argument and even violence, competitors preferred a white man's uninformed, arbitrary but impartial judgement; a feature of urban life universally familiar to Africans.

The various forms of *ingom'ebusuku* reflected degrees of cultural urbanisation, in which working-class men 'progressed' from bombing to *ingom'ebusuku* quartets influenced by *makwaya*, ragtime, and Afrikaans folk music. Some groups, like Malcolm Zwane's Kings of Harmony, eventually became the equals of the mission school ragtime choirs. The most popular of the professional *ingom'ebusuku* groups was Solomon Linda's Original Evening Birds. In the early 1940s, Linda's group recorded *Mbube* ('lion') (Singer-Gallo GE829), which Pete Seeger rearranged a decade later for his Weavers under the title 'Wimoweh'. It was a great success in the United States and Europe, and Seeger paid royalties to Linda, though not legally obliged to do so.[31] Following this overseas recognition, *ingom'ebusuku* became known as *mbube*, the most commercial of the names by which it is known today.

Street music, a part of Johannesburg's popular culture since before the turn of the century, remained a focus of communal sociability in Sophiatown. Special occasions brought some of the best-trained African brass bands down from Rustenburg. No middle-class location wedding was complete without a uniformed brass band leading the procession from the church to the reception. If two hands crossed paths in the streets, competitions often resulted, each band listening politely to the other. Untrained Pedi groups from Sophiatown bought instruments second hand and imitated the Rustenburgers, collecting coins from onlookers or accompanying a *stokfel* parade. When two of these Pedi bands met, they tried to blow each other off the street. Captain Marcus Roe of the Native Military Corps trained and led an African brass band during the 1930s, and during the '40s and '50s the City Engineers and Non-European Affairs Departments formed their own African bands to perform at hostels, parks, beerhalls and other public places.

The fife and drum bands of Scottish immigrants to South Africa, who practised regularly at Johannesburg's Union Grounds, also inspired township youngsters. African boys took up the inexpensive six-hole German metal flageolet or 'penny whistle' and home-made drums and marched as bands in Scottish dress, African boy scout (Pathfinder) drum and bugle bands added their influence. Sophiatown's Phalanzani Scots Band, with 35 penny whistlers and two drummers, dressed in Scout hats, kilts, tartan sashes, and neckerchiefs.[32] In the 1930s and '40s these 'Scottish' or 'MacGregor' bands paraded the location streets at weekends. They enjoyed the playing, the public attention, and the coins thrown by passers-by. If money were the primary object of a performance, they invaded the white city and suburbs, where takings were considerably better.

Most MacGregor bands continued in the tradition of the Ninevite and *Amalaita* street bands. In other contexts, many of these youngsters would have been called Blue Nines, for most urban Africans regarded the bands as cover organisations for gangs of school dropouts who drank liquor and smoked *dagga*. Veteran saxophonist Ntemi Piliso remarked, 'These boys were muggers at night but sat around during the day playing penny whistles and looking innocent'.[33] Yet the bands included many middle-class, school-going youngsters as well.

These penny whistlers often played for *stokfel* parades of 'MacGregor women' dressed in tartan skirts and white gloves. Sometimes the women played drums and trumpets (not penny whistles) themselves. Huddleston writes of the street parades of these female 'Sophiatown Scottish':

> Behind them will come the spectators, not marching in step but dancing with complete abandon, and surrounding them, as always when there's a sight, a crowd of children dancing too, and singing as they dance.[34]

The MacGregors became established in other South African cities as well. They are mentioned in Wilson and Mafeje's study[35] of Cape Town's Langa Township, where proletarian young men are categorically known as the 'ooMac'.

Street bands of Coloured 'coons' also inspired younger township boys, who were often no more than ten years old. They formed a different kind of penny whistle band that also contributed to the development of township music. The penny whistle's history as the favoured instrument of young urban African boys is based firmly in traditional antecedents. As early as 1812, Burchell witnessed a performance of Tswana reed pipes (*lithlaka*) when exploring the Western Transvaal. He returned the favour by playing the European flute for the Tswana musicians:

> The attention with which they listened to the flute, evinces that more varied music affords them pleasure, and renders it probable that he who should put into their hands the flageolet and teach them to play a few simple airs, or to combine together into one instrument, an octave of their reed pipes, would long be remembered among them.[36]

Unknown to Burchell, the neighboring Zulu must already have possessed such a flageolet, called the *umtshingo*. It spread to the Tswana during the Matabele (Zulu) invasion of the late 1820s and is found among the Sotho, Swazi, Xhosa, and other peoples.[37] Although it lacks fingerholes, it can produce a complete scale of partials 4 to 12 of an harmonic series, sounded by varying the wind pressure and by opening and stopping the end of the tube with a finger. The *umtshingo* was closely identified with young herd-boys, who used the instrument to call their cattle or signal other boys. Saxophonist-arranger Reggie Msomi and many other townsmen were born or spent periods of their childhood in rural areas where they herded cattle and made their own *imitshingo*. In the cities, the low cost (6 to 8 shillings), durability, and expanded technical possibilities of the six- hole penny whistle made it a natural successor to the *umtshingo*. Because it was regarded as the instrument of 'herd-boys', 'street urchins', and 'petty criminals', it had very low prestige.[38]

At *stokfels* during the early 1940s, the juvenile musicians added a home-made guitar (*isiginci*), milk-tin rattles, and a one-string bass with a wooden-box resonator to one or more penny whistles. Unlike the MacGregors, who copied Scottish marches, they imitated the popular local and American swing jazz orchestras. Although the penny whistle is designed for two full octaves, young Africans developed a fingering system that allowed them to produce 'glides, blue-notes and chromatic passing notes in a combined technique of fingering and blowing which goes beyond the factory tuned seven-note diatonic scale'.[39] Brought up on *marabi* and the clarinet of Americans like Artie Shaw and Benny Goodman and locals such as Zacks Nkosi they developed an authentic, highly vocal style of jazz improvisation within African urban music. They drew from available materials in much the same way as the shebeen musicians did and extended *tsaba-tsaba* and other African jazz styles in new directions. Ultimately they blended indigenous and imported musical elements into a unified form based on African principles. This form developed from an improvisational 'street music' to a staple of the South African recording industry – the first distinctively South African style to achieve international recognition.

This music came eventually to be known as *kwela*, a term given currency by mass-media distribution. The influence of the recording industry on *kwela* street performance was evident, as penny whistlers walked about the streets playing requests for 'a tickey per record'. They identified song tempos as '78' or '82' from the rpms of commercial discs, and ended their street 'records' with a fade-out.[40] Donald Swanson's 1950 film, *The Magic Garden*, one of the first to use African actors and a location setting, featured penny whistler Willard Cele playing his own compositions in an Alexandra street. These were later released as 'Penny Whistle Blues' and 'Penny Whistle Boogie' (Gallotone GE1123), highly popular with African audiences. Recognition by the entertainment media greatly increased the respectability of penny whistle music among urban Africans,[41] who began to regard it as an authentic expression of their urban culture rather than as an indolent pastime of juvenile delinquents.

By the 1950s penny whistle music and dance parties were a major recreational activity of young urban Africans. Like other popular musical styles, it generated a distinctive dance form – *patha patha* ('touch touch'). This was an individualised, sexually suggestive form of jive dancing for young people in which partners alternately touched each other all over the body with their hands, in time with the rhythm. The dancers often shouted the word *kwela* (Zulu: 'climb on', 'get up') as an inducement to others to join in. It appears, however, that the term was not clearly or widely associated with the music itself until the release of the recording 'Tom Hark' (Columbia YE164) by Elias Lerole and his Zig-Zag Flutes in 1956. The record begins with a short scene spoken in the Afrikaans-based urban African dialect, *flytaal*: A gang of street-corner gamblers pack up their dice and pull out their innocent-looking penny whistles at the sight of a police van. One shouts '*Daar kom die khwela-khwela*' – the African name for these large pick-up vans. Some Africans argued that it was whites, who by 1956 were buying penny whistle recordings also, rather than Africans who first picked out the word *kwela* from 'Tom Hark' and used it as a general term for the music.

It was the penny whistle bands, rather than the large swing orchestras and jazz vocalists, who were the first urban African recording artists to become widely popular among whites as well as blacks. The success of 'Tom Hark' in the United Kingdom (on Columbia DB4109) and its jazz orchestration by clarinetist Ted Heath greatly enhanced the popularity of *kwela* in South Africa. Media distribution strongly affected the success and later development of *kwela*. African talent scouts Cuthbert Matumba of Troubadour Records and Walter Nhlapo of Gallos brought young penny whistle virtuosos such as Elias and Aaron Lerole and Spokes Mashiyane into the studios, where they made some of the best-selling records in the history of the local industry.

Kwela music consisted of a rhythmic ostinato chord sequence, usually C-F-C-G^7,[42] on string bass and guitar, backed by a standard drum set in place of shakers. Above this was a strong repetitive melodic line played by several penny whistles. This line was divided into the antiphonal two-phrase, four-bar sequence typical of African studio arrangements, and derived ultimately from the phrase structure of Nguni traditional bow songs.[43] An excellent example of this melodic structure is Aaron Lerole's 'Lion Killer'. Above the two parts played by the rhythm section and penny whistles, a solo penny whistle improvises a third part, following the part structure of traditional vocal music. Along with the lively rhythm, it was these solos that caught the ears of both the South African and international audiences, and made *kwela* a success.

The penny whistle was perhaps an ideal instrument on which

Lion Killer

Aaron Jake Lerole

to build the foundations of an indigenous South African jazz. Despite its relatively low volume and thinness of tone in comparison to the clarinet, the penny whistle's very simplicity of construction allowed for a tonal flexibility and vocal quality that was harder to produce on more tonally stable Western band instruments. Players like Aaron Lerole eventually had to switch to the saxophone to remain in the professional music business after *kwela's* popularity declined. Yet they continued to prefer the penny whistle because, as Lerole explained, 'I could master it; I could make it talk any sound I wanted'.[44]

During the 1950s studios used professional jazz musicians to back the penny whistlers, adding saxophone and piano to *kwela* instrumentation. Though they preferred to play American music, many jazzmen admired the inventive virtuosity of the penny whistle soloists. *Kwela* was recognised as the basis of a local style that could compete commercially with imported music. Musically illiterate jazz players who had performed *marabi* on the penny whistle as youngsters readily adapted to the new style, creating a *kwela*-jazz in which the penny whistle was replaced by the saxophone. Overseas audiences had taken only a passing interest in the penny whistle. For urban Africans, this reinforced its permanent classification as a child's instrument. Even the great Spokes Mashiyane had to change to the saxophone (*New Sounds of Africa*, Fiesta FLP 1358-B). The new jazz-*kwela* style was already crystallising by 1950. Innovators included Ntemi Piliso and his Alexandra All-Star Band as well as the Jazz Maniacs, whose popular recording, *Majuba*, gave a generic name to the style. By 1954 even the penny whistlers were described as performing in '*Majuba* tempo'.[45] *Kwela* is only one among the many forms that Africans created in the streets and locations of Johannesburg that commercial studios have reprocessed and redistributed at great profit.

Though Africans had been listening to white municipal radio stations since the 1920s, broadcasting for Africans only began in 1941 in Durban with a five-minute report of war news in Zulu by K. E. Masinga. This service was extended to Johannesburg and the Eastern Cape, increased to 15 and then 35 minutes, and made available to migrant workers through ground-line rediffusion hook-ups to their hostels. Masinga, a talented writer, introduced African radio drama with the help of the broadcaster and ethnomusicologist Hugh Tracey. The first play was Masinga's musical script of a Zulu folktale, *Chief Above and Chief Below* (1939), with original songs by the author in traditional idiom. Tracey was a purist, dedicated to rescuing traditional forms from imported and urban musical influences. Musical dramas based on folk sources and rural settings enabled him to insert traditional music into urban radio programming. The plays proved popular, especially among the migrant hostel dwellers. For more urbanised listeners, the Gay Gaieties leader J. P. Tutu composed a number of musical plays in Zulu for the Johannesburg branch of the South African Broadcasting Corporation.

Town music forms dominated the SABC programmes while the rediffusion hook-ups emphasised neo-traditional and syncretic styles popular with non-literate workers. Tracey[46] recalled that at first Zulu hostel residents complained about items from other African ethnic groups on 'their' service. By the late 1940s, however, they admitted enjoying the variety, a reflection of African workers' increasing ethnic tolerance.

The SABC had a regular programme on Tuesday, Thursday, and Saturday, from 9.45 to 10.20 am. Its wide variety of African musical styles did not entirely please any sector of the Johannesburg audience. As the only African programme, however, it was extremely popular. It also increased cultural communication, exposing urban Africans to traditional music and migrants to African 'township jazz'. Radio dramas of all kinds enjoyed general popularity. Following his election to the International Mark Twain Society for his adaptations of Shakespeare in 1953, K. E. Masinga's Zulu translations of *King Lear* and *The Tempest* were serialised over SABC.[47]

By the early 1950s the SABC was presenting different African languages and musical styles on separate days. Once a week jazz pianist-composer Gideon Nxumalo entertained urban Africans with his regular feature, 'This Is Bantu Jazz'. He was principally responsible for the wide distribution of a new term for the *majuba* African jazz, *mbaqanga*. This term, coined by Jazz Maniacs' trumpeter Michael Xaba, originally referred in Zulu to a kind of traditional steamed maize bread. Among musicians, it meant that the music was both the Africans' own, the homely cultural sustenance of the townships, and the popular working-class source of the musicians' 'daily bread'.

Another name for this blend of African melody, *marabi*, and jazz was *msakazo*, a derogatory term meaning 'broadcast'. The record companies, taking advantage of the commercial possibilities of radio, processed or 'mass produced' the music in the studios, pursuing a common denominator of urban African taste. In 1952, a commercial company installed a rediffusion service in Soweto's Orlando township, even though residents objected[48] that Orlando needed lights, schools, paved streets and adequate housing more than rediffusion. The African National Congress feared that radio would become an instrument of government propaganda. Others attacked it as a 'back-to-the-kraal, apartheid and never-never-land service' that used African languages (rather than English) and migrant and *msakazo* music in a 'develop-along-your-own-lines pattern'.[49]

The co-ordinated expansion of radio and recording studios for Africans increasingly swallowed up the performers. African journalists decried white exploitation and urged greater community support

161

for artists.[50] In the late 1940s and '50s, however, political and social pressures pushed professional African artists into the arms of white entrepreneurs.

As early as the Second World War, a few African bands performed unofficially at white nightclubs in Johannesburg. In 1942, white musicians who feared cut-rate African competition managed to get the Jazz Maniacs expelled from the Paradise Nightclub, claiming that the band were not members of the fledgling white musicians' union. Offering to join the union and pay dues, the Maniacs found themselves barred from the union also.[51] African musicians did continue to find work at white clubs until the late 1950s, but their position remained tenuous and insecure.

In the meantime the population of Johannesburg continued to grow. Whites agitated for the removal of the Western Areas and other so-called 'black spots' located in the path of white expansion. In 1945 yet another amendment to the Urban Areas act greatly increased the pressure on the urban African community by strengthening influx control regulations. Professional performing without white supervision was not considered 'gainful employment', and artists suffered along with the unemployed from the rigid application of the pass laws.

Most important, these pressures led to a major expansion of criminal activity in the African areas. General socio-legal insecurity among urban Africans had by the late 1940s produced a new anti-social type, the *tsotsi*. Tsotsis were originally young, city-bred African 'confidence men' able to speak some English and Afrikaans and to manipulate the white system. Aided by female counterparts called *noasisas* ('watchers'),[52] the *tsotsis* initially relied more upon their wits than violence to plunder the white economy. The term *tsotsi* itself was an urban African pronunciation of 'zoot suit', a symbol of urban sophistication drawn from American popular culture, with its ready money and flashy clothes. *Tsotsis* were part of the ethnically mixed society of the locations. Among themselves they spoke the Afrikaans dialect *flytaal* or *mensetaal*, which by the late 1940s had become known more widely as *tsotsitaal*. Borrowing heavily from American slang, Johannesburg *tsotsitaal* was eventually spoken by most urban workers and became the language of African working-class culture. As conditions worsened, *tsotsis* turned to robbery, mugging and other violent crimes. Meanwhile, the label broadened to include all urban criminals except for the gangs of migrants such as the maRashea (Russians) and *Amalaita*. The *tsotsis* were successors to the infamous Blue Nines.

During the 1950s, the *tsotsis* developed into a well-organised counter-society of urban gangs who adopted fashions pictured in *Esquire* magazine and copied the style of American cinema gangsters like Richard Widmark in *Street With No Name*. Their ethos was best

162

expressed in Willard Motley's locally popular American crime novel *Knock On Any Door*: 'Live fast, die young, and leave a good-looking corpse'.[53] Major gangs such as the Americans, Berliners, Koreans, and Green Archers marked out territories over which they tried to exercise general control. The Americans controlled much of the criminal activity in Sophiatown, and their encounters with rival gangs such as the Spoilers of Pimville often ended in bloodshed. Alexandra Township's dreaded Msomi gang began as vigilantes 'protecting' the community, but quickly turned into a paramilitary criminal administration, holding public executions in the streets of the location.

The Sophiatown gangs were the most sophisticated and integrated themselves into the socioeconomic life of their community. Working-class urbanites lived with violence and even romanticised the gangs. They saw them as leaders of their own 'shebeen society', culture heroes courageous and clever enough to become wealthy at the expense of whites.

The gangsters and *tsotsis* themselves greatly admired professional jazz musicians, who expressed their urban lifestyle. Gang leaders often controlled local cinemas and concert halls, where they sponsored shows. Bands counted specific gangs among their local followings, and certain venues became the 'strongholds' of particular bands. The Jig Club in WNT, for example, was hospitable only to the Jazz Maniacs and Harlem Swingsters; it was a courageous group of players who consented to perform there in their stead. Top bands like the Maniacs and Swingsters, and vocal groups like the Manhattan Brothers and African Inkspots were considered great rivals, and their appearance on the same bill could cause a near riot.

Criminal involvement damaged professional performance. Gangs that supported one band often tried to suppress others, and many shows turned into violent confrontations as *tsotsis* attacking the musicians were met by others rising to their defence.[54] Gangsters often pressed their friendship on popular musicians as a means of enhancing their own prestige. Zuluboy Cele, murdered in 1944, was only one of numerous performers who suffered from involvement with gangsters. Female vocalists were particularly vulnerable. Miriam Makeba recalled in a 1962 interiew 'the nights when thugs would invade dance halls and "claim" them as girlfriends for the greater glory of appearing in public with them'.[55] Nationally popular performers such as Makeba, Thoko Thomo, and Susan Gabashane were all victims of kidnapping or assault during the early '50s. After a stabbing by a jealous fan, South Africa's most popular singing star, Dolly Rathebe, retired in fear for her safety at the height of her career and moved from Sophiatown to Port Elizabeth in the Eastern Cape.

Ordinary working-class and middle-class concert-goers began to stay away out of fear of knife-wielding *tsotsis*. Major shows regularly failed to make a profit, and musicians went unpaid when *tsotsis* chased dancehall patrons or forced bands to play at knifepoint until 6 am. The Merry Blackbirds, who preferred inner-city venues and often played for white audiences anyway, vowed never again to play in the locations. While violence was destroying concerts and dances in the locations, the police made it increasingly more difficult for Africans to use concert halls in the city centre. The destruction by fire of the Ritz Palais de Danse, Inchcape Hall in November 1951, both hastened and symbolised the decline of the independent African entertainment world. Apart from the BMSC and white clubs, well-supervised venues were no longer easy to find.

This situation prompted many bands to undertake extended tours of towns around the country; but pass regulations, organisational problems, entertainment taxes, and travel expenses limited their chances of success. Combined with inevitable personality conflicts and strains on home life, these difficulties made tours a threat to group loyalty. Many bands disintegrated on the road and never reformed.

The decline of large dance orchestras in America in the 1950s helped to produce a similar trend in South Africa. More directly responsible for the death of South Africa's big bands, however, were the destruction of the Western Areas and regulations forbidding Africans to appear at venues where liquor was served. As Sophiatown and its dance halls were destroyed, musicians were shut out of the inner-city clubs and halls, and jazz was gradually deprived of its multi-racial audience.

At the root of these difficulties was the government's relentless effort to destabilise urban African society and to deny Africans any hope of permanent identification with the urban environment. In 1948, the Nationalist Party took control of Parliament and set about institutionalising and systematising the racial segregation and stratification of South African society. The Group Areas Act of 1950 enforced residential segregation, shifting large numbers of black people into separate living areas. The Western Areas Resettlement Act of 1953 signalled the end of African hopes for social recognition. Sophiatown was to be destroyed and its residents moved to the new government townships of Soweto (Southwest Townships), there to be divided according to language group.

Johannesburg Africans put up stiff cultural resistance to this policy. Despite the disruptions, the 1950s were a period of great activity and achievement in black music and theatre. Jive dancers competed aggressively, but bands shared engagements. The constant changing of band names and personnel[56] actually reflected the splitting and shuffling of band members to cover multiple bookings. Saxophonist Zakes Nkosi's City Jazz Nine was originally formed by some members of the Jazz Maniacs who wanted to play for afternoon *stokfel* parties in the locations, and they later recorded on their own. Internal quarrels in the bands centred more on money, authority and professional reliability than on antagonism between rival groups. Disregarding the dangers, large numbers of followers travelled twenty or thirty miles to hear their favourite bands at outlying townships. Recordings had not dampened enthusiasm for live music; on the contrary, fans often attended concerts hoping to hear a favourite band perform its latest release.

Bands acquired their devoted followings primarily by showing off their creative virtuosity. While the Manhattan Brothers were a Pimville troupe and the Jazz Maniacs a Sophiatown band, every location had its own favourite soloist or 'hero' on each of the solo instruments. Jazz skills brought prestige, solo improvisation was encouraged, and widespread musical literacy helped bands to bridge the social gap between their different audiences. In the early hours of the morning, musicians would put away their written orchestrations of tunes like Count Basie's 'One O'clock Jump' and 'Bring it back home' with African jazz (*mbaqanga*) and hot solo choruses. These torrid displays gained the bands and players their ranks of loyal followers. Audiences based their judgements on local compositions with African musical features, displaying their approval with nearly hysterical excitement. These late night 'do or die' sessions helped forge *marabi*, *kwela*, and American jazz into *mbaqanga*, the people's own jazz, an expression and celebration of their new cultural identity.

The 1950s were the heyday of passive resistance and anti-pass campaigns, and each had its special protest songs.[57] Despite censorship, musicians and African broadcasters used recordings to spread the message and inspiration of protest, and heartened the resistance. The successful Alexandra bus boycott of 1957 inspired *Azikwelwa* (We Won't Ride), banned by the SABC, and broadcaster Joseph Makhema was dismissed for playing Masiza's *Vukani Mawethu* (Awake My People) over the radio. The Sophiatown removals, begun in February 1955, were bitterly protested in the Sun Valley Sisters' 'Bye Bye Sophiatown', and *Asibadali* ('We Aren't Paying'; i.e., rent) (RCA 74042). Residents sang Strike Vilakazi's 'Meadowlands' as government trucks hauled their belongings away to Meadowlands Township in Soweto.[58]

Meanwhile, performers continued to use song lyrics to comment upon social issues and behaviour within the urban African community itself, a tradition established by Reuben Caluza with his recordings for HMV in 1930. Their targets were the location police (e.g., 'Black List' by the Three Fools, BB1014), *tsotsism*, prostitution, and physical and social conditions in the African areas.

The performers' expression of an urban African cultural identity and values contributed to united political action.[59] Public performances became occasions for expressing political solidarity. At the Durban première of the first commercial film about urban Africans, *Jim Comes to Joburg*, its star, Dolly Rathebe, was greeted by a crowd shouting the African National Congress' Defiance Campaign slogan, *Mayibuye iAfrika!* ('Come back, Africa!').[60]

While performers to some degree maintained their role as interpreters, spokesmen, and representatives of their community, apartheid and internal social disruption were threatening to rob urban Africans of their remaining cultural autonomy. During the 1950s, both working-class and middle-class performers had to rely increasingly upon white producers and management for the advancement of their careers in live performance as well recording and broadcasting.

Most professional musicians admired American jazz, but only a few acquired the reading skills necessary to perform imported orchestrations. At the same time, local record sales rose when the *Kwela* penny whistlers brought their urban African transformations of popular American styles to the studios. Turning *Kwela* into *mbaqanga*, nonreading groups produced top-selling recordings such as *Baby Come Duze* by the Alexandra All Star Band. Yet without royalty agreements, recording alone did not provide an adequate income. Musicians had either to take non-performance employment or to depend on intermittent studio freelancing as sidemen. When royalty and copyright conventions did appear in South Africa in the late 1950s, they benefited recording companies rather than performers. Like African labourers, musicians could neither join white unions nor form their own collective bargaining agencies and were thus at a serious disadvantage in dealing with the white entertainment industry. Record companies often refused to pay royalties, citing technicalities or alleged contract violations, as was the case with *Baby Come Duze*.

A case in point is that of Spokes Mashiyane, penny whistler turned *mbaqanga* saxophonist, and one of the first African musicians to become widely known among whites. Though his recordings made the equivalent of hundreds of thousands of dollars for Trutone, his flat fees for each one ranged from seven to fifty dollars. He could not earn a living through recording, so he performed at white parties and public occasions, helped by white management[61]. When he pressed his demand for royalties, he was assaulted by thugs. Finally, the fledgling Union of Southern African Artists helped, and Mashiyane's income soared because of the royalty provisions in his new contract with Gallo in 1958.

More important for the development of urban African music was the new studio production system. Earlier, in the late 1930s, performers had accused Griffiths Motsieloa, the Gallo talent scout, of exploiting them economically. But there was no question of interference with their music-making, either from him or from his successor, Walter Nhlapo, who was respected among musicians for his fairness and concern for their welfare.

In the early 1950s, however, Troubador Records hired Cuthbert Matumba as talent scout/producer, and within six years they commanded 85 per cent of African record sales. Matumba's system resembled that of the black producer Clarence Williams in America, who used a stable of salaried musicians to mass-produce dozens of popular blues and jazz recordings during the 1920s.[62] Matumba shifted his musicians around in different recording combinations. Using a standard musical formula, he produced numerous *msakazo* (African jazz) recordings popular with urban working-class Africans. Troubador and other companies bought rights to the names of popular bands, so that troublesome members could easily be replaced.[63] For the migrants, Matumba hired neo-traditional players such as John Bhengu ('Phuzhushukela'), and urbanised their style by backing them with studio sidemen.

Matumba had little use for the literate Sophiatown jazzmen. The jazz audience, declining in an age of American 'bop' and 'cool' in any case, preferred imported recordings. Skilled professional jazz players and singers had three alternatives. They could leave the studios and the professional music world, adapt to the *mbaqanga* trend in popular music, or seek a wider multi-racial and international audience. Many retired, especially members of stage song-and-dance companies who had depended so greatly on swing orchestral music and live performance. Those who remained in the studios were told to stick close to superhits like *Pola Rapopo* (Sit Down Old Man) a monotonous, formulaic *msakazo* released by Kenneth Mangala in 1955 (Troubador AFC 30). In response, jazzmen combined *msakazo* with jazz improvisation, much as they had formerly done in the dance halls. They created an authentic and complex *mbaqanga* or Africanised jazz that appealed broadly to all classes of Africans. Among these recording units were King Force Silgee's Jazz Maniacs Quintet ('Tickey Line' Gallotone GB1992); the King Cole Basies (*Umdudo* Gallotone AJ3); and Mackay Davashe's famous Shantytown Sextet, with alto virtuoso Kippie Moeketsi, Jacob Lepere, bass, Norman Martin, drums, General Duze, guitar, Boyce Gwele, piano, and Mackay himself on tenor (*Msakazo* Gallotone GB1955) (see plate 20). Vocal groups also took part in the studio-sponsored indigenisation of jazz. Miriam Makeba, an international star for the past twenty years, first built her local reputation with *mbaqanga* as lead singer with the Manhattan Brothers (*Tula Ndivile*, Gallotone GB2034) and later with her own female quartet, the Skylarks (*Laleni Bantwana*), Gallo-New Sound GB2999). The Skylarks included three other great talents; the current international sensasation Letta Mbulu, along with Abigail Kubheka, and Mary Rabotapa.

To fill the vacuum created by the decline of the independent

African concert industry, the record companies hired black cinemas and some of the remaining location halls to present their stable of performers. With their superior authority and resources, the companies could provide security for their performers and reduce the potential for violence by keeping audiences seated throughout the show. Along with the elegant suits and tuxedos worn by the Manhattan Brothers and Jazz Maniacs, groups like LoSix performed part of their shows in traditional African costume to entertain less urbanised audiences.

Between 1949 and 1957, African jazz vocalists were able to increase their popularity by appearing in local films that dealt with urban African life. These included *Jim Comes to Joburg* (1949), *The Magic Garden* (1950),*Song of Africa* (1953) and the film version of the *Zonk* show (1953). Though shown exclusively in black cinemas, all the films depicted Africans from a romanticised liberal white point of view. The single exception was Lionel Rogosin's *Come Back Africa* (1957), which portrayed not only the reality of Sophiatown but the desperate plight of black workers in South African cities, and was promptly banned. The other films' image of urban Africans as simple-hearted, dogged and irrepressible in the face of hardship certainly falsified their experience. Even so, Africans were pleased to see their communities and performers represented in this prestigious medium.

The sense of glamour and excitement that pervaded the Johannesburg black entertainment world in the 1950s was largely created by African journalists like Todd Matshikiza, Walter Nhlapo, Can Themba, Stan Motjuadi, Casey Motsitsi, Henry Nxumalo, Mike Phahlane and others writing for *Drum, Bantu World, Zonk,* and the *Golden City Post*. Their evocative and penetrating commentary on the Johannesburg cultural scene helped give black communities a dynamic, resilient self-image and a positive sense of achievement despite the government's tightening stranglehold on everything they valued. Without these writers no coherent, authentic account of Sophiatown's culture would be possible.

Major changes were brought about in the 1950s by agents of white society, who placed themselves between the African community and its performing artists. Their interposition was both commercially and politically motivated, and inevitably alienated performers from their audiences and their creative work. They operated in both amateur and professional performance fields, and in the context of apartheid helped isolate performance from community aspirations. Not all efforts by whites were negative, though, and until the 1960s possibilities for fruitful interracial cooperation still existed.

Reflecting the ongoing concern of liberal whites for urban African social welfare, the bandmaster Marcus Roe and other officials of the Johannesburg Non-European Affairs Department (NEAD) began the Johannesburg Bantu Music Festival (JBMF) in 1947. With an impressive list of elite African cultural leaders among its committee members, the Festival sought to take over and revitalise the old Eisteddfodau of the Transvaal African Teachers' Association. Its official aims were:

1 to encourage a love of music and promote talent among the African people;
2 to raise the standard of performance and sense of appreciation;
3 to introduce to Johannesburg audiences the best African and European music.[64]

Beginning with six prominent choirs competing under the supervision of choirmaster Lucas Makhema, the JBMF gradually enlarged the programme to 84 separate sections. The interracial committee agreed to expand the programme beyond 'serious' choral music and include other kinds of performance, including miners' dancing, *ingom' ebusuku*, jazz, brass bands, ballroom dancing, and drama.

In the beginning, the JBMF served a genuine need and provided the kind of cultural outlet that urban black South Africans wanted (see plate 21). Hundreds of choirs and other ensembles poured into Johannesburg for the festival, which became the most important national black cultural event of the year, with the winners' concert held in City Hall. The key to its initial success was the good will and good relationships between white civic officials and leading blacks. As time went on, restrictive and petty apartheid regulations poisoned the atmosphere and made attempts at interracial cooperation frustrating and sordid. The fate of the JBMF is a good example of how South Africa's larger tragedy has stunted and embittered its culture as well its spirit and national health[65].

After a few years working-class Africans began to see the festival as an affair for the 'whites' good boys,' a place where 'the whites tell us how to perform our music'[66]. Certainly, raising ' the standard of performance' meant encouraging conformity to European criteria, not only in ballroom but even in African traditional dancing.

Middle-class cultural leaders like Khabi Mngoma, a classical musician and music educator active in the festival, complained that programme and artistic decisions were indeed made by whites, albeit with good intentions. In frustration, Mngoma and writer Ezekiel Mphahlele formed the Syndicate of African Artists, an African community-based performing arts group dedicated to African classical music and literary drama in Soweto. Harassed by police and government from the start, the Syndicate turned to political agitation. Mngoma appealed to urban Africans: 'We are beginning to create a cultural front in our struggle towards self-determination and we rely on you to help'[67]. Their magazine of cultural opinion, *Voice of Africa*, was banned in 1952, and Syndicate members brought to court for subversion. Still, the organisation was perhaps the first formal urban cultural movement actively promoting the cultural identity and socio-political aspirations of Johannesburg's blacks.

The Syndicate sponsored concerts by South Africa's black Western classical musicians and political plays such as Lucas Nkosi's *Now I Know*. When possible, they paid their performers in an effort to counteract the patronising taint of amateurism attached to the trophies awarded by the JBMF to mine dancers and classical pianists alike. By 1954, the JBMF's artistic co-ordinator, Lucas Makhema, saw that whites were replacing blacks in the NEAD and left to become a choirmaster in Bulawayo 'before I was booted out'[68]. Until 1956, the JBMF remained a major cultural event for the African middle class. It commissioned such works as Todd Matshikiza's Xhosa cantata, *Uxolo*, for 200 voices and a 70 piece African brass band. In that year, however, resentment over the shoddy arrangements for segregated concerts for blacks by foreign classical artists including Dame Margot Fonteyn, Yehudi Menuhin, La Scala Opera, and the London Symphony Orchestra poisoned the spirit of the festival. Middle-class Africans, sharing the general bitterness over the destruction of Sophiatown, lost interest in the festival, which they now regarded as an attempt to divert Africans' attention from their real problems.

Professional African jazz musicians disliked both the white artistic interference and the ethos of amateurism at the JBMF. The jazz band and instrumental soloist competitions at the festival in 1950 drew no entrants, and by 1953 the jazz category was dropped altogether. Jazz players had little interest in rehearsing a 'set piece' in pursuit of a trophy when recordings and live performances in the white-controlled entertainment field paid real money.

These opportunities were dwindling, though, as permits to perform at white nightclubs, private parties and university concerts became harder to obtain. A few concert troupes, including the Synco Fans and Gay Gaieties, kept stage variety traditions alive. In 1951, Eric Nomvete's Foundation Follies visited Johannesburg from East London, Cape. Sponsored by the National War Memorial Health Foundation, they were the first professional African company to perform at the City Hall in Johannesburg.

In 1952, white promoter Alfred Herbert organised his first *African Jazz and Variety* show at Johannesburg's Windmill Theatre, presenting some of the city's best performers before white audiences. The promise of regular pay and exposure to a wider audience attracted the professionals, particularly since Herbert allowed them to organise their own programme, based on the established African stage company format. The show was highly successful. Like Ike Brooks,

Herbert himself was a product of the South African Anglo-Jewish music hall tradition. He began to take a more sophisticated directorial approach, tailoring succeeding shows to the tastes of his liberal white and largely Jewish audience. By 1956, *African Jazz* and *Variety* was featuring Dolly Rathebe singing in Yiddish. The show's programme for the late 1950's read like a roster of the most famous names in black Johannesburg show business, and featured performers were paid £35 a week.

As a producer, Herbert exploited his performers, even abandoning them to their own devices when tours to Central and East African or others parts of Southern Africa ran into financial trouble. Nevertheless, his efforts to keep their personal as well as professional lives on an even keel and the lack of other performance opportunities kept performers with him up until the mid-'60s. Herbert's directorial influence on the development of urban African performing arts and on the relation of professional performers to the African community was more significantly harmful than his financial misdealings. *African Jazz and Variety* became more a burlesque than a representation of the traditions of urban African artistry. In 1959, the show included a rural pastiche written by Herbert entitled 'Kraal Tone Poem', presenting 'the songs, the dances, the life and the laughter from the home of jazz, the Kraal'[69]. Though billed as an 'original vernacular ethnic' show, its central feature was 'sexy dancing [by] a crowd of snappy-looking African lovelies clad in leopard-skin bikinis'[70], and Herbert described his 1961 show, *Drums of Africa*, as showing off 'the sexulating rawness and glamour of some of the most beautiful non-European women'[71]. None of these talents, of course, was shown to blacks.

Clearly black performers could not serve the cultural needs of the black community under Herbert's direction. But professional artists who wanted to reach out beyond their local audience had few alternatives. Only a white employer could easily get performance permits and the vital 'musicians' pass' entitling performers to 'go to any town under the European promoter, who is held responsible for their activities'[72].

Performers were caught between the recording studios and the promoters in an apartheid society. Walter Nhlapo advised that 'unless music lovers band together and offer employment to musicians in the form of concerts and record clubs, commercialism will kill music as we know it'[73].

Sophiatown's culturally self-conscious, American-oriented elite had taken steps to support local jazz by forming the Sophiatown Modern Jazz Club in 1955 (see plate 172). By that time, the bebop styles of Charlie Parker and Dizzy Gillespie were a powerful influence on local musicians. A number of innovative groups were playing the new jazz, including Mackay Davashe's Shantytown Sextet, and trumpeter Elijah Nkonyane's Elijah Rhythm Kings. During the next two years, led by jazz enthusiast Cameron 'Pinocchio' Mokaleng (see plate 19), the Modern Jazz Club sponsored a series of well-organised Sunday 'jam sessions' at the Odin Cinema Sophiatown (see plates 24 and 25). After the initial session, 'Jazz at the Odin' involved white as well as black musicians. The series was a milestone for jazz and creative interaction across racial lines in South African music. This new music was not well understood by the urban African population as a whole. Yet the prestige of jazz and of black American performance culture drew in the most urbanised people of Sophiatown. To appreciate jazz was a mark of urban sophistication and social status, even among *tsotsis* and gangsters; and by the late 1950s a genuine appreciation of the new styles had taken hold. By then, however, the Modern Jazz Club was dying along with Sophiatown. Forced to leave Johannesburg because of pass regulations, Pinocchio Mokaleng fled into bitter exile in Britain.

Though 'Jazz at the Odin' involved individual musicians and not formal bands, the sessions did lead to the formation of the Jazz Epistles (*Verse 1*, Continental 14. ABC18341). They included bop stylist Dollar Brand (piano), Kippie Moeketsi (alto), Jonas Gwangwa (trombone), Hugh Masekela (trumpet), Johnny Gertse, (guitars) and Early Mabuza (drums). The Jazz Epistles helped to establish an influential 'main stream' modern jazz movement, which claimed national attention among urban black South Africans during the 1960s.

Not all the effects of white involvement in urban black performing arts were negative. During the late 1950s, inter-racial cooperation helped to keep musical professionalism alive in South African jazz and set the stage for international recognition of black South African performers. Nor were all whites exploitative or patronising. The Anglican missionary Father Trevor Huddleston, an energetic religious leader, social worker, educator, fund-raiser, and champion of urban African rights, also took an active interest in the welfare of black performing artists in Johannesburg. His encouragement of Hugh Masekela, Jonas Gwangwa, and many others led to the formation of the Huddleston Jazz Band during the '50s. When Huddleston was recalled in 1954, a farewell concert attracted more than 200 performers and netted more than four thousand dollars for its sponsor, the Union of Southern African Artists ('Union Artists').

Union Artists began as an inter-racial effort to protect the professional rights of black performers. Under the leadership of clothing workers' trade unionist, Guy Routh, and later, the theatrical personality Ian Bernhardt, Union Artists successfully arranged royalty payments to Solomon Linda, Spokes Mashiyane, and Mackay Davashe. They also engineered the boycott by British Equity of all segregated shows in South Africa.

After Routh departed for England, Bernhardt emphasised the promotional aspects of Union Artists. The Huddleston concert provided the means to acquire permanent premises in Dorkay House. There Bernhardt initiated a programme to locate, train, and present African musical performers, before a multiracial audience. So began a series of talent contests and small 'festivals' leading to the production of the famous Township Jazz and Dorkay Jazz concert series, which began at Selbourne Hall in 1957 and continued until 1966. The concerts were highly successful, and many top African performers including Dolly Rathebe, Thandi Klassens, Letta Mbulu, Sophie Mcina, Patience Gqwabe, the Jazz Epistles, and Jazz Dazzlers appeared. Among the early highlights was a benefit in 1957 for the families of the murdered journalist Henry Nxumalo and stage comedian Victor Mkhize. The city took one-third of the proceeds as entertainment tax.

These concerts allowed musicians to perform in secure, well-organised circumstances, but without artistic interference from whites. Though audiences were segregated, the series did gain African jazz musicians a wider multi-racial following and greatly revived interest in jazz within the Johannesburg black community. In addition to concerts, Union Artists organised the African Music and Drama Association (AMDA) at Dorkay House, where performers such as Wilson Silgee could instruct their younger colleagues. Some performers accused Union Artists of exploitation and its African management committee members of favouritism, but most were pleased with their artistic freedom and broadened opportunities. Artists received some cash for concert appearances, though some resented the condescending taint of amateurism implicit in the talent search. Pianist Dollar Brand (Abdullah Ibrahim) complained, 'Ian Bernhardt only gives out trophies, and one is enough!'.[74]

Township Jazz was at best a pale and somewhat disembodied shadow of the old concert-and-dances of the black community. Todd Matshikiza remarked in 1957 that he would gladly have given up the opportunity to play in City Hall to perform again with the Harlem Swingsters at the old Jig Club in WNT.[75]

The culmination of this phase in the history of Dorkay House as a centre of black performance activity was the birth of the musical play, *King Kong*, in 1959. *King Kong* was based on the tragic career of South African black heavyweight boxing champion Ezekial 'King Kong' Dhlamini. Its creators intended it to be a model of fruitful co-operation between blacks and whites in the international entertainment field. With production, direction, script, and musical direction by whites, but using black musical actors and musicians and a score by Todd Matshikiza, the show proposed to combine the polish and style of Broadway with the cultural vitality and resources of the townships. The musical actors included the members of the Manhattan

173

Brothers and Woody Woodpeckers vocal groups, with Nathan Mdle-dle as King Kong and Miriam Makeba as his lady love, Joyce (see plate 26). The fiery Jazz Dazzlers Orchestra, led by Mackay Davashe, included members of the Shantytown Sextet, Harlem Swingsters, and Huddleston Jazz Band. The music was big band, but ten-year-old Lemmy Mabaso was also on hand, electrifying audiences with his penny whistle *kwela* solos (see plate 27). The play did not make a strong political statement; but it did show something of the hardships, violence, and frustration of African township life. The show infused African musical and dramatic stage traditions into a narrative structure, and presented a mixture of African and Western song and dance. There was jazz, a *tsotsis* knife dance based on Sotho *mokorotlo* war dancing, and a dance celebrating King Kong's release from prison that echoed the traditional Zulu welcome for a returning hero.[76]

King Kong was an immediate, overwhelming success with Johannesburg people of all races. A broadly South African production, it challenged the best of international musical theatre. The show's producer, Leon Gluckman, naively imagined it might create a more sympathetic attitude among whites towards urban blacks:

> Any white person who has seen the show will think twice now before he pushes an African out of the way on a street corner. It's not politics, but a question of human relations.[77]

King Kong arrived in London, where its black performers believed they had left the restrictions and parochialism of the townships and entered the international performing world for good. But international attitudes towards Africa had left South Africa behind. In 1960, African nationalism, independence and cultural resurgence were already dominant movements. White as well as black critics complained about the show's lack of political force:

> Politically, *King Kong* is about as dynamic as a bag of laundry. Everything, including the gangsters and the social misery, has been agreeably prettified . . . A full-blooded entertainment this may be but a whistle and a wiggle are no match for the policy of *apartheid*. One swallow of black and white collaboration doesn't make a summer of South Africa's bleak shame.[78]

In fairness, the show would never have been granted wide public exposure in South Africa if the system had been frontally attacked. Implicit in the production was the dream, no less than the illusion, of a better, more humane South Africa. The financial rewards for performers were hardly a dream come true, however. While Todd Matshikiza got £80 per week and the leading instrumental soloist Kippie Moeketsi got £35, most actors and band members made only £15.[79]

Artistically, white playgoers expected an 'African' (traditional) display, and so were disturbed by its modern, hybrid nature and considered it inauthentic. Because *King Kong* was presented in the style of European musical theatre, the actors appeared amateurish to London audiences. Nevertheless, the show ran for a year; and many of the cast, including Miriam Makeba and the four Manhattan Brothers, stayed on to pursue performing careers outside South Africa. Matshikiza's music underwent significant transformation at the hands of the music director, Stanley Glasser, who essentially removed the African township character from the London arrangements. This change was clearly perceived by urban black South Africans back home, who gave the London cast album an indifferent reception. Ethnomusicologist A.A. Mensah noted:

> The White collaborators . . . had managed to gain the upper hand and had introduced splendid arrangements but in doing so had missed some of the basic elements in the conception of modern entertainment music held by Black South Africans.[80]

In the Johannesburg of 1959, *King Kong* represented at once an ultimate achievement and final flowering of Sophiatown culture. The white suburb of Triomf rose where Sophiatown had stood. *King Kong* was both a presentation and a symbol of the character and indestructibility of Johannesburg urban African community. The show was imitated by Alfred Herbert and other producers, but the most important was the tireless Wilfred Sentso, whose productions *Washerwoman* (1959) and *Frustrated Black Boy* (1961) unflinchingly portrayed African suffering through the medium of musical theatre. During the 1960s, African director-playwrights adopted the *King Kong* model. Without white interference or assistance, they produced a self-supporting, indigenous urban musical theatre. Today, this theatre represents the most socially and politically significant art form in the black townships.

The 1950s witnessed changes in the social personality, status, and self-image of professional performers in the urban community. Opportunities in performing for white and black audiences, recording, and broadcasting continued to offer at least some African musicians the chance to earn a living from performance activity alone. The Manhattan Brothers, for example, earned five hundred dollars a week as a group during the best periods of the early 1950s, despite the violence at African shows. Still, performers' efforts to get out of the township environment and into the white and international arenas reinforced the ambivalence that many urban Africans felt towards them.

Ever since the emergence of the African dance musician around the turn of the century, urban and mission school Africans had looked upon professional popular musicians as social deviants, drinkers, gamblers, and womanisers unaccountable to either traditional or

Christian social morality. In contrast, amateur choral and keyboard musicians who were active in the schools and churches and middle-class professions were highly respected. So were performers who appeared exclusively at middle-class minstrel concerts and European-style dances. Middle-class youngsters who showed an interest in professional performance, however, were warned against leading the dissolute life of a 'ragtimer'.[81] Dambuza Mdledle recalled that the Manhattan Brothers' parents 'could not foresee a future for their clean-living lads "eating music" and mixing with musicians, whose bad behaviour and drunken habits were legendary'.[82]

During the 1940s, African jazz musicians benefited from their associations with black American performance culture and from their ability to express the cultural aspirations of their audiences. Nevertheless, working-class dance forms such as *tsaba-tsaba* and the occasions where they were performed perpetuated the 'ragtimer' image. Like their black American counterparts,[83] professional black South African musicians began to complain that their performances were socially accepted but that they as persons were not:

> It seemed to us that musicians were only regarded as human beings while they were on stage and performing. After that nobody cared about them.[84]

H.I.E. Dhlomo defended performers, saying,

> We either do not appreciate the value of or we expect too much of our creative artists. We ignore their contributions and do not think them 'Leaders' and patriots unless they play a prominent part in our social and political life.[85]

The attempt to model themselves upon Duke Ellington or Lena Horne and to cultivate the image of the impeccably dressed, smoothly mannered, glamorous American jazzman or woman heightened both the status and popularity of African performers during the 1940s. Amid the bitterness and fragmentation of African society in Soweto in the late 1950s and 60s, the image of the hard-drinking, *dagga*-smoking 'hep cat' reduced jazz musicians once again to the status of social marginals.

The performers' desire to escape the urban African community professionally aroused resentment among many of their fellow Africans, who saw no chance of doing so themselves. People being strangled by the wider system criticised musicians who played in white nightclubs and City Hall concerts as self-important and some-times violently attacked them. Bloke Modisane noted bitterly:

> The African directs his aggression, perhaps more viciously, against his own group, particularly against the more successful Africans who are resented for being successful.[86]

The notion that African professional performers had sold out to the white entertainment industry and abandoned their people persisted alongside genuine admiration of the *African Jazz and Variety*, *Township Jazz*, and *King Kong* performers.

Internally, the jazz performance community itself suffered from exploitation, professional insecurity, and modes of cultural production that discouraged group integrity and stylistic development. Both black and white promoters frequently violated the terms of their agreements with musicians. Non-professional promoters could simply withdraw from the entertainment field after a more or less successful attempt to make a quick profit. They could always find new performers to replace those unhappy with past treatment.

Working conditions contributed to a rapid turnover of personnel within the bands despite the high level of demand for their services. With so few outlets for independent achievement and public recognition, band members often quarrelled over money, leadership and personal prestige. Promoters found this lack of unity easy to exploit. Performers frequently left established groups and set up new ensembles of their own, since a disproportionate amount of revenues, recognition and authority normally went to the group leader-manager.

Professionally insecure younger musicians were no longer taking the time and effort to develop reading and other technical skills common among the older generation. This trend was reinforced by the new system of Bantu Education, which in the late 1950s closed some mission schools, brought others under government control, and replaced their curriculum with one designed to educate Africans for subservience. Music education suffered along with instruction in all other fields. Even earlier, however, the *Voice of Africa* complained:

> African artists are talented but fail to reach the top because they are intoxicated by immediate success to the extent of leaving off the hard work of practising, and depend on inspiration in their performances, which invariably results in failure and the artists' disappearance and despair.[87]

The development of African broadcasting did nothing to encourage stylistic innovation or continuity. Producers like the SABC's Michael Kittermaster insisted on making their own artistic judgements over the protests of African performers. Most often, temporary ensembles were created at Broadcasting House for specific programmes. The Radio Rhythm Boys, for example, included King Force Silgee (tenor), Todd Matshikiza (piano), Thomas Khoza (drums), and Fats Dunjwa (bass), all drawn from different local bands.

New African record producers like Rupert Bopape preferred to hire musicians individually for standard *msakazo* recordings. Professional urban musicians expressed disgust with the new system[88], while the producers disliked the jazzmen's sense of artistic and professional independence and found their demands for better pay and working conditions troublesome. Bopape replaced the middle-class players with working-class and migrant performers and instituted a system of rigid studio control. Performance units were rehearsed incessantly and the musical results became his property. Bopape, though not a musician himself, has more than 1 000 compositions copyrighted in his name, including Aaron Lerole's 'Tom Hark'. Lerole received about £8 for 'Tom Hark', and performers got about £6 for a recording.

Bopape built on the vocal *mbaqanga* of Miriam Makeba, Letta Mbulu, Susan Gabashane, Sylvia Moloi, and Thandi Mpambane's (later Klassens) Quad Sisters to create a style called *simanje-manje* (Zulu: 'now-now'). Makeba and the others performed African melodies in the close harmony style of the American Andrews Sisters. The new music, pioneered by Joyce Mogatusi's Dark City Sisters, coached by Aaron Lerole, showed less American influence. It employed a simplified version of traditional part structure, set rural songs to urban rhythms derived from *marabi* and *tsaba-tsaba*, and was played at a rapid tempo by back-up groups of three reeds plus electric bass, guitar, and drumset. Musicologist Andrew Tracey notes that the 'principle of parts cutting a cycle at different points is very noticable in black urban *mbaqanga* bands'.[89]

Bopape used spoken introductions in *tsotsitaal* to liven up recordings by the female quartets and Lerole's Black Mambazo group. Searching the mines, hostels, and even the rural areas, Bopape discovered some outstanding talents whose neo-traditional music could be processed into the new style. These included Simon 'Mahlathini' Nakbinde, who developed his remarkable sense of rhythm and phrasing as well as his talents as a composer and choreographer as the leader of a group of eighteen traditional wedding singers during the 1950s. At that time, deep-voiced Aaron Lerole led the pioneering Black Mambazo, which included Mahlathini's cousin Zeph Nkabinde. Influenced by Lerole, Mahlathini developed his rasping bass 'goat voice' (*ukubodla*; Zulu 'to bellow, roar')[90] and sang in praise of traditional values. The goat voice had roots in Nguni male traditional singing.

After Lerole quit Bopape at EMI in 1961, Bopape went to Gallo where he helped make Mahlathini famous. Soon every *simanje-manje* group had to have its male 'groaner', as they are called, leading a female quartet with solos sung in the goat voice style. Mahlathini performed in traditional animal skins as well as in Western costume, and with the help of his female group, the Mohotella Queens, innovated new stage dance routines based on traditional steps and urban jive.

178

This was music for people who were urbanising but not Westernising, as well as for migrants and even rural listeners influenced by urban culture. The new *mbaqanga* sold well in both urban and rural South Africa and in other countries of Southern and Central Africa. Performers such as Mahlathini still enjoy enormous prestige among urban workers who maintain strong links with the rural areas. Mahlathini sings nostalgically of the moral superiority and social security of traditional society, and reminds audiences of their rural roots. In the midst of urban hardship and insecurity, this musical glorification of African traditions appeals strongly to landless proletarians. For them, Nkabinde is *Indoda Mahlathini* ('Mahlathini The Man'), and his deep groaning voice embodies all the masculine power of the traditional Nguni *imbongi* (praise poet).

The commercial success of this music was based in part on the new social and demographic realities of urban African communities. As rural people continued their townward migration, the old locations of the Western Areas, Pimville, and Eastern Native Township were destroyed, and the people redistributed in the vast, anomic rental townships of Soweto. With the possible exception of Orlando, begun in 1932, there was as yet no feeling of community in Soweto, whose endless rows of identical brick 'matchbox' houses reflected the authorities' view of the urban black population as mere 'temporary sojourners' in the towns.

Urban Africans lost, at least temporarily, the sense of direction and identity once embodied in Sophiatown and its way of life. Africans protested against the destruction of Sophiatown far more strongly than they had objected to removal from the slumyards, because its streets, houses and institutions seemed so much more truly their own. As Father Huddleston lamented, 'When Sophiatown is finally obliterated and its people scattered, I believe that South Africa will have lost not only a place but an ideal'.[91]

Even as government bulldozers were levelling its houses, Sophiatown generated a cultural flowering unequalled in the urban history of South Africa. Principally in the pages of *Drum* magazine and the *Bantu World*, Henry Nxumalo, Can Themba, Stanley Motjuadi, Casey Motsisi, Arthur Maimane, Todd Matshikiza, Walter Nhlapo, Nat Nakasa and many others produced the best investigative journalism, short fiction, satirical humour, social and political commentary, and musical criticism South Africa had ever seen. Musical creativity and appreciation and intellectual discussion flourished in the backyards and shebeens. The great dance orchestras, soloists, and song and dance groups of the day packed Sophiatown's clubs, cinemas, and halls. Even as a memory, Sophiatown serves as a symbol; a legendary point of reference for an older generation of black writers and artists of every sort. Today, amid growing racial and pol-

itical tension, a number of African performers and organizers are re-
newing the quest for artistic and professional autonomy that
Sophiatown embodied. Watered by the spirit of Black Consciousness,
a new creative growth has sprouted and, like the thorny aloe, flourishes in the barren landscape of apartheid.

Notes

1   Andre Proctor, 'Class struggle, segregation and the city: a history of
    Sophiatown, 1905–1940', in B. Bozzoli, Johannesburg, 1979, p. 57.
2   Ibid., p. 62.
3   Ibid., p. 81.
4   Ibid., p. 76.
5   Mia Brandel-Syrier, Reeftown Elite, London, 1971, p. 60.
6   Inkundla ya Bantu, 17 June 1944.
7   John Storm Roberts, Black Music of Two Worlds, New York, 1972, p. 245.
8   Alan P. Merriam, 'African music', in W. Bascom and M. Herskovits
    (eds), Continuity and Change in African Cultures, Chicago, 1959.
9   Charles Adams, Ethnography of Basotho Evaluative Behavior in the Cognitive
    Domain Lipapadi (Games), Phd thesis, Indiana 1974, p. 209.
10 E. J. Collins, 'Post-war popular band music in West Africa', African Arts
    10 (3), (1977).
11 Bantu World, 23 September 1939.
12 Ibid., 11 January 1941.
13 G. P. Lestrade, 'Traditional literature', in I. Schapera (ed.), The Bantu-
    Speaking Tribes of South Africa, London, 1937, p. 194.
14 Robert Toll, Blacking Up, New York, 1974.
15 Bantu World, 4 February 1940.
16 Ibid., 27 May 1944.
17 Ike Brookes, interview, 23 May 1977.
18 Ilanga Lase Natal, 18 May 1946.
19 Essop Patel (ed.), The World of Nat Nakasa, Johannesburg, 1975, p. 21.
20 Proctor, 'Class struggle, segregation and the city', p. 81.
21 A. A. Mensah, 'Jazz – the round trip', Jazz Forschung (Jazz Research),
    1971/1972, p. 128.
22 Todd Matshikiza, Drum, July 1957.
23 Drum, August 1955.
24 Bantu World, 12 July 1941.
25 Ibid., 19 April 1941.
26 Ralph Trewhela, interview, 9 August 1976.
27 Elkin Sithole, Zulu Music as a Reflection of Social Change, M.A. dissertation
    Wesleyan, 1971.
28 D. K. Rycroft, 'The new "town" music of Southern Africa', Recorded Folk
    Music, 1, September/October (1958), p. 55.
29 D. K. Rycroft, 'Zulu male traditional singing', African Music, I, 4 (1957),
    pp. 33–5; and personal communication, 1981.
30 Ibid.
31 Bantu World, 20 August 1954.

32 *Drum*, November 1957.

33 Ntemi Piliso, interview, 22 November 1976.

34 Trevor Huddleston, *Naught For Your Comfort*, New York, 1956, p. 34.

35 M. Wilson and A. Mafeje, *Langa*, Cape Town, 1963, p. 22.

36 W. J. Burchell, *Travels in the Interior of Southern Africa*, volume II, London, 1822, p. 421.

37 P. R. Kirby, *The Musical Instruments of the Native Races of South Africa*, Johannesburg, 1965; orig. 1934, p. 112.

38 *Drum*, November, 1957.

39 Roberts, *Black Music of Two Worlds*, pp. 257–8.

40 Gerhard Kubik, *The Kachamba Brothers Band*, Manchester, 1974, pp. 1, 10–13.

41 Rycroft, 'The new "town" music', p. 56.

42 Kubik, *The Kachamba Brothers Band*, p. 24.

43 Fr. Dave Dargie, 'A theoretical approach to composition in Xhosa style', in *Papers Presented at the Second Symposium on Ethnomusicology*, ILAM, Grahamstown, 1982, p. 20.

44 Aaron Lerole, interview, 28 December 1976.

45 *Bantu World*, 8, 22 May, 1954.

46 Hugh Tracey, interview, 10 June 1975.

47 *Cape Argus*, 12 November 1954.

48 *Bantu World*, 9 August 1952.

49 *Ilanga Lase Natal*, 16, 19 August 1952.

50 *Ibid.*, 11 January, 2 April 1947.

51 Peter Rezant tells a similar story about the Merry Blackbirds *cf.* Muff Andersson, *Music in the Mix*, Johannesburg, 1981, p. 24.

52 Anthony Sampson, *Drum*, London, 1956, p. 108.

53 *Ibid.*, p. 103.

54 Nathan Mdledle, *Weekend World*, 12 June 1954.

55 *Drum*, April 1962.

56 D. K. Rycroft, 'African music in Johannesburg: African and non-African features', *Journal of the International Folk Music Council*, IX (1959), p. 25.

57 Andersson, *Music in the Mix*, pp. 31–32.

58 Sampson, *Drum*, p. 228.

59 David Coplan, 'The African musician and the development of the Johannesburg entertainment industry', *Journal of Southern African Studies*, 5, 2, (April 1979), p. 149.

60 *Bantu World*, 19 December 1953.

61 Patel, *The World of Nat Nakasa*, pp. 89–90.

62 N. Hentoff and N. Shapiro, *Hear Me Talkin' To Ya*, New York, 1955, p. 177.

63 Andersson, *Music in the Mix*, p. 41.

64 Programme, Johannesburg Bantu Music Festival, October 1948.

65 D. K. Rycroft, personal communication, 1980.

66 Wilson, Silgee, interview, 16 September 1976.

67 *Bantu World*, 5 March 1955.

68 Lucas Makhema, interview, 22 April 1978.

69 Programme, *African Jazz and Variety*, 1959.

70 *Cape Argus*, 5 January 1965.

71   Johannesburg *Star*, 4 March 1961.
72   Alfred Herbert, *Star*, 4 March 1961.
73   *Bantu World*, 15 February 1956.
74   *Drum*, December 1959.
75   *Drum*, August 1957.
76   Harry Bloom, *King Kong*, London, 1961, pp. 52, 65.
77   Johannesburg *Star*, 7 August 1959.
78   Robert Muller, quoted in Andersson, *Music in the Mix*, p. 34.
79   Andersson, *Music in the Mix*, p. 34.
80   Mensah, 'Jazz – the round trip', p. 134.
81   *Bantu World*, 15 May 1954.
82   Quoted in Y. Huskisson, *Bantu Composers of Southern Africa*, Johannesburg, 1969, p. 98.
83   Hentoff and Shapiro, *Hear Me Talkin' To Ya*, p. 330.
84   Nathan Mdledle, *Bantu World*, 13 March 1954.
85   *Ilanga Lase Natal*, 16 August 1952.
86   Bloke Modisane, *Blame Me On History*, London, 1963, p. 59.
87   *Voice of Africa*, May 1950.
88   Oscar Mvungana, *Bantu World*, 20 August 1955.
89   Andrew Tracey, quoted in Andersson, *Music in the Mix*, p. 13.
90   *cf.* J. Clegg, 'The music of Zulu immigrant workers in Johannesburg – a focus on concertina and guitar', in *Papers Presented at the Symposium on Ethnomusicology*, Grahamstown, 1981, p. 6.
91   Huddleston, *Naught For Your Comfort*, p. 137.

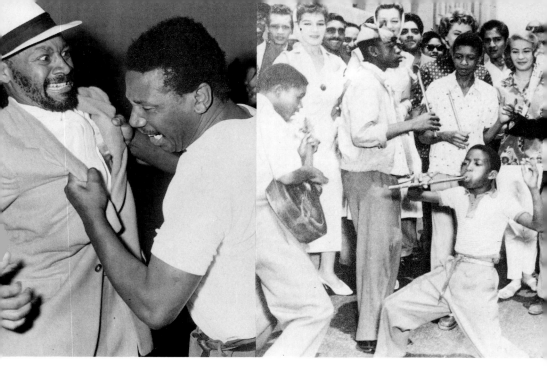

26 Nathan Mdebele (right) in the title role of the
musical King Kong, rehearses with Stephen
Mallow, who plays his manager

27 Famous at ten years old: Lemmy Mabaso,
penny whistler in King Kong

28 Soweto: a view of the prison-like housing of the migrant single men's quarters

29 Early Mabusa, great jazz drummer, in the 1950s

30 Kippie 'Morolong' Moeketsi, virtuoso alto saxophonist, in Soweto 1975

31 Chris McGregor's Blue Notes, winners of the 1963 Cold Castle festival jazz band prize, visit Britain: Dudu Pukwana (alto saxophone) Mongezi Feza (trumpet), Johnny Dyani (bass) Chris McGregor (piano), not shown Louis Moholo (drums)

32 *Abdullah Ibrahim (Dollar Brand)*

33 *The author performing with Malombo: percussionist, Gabriel 'Mabee' Thobejane and virtuoso guitarist, Philip Thabane*

34 *The Drive, Soweto, 1975*

35 *Hugh Masekela, internationally successful trumpeter*

7 Township music and musicians

THE year 1960 witnessed the end of Sophiatown, the departure of *King Kong*, and the massacre at Sharpeville. The bleak, dusty subdivisions of Soweto took centre stage in the struggle for urban black culture in South Africa. By 1970, Soweto's population approached one million, half of whom could be considered fully urbanised, with no rural ties. Yet almost a third had no legal right to live there, and two-thirds were officially below the Poverty Datum Line, the level of income needed for minimal family subsistence.[1] Today, wages have risen considerably, but the quality of life in Soweto is not much improved. The townships have no centre, no downtown, few stores and fewer public amenities, and only a few thousand jobs in small neighbourhood businesses. Each day hundreds of thousands of Sowetonians ride the dangerous, overcrowded trains to work in Johannesburg. Any person who was not born in the area or has not worked continuously for a single employer for ten years, can be 'endorsed out' – forced to leave the area – if he cannot find work. All face the threat of immediate arrest of their passes are not in order, widowed or divorced women face eviction, and the waiting list for housing grows daily. In apartheid's final solution to the Native Problem, all urban Africans may lose their South African citizenship and be deported to 'independent homelands' they may never have seen.

Since Soweto is divided into twenty-two sections for Sotho, Tswana, Pedi, Zulu, Xhosa, Swazi, Ndebele, Venda, and Shangaan speakers, with only five mixed areas, neighbours from the old locations were most often separated in the move to the townships. Living among strangers in individual houses, families easily become suspicious, antagonistic, and afraid of one another. Guns are scarce and illegal, yet Soweto has long had a higher rate of murder and serious assault than most large American cities. The efforts of the houseproud middle class to improve their dwellings and establish peaceful, affluent neighbourhoods in Dube and Mofolo can do little to counteract the atmosphere of insecurity that pervades the townships.

Time and again Africans have created genuine communities in South African cities out of a determination to establish a permanent place as recognised members of urban society, and each time the government has knocked their neighbourhoods down. Recently even distant Alexandra was partly destroyed, many of its families endorsed out of Johannesburg, packed off to Soweto, or divided; husbands and wives made to live apart in single-sex workers' hostels. The government does this not merely to make room for white expansion and to spare white communities the psychological discomfort of proximity to black residential areas. Soweto and the dozens of more or less identical townships throughout South Africa are physically designed to facilitate the control of urban Africans and the suppression of violent protests like the 'Soweto Uprising' of 1976–7 (see plate 28). Just as deliberately, their very barrenness and lack of amenities, their labour camp atmosphere, are intended to discourage Africans from identifying with the urban areas, from calling the city their home.

Despite these conditions, authentic community life has taken shape in Soweto and some other urban townships over the past two decades. Social institutions like the *stokfel* and shebeen still flourish, despite municipal bar-lounges and liquor stores that have operated since 1962. Voluntary associations abound, including independent and mission churches, sports, school, and youth clubs, welfare societies, amateur choirs, and in some areas, newly powerful labour unions that have fought for and won official recognition. Class differences have become more pronounced due to the growth of a skilled professional, salaried, or entrepreneurial middle class, and influx control enforcement that hinders the urbanisation of industrial workers. There are several large male hostels in Soweto, though most migrants are housed nearer to their places of work. Class is expressed in lifestyle, particularly in modes of recreation and entertainment, and the celebration of family events such as weddings and funerals, as well as in material possessions.[2]

With the significant exception of popular township musical theatre, treated in the next chapter, there is little in the way of autonomous black show business in Soweto or Johannesburg itself. Soweto in the late 1970s had one established nightclub, one hotel, one cinema, a few discos, Jabulani Amphitheatre and Orlando Stadium for outdoor concerts, and a small number of community halls. Most of the musical shows are sponsored by recording companies displaying their top recording artists. During the 1960s and 1970s, the staple of these ever-popular shows were the *mbaqanga* or *mqashiyo* song and dance groups like Mahlathini and his Queens, backed by the Makhona Tshole Band, the all-male Abafana base Qhudeni, and many others. Whether presented in the townships or at black cinemas in the city like the Rio, whites cannot attend these shows without special permission, and few indeed would choose to go. The *mbaqanga* shows are directed at migrants and partly urbanised industrial and domestic workers who retain ties to rural culture and take little interest in the American influenced soul, pop, and jazz music more popular among fully urbanised Sowetonians. Under the direction of music and dance coaches working for record company producers like GRC's H. V. Nzimande, the *mbaqanga* groups rehearse constantly, and put more energy into their stage routines than into the making of recordings.

Most vocalists are drawn from Soweto's working class, and some are even migrants in search of better paid, more enjoyable, and prestigious employment than in the mines, offices, and factories. On a given evening you can find any number of neighbourhood 'backyard bands' in Soweto, practising for a chance to audition for black studio talent scouts. Rupert Bopape of Gallo-Mavuthela searched for talent in the mines and hostels, and his successor West Nkosi actively recruits performers in the rural areas, like the Basotho Lihoba Group. Even if singers, dancers and musicians present themselves at the studio as a unit, they are most often regrouped according to the producer's concepts of sound, style, and presentation. New groups are given copies of recent *mbaqanga* hits to imitate, and rehearse for a year before they can go on tour.

Groups tend to be multi-ethnic, reflecting the blending of various local African musical traditions in the urban areas over the past several decades, as well as producers' efforts to find musical 'common denominators' among the heterogeneous urban audience. Vocalists are kept as a unit for all performances. Instrumentalists, on the other hand, are used independently according to the demands of a particular recording or live show. The months of practice that go into the most polished acts encourage producers to keep groups together, particularly once they have become popular and recognisable to the public. No such group integrity is necessary for recordings, of course. Average pay in the late 1970s for *mbaqanga* performers was £12 10s per show for women and £19 for men, with £10 flat fee plus 2.5 per cent royalties and £8 10s monthly allowance, with no pay for rehearsals. Clearly a lot depends upon record sales and the willingness of the record companies to abide by reasonable royalty agreements. Stars like Mahlathini are not only wealthy but can afford to resist interference from studio producers by switching companies or setting up production arrangements of their own.

Mbaqanga shows generally have several segments, proceeding from the most traditional in music, dance, and costume towards the more Westernised. Songs in the opening segment begin with a lead guitar introduction, followed by the bass melody pattern based on the F–C–G⁷–C ostinato formula played over a bouncing 8/8 township rhythm. Piano or accordion lines are laid on top in African staggered fashion, each part entering the phrase cycle at different points. The traditional appreciation for incremental repetition with slight but important variations is basic to *mbaqanga* as well. Song lyrics consist of a few short couplets, for example:

> The girls of this time
> They slip into the bush
>   and get pregnant
> And then come to the mother
>   and say 'help me'.

Most arousing for the audience is the correspondence between body movement, gesture, melody, and rhythm. Steps and movements are taken from both traditional and township dances, and in a manner at once forceful, humorous and erotic, make visual the bounce and drive of *mbaqanga's* constrasting lines and rhythms. In later segments, vocalists change from sneakers, shorts, tee shirts and visored caps to colourful clerical robes for an upbeat *mbaqanga* zionist hymn, disco gear for a soul number in Zulu, Sotho or Xhosa, and evening wear for a recent black American hit in English. Most shows include a variety of performers and soul and rock styles as well as *mbaqanga*. Many have a stand-up comic as master of ceremonies, and musical segments are separated by comic skits. The emphasis is on heavily physical, even acrobatic satire of snobbish, educated Africans, police, township hipsters, the war between the sexes, and other familiar characters and themes. Explicit satire of government policy or whites is carefully excluded, though during the period of unrest in 1976–7, songs using words like 'power' or 'freedom' were often greeted by raised-fist salutes and shouts of *amandla eyethu* ('power is ours') from the audience.

Among the most authentic and intriguing *mbaqanga* performers are the Zulu guitarist John Bhengu (Phuzhushukela) and his male dance group. The Zulu solo guitar song tradition goes back at least to the *amagxagxa* proletarian guitarists of the 1920s, and *mazkande* (from Afrikaans: *musikant*; 'musician') music, traditional tunes performed on Western instruments, may have started in the nineteenth-century. The early mode of performance called *ukuvamba*,[3] which involved only the strumming of a few basic chords, was first widely popularised in the 1940s by two Ndebele singers from Bulawayo, Geroge Sibanda and Josaya Hadebe. Both these pioneers sold their composers' rights for flat fees and died penniless, confirming the old

Zulu proverb, *Isiginci asakh'umuzi*; 'a guitar does not build a homestead'.[4]

The guitarists of that period constructed their self-image, though not their music, or the model of singing cowboy guitarists in American Western films. In the late 1940s, a young Zulu guitarist, John Bhengu, who was much influenced by Hadebe, appeared in Durban and began winning street guitar competitions with his innovative picking (*ukupika*) style. These competitions still take place wherever migrant Zulu musicians gather, and as in competitive dancing, the prize is prestige and the assertion of superior manliness (*ubudoda*) rather than money. Among the criteria of excellence are first the inventiveness of the *iihlabo*, a short introduction of virtuoso plucking, popularised by Bhengu, that runs over the melody and scale that the player will use for his song. Second is *ubugaku*, the originality of melody and lyrics in a new song; and third *ukubonga*, the way a player praises his people, his home, his chief and himself. Early songs were traditional one-string bow (*umakhweyana*) tunes adapted to the guitar. Before long the nostalgic songs about country life were replaced by lyrics that confronted the problems of urbanism, apartheid, and migrant working conditions.[5]

On a visit to Johannesburg in the early 1950s, John Bhengu met the Troubador producer Cuthbert Matumba, and the result was his first recording, *Ilanga Libalela* (The Blazing Sun). Later he moved over to Trutone and then GRC under H. V. Nzimande, who took Bhengu's austerely authentic style and backed it up with a full *mbaqanga* band and three male dancers in traditional dress for live concerts. The result was immediately popular and Bhengu became both famous and wealthy enough to buy cars as well as a homestead, under the stage name Phuzhushukela ('drink sugar'). The amplified instrumentation provided Phuzhushukela's music with compelling, danceable rhythms and improved its appeal to African working-class audiences.

Though his playing and singing retain their original integrity, Phuzhushukela's current stage appearances and recordings clearly represent an artistic compromise with commercial hype. Significantly, his dancers do not reproduce but rather broadly satirise traditional dance. Acrobatic turns by male dancers in warrior dress are greeted by screams of laughter from the appreciative audience. This kind of traditional burlesque began with early mine dancers and developed in urban competitions between Zulu migrants, in which losers performed comic steps to ease their discomfort.

Under Bopape, Mahlathini too originally performed in traditional dress, backed not by males but by an urban all-female quartet, thus originating the now pervasive *simanje-manje* style. *Mbaqanga* audiences enjoy traditional performance styles, but in their urban circumstances also require some psychic distance from its 'primitive' associations.

Displayed on a stage backed by electric guitars and saxophones, it takes on the appearance of unreality, a satire in which the listener takes pleasure while maintaining a comfortable cultural distance. Other popular all-male *mbaqanga* groups, Amaswazi Ermelo and Abafana Basishingishane, also specialise in comical parodies of traditional dance.[6]

Educated Africans do not attend *mbaqanga* shows or buy Mahlathini's records, but they are at least in two minds about them. On the one hand they regard *mbaqanga*, with some justification, as the stagnant, commercially processed performance aspect of apartheid homelands ideology, the musical equivalent of Bantu Education. On the other hand, *mbaqanga* retains some of its original meaning as the Africans' own music. It has been developed by Africans out of their own cultural resources, and the size and enthusiasm of its mass audience are too great to be dismissed as mere self-deception. As a result, some of the most popular, talented and innovative black rock and fusion groups such as Harari have derived creative inspiration from *mbaqanga* musicians like Phuzhushukela.[7]

A case in point is the contemporary *ingom'ebusuku* group Ladysmith Black Mambazo, who sing in the style called *isicatamiya* ('a stalking approach; a surprise attack') or *cothoz' mfana* ('sneaky boy'). This twelve-member Zulu–Swazi unaccompanied male choir is made up of two groups of brothers and cousins from the Shabalala and Mazibuko families. The name is derived from their hometown of Ladysmith in Natal, plus the name of Aaron Lerole's old group, Black Mambazo, added because their leader Joseph Shabalala, likens their vocal phrasing to the sharp attack of an axe (*imbazo*).[8] An admirer of Mahlathini and Lerole, Shabalala has been seriously interested in developing *isicatamiya* since his days as a migrant worker in Durban in the 1950s. After getting together in the early 1970s, his group began to harmonise and polish their vocal style after the manner of *mbaqanga* groups with the help of SABC broadcaster Alex Buthelezi.

Ladysmith Black Mambazo went on to sign with Gallo-Mavuthela, where West Nkosi turned them into one of the top-selling recording groups in the company's history. Their music is truly beautiful by Zulu or Western standards, full of soulful glides, sweet tone, rhythmic variety, and cut-and-run phrasing that befits their name *Mambazo*. The term *isicatamiya* fits their lyrics as well as their vocal style, as they creep up by indirection and then stun with sudden clarity. Though they are favourites of the SABC because they sing mostly of religious and idyllic rural themes[9] in elegant, figurative Zulu, there is more to Ladysmith Black Mambazo than first meets the ear. Joseph Shabalala is highly respected among his listeners because he is *qinile*; worldly-wise, cunning, with a wiry voice that sounds older than his modest years. His tone and lyrics are a blend of melancholy, wistfulness and self-assertion that ineffably captures the dilemma, the trapped, contingent quality of migrant life. The title song of the group's album *Isitimela* (Train) laments:

Here is the train; it has gone, O father
It is going to Pietermaritzburg
They will weep, they will remain behind,
Sorrowful over us . . .

The heavens are trembling
If you marry a lady, she will remain behind weeping
They will remain behind, sad over us . . . .

and in *Khulekani we Zinsizwa* (Salute, Young Men!):

We see you young men
We see you young girls
Says brother Mshengu
We don't sing songs
We blaze away!
There in Johannesburg,
They know of us . . . .[10]

Ladysmith Black Mambazo are especially popular with the older generation of the semi-urbanised working class. Their more Westernised and urbanised peers remain faithful to mainstream jazz. The early 1960s were an especially difficult period for jazz musicians, yet perhaps never before or since has South Africa had as many players or as much dedication to creative expression in this art form. The veteran big band and *mbaqanga* jazz players could at first still get work in the studios backing early *simanje-manje* groups like the Dark City Sisters. Producers like Bopape and Matumba, however, disliked the independence and professional demands of the sophisticated city jazzmen.

With the new popularity of performers like Mahlathini, the producers moved to more neo-traditional players who obeyed them like studio *indunas* (headmen). King Force Silgee, Zakes Nkosi, Ellison Themba, Ntemi Piliso, and a few others stayed on to help organise and rehearse the new groups, but most had no studio contracts and changed to freelance recording with pickup ensembles. Among these were Early Mabuza (see plate 29), Eric Nomvete, Mongezi Feza, Mackay Davashe, Kippie Moeketsi, Gideon Nxumalo, Cyril Magubane, Blythe Mbitshana, Alan Kwela, Elijah Nkonyane, Dalton Khanyile, Skip Phahlane, and many other great jazz talents.

While Charlie Parker and Dizzy Gillespie were still much admired, American players who looked to Africa for inspiration like John Coltrane were leading South African jazzmen to reexamine their own indigenous resources. A major innovator in this direction was

Gideon Nxumalo, a university-trained pianist and jazz composer from Kimberley influenced by Dave Brubeck. In the late 1950s, Nxumalo composed *kwela* tunes for penny whistler Spokes Mashiyane and gained recognition for his 'This is Bantu Jazz' radio programme over SABC. In the 1960s, he taught the piano at Dorkay House and organised a series of groups using Kippie Moeketsi (alto), Dennis Nene (flute), Chooks Tshukudu (bass), Jeff 'Hoojah' Cartiers (bass), Mackay Davashe (tenor), Churchill Jolobe (drums) and Gordon Mfandu (drums). Nxumalo's efforts to use traditional instruments like the Chopi xylophone (*timbila*) and to combine traditional musical features with mainstream jazz on recordings like *Gideon Plays* (JPL02), *Jazz Fantasia*, and *Alibulali/uDanayi* (HMV JP2129) were not well understood by the public at the time, but remain among the most refreshingly experimental in South African jazz. Enduringly successful players like Dollar Brand and Victor Ndlazilwane clearly learned from him.

The untimely deaths of Nxumalo and Mackay Davashe in the early 1970s were probably hastened by their weakness for alcohol, a common problem among jazz musicians. Perhaps no personal career better represents the hardships faced by creative jazzmen and the contradictions in their relationship to the urban African audience than that of alto virtuoso Kippie 'Morolong' Moeketsi (see plate 30). Born in Johannesburg in 1925, Moeketsi had no real contact with music until he picked up his brother's clarinet at the age of 20. Over the next two years he taught himself the instrument and learned to read staff notation, while listening to the greats of American swing and local bands like the Jazz Maniacs, Rhythm Clouds, and Harlem Swingsters. In 1947 he joined the Band in Blue under Bob Twala which played *marabi*, *mbaqanga* jazz, swing and dixieland in the rough shantytown and location dancehalls.

Kippie was serious about music and the prostitution, drunkenness, and violence of the halls frightened and depressed him. Knife-wielding *tsotsis* preyed on other patrons and forced the band to play until dawn or destroyed their instruments. Kippie broke with the band in a dispute over the pay for their appearance in the *Zonk* film and after a brief stint with the Harlem Swingsters, joined Mackay Davashe's Shantytown Sextet in 1950. The band toured with the Manhattan Brothers, and Kippie earned a solid reputation for hot swing solos on his new alto sax, the instrument of his idol Charlie 'Yardbird' Parker.

Like some players in New York, Kippie not only tried to play like Bird but to dress, talk, and act like him. Kippie played the role of the hard-drinking, irresponsible, arrogant jazz genius, damaging his reputation in both the black community and black show business, where the erratic, alienated hipster image seemed conceited, anti-social and amoral. On tour in the Cape in 1954, pianist Todd Matshikiza suddenly left the band and was replaced by Dollar Brand, who became Kippie's closest friend. Together they listened and experimented with the music of Parker, Thelonius Monk, Duke Ellington, Bud Powell, Coleman Hawkins, Don Byas, Lester Young, Ben Webster, and other Americans. Together with Hugh Masekela (trumpet) and Jonas Gwangwa (trombone), they formed the Jazz Epistles and at last played with complete artistic freedom, though most often before a white or integrated audience.

When Mackay Davashe formed the Jazz Dazzlers Orchestra for *King Kong*, Kippie was all set to go to London as star soloist. Just before the show left Johannesburg in 1960, *tsotsis* who thought Kippie too conceited hit him on the head with a brick and he was in hospital for several weeks. Joining the show late in London, Kippie began drinking and fighting with other members of the company and wound up in a mental hospital. Unlike his hero Charlie Parker, Kippie did not escape electric shock treatment, which he claimed badly affected his ability to send musical ideas from his mind to his fingers.

Returning to South Africa, he appeared in United Artists' Township Jazz series and then rejoined the Jazz Dazzlers on their return in 1961. But the dance halls were gone and the city clubs and auditoriums closed to black performers due to pressure from white musicians and the tightening of Separate Amenities provisions of Group Areas legislation. The only major venues left were big concerts and outdoor jazz festivals in Soweto, mostly sponsored by South African Breweries with the organisational support of United Artists.

The first of these famous Cold Castle Jazz Festivals was held in 1961, and the Jazz Epistles won first prize for jazz band, though other categories like *mbaqanga* were included as well. United Artists managed to get permission for a major series of concerts at City Hall in 1962, where Kippie played with Gideon Nxumalo's Quintet. City venues were preferred because they were safer and transport was better between the city and Soweto than around the townships themselves. At the 1962 Cold Castle festival, Kippie played with Mackay Davashe's Jazz Dazzlers, who won the £200 first prize.

The 1963 festival attracted 50 000 fans and the jazz band prize went to pianist Chris MacGregor's integrated big band, the Blue Notes, and their famous Afro-jazz composition 'Pondo Blues' (Gallotone New Sound NSC1011) (see plate 31). Unfortunately there was violence both inside and outside the stadium, and at the 1964 festival six men died outside the gates in a confrontation between township gangs. The Cold Castle series ended, but the festival format remained the only workable commercial setting for live jazz, and festivals have been held in townships near various cities every year since.

191

Festivals have always suffered from social, organisational, and programme conflicts. Those that try to attract a large audience by featuring jazz, soul, *mbaqanga*, and even choral groups on a single programme risk disruption by listeners who prefer one type of music over another. Those that present only jazz bands risk a poor turnout. The solution today seems to lie in hiring a limited number of popular, versatile groups who draw their music from a variety of local and foreign sources. Sadly, poor arrangements, bad sound systems, lack of accommodation and transport for performers and fans, no-shows, police harassment, and a get-rich-quick attitude among promoters and musicians ruin many potentially successful festivals. The ultimate problem, of course, is apartheid, which makes an autonomous, self-supporting, culturally relevant black music world impossible and creates social conditions in which frustration and violence in black urban communities cannot be excluded from major performance occasions.[11]

Disgusted with South Africa's dying jazz scene, Dollar Brand (Abdullah Ibrahim) fled to Europe in 1962, leaving a bitterly disappointed Kippie Moeketsi behind. Many smaller festivals were poorly organised, audiences were small, and players often stranded with no pay. Sickened by the violence and exploitation, Kippie was expelled from a series of groups for drinking and arguing. After finishing second to Early Mabuza's group at Pretoria's Ga Rankua township festival in 1964, Kippie had his alto confiscated during a tour to Bulairayo with Ben 'Satch' Masunga's Soweto Revue, *Back In Your Own Back Yard*. He did not pick up a saxophone again until 1971.

Large numbers of other jazzmen were also pressured into exile, retirement or an early grave. With the encouragement of Dorkay House artistic director Corney Mabaso, guitarist Alan Kwela, and others, Kippie returned to the performing scene during the last decade. Though his erratic behaviour still got him into trouble with other musicians, he freelanced regularly, and his recordings with Dollar Brand, Pat Matshikiza and others showed that the old brilliance was still there, darkened and refined by the bitter frustrations of the jazz life. His solo on 'Memories of You' from his 1973 album with Dollar Brand, *Dollar Brand + 3 with Kippie Moeketsi* (Gallo-Soultown KRS113) remains a gut-wrenching cry of the heart against what South Africa has done to its black artists. Kippie's funeral in April, 1983 attracted thousands of mourners.

Despite the frustrations, new young players continue to emerge, teaming up with the veterans to give both continuity and vitality to South African jazz. Jazz has survived the last twenty years primarily by fusing with various more popular styles of *mbaqanga*, indigenous soul, rock and popular music. The Xhosa *mbaqanga* jazz of Victor Ndlazilwane's Jazz Ministers has survived his death, and new offshoots like Dinotsi have expanded his unique style. Highly professional groups like Port Elizabeth's Soul Jazzmen and Johannes-burg's The Drive regularly won first prize at festivals in the late 1970s with their blend of jazz, American soul and *mbaqanga*. Talented free-lancers like saxophonists Winston Mankunku Ngozi, known for his Coltrane-inspired classic, *Yakhal' Inkomo*, and Mike Makgalemele also blend American funk and soul with South African jazz. Nowadays they tour with other jazz greats like Dennis Mphale (trumpet) backing popular performers like soul singer Babsy Mlangeni. Zakes Nkosi con-tinued to appear with his City Jazz Nine and record with studio *mbaqanga* groups like Abafana Besibaya right up until his death in 1982. Zakes' funeral, like Kippie Moeketsi's, was one of the largest ever seen in black Johannesburg. Many jazz performers get regular work in the popular township musical theatre of Gibson Kente and others.

In brief, jazz maintains its vitality in South Africa, now as in the past, through the versatility and professionalism of its performers. Although some might consider that backing *mbaqanga* or soul music is a waste of serious creative talent, the resulting cross-fertilisation actually reinvigorates all the styles involved. Most importantly, it ties both jazz and fusion music to indigenous roots and provides some opportunity for the continuing self-definition of black South African musical culture. A few successful groups, like the now disbanded Spirits Rejoice, play purely American jazz-fusion, but the most popu-lar jazz recordings still have something South African about them.

Dollar Brand returned to South Africa in 1968, having gained formal training and top-level experience in Europe and America (see plate 32). With great imagination and technical skill, he took an old jazz *mbaqanga* melody composed by trumpeter Elijah Nkonyane in the late 1950s, and combined it with *marabi*, Xhosa ragtime and hymn melodies, Cape Coloured folk music, *kwela*, American swing, and township rhythms to create *Mannenburg* (The Sun SRK 786134) in 1974, a record that began a new trend with old materials in black South Afri-can urban music. *Mannenburg's* enormous success was due to its com-bination of so many forms of South African music into a coherent whole with which listeners of all kinds could identify. The message to the South African music world was clear – an authentic syncretism in tune with the cultural reality of black experience is potentially the most creative and marketable direction that contemporary black music can take. Innovative performers must closely follow the cultural aspira-tions of their communities if they are to play an important role in Afri-can self-definition.

The most popular forms are of black city music today is imported from the United States and Jamaica, but local soul, rock, and fusion styles also have a solid and growing following. Unlike jazz, these popular styles and performers cannot be discussed without reference to South African's white-controlled recording, concert and broadcasting industries, which greatly determine what black people will perform and hear.

Jazz is not as susceptible to media industry control, since instrumental music is not censored and most jazz players either stay out of the studios or record with independent black producers like Rashid Vally or small recording companies seeking to provide alternatives to the music of giants like Gallo-Africa. The lack of studio access and effective distribution for serious jazz is, of course, a form of interference and censorship in itself.

I have reviewed the ways broadcasting and recording industries reinforce the ideology and goals of apartheid both here and elsewhere,[12] and Muff Andersson[13] provides an excellent account of how capitalist media and state broadcasting combine to alienate performers from their art and their communities and exploit black performing arts and artists for economic and political profit. Briefly, musicians can only hope to achieve professional security through the recording industry, which prefers to regard music as a commodity without cultural integrity. Despite new royalty provisions, contracts are written to protect the profits and rights of the companies, not the performers, the majority of whom see their contracts only once – when they are signed. The state Radio Bantu rigorously censors any music referring to explicit sex, the reality of urban African existence, or social and political issues. African censors are employed to expunge any township slang or oblique reference to politics. Eager to get air time, the producers and performers pre-censor themselves or risk rejection by the SABC. The supposedly independent Swazi and homeland commercial radio stations play no music of political or cultural relevance. Radio Bantu and the new black TV channels are designed to reinforce apartheid homeland policy and inculcate the government's version of the beauties of rural life and the evil of cities among Africans. Swazi Radio, Capital Radio, Radio 702, and Bophutatswana Radio do play more progressive groups, like Harari, and exercise less censorship. The bulk of their fare, however, like that of the white-oriented Radio 5, is more on the order of musical pacification, 'entertainment' to make the frustrations of urban youth and workers more immediately bearable.

Despite efforts to expropriate African performance culture and to use it to impose an apartheid version of African identity, there are ways of resisting. Many of South Africa's most popular and progressive groups, like the Drive, Juluka, and the Afro-rock group Harari, began with independent black producers and resist signing with the major studios unless they are given full control of their music (see plate 34). Many groups continue to produce political, socially relevant, authentic township music even though it will never be played on radio. African record shops have great influence on sales, and once word gets out about a politically meaningful recording like the Minerals' *Sweet Soweto* or Era's *Manyano*, it will sell thousands of copies despite lack of airplay. Explicitly political foreign styles like the reggae of Jimmy Cliff, Bob Marley, and Peter Tosh also sell well in the townships. Musical cries for justice, recognition and social action from black American performers drawing on the spiritualistic tradition of black religious music, like those of Harold Melvin and the Blue Notes and the Staple Singers, become anthems for township youth.

The most popular South African soul performers, including Steve Kekana, The Soul Brothers, Kori Moraba, Babsi Mlangeni, and the late Mpharanyana sell hundreds of thousands of records with music that combines the American soul ballad with *mbaqanga*. Andersson[14] regrets the lack of politically relevant lyrics in their songs, but they have established a new style based on rhythmic and emotional appeal that may be put to more critical use by new performers less concerned with media exposure or sales. What Andersson fails to recognise is the importance of musical form as well as lyrical content in the cultural politics of black South African music. Songs whose words have little explicit political reference may communicate a sense of cultural pride and creative development vital to African identity formation and black political consciousness. The two groups most representative of this developing African cultural self-consciousness are Malombo and Harari.

Philip Thabane, founder and guiding spirit of Malombo, is the son of an Ndebele mother and Tswana father who grew up in Pretoria's Mamelodi Township. As a youngster Philip began playing the guitar by himself, picking up a variety of musical ideas from the neo-traditional, *mbaqanga*, African Christian, and American jazz styles that floated about the township. Leaving school after Standard One, Thabane spent his time improvising and blending musical elements into an impressionistic, loosely structured and intensely personal style.

He first appeared publicly at the age of thirteen in 1958 at a variety show in Pretoria, and in 1959 formed the Lullabyelanders, a group with four male voices backed up by Philip's idiosyncratic guitar. The group disintegrated but in 1960 Philip began working with another member of the group, Abie Cindi, who now played silver flute, and African mallet drummer Julian Bahula to create the unique Afro-jazz sound of the Malombo Jazz Men.

Malombo is a Venda word referring to ancestral and other spirits consulted by traditional diviners, and signifies the deeply African spiritual attitude that the group brought to their music. While they rehearsed, developing a new, expressionistic, multi-traditional

African music, Philip won successive first prizes in the solo instrumental category at the 1961, '62 and '63 Cold Castle Jazz Festivals in Soweto. Encouraged by radical poet Sidney Sepamla, the Malombo Jazz Men played as a group at the 1964 festival, sharing the prize with Early Mabuza's Quartet. The music of both groups is immortalised on the now classic recording *Jazz Festival 1964* (EMI Number One N9033).

The music's loose progression of improvised phrases, disjunct melodic and rhythmic lines, and poeticised chanting was puzzling to listeners, who had difficulty explaining its unique appeal. Its roots in neo-traditional music, African church melodies, *marabi*, *mbaqanga*, and the jazz guitar work of Wes Montgomery and John McLaughlin gave it a feeling at once indigenous and rural, contemporary and urban. The key, however, was the powerful and visually dramatic style of live performance. Intensely theatrical poetic recitation was vital to Malombo's music, and the group soon became associated with African cultural nationalism and the emerging political aims of the Black Consciousness Movement. Their initial success led to conflicts within the group, and Julian and Abie were more interested in direct political involvement than was Philip. They split up in 1965, Julian and Abie forming the Malombo Jazz Makers with guitarist Lucky Ranku. This group played for the rallies of the radical South African Students' Organisation (SASO) led by Steve Biko, and Julian and Lucky eventually fled to London in the early 1970s. There they formed a large new group called Jabula, officially linked to the exiled African National Congress.

Philip Thabane meanwhile involved the brilliant natural drummer and dancer Gabriel 'Mabee' Thobejane in his music, and as Malombo this duo revolutionised progressive indigenous music in South Africa from 1965 to 1977. Their first recording appeared in 1968, and in 1971, Philip and Gabriel travelled to the United States where they appeared at clubs and concerts around the country for two years, playing with Miles Davis, Max Roach, Pharoah Sanders, McCoy Tyner, and other first rank jazz musicians. Free of apartheid restrictions, Malombo achieved musical recognition and financial success in America, but Philip, a true son of the townships, began to suffer from creative isolation from the sources of his inspiration. In 1973 he and Gabriel returned home to perform for and learn from their own people in the Transvaal townships. Their international reputation has been enhanced by their album *Pele Pele* (WEA ATC 8003) and their appearance at the New York Newport Jazz Festival in 1977.

Good as they are, their recordings are a poor representation of the electricity and spellbinding virtuosity of their live performances. I had the unique privilege of performing with Malombo as a second percussionist at many of their concerts in the townships and at the Market Café, Johannesburg, during 1976–7 (see plate 33). Philip and

Gabriel kept up a constant, almost competitive musical dialogue on guitar, kalimba ('hand piano'), flute, pennywhistle, and drums. The intensity of Philip's guitar solos and melodic poetic recitation, and Gabriel's percussive power and dynamics with drums, dance, and ankle rattles kept black and white concertgoers alike jumping and shouting on the edges of their seats.

The content of Malombo's music remains a unique contemporary blend of traditional and imported resources symbolising the cultural orientation of Black Consciousness. Thabane's songs, however, refer not to political issues but to a deeper cultural and spiritual sensibility. The song *Khoedi* ('The Moon'), for example, poetically evokes a conflict in the relationship between the singer's own lineage and that of his maternal uncle:

> The moon is out
> My uncle's wife
> You talk too much.[15]

In 1977, personal conflicts led to the dissolution of Thabane and Thobejane's musical partnership, and Philip has now expanded his group to anywhere between five and eleven members, with more traditionally-oriented choreography, percussion, and vocal work. Abie Cindi and Gabriel Thobejane are currently struggling to succeed with their own groups of a similar kind, Afrika and Sakhile respectively. Thabane has been remarkable for his ability to capture a multiracial and international audience while still retaining the respect and goodwill of his township community. Now that Dollar Brand has chosen permanent exile in New York, Thabane is among the few prominent black South African musicians who can move freely between the townships, the white theatre and concert halls, and America and Europe. He accomplishes this by continuing to follow the same unpretentious lifestyle as his Mamelodi neighbours, while avoiding political involvements that might cause the authorities to restrict his appearances or his travel. At the same time, his faithfulness to urban African cultural identity has saved him from social and creative alienation and made him a leader in the musical realisation and shaping of that identity.

A second important group in this respect is the Afro-rock band Harari. Harari began in 1968 with Selby Ntuli (drums) Sipho Mabuse (flute, keyboards) and Alec Khaoli (bass), who called themselves the Beaters until after their successful tour of Zimbabwe in 1976. Changing their name to that of the famous African township near Salisbury (now also called Harari), they continued to develop their exciting and accessible combination of black American funk, progressive rock and African traditional and *mbaqanga* music. Their willingness to forego premature stardom in favour of musical integrity greatly aided their creative development and social integration in their Soweto community. Given freedom by independent producer Rashid Vally, they produced successful albums like *Rufaro* (The Sun – Independent Record GL1874) that spawned a new movement in black South African music.

With the death of Selby Ntuli in 1978, the group had to reorganise, but have emerged stronger than ever with a string of popular live appearances. Moving from Vally to the more commercial Gallo-Africa company has led to some artistic compromise, but songs like *Jikeleza* ('surround') on their album *Kalahari Rock* (Gallo ML4303) match the freshness, power and cultural authenticity of their best previous work. Ostensibly addressed to a 'witch' who is troubling the community, *Jikeleza's* English refrain confronts the white colonial mentality;

> You're surrounding another man's home,
> Why did you leave yours alone?
> You're casting your spell on my soul,
> Why don't you leave me alone?[16]

The group currently features Sipho Mabuse, Alec Khaoli, Oupa Segwai, Thelma Segonah, Masike Mohape and Doc Mathilane. Harari appeals to working-class as well as middle-class Africans, and whether or not their unlooked-for identity as a leading Black Consciousness band can survive the conflict between apartheid cultural repression and the expressive demands of the township audience remains to be seen.

Another group that has learned to walk the political and cultural tight rope with surprising success is Juluka, created by Johnny Clegg and Sipho Mcunu. Clegg is a young white social anthropologist and performer of Zulu guitar, song, and dance who learned Zulu language and performance in the workers' hostels of Johannesburg. During the 1970s, he and his friend Mcunu, a Johannesburg gardener, composer and dancer from Natal, put together an original blend of Zulu rural music and dance, *mbaqanga*, and Western folk guitar music. After some years of struggling, during which Radio Bantu refused to play their records because they considered Clegg's efforts 'an insult to the Zulu and their culture', (really a threat to cultural apartheid) Sipho and Johnny have lately begun taking the multi-racial concert and record scene by storm. With his vast store of knowledge and mastery of Zulu performance culture, Clegg is truly bicultural – a remarkable example of what can be done despite apartheid, and of what might be possible without it.

Of the South African popular groups, Harari or Juluka might be the most likely to achieve significant international success, with their polished yet authentic African-American sounds. Under present conditions, however, it is difficult for any resident South African band to achieve what record companies call the 'Big Overseas'.[17] It is not merely that producers promote imported artists over local talent, encouraging South Africans to play American music better than the Americans even though international audiences are looking for something African as well as accessible and contemporary. It is simply that the international ostracism of apartheid necessarily extends to the performing arts.

In Britain, birthplace of the modern colonial mentality, audiences may accept South African shows, but artists travelling to the United States and continental Europe will be asked about their politics and expected to express opposition to apartheid in their work. If they do so they can expect police harassment and loss of their passports on their return. Many black South Africans cannot travel overseas in any case, thanks to the government's insistence that they get passports from homeland governments which are not recognised internationally. Any successful artist who is allowed to travel overseas and return regularly will be suspected by people in the townships of 'selling out' in some way to the government.

In South Africa, an 'international' black group really means one that appeals to South African whites. Black performers must then choose between limited careers and second-rate treatment in South Africa or exile abroad. The Manhattan Brothers, Miriam Makeba, Letta Mbulu, Hugh Masekela, Dollar Brand, Jonas Gwangwa, Dudu Pukwana, Louis Moholo and Julian Bahula are just a few of the superb talents who have chosen exile, and South Africa is of course the poorer for it (see plates 35, 36 and 37). This most extreme form of alienation of artists from their home communities is in itself a powerful indictment of apartheid. Meanwhile the 'star system' of musical commoditisation aborts personal and artistic development among aspiring performers and discourages artistic professionalism. The political myopia of the white ruling class is revealed in record producers' obsession with finding a black group who can make the Big Overseas, while apartheid prevents international acceptance short of self-exile and strangles the aspirations of black artists at home.

Black city music in South Africa, of course, is not confined to the world of recording professionals. The black recording and concert industry itself still ultimately depends upon the new talent and styles produced in the townships. With the rise of Soweto, the street singers and penny whistle bands finally vanished, since neither the township nor the city streets offered hospitality to music and dancing any longer. They took refuge in the shebeens, backyard parties, servants' quarters and hostels, where amateur instrumentalists still get together for sociable entertainment. The brass bands and the marching MacGregor women also disappeared, though *stokfels* still function.

African brass bands are now sponsored only by the police and by independent African churches in the homelands. On Sundays, African Zionist Christians still parade in both the city and the townships in their multicoloured uniforms bright with sacred symbols. In the backyards, amateur vocal groups and neighbourhood youngsters still sing for the weddings and other family occasions of their friends. Social workers organise youth clubs where urban children come to appreciate their heritage by learning rural-traditional songs and dances from migrant workers. In the backrooms of the Donaldson Centre in Orlando aspiring soul singers and *mbaqanga* bands practise for a chance to audition at the recording and broadcasting studios. Young jazz enthusiasts hold all-night *akulalwas* ('we don't sleep'), talking, listening to records or serious jazz performers, taking refuge in good music and good company. Veteran swing bands still perform the jazz 'evergreens' for ballroom dance clubs in townships all over South Africa. Professor Khabi Mngoma's Soweto Symphony Orchestra and Ionian Male Choir provide an outlet for Africans interested in Western classical music. At political marches, students still produce powerful new songs of protest based on the melodies of African school songs and hymns.

Despite this activity, the wellsprings of amateur music-making have probably never been so dry as they are in today's urban black communities. Music is not included in the Bantu Education curriculum, and few of the overworked, underpaid African teachers can organise school choirs on their own time. Transportation problems and lack of money make it difficult to put together adult choirs and choral competitions. The sense of cultural progress that inspired previous generations of choral composers, conductors and singers has died with the faith in liberal ideals and government promises of a better life. Some fine choirs, such as those of James Kumalo and Wilby Baqwa, still carry on, but disruption, disorganisation, and even violence still plague amateur as well as professional concerts. Dorkay House, the only non-commercial show promoter, and sponsor of African talent, is closed. University students have little music, rejecting African folksong as homeland culture and modern music as politically irrelevant. Committed Black Consciousness Movement musicians, such as Molefe Phetoe or Lefifi Tladi, who read virile poetry to Malombo-style instrumental music, have been driven into exile. It may be, perhaps, that in the sombre social landscape of Soweto, the people are too sad or angry now to sing.

Yet Mtutuzeli Matshoba, in an autobiographical account of the life of industrial labourers in Johannesburg, writes movingly of the musical response of migrants to the squalor of the hostels:

At least two days a week they sang traditional choral music. After supper they would assemble in the adjoining closet and start singing with

the conscientiousness of a stage group rehearsing for a fete . . . . Some
of the songs were performed with graceful dances, so elegantly carried
out that I wondered where they could all have learnt the same paces.
When they sang, it was from the core of their souls, their eyes glazed
with memories of where they had first sung those lyrics; and inter-
ruptions were not tolerated. Sometimes I was so moved by their music
that I yearned to join them . . . . After an evening of invigorating talk
and untainted African traditional song I went away feeling as if I had
found treasure in a graveyard.[18]

No matter how many concerts fail, amateur promoters still try
to put together the best township talent for an afternoon of community celebration. Though the inter-racial nightclubs that flourished
in Johannesburg's Hillbrow district in the late 1970s have been closed,
recent liberalisation of so-called 'petty apartheid' now allows black
and white performers on the same stage together, even in the townships. While jealousy, mistrust, and self-aggrandisement have ruined
attempts to create a black musicians' union, the South African Recording Rights Association and the South African Music Rights Organisation now protect the contracts, royalties and copyrights of
hundreds of black members. The Federated Union of Black Artists
works within the Black Consciousness Movement to provide training
and financial support to aspiring black musicians. Producer Ray
Nkwe's Johannesburg Jazz Appreciation Society and Black Music
Foundation attempt to reignite interest in serious jazz and all forms of
indigenous African music.[19] The most hopeful development, and the
place where live jazz and many other kinds of black music have taken
refuge, is township musical theatre, which more than any other art
form still flourishes amid the dust and heat of apartheid.

NOTES

1   Julian Kramer, *Self-help in Soweto: Mutual Aid Societies in a South African City*,
    MA dissertation, Bergen, 1975, pp. 6–23.
2   Ellen Hellmann, *Soweto: Johannesburg's African City*, Johannesburg, 1967,
    p. 19.
3   J. Clegg, 'The music of Zulu immigrant workers in Johannesburg – a
    focus on concertina and guitar', in *Papers Presented at the Symposium on
    Ethnomusicology*, Grahamstown, 1981, p. 3.
4   *Ibid.* p. 6.
5   *Ibid.*, pp. 3–5.
6   Muff Andersson, *Music in the Mix*, Johannesburg, 1981, pp. 124, 127.
7   See *Uzulu* on *Rufaro – Happiness*, Harari, The Sun – Independent Records
    GL1874.
8   Andersson, *Music in the Mix*, p. 125.
9   *Ibid.*, p. 123.
10 Translation J. Clegg. Copyright Gallo-Mavuthela Music, 1975.
11 Johannesburg *Post*, 7 February 1978.

12   David Coplan, 'The African musician and the development of the Johannesburg entertainment industry', *Journal of Southern African Studies*, 5, 2, April, (1979).

13   Andersson, *Music in the Mix*, pp. 45–99.

14   *Ibid.*, pp. 128–131.

15   Copyright Philip Thabane, 1977.

16   Copyright Gallo-Africa, 1979.

17   Andersson, *Music in the Mix*, p. 49.

18   Mtutuzeli Matshoba, 'To kill a man's pride', in Mothobi Mutloatse (ed.), *Africa South: Contemporary Writings*, London, 1981, p. 123.

19   Andersson, *Music in the Mix*, pp. 173–4.

8

Twenty years of black theatre: the struggle for black city culture

BEFORE *King Kong* burst upon the scene in 1959, there was little formal theatrical activity among urban Africans. Phoenix Players (Union Artists) artistic director Corney Mabaso went so far as to declare that there was no African drama in Johannesburg until the young Athol Fugard arrived from Port Elizabeth in 1957.[1] This judgement is too sweeping. Though there was not yet an African mass audience for literary drama, quiet experimentation by a number of African dramatists was setting the stage for the theatrical renaissance of the 1960s and '70s.

The Bantu Dramatic Society continued its efforts to promote literary drama at the BMSC during the 1940s, and African authors turned to themes more relevant to urban life. After the failure of H.I.E. Dhlomo's *Moshoeshoe*, which was too rural and folkloristic for urban taste, his company, the African Dramatic and Operatic Society wrote and produced *Ruby and Frank*, a 'vivid picture of the trials and experiences of modern Africans'.[2] The overriding themes of literary dramas at this time were the clash of traditional values and institutions with Western culture and the necessity of townward migration and urban cultural change, themes that remain a staple of working-class township theatre today.

Among the most interesting of these experiments was *Izinkwa* (bread), first written and produced as a radio play for Johannesburg Broadcasting's African programme by the multitalented Dan Twala and his Bantu Sports Club Choristers. The play begins with scenes depicting the rural village life of African Christian peasants. In Part Two, one family is forced to move to a nearby town, where their son gambles away their small savings. Failing to survive as a petty trader, the father works himself to death in the mills while his wife is arrested for brewing. As the son gives himself over to drinking and gambling, the daughter disappears in the location of a larger city, and the family disintegrates: 'The end of the play finds the mother on her knees in prayer by the bedside of the dying old man'.[3]

To whites like Twala's producer Michael Kittermaster, such stories emphasised the moral superiority of rural life and the dangers of the city for Africans. The dark vision of African urbanisation portrayed in *Izinkwa*, however, contains an implicit indictment of a system which forces African peasants off the land and into the unrelenting struggle for existence in the urban labour market and the locations. Other attempts to dramatise the squalor of African working-class life, such as James Jolobe's *Amathunzi Obomi* (1958) tended to emphasise individual moral responsibility for personal destiny among urban Africans, and suggested ethical behaviour as a solution to the problems of poverty and social disorganisation.[4]

Within the urban community, the schools continued to provide performance training, and comic sketches, scenes from English plays, and dramatised African folktales were featured at school concerts and area festivals. Khabi Mngoma and Ezekiel Mphahlele's efforts to catch the attention of the general African public with this kind of material failed. When police harassment forced their Syndicate of African Artists to disband in 1956,[5] there was no black-run theatrical organisation left in Johannesburg. Amateur dramatic societies and teachers like Bob Leshoi of Lady Selbourne High School in Pretoria continued to organise dramatic scenes for community concerts and some full-scale productions. African variety stage troupes laid the foundation for township musical theatre with comic sketches and folkloristic displays until the death of the old locations and the success of *King Kong* put an end to this medium of black performance.

Though they produced little in the way of drama relevant or authentic to African social experience, white producers were responsible for much of the theatrical activity among Africans during this period. The multi-racial, socialist-oriented Bantu People's Theatre of Andre van Gyseghem was reorganised by labour organiser Guy Routh in 1939. Under their new name, the African National Theatre, they produced Routh's *Patriot's Pie*, about a young African enlistee, and *The Word and the Act*, a satire of Prime Minister Herzog's Native Administration Acts, along with some Eugene O'Neill one-acters and G. Radebe's *The Rude Criminal*, a play about the pass laws. Though the company disintegrated during the Second World War, they must be considered South Africa's first radical, committed theatrical organisation.[6]

During the 1950s a good deal of black dramatic talent was tied up in the exploitative burlesques of African culture purveyed to whites by show producers like Alf Herbert, but other efforts were more positive. Beginning in 1941, the drama teacher Teda de Moor produced African dance dramas acted by students from the Jan Hofmeyr School of Social Work in Johannesburg. Though naive and patronising in her approach to African performance, insisting that 'Africans are born actors; they do not need to be taught'[7], de Moor made honest attempts to have rural, migrant and urban African culture portrayed authentically. While teaching at the Witwatersrand Technical College, she involved urban labourers and domestic servants in dramatising their own experience as a means of easing their adaptation to city life.

In 1952 she teamed up with herbalist, dancer, and variety actor George Makanya to found the Bantu Theatre Company of Cape Town. The company toured South Africa, staging Hugh Tracey and K. E. Masinga's *Chief Above and Chief Below*, with its traditional themes; and scenes from African life on the railways, mines, and locations, with their inevitable focus on the transition from country to town, often in Zulu or Xhosa. This theme was treated most fully in their full-length production, *George's Journey*, in 1961. Although their plays seldom dealt with the reality of urban conditions and reflected an uneasy mix of folkloristic revival, migrant culture and black performance for white audiences, the Bantu Theatre Company helped to make Africans aware of the potential of theatre as a medium of self-realisation and cultural development.

Ian Bernhardt, who was to become one of the most important organising personalities in multi-racial showbusiness in South Africa, also became involved in black theatre through his interest in social work. African schools kindled interest in drama but there was little professional theatre for township Africans to see. In the early 1950s Bernhardt and a troupe of young white fellow actors toured the Witwatersrand townships with a programme of three one-act plays. Following this the Public Transport Corporation's welfare officer asked Bernhardt to help form a drama group among its African employees. The result was Bareti Players, who staged Shakespeare's *Comedy of Errors* and a series of one-act plays on South African themes in the Johannesburg townships from 1953 to 1955. At that point Guy Routh, Bernhardt, the actor Dan Poho, the musician Gwigwi Mwrebi, Bob Leshoi, Sidney Sepamla, Meshack Mosia and others founded Union Artists.

At Dorkay House, Union Artists made *Township Jazz*, *King Kong*, and dozens of other innovative black variety and theatrical productions possible. Bernhardt's aims were not only to protect black performer's rights and to provide non-commercial, artistically free outlets for their talent but to facilitate creative exchange between artists and communities of all races, and to develop a broadly South African urban performance culture. In line with this ideal, Union

Artists secured a boycott by British Equity of all segregated performances in South Africa. The high point in black-white cooperation in the field of musical theatre reached in the late 1950s were largely a result of Union Artists' efforts and influence. Among the most important events in the theatrical history of Dorkay House and all South Africa for that matter was the arrival in Johannesburg in 1957 of a young director and playwright from Port Elizabeth, Athol Fugard.

Fugard had been involved with amateur drama in Port Elizabeth's Korsten location, where he later helped organise a black company, Serpent Players. In Johannesburg he soon familiarised himself with Sophiatown and its way of life. The result was his first play, *No Good Friday* (1958) which dealt with an individual's stand against the gangsterism and extortion practised in the locations. The play opened at the BMSC and drew upon Union Artists for its cast, which included Bloke Modisane, Dan Poho, Steve Moloi, Corney Mabaso, Sol Rachilo, Ken Gampu, Zakes Mokae, Gladys Sibisa, and Fugard himself. *No Good Friday* avoided larger political, economic, and racial issues, but it authentically reflected black urban experience and inspired some electrifying acting from Modisane and the others. Fugard's success with the cast was due in part to his innovative composing and directing methods. Drawing on African tradition, he developed scripts through actors' extemporaneous performing, or by giving them skeletal scenes to work up through their own improvisational treatment.

The play attracted the attention of white theatrical people, few of whom had thought such a production possible, and enjoyed a moderately successful run at Johannesburg's Brooke Theatre. One result was that Fugard and his talented actors left the township audience behind. There was no mass African audience for theatre, and the majority of Africans were not prepared to accept Western dramatic forms, even though their content might be familiar. In his succeeding plays, including *Nongogo* (1959), *Boesman and Lena* (1960), and *The Blood Knot* (1962), Fugard addressed black experience but not black audiences. *The Blood Knot*, perhaps his finest play, was a success in the United States, gaining Fugard an international reputation and his co-star Zakes Mokae an acting career in London and New York, but bypassed the townships. The overall success of the play did, however, inspire a group of young Africans in Port Elizabeth to ask Fugard to help them start Serpent Players. Not until Fugard teamed up with two members of Serpent Players to create *Sizwe Bansi is Dead* in 1972 did he successfully place his work before black South African as well as international audiences.

Despite the indirectness of his connection with black playgoers, Fugard exerted a powerful influence on the development of black theatre. His plays produced the first cadre of African professional dramatic actors. The success of *No Good Friday* not only attracted the support of Union Artists, but convinced Bernhardt, author Harry Bloom and others that the staging of a major black production, *King Kong*, was artistically feasible.

King Kong itself, of course, inspired a variety of productions intended to capitalise on its success. *King Kong* director Leon Gluckman followed up with Union Artists' staging of Eugene O'Neill's *Emperor Jones*, starring Manhattan Brother Joe Makgotsi. In Durban, the novelist Alan Paton scripted *Mkumbane*, a musical portrayal of the daily life of Africans in Cato Manor, one of the poorest, crime-ridden yet socially vibrant of the old urban locations. At the time, Africans protesting against government resettlement policies were being expelled from Cato Manor, and the community was already marked for destruction. Paton used traditional African forms of choral verse chant (in English), and dialogue alternated with an emotionally exhilarating score for 200 voices by *King Kong* composer Todd Matshikiza. Though production difficulties, police harassment and mixed reviews combined to allow *Mkumbane* only a short run, its particular uses of theme and musical dramatics made it an important forerunner of the popular working-class township theatre of today. Among those most influenced by these developments was a young musical composer-arranger from Grahamstown, Gibson Kente, who revolutionised urban African popular theatre during the 1960s.

In 1962, *King Kong* veteran Ben 'Satch' Masinga produced his own jazz musical in Zulu, *Back in Your Own Back Yard*, for Soweto audiences only, and Union Artists declined to help him. Yet Masinga was more realistic and forward-looking than Ian Bernhardt, for changes in black urban attitudes and white apartheid legislation would soon make black-produced, black-acted shows for black audiences the only viable direction for black theatre to take. It was Gibson Kente, who had worked with drama at the Jan Hofmeyr School before writing and arranging for Miriam Makeba and other vocalists, who grasped most fully the theatrical implications of urban South African society in the early 1960s (see plate 39).

Kente soon became aware of professional black performers' bitter feelings of artistic and financial exploitation, not only by Alf Herbert and Bertha Egnos, but by Ian Bernhardt, the *King Kong* organisation, and Union Artists itself. Artistically, despite their good intentions, Union Artists' productions tended to fall into the gap between the cultural expectations of white and black audiences. As a result, Union Artists mounted fewer shows, but continued to provide rehearsal facilities, talent, and organisational support for African producers with fresh ideas of their own.

One of these was Kente, who used the talents of singer Letta Mbulu and others trained in the white-sponsored musicals to produce *Manana, The Jazz Prophet* in 1963. In every way, the show was designed to succeed with the African township audience. *Manana* was scripted in English, the language of international showbusiness and the one that symbolised urban Africans' desire to overcome ethnic division, local parochialism and the implications of apartheid. The plot was a straightforward melodrama about the efforts of an evangelistic African minister to mobilise the energies of delinquent township youth for religious and community service by bringing jazz and other forms of popular music into his church. Heavily influenced by Afro-American music, Kente used this story line to blur the boundaries between gospel, jazz, and local musical styles, creating an uplifting spectacle of township dance and song. Equally effective was the expressive tension he created between rhetorical exaggeration and the thoroughly realistic portrayal of the conditions of urban African life. *Manana* was a black play, produced, directed, written, and scored by a black playwright, using black actors to dramatise their experience according to emerging black urban aesthetic conventions. Most important, it created a theatre of self-realisation, in which black audiences could see themselves and their concerns brought to the stage in a victory of the human spirit.

In this post-Sharpeville era of government repression, Kente carefully avoided dramatising the wider political issues underlying the suffering and frustrations of urban Africans. He concentrated instead on personal morality and social responsibility based on African Christianity as the foundation of community life. While his art did little to raise the political or class consciousness of his audiences, he did achieve the important goal of developing a theatre faithful to African daily experience that for the first time reached thousands of township residents. In so doing he formulated a new theatrical language for the townships and provided black theatre with its first mass audience.

In 1966 Kente produced *Sikalo* ('Lament'), another musical melodrama that dealt with gangsterism, intergenerational conflict, social disorganisation and physical suffering in the townships. Once again the stereotypical scenes and characters were just sufficiently larger than township life to capture the popular imagination, and the music played by Mackay Davashe and his band was a further development of Kente's own stylistic blend of African gospel and township jazz. Kente developed *Sikalo* on his own, using Cocky Thlothalemaje, Kenny Majozi, Siman Sabela, and Margaret Mgcingana in leading roles. United Artists produced the show for integrated audiences at the Witwatersrand University Great Hall, where it enjoyed moderate success. The première at Soweto's Mofolo Hall, however, was a major cultural event in Johannesburg African society, and the play made an overwhelming and seemingly permanent impression on African playgoers. To this day, *Sikalo* is recognised as a milestone by the African theatrical community, where the show's political shortcomings are less remembered than its artistic dynamism and social authenticity.

From that point on, Kente dissociated himself from Dorkay House and set out on his own. Based in Soweto, he achieved independent artistic and financial success with *Lifa* (1968) and *Zwi* (1970). Kente recognised that the costly sets, crew, and equipment required by white theatre were not necessary in the townships and would serve only to reduce his mobility. Packing young, newly-trained actors, simple costumes and a few crudely painted flats and backdrops into an old bus, the company performed under the house lights to standing-room-only audiences in township halls all over South Africa, and so became a major force in a rejuvenated black community showbusiness.

Kente was no isolated innovator, but a talented man able to grasp and synthesise the right cultural and organisational elements to develop township theatre. Working independently, a young student, Sam Mhangwane, and his Sea Pearls Drama Society produced a township melodrama in 1963 called *Crime Does Not Pay*, with dialogue in Soweto *tsotsitaal*. After competing successfully in a Union Artists' black drama festival in 1964, Mhangwane wrote his sexy musical portrayal of social immorality and retribution, *Unfaithful Woman*, mostly in English, which toured continuously for the next twelve years.

Simultaneously, apartheid was putting up barriers to interracial cooperation in the arts in every direction. Beginning in 1964, separate amenities and community development provisions of the Group Areas legislation outlawed multi-racial performance companies, required permits for blacks to perform in or attend shows in the white areas and for whites to do the same in the townships. Union Artists had to give up doing shows altogether, though the African Music and Drama Association (AMDA) retained its separate teaching functions under black leadership. Ian Bernhardt helped to form a new black company at Dorkay House, Phoenix Players, for the initial purpose of presenting Athol Fugard's *Hello and Goodbye* to blacks. Fugard himself was despondent, declaring in 1968 that 'the legislation that governs the performing arts in various forms makes it impossible for an African and me to get together on the stage as we did five or six years ago . . . It's an appalling deterioration'.[8]

Alan Paton tried again with his rousing musical *Sponono*, starring Cocky Thlothlalemaje, with music by Gideon Nxumalo, which finally enjoyed some success at the New York World's Fair in 1964 and launched Letta Mbulu on her international career. With the exception of the doggedly courageous director Barney Simon, most whites simply gave up as the darkness of apartheid dimmed the lights of inter-racial theatre in Johannesburg. Athol Fugard returned to Port Elizabeth to work with Serpent players. The aptly named Phoenix Players carried on with the effort to resurrect an international black show business out of the ashes of the legacy of *King Kong*. Corney Mabaso briefly revived H.I.E. Dhlomo's Zulu drama, *Chaka*, there, and Barney Simon continued to train African actors using British and American plays. But in Soweto, an autonomous, community-based black show business again began to flourish in the very teeth of apartheid. Its medium was musical theatre, and its exponents made it a major cultural force in the 1970s.

This decade witnessed the division of black theatre into three performance areas, distinguished by audience, venue, expressive style, and political and thematic focus. These divisions have been loosely labelled 'township theatre', 'town theatre', and 'Black Consciousness theatre'.[9] Until almost the end of the decade, township theatre was dominated by Gibson Kente, followed closely by Sam Mhangwane and trailed by a number of younger playwright-directors who have recently begun to reorient, diversify and politicise his basic style.

Kente is, of course, a member of South Africa's emerging black entrepreneurial middle class, and financial success, cultural leadership, and public recognition have always been among his priorities. Unlike some white companies, black theatre receives no public subsidy and can only be seen in the townships if it attracts a large paying audience, makes a profit and escapes government censorship. Kente accomplished the first requirement by developing the synthesis of narrative, mime, movement, vocal dramatics, music and dance found in traditional oral literary performance into a township melodrama using urban experience and cultural resources.

He used virtually every medium and style of performance found in the streets and social occasions of the townships, so that working-class Africans unfamiliar with formal theatre could recognise themselves up on the stage. He kept admission prices and expenses low, establishing a circuit of seemingly endless one-night appearances in township halls all over the country. By 1974 he had three travelling companies and was paying actors between £25 and £50 a week. The professional experience and regular salaries he offered kept many performers with him despite the enormous disparity between his earnings and theirs. Kente's greatest challenge, in fact, has been in meeting his audience's increasing demands for political expression while keeping the authorities from shutting him down completely.

Interestingly, it was the success of Athol Fugard's *Sizwe Bansi is Dead*, first produced in 1972 in Port Elizabeth in collaboration with Serpent Players' actors John Kani and Winston Ntshona, that helped convince Kente to bring more explicitly political themes into his plays. *Sizwe* and its cast went on to national and international acclaim, but Kente remained in the townships. There audiences were no longer satisfied with the simple representation of their experience; they wanted an exposure of the political and economic system that produced their condition and a suggestion of what they were to do about it. In response, Kente produced a series of political melodramas between 1974 and 1976, *How Long, I Believe*, and *Too Late*, that squarely placed the blame for the suffering and squalor of the townships on apartheid, while compassionately heroising the resilience, vitality, and essential humanity of their people.

How Long has become a township classic and its title song (Record and Tape RTL4033) has been used by other playwrights. It emphasises the importance of African education and family unity as sources of strength in a predatory environment. *I Believe* used elements of traditional Xhosa performance culture in presenting a call for black political unity, and *Too Late* served as a theatrical warning to the government to do something before it is too late.[10] *Too Late* also introduces a second theme central to Kente's later work, the 'generation gap' in the township community. Proletarian characters of the younger generation are used to present the radical, bitterly militant critique of South African society, a position the playwright finally discredits in favour of the reformist moderation advocated by the older, more bourgeois characters.[11]

The poignance of Kente's warning was demonstrated in the Soweto uprising of 1976–77, during which he was detained while attempting to film *How Long* in Kingwilliamstown. Though the film was completed, the producers have so far not released it for fear of government retaliation. Following his release, Kente produced *Can You Take It* (1977) a township love story in the presentational style of American Broadway musical theatre. Though this show was the first to use coloured stage lighting, which enhanced wonderfully colourful costumes and beautifully choreographed chorus routines, the innovations in form and *mise-en-scène* pleased only those playgoers who identify Americanisation with 'raising the standard' of local black productions. The play's single thematic focus on the urban black generation gap could not satisfy the growing political consciousness of township audiences, so in *La Duma* ('It Thundered') (1978), Kente created a direct confrontation between radical political organisation and family and community solidarity.

The conflict between the Marxist urban guerrilla Paul and his police constable brother in *La Duma* ultimately resolves in the rejection of the radical position as contrary to African religious and family values. Yet the ambivalence of Kente's position is revealed in the very identity of Paul's brother as a policeman; a kind man but a stooge and a sell-out whose job makes him as much of an enemy of the black community as the thoroughly vicious Constable Pelepele in *Too Late*. In *La Duma*'s dénouement, the radical Paul's ultimate fate is not resolved. This ambivalence has become characteristic of current township dramas, and in this instance serves to express the unwillingness of the township community to give up even its most violent and anti-social militants to the common enemy, the state.

The theatrical style of *La Duma* is a creative compromise between the brash colour, polished choreography, but rather static action of Broadway productions and the almost acrobatic movement and expressive realism of township drama; yet another indication of Kente's innovative leadership in popular theatrical form. One recent production, *Mama and the Load* (1980), uses visible stage imagery to illustrate its central themes of poverty and family disintegration, the decline of adult moral authority and guidance, and the need for renewed kinship and community unity among urban blacks.[12] Clearly, Kente continues to be caught in the contradiction of his own class position, which is becoming increasingly untenable in relation to the continuing polarisation of South African society.[13]

Playwright Sam Mhangwane has dealt with similar problems in a different way. Following *Crime Does Not Pay* and *Unfaithful Woman* came *Blame Yourself* (1966). The melodramatic realism of this play resonated with Africans' experience in the townships, and it remained popular with black audiences until the late 1970s. Mhangwane studied stagecraft in both the United Kingdom and America in 1974, and his plays have consistent, 'well-made' plots and believable township settings and characters. His Sunday acting workshops at Soweto's Donaldson Centre generously serve the theatrical community by recruiting and training fresh young talent (see plate 38). In Mhangwane's plays, music and dance are used for comic and dramatic relief rather than as integral parts of the story, but the acting and action are pure township – acrobatic, rhythmical, electrifying and bombastic; running the gamut of emotions from the maudlin to the satirical, angry, or deliriously celebrative – communicated through the actors' faces and bodies as well as their words and voices.

Mhangwane's actors switch from dialogue to soliloquy to dance to frantic activity with practised ease. Everything one might see in the township streets, from traditional Shangaan dancing and zionist church parades to tsotsi gangs and – Mhangwane's speciality – explicit sex and the war between the sexes, is done with comic naturalism and rhetorical flair. The lead character, Paul, in *Blame Yourself*, displays an uncanny ability to turn a soliloquy into a heated dialogue with the audience, breaking down the 'third wall' and achieving an identity between the artist and his audience-community. Mhangwane, Kente, and followers such as Boykie Mohlamme (*Mahlomola*) have recognised that the essence of African theatre is tragicomedy; the genius for exploring physical and emotional suffering through satirical mime and dramatic irony.

The stories of *Unfaithful Woman* and *Blame Yourself* are like mirror-images of each other, the first portraying a township woman's fall into promiscuity and degradation, the second a rake's progress from hardworking, churchgoing township husband to penniless, suicidal wretch through moral weakness, philandering and alcoholism. These plays avoid direct confrontation with the authorities, resolving the black playwright's political dilemma by concentrating on personal responsibility and social morality as the primary need in urban African communities, a prerequisite for united struggle for change. Africans, say Mhangwane and Kente, must put their own house in order before transforming the wider society. In another production, *Thembi* (1978), Mhangwane treats the problem of generational conflict, family relationships and changing social consciousness among Africans and xenophobia among whites through the themes of youthful sexuality, sex education and family planning. The success of *Thembi*, despite its hours of dialogue almost unrelieved by music, dance, or visual display, demonstrates the concern that Mhangwane and his audience share for the creation of new social values, patterns of integration and communal identity in the townships.[14]

The preoccupation of township playwrights with social tension and reintegration is most often expressed in the narrative idiom of kinship relations against a background of cultural change and the urban-rural dichotomy. In Solly Mekoe's well-known *uLindiwe* ('The Awaited One') for example, a city man, Dabula, sells his virility to a traditional African doctor in exchange for the power to acquire wealth. Childless, Dabula arranges for his rural brother, Dumdum, to impregnate his wife for him according to traditional custom. A child, uLindiwe, is born, but Dabula is robbed, framed on a dagga-selling charge by his girlfriend and her lover, and sent to prison. After his release Dabula is killed in a shebeen knife brawl, but the sufferings of uLindiwe for her social father are somewhat relieved when she discovers the identity of her true biological father, a good man of traditional outlook who cares for her and her mother. A degree of family harmony is restored in an uneasy compromise between modern and traditional values typical of township society.[15] The implication is that city life leads to greed, moral degeneration and impotence among Africans, and that traditional family values may serve to strengthen the social foundations of township community life, despite the social destruction wrought by South African political economy.

The popularity of such themes is paralleled on the formal level by the uses of language, music, and dance in township theatre. Despite the widespread use of *tsotsitaal* and urban dialects of Zulu, Sotho, and Xhosa in the townships, playwrights almost always write in English, interlarded with jokes, exclamations, song texts, and throwaway lines in a variety of African languages and polyglot slang.

When questioned, playwrights respond that English is the only *lingua franca* understood in townships throughout the country, but their preference for it as a medium of communication has a deeper significance. Some theatre companies have given their productions a more indigenous feel by using *tsotsitaal*, changing from urban Zulu to Sotho or Xhosa depending on where they were performing, or simply stuck to a single African language and relied on the multilingualism so prevalent in the townships to help them in areas where that language was not predominant. This last strategy is most prevalent in West Africa, where popular 'concert party' and 'folk opera' is always presented in widely distributed African languages such as Twi in Ghana and Yoruba in Nigeria.

English, however, has both political and psychocultural advantages in urban South Africa. Firstly, in any African art form, retreat to the more localised and traditional smacks of the separate development, homeland culture promoted by the white nationalist government. Secondly, playwrights (like musicians) suffer from a sense of cultural isolation that the international theatrical medium of English helps to overcome. Fighting government censorship and control of the channels of intergroup and international communication, black playwrights desire, psychologically at least, to create a theatre that can bring their message to white South Africa, Europe and America, even if their plays are rarely performed outside the townships.

As regards acting, the expectations of white and overseas audiences differ from those of township playgoers, who demand the vigorous, broadly gestural and rhetorically commanding style of presentation handed down from traditional oral and choreographic narration. The missionary Frances Gardiner remarked in 1836 that the brave deeds of Zulu soldiers were always recounted in mimetic dancing, full of 'energetic gesticulation . . . violent leaping, and sententious running' supported by 'displays of muscular power in leaping, charging, vaulting several feet into the air, drawing up the knees towards the chin, and at the same time passing the hands between the ankles'.[16]

Township actors don't always go quite this far, but emotional and dramatic conflict are more often expressed through vocal quality and physical movement than in dialogue or psychologically intense posing or naturalistic action. As in traditional performance, music, dance, and costume are integral to dramatic action and character development. A number of academic and radical black dramatists argue that such rowdy, colourful display subverts the socio-political focus of black theatre, and turns it into mere entertainment that pacifies rather than arouses political consciousness. In addition, the township performance aesthetic is not easily understood by white and overseas audiences and critics, and must be blended with European modes of

36 Julian Bahula of Jabula, formerly
with the Malombo Jazz Men, now
in exile in London

37 Louis Moholo, drummer, one of the
many South African musical talents
in exile

38 Theatre workshop in Soweto started
by Sam Mhangwane, playwright and
director

39 Gibson Kente, an innovative writer
of musicals and plays, a central
figure in the development of black
theatre

theatrical expression and techniques, as in *Sizwe Bansi is Dead* and Workshop 71's prison drama, *Survival,* to gain acceptance outside the townships.

Yet in part, the success of *Sizwe* and *Survival* as drama derives from their actor-creators' ability to communicate a strongly political, universally human social message by blending Western dramatic structure with genuine township performance style. The audience, notes John Kani, is like a third actor who must be constantly wooed 'to cross the barriers of illusory distance, to feel his plight as theirs'.[17] It was largely this expressive vitality that brought Tony Awards to Kani and Ntshona for their performances in *Sizwe* on Broadway in 1974, an achievement repeated by Zakes Mokae in 1982 for his role in Fugard's *Master Harold and the Boys*. Fugard has succeeded in adapting black South African acting to Western plays as well, including two highly regarded productions of Samuel Beckett's *Waiting for Godot*; the first featuring Zakes Mokae, Fats Bookhalane, Corney Mabaso, and Gilbert Xaba in Johannesburg in 1963, and the second starring Kani, Ntshona, and two white actors in Cape Town and London in 1981. In these productions, *Godot* immediately becomes a political play, an indictment of the barren, oppressive callousness of South Africa's human landscape.[18]

Black playgoers, however, complain that despite the high quality of *Sizwe* and the strength of its protest against homeland policy, influx control, and the pass laws, it is too complex in structure and expression, too 'talky', and too unmusical – in short, too Western in form – to be worth seeing more than once. As one theatrical promoter in Port Elizabeth told me, Africans might return any number of times to Kente's *How Long*, but *Sizwe* was not 'a renewable experience'.[19] Other African critics complain that characters representing the African 'common man' in Fugard's plays like Zack in *The Blood Knot*, Willie in *Master Harold*, and even Robert in *Sizwe* are too shuffling, unintelligent, and unconscious; not proud enough or admirable enough to represent black sufferings, values, and aspirations.[20]

Workshop 71's *Survival*, on the other hand, has fully conscious characters and uses tuneful township music, dance, and tragicomedy to get across the message that South Africa is a prison. Similarly, the Reverend Mqina's remarkable, frequently banned *Give Us This Day* (1974) passionately condemned apartheid in pure township musical theatrical style, revealing its potential for the transformation of mass political consciousness. Ironically, *Survival* was allowed to tour abroad *because* it had not developed a mass black audience, while the far more moderate Gibson Kente play *How Long* did command such a following and so got its author jailed for putting it on film in 1976. When *Survival* finally began to tour successfully in the townships in 1978, it was promptly banned.

A last issue of perennial concern to township playwrights is the proper role of traditional culture in contemporary theatre. On the one hand, urban cultural disorientation, social disintegration, and the philosophy of Black Consciousness have fostered the positive reassessment of traditional culture among urban Africans. On the other hand, the success of Welcome Msomi's Zulu Macbeth, *uMabatha*, (1972) and of exploitative displays of African tradition by white producers, *Ipi Tombi* (1974), have nonetheless inspired township playwrights to blend traditional music, dance, and divination scenes into their plays. The verdict of township audiences on these attempts seems to be that traditional culture is acceptable, even rousingly effective, provided it is done authentically and well. Examples of successful reintegration include the Zulu roadworkers' poignant lament over their families' sufferings in Mohlamme's *Mahlomola* ('Suffering'), and the Shangaan dance scene in Mhangwane's *Blame Yourself*.

Probably the most exciting and innovative use of traditional forms of language, dramatic narrative, legend, history, music, dance and setting are Credo Mutwa's *uNosilimela* (1973) and Fatima Dike's *Sacrifice of Kreli* (1976). *uNosilimela* is an African romance modeled on Zulu folk narrative (*inganekwane*) and traditional mimetic dramatisation (*umlinganiso*). Its protagonist is an outcast and time-traveller, a young princess whose historical sufferings have the ultimate purpose of re-establishing traditional values in African life. The positive revaluation of the African past and its reintegration into contemporary consciousness is intended not only to reduce the self-alienation of urban Africans but to provide a cultural pattern for the eventual peaceful regeneration of South African society as a whole.

Staging in *uNosilimela* attempted to recreate the physical setting of dramatic narration and episodic mime in traditional villages. The play is a festival of movement, song, dance, declamation and dramatic action, but the demands of creating such a setting in inflexible, ill-equipped, poorly lit township meeting halls proved too much for its sponsors, Workshop 71. In addition, the elements of pure fantasy, the whirl of action and plot, and the unfamiliar settings themselves seem to have proved too innovative for township audiences at that time, and the run of *uNosilimela* was regrettably short. Credo Mutwa's personal brand of cultural politics may have puzzled township playgoers as well. A religious visionary who thoroughly rejects the city and its human environment, Mutwa is a conservative traditionalist manqué who publicly denounced the youth of Soweto as they fell to police gunfire during the uprising of 1976.

A more realistic, historically accurate, and dramatically satisfying recreation of the African past in relation to the concerns of the present is Xhosa playwright Fatima Dike's *Sacrifice of Kreli*.[21] Based on historical research by the play's producer, Rob Amato, the story takes place in 1885 and recounts the efforts of Gcaleka Xhosa chief Kreli to revitalise his nation after yet another defeat by Cape Colonial forces in 1877–8.

Hidden with his followers in a deep canyon far from his former domain, Kreli sends his trusted *iqira* (diviner) Mlanjeni into the nether world of the ancestors to discover what course of action he should take. Beset by defeatism and threats of desertion among his men, Kreli uses Mlanjeni's miraculous return from the land of the dead to rally his people to return to their glorious traditions, reclaim their children from the foster care of the neighboring Bomvana, and renew their resistance to dispossession and national disintegration. Makwedini Mtsaka and Barney Simon's clear, austere direction gave the play a feeling of disciplined power. Mtsaka's shrewd portrayal of Kreli, the aging outlaw king, was at once pathetic and magisterial, an unbending spirit in a bowed and grieving body. Chris Baskiti's Mlanjeni was equally spellbinding; a muscular, uncanny evocation of the mystical power of Xhosa spiritual consciousness. Sets were almost painfully simple, calling for the imaginative participation of the audience, who were carried seamlessly from the seen to the unseen, from knowledge to imagination.

In the hands of Dike and Cape Town's Sechaba Theatre Company, the story of Kreli becomes a commentary on the nature and challenge of African leadership relevant to contemporary struggles for national regeneration. The play was performed in Xhosa for African audiences in the Cape and Transkei, and in Xhosa and English for racially mixed or non-Xhosa audiences elsewhere. Fatima Dike is clear about the use of English not as a convenience or a compromise, but as a creative tool for translating the beauty and rhythm of Xhosa into an international poetic medium. Though the play was more successful in small Xhosa towns than in large cities like Johannesburg, it remains a model for the effective mobilisation of traditional and historical resources in a modern cultural and political context.

In stark contrast, the successful efforts of white theatrical producers to package African traditional performing arts for the musical stage reached new depths of cultural and economic exploitation and political misrepresentation in the 1970s. Perhaps the most notorious example is Bertha Egnos, who first came to public attention as the composer and director of 'original African music' for Jamie Uys' film *Dingaka* in the 1960s (Gallotone SGALP 1385). Bertha Egnos achieved fame and fortune in South African show business with her production *Ipi Tombi* (incorrect Zulu for 'where are the girls?') in 1974, which eventually supported three touring companies and played longer, both in Johannesburg and London, than any other South African show ever.

On the cultural level, *Ipi Tombi* is an inauthentic burlesque of

African urban and rural life which portrays Africans as happy children better suited to the pastoral joys of the homelands than to the corrupting evils of the city. African men must come to the city for work, of course, but they should return as soon as possible to the bosom of their rural families and the land. In this apartheid-inspired vision, African culture as represented by traditional song and dance is good, but the traditional religion which nurtured them is bad.[22] In one menacing scene, the traditional diviner is represented as a dark, evil witchdoctor from whom the soul of a Zulu maiden is rescued by the minions of Christian light.

Despite producers' claims that, like the government, they are promoting the value of traditional African culture, *Ipi Tombi* shows little respect for it. Ethnic traditions are mixed haphazardly throughout the show for sensational effect. Blanketed Basotho sing Zulu traditional songs, scantily-clad young girls wear married women's beaded headdresses, dancers at an urban wedding wear beads and tiny skirts never seen in rural or urban celebrations, and the whole is pervaded by a coy semi-nudity and licentious display that would be unacceptable at the most rowdy shebeen party.[23]

From the start, *Ipi Tombi*'s producers were aware of the show's potential for polishing up apartheid's international image. As the original programme stated:

> When it goes overseas *Ipi Tombi* may well become South Africa's most valuable export, and the cast our most exciting ambassadors. The commodity it sells is happiness, which surely must compare favorably with the export of our gold and our diamonds.[24]

The producers did not then anticipate the political sophistication of New York (as opposed to London) theatregoers, or the angry public protests that would quickly end *Ipi Tombi*'s Broadway run in 1976.

When the producers of *Ipi Tombi* finally arranged for special blacks-only performances as the show neared the end of its Johannesburg run in 1975, few black theatregoers were interested. Nevertheless, the international success of *Ipi Tombi*, *Meropa*, and other shows of this kind has inspired young black playwrights to bring traditional music, dance, and cultural themes back to the township stage.[25] Brown Keogotsitse worked with migrant mineworkers in creating dances and settings for *Mbube – The Warrior* (1978), a play about political conflict in a traditional chiefdom. Bapupi Mothlahane revived the familiar theme of the inconclusive struggle between tradition and modernity in African life by juxtaposing traditional and urban dance styles and music in his 1977 production, *Asazi* ('We Don't Know').

The paternalism and cultural exploitation of *Ipi Tombi* itself is paralleled in the apparent economic and professional exploitation of Miss Egnos' African musicians, choreographers and performers. The procedure in both *Ipi Tombi* and *Lulu Wena* (1977) has been to audition and hire African singers, composers and dancers, and ask them to display their materials. These artists have been paid as little as £3 per day and signed to contracts that put their contributions under Egnos copyright, with the understanding that better pay and opportunities will follow once the show has opened. Other songs are appropriated from 'traditional' African music supposedly in the public domain, but in some cases the recorded or published work of professional African musicians. In 1976 a panel appointed by the South African Music Rights Organisation (SAMRO) concluded that composer Strike Vilakazi was justified in charging that the hit song from *Ipi Tombi*, 'Mama Thembu's Wedding', was indeed based upon one of his published compositions, but he was unable to win his case in court. In some cases, it is alleged that artists who develop the show in rehearsal are fired and paid off when the show opens, and their contributions copyrighted by Miss Egnos.[26]

Those who do perform on stage, as well as artists who do not, are then forbidden by their contracts to take any of the techniques or materials involved in the show to any other production. When a group of former *Ipi Tombi* cast members tried to take their own new show, *Sola Sola* on a tour of Australia in 1977, Miss Egnos threatened them with a law suit.[27] What she seems to be doing, in effect, is hiring African talent at bargain rates, appropriating African performance culture, debasing it for sale at a huge profit, claiming it as her own legal property, and preventing her performers from marketing their own talents and resources freely thereafter.

In return, performers display their bodies and talents in eight shows per week, for a salary which in 1975 stood at an average of £50, £35, and £25 per week, for the first, second, and third casts respectively. Miss Egnos, of course, denies the allegations of those who have worked for her, proclaiming her dedication to the welfare and professional advancement of black artists:

> I would like to see a strong actors' union to protect Black theatre. You all know that Black artists are being exploited by their own people too. We will be working to form a union to protect them.[28]

With friends like Bertha Egnos, black theatre needs no enemies.

The real spirit of *King Kong*, of interracial artistic collaboration in the development of a fully South African as distinct from black theatre, has lived on in the productions of a 'fringe circuit'[29] of university and 'off-Broadway' companies and theatres in Johannesburg, Cape Town, and other cities. Dorkay House's Phoenix Players made a major effort 'to promote cultural exchange between township and city'[30] with *Phiri* early in 1972. *Phiri* was an African jazz musical which revived Ben Jonson's *Volpone* in a township setting. With stage direction and script by Barney Simon, music by Cyril Magubane and Mackay Davashe, choreography by Gordon Wales, and musical acting by such talents as Stanley 'Fats' Dibeco, Willie Moloisi, Sophie Mgcina, David Phetoe, Corney Mabaso, Sam Williams and many others, *Phiri* presented black Johannesburg culture and social experience with the highest theatrical professionalism.

The social and critical environment of the time was not good, however. The official closing of the BMSC following *Phiri's* last rehearsal there was a bad omen for supporters of black culture in the city, and stylistically the show effected an uneasy compromise between black and white production values and aesthetics. The show opened to white audiences at the Witwatersrand University, but patronising, ethnocentric theatre critics like Percy Baneshik[31] failed to comprehend or appreciate the tragicomedy, earthiness, physicality, visible emotionality and episodic structure that are the soul of African drama. Lengthened and revised for black audiences, *Phiri* attracted a good following, but its expensive equipment, sets and other white production values condemned it to a short run. Inevitably, perhaps, interpersonal rivalry among its many powerful talents tore apart the cast and prematurely ended the show. In retrospect, *Phiri* helped to raise artistic and production standards in black theatre, and several of its songs, including Sophie Mgcina's impassioned servant's complaint, 'Madam Please', have become classics of the South African musical stage.

The year 1972 was a productive one for Phoenix Players, who sponsored Corney Mabaso's *Black and Blue* (I and II); poetry readings by Soweto intellectuals set to contemporary blues and percussion, soon followed by *Isintu*, a 'traditional' stage musical that later toured Japan as *Meropa* and London as *KwaZulu*, and most significantly by the first Johannesburg performances of Fugard's *Sizwe Bansi is Dead*. The success of *Sizwe* helped to nurture the township-to-Broadway dreams of black actors and playwrights, but the failure of *Phiri* discouraged the artists at Dorkay House and destroyed their faith in the professional value of white theatrical training and expertise. Boxed in by Group Areas restrictions and pressured by the growing racial polarisation of the mid-seventies, Dorkay House and Phoenix Players slowly died.

Fortunately there were newer, more forward-looking and vigorous fringe companies working to provide an outlet for socially relevant black theatre in the white cities. These included Workshop 71, who combined Western improvisational 'workshop' drama techniques with township acting, dance, music and a satirical social consciousness to create *Crossroads*, *Zzzip*, *uHlanga*, *uNosilimela*, and *Survival* in the early and middle 1970s. Director Robert Mshengu Maclaren asserted in 1976 that 'Workshop 71 attempts to create South

African theatre out of a composite culture of all South Africans at a time when there is not a meeting of cultures but a confrontation of cultures'.[32] But the seed of such a theatre could not grow in such poor political soil, and with the departure of Maclaren for England and the cast of *Survival* for California in the wake of the Soweto uprisings, Workshop 71 ceased to function. Undaunted, the Market Theatre in Johannesburg and the People's Space in Cape Town moved rapidly to provide homes for both multi-racial and township theatrical productions in the white cities.

With the lifting of the ban on multi-racial companies in late 1977, the Market began to feature integrated productions. These included the biting political comedy *Woza Albert* (1981), which played in Soweto as well as Johannesburg and London, and Hilary Blecher's adaptation of Elsa Joubert's Afrikaans novel about the pathetic life of a black domestic servant, *Die Swerfjare van Poppie Nongena*. This last play was brought to New York in 1982 as *The Long Journey of Poppie Nongena*, and has had a successful run both off-Broadway and subsequently in London. In addition, the Market and Witwatersrand University's small experimental theatre, The Nunnery, have begun to exhibit township plays like *uLindiwe* and Makwedini Julius Mtsaka's powerful allegory of traditional and contemporary African values in conflict in the context of homeland politics, *The Last Man*.

Such exposure and support has encouraged a new, post-Kente generation of young township playwrights to confront the social, political and economic realities of African life more directly, using the performance culture of the townships to raise popular political awareness with less metaphorical self-concealment. The People's Space theatre in Cape Town became a centre of this new effort to infuse by now familiar township forms and themes with political consciousness and naturalistic theatrical expression. In 1979, the Space produced Matsemela Mànaka's lucid, imagistic evocation of black economic exploitation, *Egoli*, a play about the daily degradations of migrant mineworkers in Johannesburg, originally staged at the Market.

Like traditional African theatre, *Egoli* is plotless, episodic, and improvisational, but like the productions of Workshop 71, it employs flashbacks, dream sequences, and other non-naturalistic techniques as it attempts to break down the physical barriers between actors and audience.[33] *Egoli* was followed by two plays by Zanemvula Mda, *We Shall Sing for the Fatherland*, which considers the outcome of a revolution and questions whether it can achieve fundamental change in social values, and *Dark Voices Ring*, a portrayal of the damage done to individual lives by the apartheid system and exposes the immediate sources of the revolutionary impulse.

Another 1979 production was Maishe Maponya's *Hungry Earth*

by Soweto's Bahumutsi Drama Group. The title refers to the soil of the townships, which seems hungry for the bodies of African working-men, who die in such numbers from mine and industrial accidents and other slings and arrows that the flesh of black South Africans is heir to. Here, episodes of working life are linked by songs, chants, and monologues on political topics. Naturalistic sound and mime are used and actors switch roles from scene to scene, often talking to the audience directly in order to destroy the rhetorical and illusionary frame of the drama and jolt the audience into critical appraisal of the action.[34]

Techniques of this kind were first pioneered in South Africa by Workshop 71, and playwrights like Manaka and Maponya are clearly reacting against the stylistic and thematic orientation of the theatre of Gibson Kente. Their perspective is influenced also by the radical theatre movement generated by the South African Students' Organisation (SASO) and other Black Consciousness groups during the 1970s. Kente's popular success as well as his shortcomings helped to make student leaders aware of the uses of theatre in formulating and communicating an ideology of African cultural re-evaluation and rehabilitation. In setting up a Culture Committee, SASO had recognised that 'culture is tied up with the aspirations of a people', and charged the committee to deal with the 'awakening and heightening of cultural awareness and of the involvement of the black people in their struggle for identity, self-respect, and liberation'.[35] The government, of course, uses its own version of African culture to promote ethnic division and retard modernisation among Africans. The Black Consciousness movement had therefore to attempt to restore cultural identity and autonomy without playing into the hands of government policy.

Pascal Gwala, editor of Durban's radical *Black Review*, regards 'authentic' black theatre as a blend of the performance culture of the African past with modern theatre techniques and the 'black ethic'[36] of full, equal humanity recognised for all people. He thus makes a distinction between 'black drama' and 'drama for blacks'.[37] Black drama Gwala identifies with a theatre that promotes dignity, self-reliance, and critical self-assessment among Africans on their own cultural terms, and with heightened political consciousness in the service of a national black liberation movement. Drama for blacks he identifies with both white-sponsored theatrical areas of economic and cultural exploitation of blacks, and with the theatre of Kente and other popular dramatists who emphasise internal community problems and personal morality over the external system of repression and the need for political consciousness and action.

Among the first radical theatre groups to attempt to operate within the townships themselves was the Music, Dance, Art, Literature Institute or MDALI (Zulu: 'creator') of Soweto, an offshoot of

Union Artists and Phoenix Players formed in 1972. Led by such talented people as the actor David Phetoe, MDALI sought to promote self-determination, self-realisation, and self-support in theatre arts, to create an audience for committed theatre, to form an actors' union, and to recruit talent from the townships through local performance festivals. Perceiving apartheid as a total system, MDALI and the associated Mhloti ('tears') Black Theatre, led by David Phetoe's brother Molefi, now in exile in England, rejected white artistic leadership, criticism, financial sponsorship, and inter-racial front organisations such as the abortive South African Theatre Organisation (SATO).[38]

To differentiate black drama from the popular theatre of Kente, Pascal Gwala asserts that it is not a theatre of protest or complaint, but one which negates old stereotypes and affirms new, positive self-images for blacks. The cultural dialectic of negation and affirmation is to provide the dynamic for social and political change.[39] Mhloti Black Theatre has vowed never to

> present plays that tell you how unfaithful our women are . . . of our broken families, of how black people fight and murder each other, or bewitch each other, pimp, mistrust, hate and despise each other . . . this kind of theatre leaves the people broken and despaired. We tell the people to stop moaning and start doing something about their valuable and beautiful black lives.[40]

The difficulty here is that those things which Mhloti promises not to tell the people do in fact occur – social consequences of colonisation, economic deprivation and apartheid. Therefore productions by MDALI of Peter Weiss' *Marat/Sade* or Mhloti's of West African plays like those of Soyinka have had little impact on township theatre or theatregoers.

In 1973 an Afro-Indian theatre group, People's Experimental Theatre (PET), was formed in Lenasia, an Indian suburb of Johannesburg, to perform *Shanti*, an overtly political play by the recently murdered Vice President of the Black People's Convention, Mthuli Shezi.[41] While this play about revolutionary struggle and love is set firmly in South Africa, the characters are not realistic by township standards, and their tendency to preach radical ideology rather than personify the conditions of black existence again limit its potential appeal. Despite the desire for better 'grass-roots contact' between artist-intellectuals and the African working class, none of these plays or even Mhloti's increasingly popular musical poetry readings have brought this about.

More disappointing has been the reluctance of radical dramatists to re-examine African history or cultural tradition, especially in view of the greater identification of township residents with the cultural rather than the political dimensions of the Black Consciousness movement.[42] That this can be done without fostering ethnic parochialism or artificial revivalism is clear from the artistic success of Dike's *Sacrifice of Kreli* and actor James Mthoba's *uHlanga* ('The Reed'), a gripping one-man dramatisation of African history produced by Workshop 71 in 1975. The play argues that historical understanding and cultural rediscovery and self-confidence are part of the essential groundwork of liberation, and 'directly states to all of us that no man is without his peculiar indestructible form of culture even if there may be external forces seeking to eradicate it'.[43]

Black Consciousness theatre might of course become more familiar and accepted by township audiences if its leaders and productions were not so promptly banned under the Publications and Entertainments Bill or even the Terrorism Act. The arrest of Black Consciousness movement activists Saths Cooper, Mrs Sam Moodley and Strini Moodley in 1973 effectively silenced the Theatre Council of Natal (TECON), and in 1975 PET disintegrated after the banning of its newsletter and the arrests of Sadecque Variava, Solly Ismail and Nomsisi Kraai Kuzwayo. Included in the charge sheet at their arraignment under the Terrorism Act was the accusation that these leaders did 'stage' present, produce and/or participate in inflammatory, provocative, anti-white, racialistic, subversive and/or revolutionary plays or dramas'.[44] In the same year, Port Elizabeth playwright Khayalethu Mqhayisa's dramatisation of the social re-entry problems of prisoners released from Robben Island, *Confused Mhlaba*, was banned just as its popularity began to grow in the townships.

Outright banning is not the only problem faced by committed political theatre. While white provincial arts councils get heavy government subsidies, financial sponsorship is virtually non-existent for black theatre companies, radical or otherwise. White producers still siphon off black talent, and it is still illegal for an African to be registered as an independent professional actor. As a result, actors of internationally recognised talent such as John Kani and Winston Ntshona are still listed officially as clerks for Athol Fugard.[45] The lack of sponsorship is probably a good thing both artistically and politically, of course, since the course of this entire narrative proves nothing so much as that he who pays the piper calls the tune. But it also means that the development of an effective political theatre in South Africa depends upon the willingness of radical playwrights to establish continuity with the existing indigenous traditions of popular theatrical performance developed over the past century. Committed theatre must survive economically in the manner of all modern African performance culture; through the paid support of its audience. Furthermore, the effectiveness of theatrical communication is determined by the ability of plays to fulfil the cultural as well as political values of a broad range of urban Africans.

The clear path for committed playwrights who seek to create a mass audience for politically conscious theatre is to follow the lead of the young township playwrights including Manaka, Mda and Maponya. Though their productions may appear to the outsider as naive or poorly constructed, they are based in fact on the recognition that theatre is

> the most accessible and forceful medium through which the black working class is able to articulate its ideology, expose the contradictions of apartheid, and communicate a more accurate portrayal of their actual conditions of existence to members of their own and other classes.[46]

Emerging directly from the townships, these dramatists understand that for African playgoers, theatre is not a matter of creating an illusion, suspending disbelief, or identifying with metaphoric representations of experience.

The working-class aesthetic of the townships is that theatre is a direct extension of the actual conditions of black existence, with no necessary boundaries between art and life, performer and audience. This perspective is revealed in spontaneous audience responses to cathartic episodes such as the attempted suicide of Paul in Sam Mhangwane's *Blame Yourself* ('Is he really dead?') or the structure of Aby Madibane's play, *Black Tears* (1977):

> He simply draws his ideas by letting the lead actor, Sello, loose into the society and notes his development without leaving out important effects on him . . . The society is to be blamed for each individual . . . and somebody up there (on stage) is to be blamed for the society.[47]

Township playwrights are reacting implicitly against the view of white theatre critics who are driven by their class position to argue that plays like Manaka's *Egoli* are not theatre at all but mere forms of political statement.[48] For Manaka and Maponya, the more their work approaches the metaphoric structure of the well-made play the less effective as theatre it becomes. Drama theorists like Michael Etherton[49] are wrong in regarding the breakdown of barriers between real time and performance time, between lived experience and theatrical reproduction, and between performers and audience that occurs in popular theatre as retarding the development of coherent aesthetic principles and forms of presentation. As artists, township playwrights are aware that drama achieves its affecting power through a dialectic between rhetoric and authenticity.[50] Building on the audience expectations created by Gibson Kente, these authors are using theatre to transform political consciousness by the reflexive heightening and intensifying of black experience on the stage:

> The drama arises out of performance within the play itself and the concurrent real world. The text is rarely recorded but is nurtured in the

225

mind of its creator and is constantly updated and modified in terms of the lived relationship between people and their physical and social environments.[51]

Despite repression and the lack of facilities, training, and capital, black theatre flourishes in South Africa. Kavanagh[52] has counted no less than 150 separate productions between 1953 and 1977, and the proportions are growing. Apartheid may even have served to encourage this outpouring, for as John Kani explained, repression is like

> some kind of gangrene within you, inside of you, that eats your soul, that forces you to save your soul. I couldn't really say that a repressive society would result in creative art. But somehow it does help, it is an ingredient; it acts as a catalyst to a man who is committed.[53]

Among the most significant areas in which South Africa's political economy has inspired spontaneous theatre is among black miners, industrial workers and urban squatters. McNamara noted recently how Mozambican migrant workers have begun to use performance as a means to express the common values of their fellow miners during compound recreation:

> In one such situation, a group of Ndau dancers from Northern Mozambique used the dance arena as a platform for the dramatization of the common involvement of all in the underground work process. In their dance they recreated an 'accident' underground, from which the victim miraculously recovered after certain rites had been performed over him by an individual wearing the steel arm badge of an underground 'boss boy' or team leader. This was followed by a sequence in which the lead dancer, wielding a spade, lashed 'rock' into a 'cocopan rail loader' (in reality a tomato box). When lashing was completed the dancer suddenly turned up the box onto the arena floor, an action which represents the tipping of ore-bearing rock into the orepass. The action also appeared to have subversive intention in terms of sabotaging the products of labour, judging from the approving roar of the crowd which followed.[54]

White theatre activists like Hilary Blecher have found new and more meaningful outlets for their efforts in conducting theatre training and appreciation workshops in the sprawling, ramshackle squatter camps of Winterveld, near Pretoria, and Cape Town's famous Crossroads.[55] In 1978 the women of Crossroads created their own play, *Imfuduso*, dramatising the efforts of the police to remove the camp and deport its residents to the Ciskei, and the women's own successful resistance, for the edification of their neighbours.[56]

Perhaps the best example of the potential of theatre for the articulation of experience, the raising of consciousness, and the creation of solidarity among African workers is the Zulu play, *Ilanga*.[57] This play developed initially out of the efforts of trade union lawyer Halton

Cheadle to defend 55 Zulu foundry workers arrested for striking illegally in 1980. Among the immediate provocations for their brutal arrest by police was a dance they performed before Department of Labour officials outside the foundry enacting some of the conditions which prompted them to down tools. Finding it difficult to get the strikers to clarify their version of events for the purposes of their defence, Cheadle had them act out the story, an exercise that led to the elaboration of these roles into a full-scale play.

In reconstructing statements and events, the workers demanded exact recreation of reality from each other, debating each enactment until consensus was reached. No one was allowed to embroider his reconstruction to show himself or others in a better or worse light than they deserved. With the help of Johannesburg's multi-racial Junction Avenue Theatre Company, these re-enactments were adapted to courtroom procedure and actually performed for the magistrate during the trial. Finally, *Ilanga* emerged as a real piece of theatre, performed for co-workers in the evening at the Metal and Allied Workers' Union hall by the original actor-defendants in the strike.

The play as theatre thus achieves an almost seamless reflexive continuity with African experience, as 'the characters play themselves and enact their lives before a participant audience which is drawn into the structure of the play'.[58] Characters directly address the audience as well as each other, and actors sit and act among the audience as a means of encouraging individual engagement and response. The natural evolution of *Ilanga* from a legal strategy to a theatrical vehicle of collective consciousness demonstrates the social vitality of African theatre and its central role in contemporary cultural reintegration.

The creative involvement of white directors, actors, and theatre managers in some of the most progressive forms of African theatre also suggest that there may yet be hope for both inter-racial artistic collaboration and a socially relevant, broadly South African performance culture. For the time being, at least, South Africans of all races will find the most innovative and committed talents and productions at Barney Simon's Market Theatre, Johannesburg, the University of Cape Town's Baxter Theatre, and in union halls in cities throughout South Africa. Inspired by the critical History Workshop movement at the University of the Witwatersrand, the Federated Union of Black Artists (FUBA) has begun to sponsor popular drama that reclaims the whole of African social history for township audiences. A competition in 1978 produced well-researched plays dealing not only with ancient traditions of African kingship but with African life and resistance in the diamond fields of Kimberley, the goldfields of Johannesburg, and the Boer War.[59]

The Junction Avenue Theatre Company, also an outgrowth of

the History Workshops at Wits, recently produced a dramatisation of Modikwe Dikobe's novel of African working-class life in Johannesburg in the 1930s, *The Marabi Dance*[60] for the festival-symposium on Culture and Resistance held in Gaberone, Botswana in July 1982. A number of participants argued that aesthetic and political goals in committed theatre are mutually exclusive, such that the more artistically structured and metaphorical in expression a play is, the less authentic and politically effective it becomes. While I concur in the implicit rejection of class-based, socially emasculated Western formalist drama criticism, my experience compels me to maintain that a consciously formulated performance aesthetic is as important as social realism and ideological content in heightening the political and cultural consciousness of black audiences. The history of black theatre in South Africa strikingly illustrates that it is not only what but how performers communicate that gives performing arts their revelatory, transformative power.

Notes

1   Corney Mabaso, interview, 22 December 1976.
2   *Bantu World*, 7 October 1939.
3   *Bantu World*, 21 February 1948.
4   A. Gérard, *Four African Literatures*, Berkeley, 1971, pp. 80–81.
5   *Bantu World*, 4 February 1956.
6   Guy Routh, 'Bantu People's Theatre', *Trek*, October, (1950), 14 (10).
7   Teda de Moor, *Forum*, 11 October 1941.
8   *Sunday Times* (Johannesburg), 31 March 1968.
9   Robert Mshengu Kavanagh, 'Introduction', *South African People's Plays*, London, 1981, p. xiv.
10 *Ibid.*, p. xxvi.
11 *Ibid.*
12 P. F. Larlham, *Black Performance in South Africa*, unpublished Ph.D. thesis, New York University, 1981, p. 141.
13 Kavanagh, *South African People's Plays*, p. xvii.
14 E. Hellmann, *Soweto: Johannesburg's African City*, Johannesburg, 1967, p. 16.
15 Elliot Makhaya, *Post* (Johannesburg), 24 February 1978.
16 Frances Gardiner, *A Journal to the Zulu Country* (1836), pp. 47–50.
17 John Kani, interview with J. Marquard, *To the Point*, 23 December 1972.
18 *Sunday Observer* (London), 15 February 1981.
19 Welcome Duku, interview, 18 April 1977.
20 Larlham, *Black Performance in South Africa*, p. 163.
21 Fatima Dike, 'The Sacrifice of Kreli', *South African Drama No. 1: Theatre of the '70's*, Johannesburg, 1978.
22 Russel Vandanbroucke, *Yale/Theatre*, 8, 1 (Fall, 1978), p. 69.
23 See Mshengu, *S'ketch'*, Summer 1974/75, pp. 9–11.
24 Larlham, *Black Performance in South Africa*, pp. 166–7.
25 *Ibid.*, p. 153.
26 Saul Malapane, interview, 14 April 1977.

27   *Weekend World*, 3 April 1977.

28   *Weekend World*, 10 April 1977.

29   Kavanagh, *South African People's Plays*, p. xvi.

30   Ian Bernhardt, *Rand Daily Mail*, 6 January 1972.

31   *Star* (Johannesburg), 10 January 1972.

32   Mshengu, 'South Africa: Where Mvelinqangi Still Limps', *Yale/Theatre*, 8, 1, (Fall 1976), p. 47.

33   Larlham, *Black Performance in South Africa*, p. 173.

34   *Ibid.*, p. 177.

35   *Black Review*, (Durban) 1973, p. 210.

36   Pascal Gwala, 'Towards a National Theatre', *South African Outlook*, 103, 1227, (August 1973), p. 133.

37   Pascal Gwala, *Black Review*, 1973, p. 105.

38   *Star* (Johannesburg), 6 January 1972.

39   Pascal Gwala, *Black Review*, 1973, p. 133.

40   *Ibid.*, p. 113.

41   Kavanagh, *South African People's Plays*, p. 64.

42   Philip Frankel, 'Status, Group Consciousness, and Political Participation: Black Consciousness in Soweto', Witwatersrand History Workshop, 1978, p. 5.

43   Vincent Kunene, *S'Ketch'*, Summer, 1975, p. 14.

44   Kavanagh, *South African People's Plays*, p. 65.

45   *The Observer* (London), 15 February 1981.

46   Keyan Tomaselli, 'Black South African Theatre: Text and Context', *English in Africa*, 8, 1, (March 1981), p. 51.

47   *World*, 25 April 1977.

48   Michael Venables, 'From a Seat on the Aisle', (*Scenaria* 16, 1980, p. 19; Rosemary Raphaely, *Star Tonight*, 27 December 1979.

49   M. Etherton, 'The Dilemma of the Popular Playwright; the Work of Kabwe Kasoma and V. E. Musinga', Eldred D. Jones (ed.), *African Literature Today, No. 8: Drama in Africa*, London, 1976, p. 39.

50   James Brink, *Kote Tlon*, unpublished Ph.D. thesis, Indiana, 1980, p. 63.

51   Tomaselli, 'Black South African Theatre. . . .', pp. 51–2.

52   Kavanagh, *South African People's Plays*, p. xvii.

53   *S'Ketch'*, Winter, 1975, p. 26.

54   J.K. McNamara, 'Brothers and Workmates: Home Friend Networks in the Social Life of Black Migrant Workers in a Gold Mine Hostel', P. Mayer (ed.), *Black Villagers in an Industrial Society*, London, 1980, p. 334.

55   H. Blecher, 'Goal-oriented Theatre in the Winterveld,' *Critical Arts*, 1, 3, October, 1980, pp. 23–39.

56   Larlham, *Black Performance in South Africa*, p. 167. This play has been videotaped in Crossroads as part of Chris Austen and Peter Chappell's production *I Talk About Me, I Am Africa*, Icarus Films, New York, 1981.

57   This discussion is based upon K. Tomaselli, 'From Laser to the Candle', *South African Labour Bulletin*, 6, 8 (July, 1981).

58   *Ibid.*, p. 68.

59   *Post* (Johannesburg), 19 July 1978.

60   Modikwe Dikobe, *The Marabi Dance*, London, 1973.

9 Conclusion: the social dialectics of performance

THE story of South Africa's urban black performing arts has a good deal to say about how historical forces shape cultural expression through social process. The relationships involved are difficult to analyse, even when their components are well defined and the connections between them clear. The problem lies in attempting to isolate any form or process from its total context, to speak of one relationship without simultaneously implying another, and above all to establish lines of causation. The framework best suited to this analysis is that of social dialectics, in which social structure is treated as a network of intercommunication[1] between variables which are both products and producers of social force. While this view deprives us of any neat hierarchy of independent and dependent variables, it more faithfully reflects the actual relationship of performance to its total environment.

What seems most important, then, is to identify the concepts, processes, and methods of analysis that illuminate the relationship between performance and social action. To this end, established concepts must be re-examined to see what value they may still have. Any discussion of the development of urban performance, for example, must call the concept of urbanisation itself into question. With the exception of the issue of race itself, no social controversy has received more attention from social scientists and critics in South Africa than the process of black urbanisation. Its causes, dimensions, and consequences have been the focus of major sociological studies for more than fifty years[2].

Nevertheless, sociologists have yet to agree on the criteria that would allow them to categorise black South Africans according to their degree of urbanisation; nor do sociological criteria adequately reflect African social experience. Ever since the supply of African labour became sufficient to meet the needs of the expanding urban economy of South Africa in the years directly following the First World War, national and municipal authorities have issued 'influx control' regulations meant to stem the tide of black settlement in the cities.[3] The coercive system of labour migration has inhibited Africans from developing a self-supporting peasant economy or stable urban communities. Influx control and African resistance to it have both dramatically affected the quality of African life and made urbanisation difficult to measure. Strong ties to rural kin often coincide with long-term urban residence, social relationships and cultural values. Conversely, a low level of urban involvement and strong orientation towards rural society may coincide with nearly a lifetime of industrial employment.[4]

In the cities, differences among Africans in degree and quality of urbanisation and rural-urban contact have been significant in directing cultural process. Among the several patterns of urban life and categories of urban Africans, there are relationships structured by rural as well as urban resources and experiences. The process of urbanisation itself is a multiple one, and includes cultural as well as social and spatial aspects. For Africans, urbanisation involves commitment to permanent urban residence, and participation in relations centered in the urban social system. Culturally, urbanisation means the adoption of modes of interaction and expression developed in, but not confined to, urban situations. Mayer[5] says that an urbanised person is one fully confirmed in these modes and in valuing them positively. Yet the cities have been exporting these patterns to the rural areas for more than a century through the system of labour migration, leading to the growing phenomenon of 'rural urbanisation'[6].

From one viewpoint, urbanisation can be seen as a social process in which people acquire patterns of perception, communication, and action which are characteristic of the city.[7] Yet it is equally important to recognise that all the processes occurring in urban settings are not necessarily initiated there. Urbanisation is not identical with Westernisation, acculturation, or other kinds of change associated with contact between alien cultures of unequal material power. Missionary influence, colonial conquest and white settlement in South Africa initiated fundamental patterns of change in rural areas as well. When those affected migrated to the growing towns, those patterns were not only modified by urban experience, but exerted considerable influence over the forms that urban social relations and cultural patterns took.

While taking account of the historical complexities of rural-urban relations, this book has focused on permanent townspeople who share an urban community orientation. The notion of permanence essentially refers to an outlook; that of people with no

231

rural home, and of the country-born who have no real intention of returning there.[8]

The treatment of urbanisation as a matter of self-image and conscious behaviour is best suited to a social field in which government policy has sought to retard African urbanisation and 'detribalisation'. Specifically, the government has tried to facilitate 'Native Administration' by reinvigorating African traditional institutions once their power to threaten white domination was broken. In response to this policy, African urbanites have struggled for permanent urban status in every sphere. African Westernisation and urbanisation were seen by whites as a threat to their supremacy,[9] and by many Africans as paths of modernisation leading to their eventual emancipation. In such conditions, African urbanisation was more than a demographic process; it was an achievement.

If there is anything that characterises the dynamics of urban social relations, it is choice.[10] More than the rural areas, the cities offered black people a multitude of patterns which changed from situation to situation and encouraged flexibility. Some writers have perceived this process negatively, speaking of the 'formlessness' of urban African society.[11] A closer look, however, reveals that urban African communities are not characterised by social confusion but rather by new forms of organisation which provide a framework for understanding the behaviour of their members. The weighing of alternatives and conflicting values by individuals according to the principle of situational selection brought form out of formlessness and aided Africans' collective adaptation.

Situational selection involves choosing between conflicting principles of organisation and association. Such choices are made easier by the separation of various spheres of activity and help to resolve inconsistencies in the social field. Inconsistency, ambiguity and disharmony are part of the dynamics of urban social process, in which conflict and its resolution give momentum to adjustment and change.[12]

There is a cultural component to situational selection which underlies the urbanisation of performing arts. Choice is especially important in cultural activities which reflect social distinctions among urban residents. By examining choices made in the field of recreation, for example, one can tell the migrant who is urbanising from the one who is not. Performers also choose the styles they regard as most appropriate for specific audiences and occasions, and decide what, where and for whom they can perform. It is in leisure-time activities such as performance that one gains the clearest impression of emerging African communities and their distinctive culture.[13]

As a social process, urbanisation is promoted by the the creation of new cultural identities. In situations of change, identity is dynamic, and people manipulate its symbols in order to define who they are, who they are not, and who they wish to be.[14] The study of the interdependence of performance activity and cultural identity involves concepts of reference group behaviour and its associated structure of roles, statuses, and aspirations.[15] The importance of relevant others helps to account for the fluidity of cultural identities, and the development of role models must be seen in relation to the historical realities that underlie them.

The analysis of African status relations in urban South Africa involves oppositions – urban/migrant-rural, Westernised/traditional, and petty bourgeois/unskilled – but these relations have been ambiguous. The school-educated middle class viewed their white counterparts as a primary reference group. Yet many also admired, at a distance, the cultural vitality and social accountability of rural-traditional Africans, who they otherwise saw as a threat to their 'civilised' status. Middle-class Africans' ability to command some of the resources of white culture made them a positive reference group for the working class and increased their social and cultural influence. The actual situation of proletarians however, led them to develop their own patterns of adaptation, organisation, identity, and expression. These stemmed in part from a rejection of both the 'raw' migrant-rural Africans and the 'whiteman's good boys' of the middle class. The appeal of black American culture for members of both classes demonstrates that actual interaction with members of another group is not necessary for them to influence the formation of identity.[16] The problems of temporary migrants in working out special relationships to both urban society and to their rural communities led them to regard permanent urbanites positively in some respects and negatively in others.

The crucial point is that Africans in the towns have continually devised new patterns related to individuals' experiences and goals there. Rural ethnic background must be treated in relation to the values and interests it serves in the urban setting.[17] Similarly, ethnicity among migrant workers is not a holdover from the tribal past but reflects processes at work within the social arena of the mine compound.[18]

Sustained by shared symbols which produce their own models of social reality, cultural identities become role resources through which people participate in social interaction.[19] Culturally, adaptation to urban life is partly a process of symbolically identifying and reshaping a new environment.[20] This process guides performers in reordering expressive elements and selecting structural procedures in order to articulate their position, define performance situations, and make statements about social reality. In these ways, the flow of power is channelled into what Geertz calls the 'effort after meaning' as well as the 'effort after order'; into orientation along with consensus.[21]

Adaptation is more than a process of adjustment to external conditions, and involves attempts to create frameworks within which to resolve the dilemma of urban life. Those Africans in Johannesburg before the Second World War who wished to stay there permanently had to develop new social and cultural forms and to manipulate those they found. Even people who intended returning to the rural areas had to develop new arrangements for social cooperation and achievement under the urban conditions of their daily lives. Depending on their resources and strategies, Africans who saw themselves as permanent urbanites could be far less Westernised than some of their rural, mission-educated fellows. All categories of African urban residents, permanent or not, made important contributions to urban culture.

Understanding the search for sources of identity which reflect external conditions and bind the past to the present brings up the old problem of acculturation. Here this refers to the blending of various Western traditions into the structure of urban-based African culture patterns. Many of these patterns had their beginnings in those precursors of black urban communities, the rural and small-town mission stations. As Bastide has observed,[22] acculturation is a process involving the disintegration of the old cultural system as well as the reintegration of a new one. Acculturation in different areas of Southern Africa during the nineteenth century paralleled local power relations, with the weakest and most fragmented groups proving most susceptible to missionisation and Westernisation. There, the culture of the colonisers provided a value system that perpetuated their dominance and reinforced the structure of colonial society.[23]

Acculturation is an historical process of response to changing realities in specific situations. The emerging African middle-class has experienced Western culture primarily through church and school, while migrants and proletarians experienced varying degrees of ethnic mixing and Westernisation in the urban work place. Members of these social classes influence each other in developing syncretic cultural systems and values of their own. Acculturation therefore involves communication and exchange between sectors of the dominated social group as well as between dominant and subordinate peoples. It takes its form from the specific historical conjunction of cultures, the interrelation of various forces in the environment, and the communicative dimension of social structure. Most important is the principle of selectivity, which brings cognition to bear upon empirical reality, and makes cultural confluence a matter of meaning, decision making, and innovation.

Though Western culture was associated with colonial domination, Africans constantly searched for ways to use that culture to escape or mitigate their subordination. When these efforts failed to achieve major gains in autonomy, contrary tendencies towards cultural retrenchment emerged among urban Africans, leading to a heightened sense of cultural nationalism. The government actively promoted ethnicity and the revitalisation of African traditions in order to maintain cultural underpinnings for segregation and black racial disunity. Similarly, the policy of 'separate development' has officially discouraged African Westernisation. As a result, politically and culturally self-conscious Africans have been suspicious of movements to revive traditional culture and have had difficulty in developing the cultural component of African nationalism. Those who have done so with some success, including the leaders of the ICU in the 1920s and thirties, Anton Lembede and the Congress Youth League in the forties and fifties, and the Black Consciousness movement of the sixties and seventies, have created pan-ethnic models based on a kind of secondary acculturation; the reinterpretation of elements of traditional culture in their own adopted European terms.[24]

Acculturation is not a mechanical process, and nothing 'arises' simply from the contact of cultures or their bearers.[25] To understand what does occur in contact situations, the study of cultural processes must take political, economic, and social factors into account, and specify their interrelations. In reality, neither cultures nor their carriers are independent, but are inter-related by structures of communication, power, and exchange. Cultures meet in the minds of people who are part of networks and institutions with values, organisation, and rules for action.[26] In South Africa, acculturation has been an aspect of the quest for social status and an instrument of social mobility. Performances have reflected and reinforced changes in alignment and the status relations of groups, helping to create new urban cultural models and identities to which statuses are attached. Understanding how its involvement in social processes[27] influences the development of performance requires a close look at the schemes of interpretation that come between experience and its cultural representation. The concentration upon the forms of cultural activity pursued by members of different categories in the course of time greatly increases our knowledge of the role of performance in socio-cultural change.

Studies of long-term cultural processes such as the urbanisation of performance help to illuminate the relationship between forms of expression and all the conditions and behaviours that produce them and determine their structure.[28] Performance history must be seen as the history of human performance in society. In South Africa, social anthropology has always been historical, since indigenous peoples have had extensive contact with Europeans for more than two centuries. The reconstruction of events has therefore been both possible and necessary to the understanding of their present state.[29] In considering change, it is important to study the persistence of traditional institutions as well as the origins, development, nature and function of new ones.[30]

In ethnomusicology, 'both anthropology and history are needed for the full knowledge and understanding of music as human experience in time and space'.[31] It is as essential to recreate the development, functions, meanings, and circumstances of performance as it is to establish and analyse the musical notes in which some aspects of expression are embodied.[32] Ethnomusicology began in the nineteenth century as 'comparative musicology', centering on the cross-cultural comparison of musical thought, practices and performances. Today, the progress of the field depends upon the extension of comparison to cover all the elements which combine to produce desired artistic results. Stephen Blum has suggested[33] that 'comparative studies of the social and historical circumstances in which human beings. . .devise meaningful symbolic structures remain the most useful type of work which musicologists might perform.'

Anthropology, of course, should be comparative as well as historical since historical and comparative study are mutually illuminating. Schapera argues that 'to the anthropologists, the most convenient method of investigating and answering problems of both uniformity and variation is by comparison of social change under European influence'.[34] The study of African performance culture benefits from such comparison by examining the cultural response of Africans in different areas of Southern Africa to colonists and missionaries in the nineteeth and twentieth centuries. The conditions of contact varied widely from one region to another, producing differences in cultural outlook and modes of response that went beyond the influence of ethnic tradition. In addition to internal comparison of rates and quality of culture change, external comparison of performance culture in urban black South Africa with that of urban black America further helps to answer problems of both uniformity and variation in processes of stylistic development.

Black American performance culture figures importantly in this account not only for its comparative value but also because of its powerful influence on black South African culture. Black American music and dance, and the very ambience of communities like New York's Harlem, communicated through travelling performers and educators, print media, recordings, and films, have constituted a challenge, a model and a resource for black South Africans for more than a century. The blending of American influence into black South African culture represents neither slavish imitation of a glamorous but foreign popular culture nor the unthinking rejection of a subjugated but precious African heritage. It is rather the result of a creative syncretism[35] in which innovative performers combine materials from cultures in contact into qualitatively new forms in response to changing conditions, needs, self-images, and aspirations. In South Africa, stylistic elements from many sources have been recomposed into new frameworks of meaning, reflecting changing moral relations, systems of identity and value, and realities of power.

It is in this deeper process of syncretism that we observe the complex blending of traditions in adaptation to urban life. The analysis in this book has emphasised syncretism because its operation objectifies the relationships between historical experience, social interaction, personal agency, and cultural expression. Looking at how syncretism and related processes actually work in specific situations, as we have done, helps reveal the factors responsible for the observable form of performance and how these factors interact.

A concept which helps to place the components of syncretism – individual selectivity, innovation and reinterpretation – within the context of collective adaptation is that of the cultural broker. A cultural broker is a kind of entrepreneur in situations of acculturation, and a leader in the adoption and creation of innovations.[36] In its broadest sense the concept refers to individuals who link sectors of a society and mediate between cultures in contact. Active in creating images of changing social reality, performing artists have been among the most visible cultural brokers in urbanising African communities in South Africa.

Urban black performers have been at the centre of the processes of cultural communication and reinterpretation, creating original combinations, reinventing old forms in new contexts, and transforming performance materials in ways which reflect social forms and objectify new meanings. Performers function as cultural brokers because they provide social commentary not only in music, dance, and drama, but also in their expressive styles of dress, speech, and social interaction. Their sense of artistic personality becomes a metaphoric enactment and a realisation of consciousness in itself. Consequently, performers and performance occasions are important in re-establishing bases of social communication and order in situations of rapid transition. In such situations, an individual becomes more sensitive to

> messages that attempt to symbolise such order, and more ready to respond to people who are able to present them in terms of some broader, fundamental cosmic, social, or political order, to prescribe the proper norms of behaviour, to relate individual to collective identity, and to reassure him of his status and his place in a given collectivity.[37]

In creating such messages, performers gain prestige through their display of cultural competence and have an important influence on the flow of interaction. The display of artistic talent in relation to the total circumstances of performance brings about changes in social as well as cultural forms.[38] So the analysis of change must be concerned with questions of African aesthetic judgement and the culturally defined modes of receptivity through which any performance is experienced.[39] The value of performances and the status of performers must be seen in relation to participants' own evaluative criteria.

The overriding issue is the extent to which performing arts shape reality and the relations of people to their environment. First of all, though performing arts are bound up with adaptation to city life, their form cannot be reduced to a mere function of this process. We can speak of music or theatre only because we recognise them as modes of communication with their own principles of structure, logic of development, and patterns of elaboration. These characteristic, systemic qualities make it possible to talk meaningfully about the relation between the arts and the social field within which they occur. Of all cultural systems, the arts appear most autonomous, due to their self-focused structural logic, the inherent appeal of the integration of their forms, and the influence of artists and their works upon one another. Yet the existence of these identifying features does not make artistic behaviour an entirely separate reality.[40]

The particular appeal to the mind through the senses made by artistic expression is always conditioned by the total environment of which it is a part. The influence of one performer's activity on that of another is mediated by the context of that activity and its meaning for those involved. In the historical process of cultural exchange, external factors condition internal structural constraints in the stylistic blending of performance materials. Internal constraints include not only the nature of music, dance or drama, but also the historically similar features of different cultural systems which facilitate exchange between them,[41] and the value of specific exchanges for cultural adaptation.

The task is to understand the relationship between art and social behaviour by providing a means 'to conceptualise the dialectic between the crystallization of such directive patterns of meaning and the concrete course of social life'.[42] The key to this relationship is the role of metaphor in the formation of personal identity.[43]

Artistic performances are structured imagistic embodiments of values and qualities which people identify, at some level, with themselves. Metaphors extend as well as interpret and classify experience, giving situations both a form and an ordering significance they might not otherwise have.[44] Performance, then, acts as a social instrument by ordering experience, and by bringing values and identities to life.

People in situations of urban change use performance metaphors as instruments of social movement, order, and self-transformation.[45]

Artistic performances are cultural patterns that reflect ideas and create images of ideal personality, involving both the elaboration and learning of new modes of behaviour. By means of empathetic, emotionally charged cultural communication, they both symbolise and actualise changes in status[46] and help to bring order out of the chaos of diverse and conflicting images.

Performing arts reinforce the shift from rural to city-based principles of association and identity among urbanising Africans. Metaphors are effective in urban adaptation because they can be manipulated to achieve social movement. It is this effectiveness that underlies Peacock's[47] conception of Indonesian proletarian theatre as 'rites of modernization'. Peacock argues that urban theatrical performances promote psychocultural change among their audiences. He speculates further that the modernisation of consciousness by this means may provide a basis for collective social and political action outside the performance arena. Because his analysis is essentially static, however, it is unclear whether the performance communication he describes has the effects he proposes. A historical approach to this problem can focus on the mutual influence of social and performance processes over the course of urban development, yielding more information about the functions and effects of performance. In addition, the particular cultural style and criteria which people employ in reformulating their reality derive from complex developments requiring historical explanation.[48]

In South Africa, urbanisation has involved a gradual shift away from ethnic-regional ties towards neighbourhood residence and social class as bases of social identity and affiliation.[49] The process of change, however, is not a simple one. It involves a complex articulation between kinship, ethnic-regional, residence and class ties, as position in the emerging status system becomes increasingly important in determining behaviour.[50] For new arrivals, incorporation into urban society is a process of both personal adjustment and group identification.[51] Within this process, voluntary associations help build and reinforce values suitable to city life and provide networks of supporting relations. The social dynamics of status achievement are a driving force in urban African community life and a key factor in the organisational function of voluntary associations. Economic strategies for mutual aid, welfare services and capital accumulation are likewise organised through association membership. Equally important are the cultural activities of the associations, including entertainment occasions that provide the materials and interaction necessary for urban cultural transformation. Political organisations often develop out of welfare societies and other associations which act as committees for the holding of community events. The rich and varied associational life of urban Africans has long included performance as a major focus of identity formation and cultural patterning.

Conflicting with the role of voluntary associations in creating urban communities were powerful external and internal forces promoting disorganisation and rootlessness. Providing settings for communication and interaction, performers and performances have been vitally involved in the conflict between social order and disorder, cultural orientation and disorientation which has characterised adjustment to city life.

Within the wider field of urban South Africa, Africans actually use social uncertainty to resist white control and increase their freedom of action. At the same time, persistent social instability retards collective adaptation. Attempts to restructure social relationships are therefore part of the struggle for self-determination and political change.[52]

Since the 1940s, studies of African urbanisation have dealt increasingly with the African response to changed conditions, analysing new types of social groupings and status systems, categories, classes and patterns of organisation.[53] Often lacking, however, is any consideration of the wider system of power relations in which Africans live.[54] Yet it is these relations that integrate structure and history and mediate the creation of cultural identities and performances. The study of social history is essential for understanding how power relations have influenced cultural change.

In a plural society where common authority and not common culture defines the social system,[55] historical understanding reveals the nature of external pressures on dominated groups. Internal factors are also important, including processes of African reaction, adaptation and resistance, and patterns arising from the destruction of traditional social models and the need for new ones. History and anthropology come together once again in considering the role of power in cultural reproduction. Cultural forms are produced and reproduced through systems of rules and resources employed by individuals with definate intentions and interests. Every attempt to reproduce forms such as musical or theatrical styles in performance is mediated by the experience and circumstances of the participants. The potential for change is therefore present in any act which contributes to the reproduction of structures of performance.[56]

As a result, any treatment of performing arts as an aspect of adaptation to specific conditions must also describe power relations within which cultural change occurs. Performances derive from the cultural interpretation of experience. In South Africa, the major determinant of social experience is power, which is both the recognised ability to control the disposition of persons and things, and the transformative capacity of human action.[57] Control is physical in nature, as distinct from power, which is psychosocial. Control becomes social power only when its sources and potential are culturally recognised; that is, made relevant to some system of value and meaning. It is in the representation and enactment of emerging systems of value and meaning that performing arts have participated in power relations and in the adaptation of Africans to life in South African cities. In brief, social power provides the dynamics of urban cultural adaptation and shapes the form and function of urban performing arts.

Three aspects of the total social and historical environment provide the initiating conditions of urban cultural development.

1   the cultural, social, and economic resources that social actors have available to select from and manipulate;
2   the sources of control possessed by various groups and individuals;
3   the constraints of experience that influence thought and behaviour by demanding an adaptive response.

Each of these aspects goes through a process of cultural recognition, of assessment in terms of culturally structured values and meanings, in order to function as social instruments and as sources of individual and collective power. From their own point of view, Africans are subject to variable degrees of domination, of the exercise of power by others. The converse of this domination is autonomy, the ability to exercise power over their own environment and that of others.

Domination and autonomy exist in a dialectical relationship which initiates conflicting processes of adaptation leading towards the synthesis of social urbanisation. Among urban Africans in South Africa, external domination restricts manoeuvrability and depresses the field of social action, promoting both social disorder and broader solidarity within the community. These conditions lead to change based on the situational adjustment and social alignment involved in attempts to cope with a relative lack of autonomy, which include efforts to gain more of it.

Alternatively, autonomy in any degree leads to the creation of principles of social order, differentiation, and acceptance that provide the bases for the institutionalisation of social relations and norms of behaviour. From such institutionalisation emerges the sense and practice of community life and social co-operation. Tendencies towards both order and disorder, solidarity and conflict, influence the developing urban orientation of individuals and the emergence and maintenance of an urban social structure. This social structure is based upon a system of alignments, roles and statuses related to social identity.

Interpenetrating with these social processes are parallel cultural processes whose range of variability for individuals makes their articulation even more complex. Here, domination and autonomy produce opposed but interactive processes of acculturation and cultural retrenchment, Westernisation and cultural nationalism. It would be possible to add other processes, and I have mentioned only those most apparent in the South African situation.

The key to these processes is the flexibility of cultural traditions as sources of meaning, identity, and solidarity.[58] Such flexibility facilitates the creation of new cultural models as part of the movement towards urbanisation. The streams of social and cultural dynamics are brought together in a system of urban categories and principles of association in which differences in culture reflect and reinforce differences in status.

Finally, the production and reproduction of performances must be located within the set of political, economic, social, and cultural, relations between performers and the total context in which they perform.[59] These relationships depend on the distribution of power in the environment, economic and other returns derived from various performance alternatives, the demands of sponsors and participants, available stylistic resources and performance training, and cooperation and competition among performers. Here again the performer acts as a cultural broker, promoting his own autonomy while linking spheres of social reality with consciousness by emotional, meaningful expressions of continuity and change.

Performers accomplish these things by applying an implicit theory of composition and expression. Performance products themselves contain signs of the processes through which performers have realised their theoretical choices. In order to understand both performance and the behavior underlying it as parts of a total system, we must look at these theories with regard to: how and in what ways relationships among elements are reordered in performance; how the usage of particular procedures is restricted to one group of performers or participants as opposed to others; how particular expressive choices shift the definition of a performance situation; the means a performer uses to articulate his position in the context of social conflict.[60]

Performance has made a major contribution to the quality of life, and even to the psychosocial survival of urban Africans in South Africa. This has been recognised by authorities concerned with the welfare of the African work-force. From Johannesburg's earliest days, mine compound managers, municipal officials, missionaries, and some industrial employers have taken special interest in providing 'healthful' leisure-time occupations. Mine dancing, choir competitions, brass bands and cultural clubs helped to ease tension, soften hardship and divert energies that might otherwise have been directed against the industrial labour system itself.

Mine dancing even had the added benefit, from management's

point of view, of promoting ethnic divisiveness and hindering worker solidarity. Performance played an important role in the total process of urbanisation among Africans in part because it had been a central focus of activity in ceremonies of the life cycle, kinship and family, religion, and even political and military organisation in traditional society.

Middle-class Africans readily accepted the viewpoint of their missionary tutors, who regarded performance as a form of cultural and moral preparation for full participation in a Western society. When the right to such participation was not granted, the command of certain key aspects of Western culture remained essential in the ideology of African nationalism. Bodies such as Kimberley's South African Improvement Association and Johannesburg's BMSC used entertainment as a focus for organisational activity, social interaction, fund-raising, and the development of cultural models based upon African middle-class aspirations. Among urban African proletarians, entertainment fulfilled similar functions against a background of lower expectations but equal desperation. For them, entertainment provided a cathartic release and served as a defence against dehumanisation through the expressive sharing of experience. As entertainment, performances still provide an attraction, financial resource, and in many cases a central focus for urban associations. Entertainment is therefore an aspect of urban adaptation, which in turn provides the dynamic of change in performance styles themselves.

Performances provide images for the reshaping and reordering of cultural categories underlying the organisation of networks and communities. Performing arts have been important in Africans' attempts to find places for communities and personalised interaction to exist in South African cities.[61] African performances cannot therefore be regarded as 'mere' entertainment, since they are essential to the self-conscious pursuit of black cultural autonomy. Cultural self-definition is in turn but an aspect of the effort to create informal connections needed to unify black people in practical ways, as the South African Black Consciousness Movement has long been aware.[62]

This unifying potential again raises the question of power. Power in this sense refers to the capacity of performance to increase group support for premises on which strategies for changing society might be based. Performers, as LeRoi Jones points out,[63] are quite capable of using performance to comment critically on the power relations within which they are obliged to live and work. The logical extension of the adaptive process is the desire among urban Africans for social movement incorporating greater participation in the political process. The sources of order in urban African communities are linked to the commitment to demands for political incorporation. This is the point at which the notion of entertainment can influence and possibly work against the potential of performance to aid the restructuring of society.

To some extent, the very notion of performance entertainment was an innovation, an activity considered characteristic of modern urbanity and sharing in its general prestige. The capacity to participate knowledgeably in specific forms of entertainment became a sign of cultural competence and an instrument of identity, illustrating the social significance of evaluative criteria and expressive style. Clearly, the notion of entertainment had adaptive implications in relation to performance as both a register of, and a factor in, the play of forces determining change.

Assuming that power is by nature transformable, the question remains as to whether the performing arts can become a source of power available for use in other contexts. The dimensions of this problem are both organisational and ideological and grow out of the performing arts' adaptive significance. Organizationally, performances provide a focus for community orientation, leadership, and the emergence of social networks and institutions which in favourable circumstances serve as a basis for political activity. As Leonard Thompson rather optimistically suggested, the 'apolitical non-white associations of today may carry the germs of the South African political system of tomorrow'[64].

The role of performing arts in creating such a basis, however, is primarily ideological. African performing arts help to bring about ideological change as part of the process of urban adaptation. Yet it is uncertain whether this enhanced consciousness can become a source of solidarity clarifying the goals of cultural identity and social movement. It appears that the participants in South Africa's cultural struggle believe that it can: Africans have tried to use performance to attain these ends, while the white power structure has used it to inculcate a separate and subordinate African self-image. As Richard Adams has pointed out however,[65] cultural images and symbolic action do not so much create the potential for control as bring about the collective recognition of that potential, turning it into actual social power. Expressive culture can become a source of power, but only in conjunction with the existence and increase of the material potential for control at other levels.

Furthermore, the sources of African ideology and solidarity have been embedded in cultural models in part adopted from and mediated by the white social sector itself. The determination and capacity of white society to repress African aspirations, coupled with the contradictions inherent in the struggle for autonomy through Afro-Western syncretisation, have made urbanisation culturally disorienting for many Africans. Gerhart[66] rightly comments that 'a distinctive African urban subculture did gradually come into being, but underneath its often vibrant and gay exterior lingered a continuing crisis of the spirit'. Finally, the struggle among the urban African community, the white mass media, and the government for the control of performance reveals the interdependence of cultural with social, political, and economic autonomy and domination.

The interests of the entertainment media have been supported by political machinery limiting the performance alternatives of African artists. Consequently, they have secured increasing control over both the channels of communication and distribution of performances, and over the social and economic constraints influencing their production. The community to which the performer belongs, however, exercises whatever economic and social power it has to encourage performers to satisfy demands potentially different from those of the dominant mass media. Such conflict and relationships are of great importance in the analysis of how African performing arts have achieved their modern form in South Africa. The role of the media in African performance culture is another illustration of how the dynamics of social power influence stylistic innovation.

This book represents part of the search for 'a conceptual framework in which changes and retentions of . . . style and context can be understood within a synthesis of social and cultural change'.[67] This framework centres on the flow of social power over time, with the purpose of discovering the determinants and significance of performance process. Such discoveries can only be made through comparative accounts of this process in different periods and places. The study of artistic behaviour is essential for understanding the nature and role of cultural change in urbanisation. We will be able to assess the social importance of cultural communication only when we understand *how* as well as what meanings are communicated – a problem requiring the historical and holistic analysis of the arts.

In explaining performance development, then, we must firstly identify the material resources and limitations of the historical environment. Secondly, we must specify the power relations and interactional patterns of the social field in which performance activity takes place. These realities provide the context of cultural adaptation. After almost three centuries of settler colonialism in South Africa, for example, Schapera could speak of 'the development of a specifically South African culture, shared in by both Black and White, and presenting certain peculiarities based directly upon the fact of their juxataposition'.[68] Thirdly, we must analyse the development and function of social roles and institutions involved in the relations of performance production. Fourthly, we must discover the specific cultural principles that order elements of performance in relation to social needs. It is through principles shared by members of a culture that meanings and values are embodied in performance.

A good deal more knowledge about the aesthetic systems involved is needed in order to understand the precise relationship of composition to cultural value and meaning in black South African performing arts. The limited results of the current study, however, indicate that value and meaning guide the process of selection, synthesis and change in relation to culturally assigned qualities of expressive elements. The ultimate value of a performance is based on its effectiveness in integrating human experience[69] and in the meaning it is able to give to other levels of reality. Performance is more than a reflection of socio-cultural dialectics; it embodies and actively participates in them.

Performing arts clearly play an important role in the cultural reorientation of black South Africans in the urban setting. Consequently, performance events provide a kind of reflexive commentary on African urbanisation. Such commentary is of great value because it affords direct views of the way people present their culture to themselves.[70] In South Africa, where urban social fields have been largely composed of unintegrated sets of opposing forces and shifting elements, the analysis of performance communication can provide an important means of understanding group social existence. Additionally, understanding the process of cultural transformation requires the insights of a social history which links evolving forms of human association to changing vehicles of consciousness and expression.[71]

This account demonstrates how Africans have built new communities despite *apartheid*. Performance events have helped create culture patterns that define group orientations and help to generate new social forms. Through this process, diverse patterns and principles have been combined into new sources of order, structure and solidarity. Performers have been deeply involved in these social dialectics, acting as a force for communication and ordering, even in a world of conflict.

The struggle for cultural autonomy goes on in urban black South Africa, and the processes of cultural transformation outlined here continue to operate in relation to the external factors and power relations of South African society. Inheritors of the legacy of Doornfontein and Sophiatown, innumerable backyard bands and school vocal groups perform at weddings, funerals, meetings, and parties throughout the townships. Black and multi-racial theatre companies are creating new forms of socially and politically relevant urban drama. In Soweto and places like it, indigenous urban township jazz, popular, and religious music have found a new environment for growth. Though the government and the white entertainment industry remain powerful forces to contend with, the performing arts continue to play an active role in the evolution of black identity and the internal definition of black aspirations in South Africa.

246

Notes

1. A. F. C. Wallace, 'Revitalization movements', *American Anthropologist*, 58, 2 (1956), p. 266.
2. Among the most noteworthy studies are: Ellen Hellmann, 'The native and the towns', in I. Schapera, (ed.) *The Bantu-Speaking Tribes of South Africa*, London, 1937; and *Rooiyard: a Sociological Survey of an Urban Native Slumyard*, Cape Town, 1948; Ray Phillips, *The Bantu in The City*, Johannesburg, 1938; Philip Mayer, *Townsmen or Tribesmen*, Cape Town; 1961, and *Black Villagers in an Industrial Society*, Cape Town, 1980; B. A. Pauw, *The Second Generation*, Cape Town, 1963; D. H. Reader, *The Black Man's Portion*, Cape Town, 1961; M. Wilson and A. Mafeje, *Langa*, Cape Town, 1963; Leo Kuper, *An African Bourgeoisie*, New Haven, 1965; D. Welsh, 'The growth of the towns', in M. Wilson and L. Thompson (eds.), *The Oxford History of South Africa*, Oxford, 1971; J. C. De Ridder, *The Personality of the Urban African in South Africa*, London, 1961; and Allie Dubb, 'The impact of the city', in W. D. Hammond-Tooke (ed.), *The Bantu-Speaking Peoples of Southern Africa*, London, 1974.
3. Philip Mayer, *Townsmen or Tribesmen*, Cape Town, 1961, p. 225.
4. Y. Glass, 'The industrialisation of an indigenous people', *South African Journal of Science*, 59, 8, (1963), p. 15.
5. Mayer, *Townsmen or Tribesmen*, p. 449f.
6. M. C. O'Connel, 'Xesibe Reds, Rascals, and Gentlemen at home and at work', in P. Mayer, *Black Villagers in an Industrial Society*, Cape Town, 1980, pp. 255–307.
7. Kenneth Little, *Urbanisation as a Social Process*, London, 1974.
8. J. Clyde Mitchell, 'A note on the urbanisation of Africans on the Copperbelt', *Rhodes-Livingstone Journal*, 12, (1953).
9. D. Welsh, 'The growth of the towns', in M. Wilson and L. Thompson (eds.), *The Oxford History of South Africa*, Oxford, 1971, p. 188.
10. Mayer, *Townsmen or Tribesmen*, p. 17.
11. P. G. Koornhof, *The Drift from the Reserves Among the South African Bantu*, unpub. Ph.D. thesis, Oxford, 1953, p. 480.
12. A. Epstein, *Politics in an Urban African Community*, Manchester, 1958.
13. *Ibid.*, p. 9.
14. G. Berreman, 'Bazaar behaviour; social identity and social interaction in urban India', in G. DeVos and L. Romanucci-Ross, *Ethnic Identity*, Palo Alto, 1975, p. 71.
15. Robert Merton, *Social Theory and Social Structure*, Glencoe, Ill., 1956, p. 368.
16. *Ibid.*, p. 300.
17. Max Gluckman, 'Tribalism in British Central Africa', *Cahiers d'Etudes Africaines*, I, (1960), p. 56.
18. A. L. Epstein, *Politics in an Urban African Community*, Manchester, 1958. J. K. McNamara, 'Brothers and workmates: home friend networks in the social life of black migrant workers in a gold mine hostel', in P. Mayer, (ed.) *Black Villagers in an Industrial Society*, Cape Town, 1980.
19. Crawford Young, *The Politics of Cultural Pluralism*, Madison, Wisconsin, 1976, p. 98.

20   B. Jules-Rosette, *Symbols of Change*, San Diego, 1981, p. 6.
21   C. Geertz, *The Social History of an Indonesian Town*, Cambridge, Mass., 1965, p. 206.
22   Roger Bastide, *The African Religions of Brazil* (H. Sebba, trans), Baltimore, 1978, p. 14.
23   I. Wallerstein, 'Introduction', *Social Change: The Colonial Situation*, New York, 1966, p. 2.
24   Bastide, *The African Religions of Brazil*, pp. 387–8.
25   George Balandier, 'The colonial situation: a theoretical approach', in I. Wallerstein (ed.), *Social Change: the Colonial Situation*, New York, 1966. p. 52.
26   Roger Bastide, 'Acculturation', *Encyclopaedia Universalis* I, (1968), pp. 106–7.
27   *Ibid.*, p. 16.
28   Alan Merriam, *The Anthropology of Music*, Evanston, Ill., 1964, p. 7.
29   Isaac Schapera, 'Should anthropologists be historians?', *Journal of the Royal Anthropological Institute*, 92, 2, (1962), p. 145.
30   George Balandier, *The Sociology of Black Africa*, London, 1970, pp. 41–2.
31   Gilbert Chase, 'Musicology, history, and anthropology: current thoughts', in J. W. Grubbs (ed.), *Current Thoughts in Musicology*, Austin, Texas, 1976, p. 236.
32   Chase, 'Musicology, history, and anthropology,' pp. 238–9.
33   Stephen Blum, 'Towards a social history of musicological technique', *Ethnomusicology*, XIX, 2, (May 1975), p. 221.
34   Schapera, 'Should anthropologists be historians?', p. 151.
35   Melville Herskovits, *Man and His Works*, New York, 1984.
36   Eric Wolf, 'Aspects of group relations in a complex society: Mexico', in D. B. Heath (ed.), *Contemporary Cultures and Societies of Latin America*, New York, 1965.
37   S. N. Eisenstadt, *Tradition, Change and Modernity*, London, 1973, p. 133.
38   John Kaemmer, *The Dynamics of a Changing Music System in Rural Rhodesia*, unpub. Ph.D., thesis, Indiana, 1975, p. 50.
39   Blum, 'Towards a social history', p. 217.
40   Alan Merriam, 'Music change in a Basongye village (Zaire),' *Anthropos*, 72, 5/6 (1977), p. 825.
41   Alan Merriam, 'The use of music in the study of a problem of acculturation', *American Anthropologist*, 57 (1955).
42   Geertz, *The Interpretation of Cultures*, p. 250.
43   James Fernandez, 'Persuasions and performances: of the beast in everybody . . . and the metaphor of everyman', *Daedalus*, 1, 2, (1972), p. 43.
44   S. Hanchett, 'Five books in symbolic anthropology', *American Anthropologist* 80, (Sept. 1978), p. 621.
45   Fernandez, 'The mission of metaphor', p. 133.
46   Richard Schechner, *Essays on Performance Theory, 1970–1977*, New York, 1977, p. 73.
47   James Peacock, *Rites of modernisation*, Chicago, 1968.
48   S. Ortner, *Sherpas Through Their Rituals*, Cambridge, 1978, p. 7.
49   M. Wilson and A. Mafeje, *Langa*, Cape Town, 1963, pp. 34–8.
50   Epstein, *Politics in an Urban African Community*, p. 240.

51   Michael Banton, 'Social alignment and identity in a West African city', in H. Kuper (ed.), *Urbanisation and Migration in West Africa*, Berkeley, 1965, p. 146.

52   Balandier, *The Sociology of Black Africa*, p. 481.

53   Mayer, *Black Villagers*.

54   B. Magubane, 'A critical look at the indices used in the study of social change in colonial Africa', *Current Anthropology*, 12, 4–5, (Oct.–Dec. 1971).

55   I. Wallerstein, *Social Change: the Colonial Situation*, New York, 1966, p. 2.

56   Anthony Giddens, *The New Rules of Sociological Method*, New York, 1976, p. 102.

57   *Ibid.*, p. 110.

58   Elizabeth Colson, *The Makah Indians*, Minneapolis, 1953, p. 292.

59   W. d'Azevedo, 'A structural approach to aesthetics', *American Anthropologist*, 60 (1958), p. 712.

60   Blum, 'Towards a social history', pp. 214–17.

61   Schechner, *Essays on Performance*, p. 89.

62   G. Gerhart, *Black Power in South Africa*, Berkeley, 1978.

63   LeRoi Jones, *Blues People*, New York, 1963, p. 152.

64   Leonard Thompson, *Politics in the Republic of South Africa*, Boston, 1966, p. 150.

65   Richard N. Adams, *Energy and Structure*, Austin, 1975, p. 13.

66   Gerhart, *Black Power in South Africa*, p. 32.

67   John Szwed, 'Afro-American Musical Adaptation', N. Whitten and J. Szwed (eds.), *Afro-American Anthropology*, New York, 1970, p. 220.

68   I. Schapera, 'Contact between European and Native in South Africa – Bechuanaland', *Methods of the Study of Culture Contact in Africa*, London, 1938, p. 26.

69   John Blacking, 'The Value of Music in Human Experience', *Yearbook of the International Folk Music Council*, London, 1969, p. 34.

70   James Boon, 'Further operations of culture in anthropology: a synthesis of and for debate', in L. Schneider and C. Bonjean (eds.), *The Idea of Culture in the Social Sciences*, Cambridge, 1973, p. 19.

71   Geertz, *The Social History of an Indonesian Town*, p. 5.

Appendix A

Influenza (1918)

Key F   R.T. Caluza

```
{| m .f  :s    :     :m  | f  :s   :l  :f  | s .l  :t  :s  | d' .m :l .m |s :d' :d .r  |
 | d .t, :d .r :d .t, | l, .s, :l, :l, | f .f  :f  :f  | m :d  :d .d  |t, .t, :f .f |m :d :d .r  |
   Ngonya ka   ka       nineteen eighteen  sa qe dwa u-    ku fa  e  si   ku bi-za ngo  ku-ti ku yi
 | s  .s  :s    :s   | f  .m :f  :f | s .s  :s  :s  | s  :s :m .m |r :s :s .s |s :s :m .f  |
 | d  .r  :m    :d   | r  .m :f  :r | s .f  :r  :t, | d :d :l, .l, |r :r :f .f |m :d :l, .f, |}
```

```
{| m  :f  :r  :d  | d :— :— :— | m .f  :s    :m  | f .s  :l  :f | s .l  :t  :s  |
 | d  :d  :s,   :  | s, :— :— :— | d .t, :d .r :d .t, | l, .s, :l, :l, |f .f  :f  :f  |
   In - flu- e - nza            Ya zi  qe -  da    i zi- hlo- bo   e si zi ta-
 | s  :l  :f  :m  | :— :— :  | s .s    :s   :s   | f .m :f  :f | s .s  :s  :s  |
 | m, :r, :s, :d, | :— :— :  | d .r  :m   :d   | r .m :f  :r | s .f  :r  :t, |}
```

```
{| d' :m  :l  .m | s .f  :t  :l | s :d'  :d .r  | m  :f  :r  | d :— :s .s  |
 | m  :d  :d .d  | t, .t, :f .f | m :m  :d .d   | d  :d  :s, | s, :— :d .d |
   nda yo  a  o    ma ma na o     ba- ba  no Si  si  no Bhu- ti  Kwemnyi
 | s  :s  :m .m  | s :s  :s .s | s .m,  :f  | m :l  :f  | m :— :m .m |
 | d  :d  :l, .l, | r :r  :f .f | m :d  :l, .f, | m .r, :s, | d, :— :  |}
```

```
{| s  :f  :f .f | f :m  :m .m | f :d  :r  | m :— :s, .s, :s, .s, |s :f  :f .f |
 | t, :t, :t, .t, | d :d  :d .d | d :d  :d .d | t, :— :d .d :d .d |t, :t, :t, .t, |
   mi zi  kwaqo   tu la   a kwa  sa- la mu-  ntu kwa tat'i    nto- mbi nensi-
 | r  :t,  :r  :s :m .s :d' .ta | l :l  :l  :se :— |
                                                  kwata ta
 | :f, .f, :f, .f, | m, :  |}
```

```
{| m  :— :m .s :d' | l  :f  :l | s :— :s, .s, :s .s | s :f  :f  | m :— :d  :r .m |
 | d  :— :m .m .m | f  :f  :f | m :— :m  :m .m | r :r  :d  | d :d  :d .d |
   zwa    kwa zike   te - l'e zi- nhle  kwa ta ta   na ma bhu ngu   a ye bu
 | m .s :d'  :— | f, .l, :d' :d' | m .s :d' .d' .d' :d' .d' |t :s :s | s :— :m .s |
 | nensi zwa      kwazi ke te- l'e zi nhle kwa ta ta
 | s, .t, :r :s | d .m :s |
   kwata- ta na- mabhu- ngu
```

```
{| f  :l. :t. | d  :— .s :s .s | s  :f  :f | m :— :m :s .d' | l  :f  :l |
 | d  :l. :s, | s, :— .d :d .d | t, :t, :t, | d :— :m :m .m | f  :f  :f |
   ke ka ka- hle  Kwa ta ta   ma- jo- ngo- si   kwa ta ta   na ma- tshi
 | l  :r  :f | m :— :  | t, :s :s | m .s :d' | f .l :d' :d' |
   Kwata t'a ma- jongo si               kwata ta na
 | f. .l. :r :s. | d. :— |
   buke ka ka hle
```

```
{| s  :— .s :s .s | s  :f  :f | m :— .d  :r .m | f  :l. :t. | d :— .m :m .m |
 | m  :— .m :m .m | r  :r  :r | d :  :  | d :l. :s. | s, : : |
   tshi,  kwa tat'i   zi- ngo- du- so    e za ze te- nji si  we  Kwa tat'o
 | m .s :d' .d' :d' .d' | t :s :s | s :— .m :m .s | l  :r  :f | m : : |
   matshitsi
 | s. .t. :r :s | d .m :s | :— | f. .l. :r :s. | d. : : |
   Kwata- ti zi ngodu so         ze- te nji si  we
```

250

```
{|m    :m  :m  |m   :—.m :m .m |m    :m  :m  |m   :—.m :f .fe |s .fe :s  :l  |
 |d .t, :d  :d  |t,  :—   :    |d .t, :d  :d  |t,  :—   :     |t, .t, :t, :d  |
 |o -ma- ko-tsha na          na-ba- kwe-nya -na
 |l .se :l  :l  |se  :—   :    |l .se :l  :l  |se  :—   :     |r .r  :r  :f  |
 |l, .t, :d  :l, |m,  :—   :    |l, .t, :d  :l, |m,  :—   :     |s, .s, :s, :r, |}
```

ma ko tsha na ka nyena ba - kwe-nya-na kwa ngati ku ku n'i-f'e

```
                                                    mf
{|s .fe :s  :f  |m .r :m  :r  |d   :—   :—  |m .f :s   :m  |f .s :l  :f  |
 |t, .t, :t, :d  |d .t, :d  :s, |s,  :—   :—  |d .t, :d .r :d .t, |l, .s, :l, :l, |
 |limnya ma pe- zu kwa lo mhla ba        Kwas'onga  ti   i zo  la  nda
 |r .r :r  :l  |s .fe :s  :f  |m   :—   :—  |s .s :s   :s  |f .m :f  :f  |
 |s, .s, :s, :r  |s, .s, :s, :s, |d,  :—   :—  |d .r :m   :d  |r .m :f  :r  |}
```

```
{|s .l :t  :s  |d' :m  :l .m |s  :f :t .l |s :d' :d .r |m .f :r  |
 |f .f :f  :f  |m  :d  :d .d |t, :t, :f .f |m :m :d .d |d :d :s, |
 |i nto mbi ne-nsi zwa ya ba ngco no kwaba da -la ya ba qe -d'a ba-
 |s .s :s  :s  |s  :s  :m .m |r :s :s .s |s :s :m .f |s :l :f |
 |s .f :r  :t, |d  :d  :l, .l, |r :r :f .f |m :d :l, .f, |m, :r, :s, |}
```

```
{|d :—   :—  |m .f :s  :m  |f .s :l  :f  |s .l :t  :s  |d' :m  :l .m |
 |s :—   :—  |d .t, :d .r :d .t, |l, .s, :l, :l, |f .f :f  :f  |m  :d  :d .d |
 |sha.          A o ma     me   na o ba -ba  bashi y'i nta nda ne zihlu-
 |m :—   :—  |s .s :s  :s  |f .m :f  :f  |s .s :s  :s  |s  :s  :m .m |
 |d, :—   :—  |d .r :m  :d  |r .m :f  :r  |s .f :r  :t, |d  :d  :l, .l, |}
```

```
{|s :f :t .l |s :d' :d .r |m  :f :r  |d  :—   :s .s |s  :f  :f .f |
 |t, :t, :f .f |m :m :d .d |d  :d :s, |s,  :—   :d .d |t, :t,  :t, .t, |
 |pe ka zi no si zi zi nga nce dwa 'mu ntu.  No ko  na mhla  se si
 |r :r :f .f |m :d :l, .f, |m, :r, :s, |d, :—   :m .m |r :t, .r :s  .s |
```

```
{|f :m   :m .m |f :d :r |m  :—   :s :s .s |s  :f :f .f |m  :—.m :s .d' |
 |d :d   :d .d |d :d :d |t, :—.d :d .d |t, :t. :t, .t, |d  :—.m :m .m |
 |ko hlwa  u si z'o-lu-ku-lu  Kwa ku nje-na ke e ndu-lo   kwa ba be-
 |s :m .s :d' .ta |l :l :l |se :—   :  |t, .r :s :— |m .s :d' :— |
 |        o -lu ku lu           kwaku nje   e ndu lo
 |  :   :  |f. :f. :f. |m. :—   :  |
```

```
{|l  :f :l |s  :—.s :s .s |s  :f :f |m  :—   :d :r .m |f  .l :.t. |
 |f  :f :f |m  :—   :m .m .m |r  :r :r |d  :—   :   |d  :l. :s. |
 |y'e  Ka na-na   kwa ti nxa be hlu-pe- ka,   ba qal'u ku-zi-so-
 |f  :l :d' .d' |m .s :d' .d' :d' .d' |t :s :s |s  :—.m :f .s |l  :r :f |
 |kwaba be y'e Kana nakwa ti nxa
 |  :   :  |s, .t, :r :s |d .m :s  :—  |f. .l. :r :s. |}
```

kwati nxa be hlupe ka

Influenza (English translation by Fatima Dike)

In the year of 1918	It burnt the elderly out
We were wiped out	Mothers and fathers left orphans
By a disease which they call influenza	sad and suffering
It took friends which we loved	With no one to help them out
Mothers, fathers, sisters, and brothers	It was like this in the wilderness
In other homes, nobody survived	For those who were travelling to Canaan
It took maidens, and young men	When they started to suffer on the journey
Taking the most beautiful	They pitied themselves
It took the most coveted	Because when they ruled
The cream of our youth	They were happy
It took even handsome virile men	They forgot their maker
It took even virgins	Only those who worshipped him constantly
Who were pleasing to the eye	pulled through
It took those with home and promise	The rest were destroyed, out there in the wilderness
It took young brides and grooms	Now we want to warn our sons and daughters
It was as if there were a black cloud	Do not let your hearts rule your heads
Hanging over this earth	Because it can never be satisfied
Which had come to take our youth	

252

Appendix B

Meloli le Lithallere tsa Afrika

U ea kae?

J.P. Mohapeloa

Morija Sesotho
Book Depot, 1977 ed.

1

Key A

```
|   :   |    :l .r | l .l :s .m ,r | ld  :r .l.
        Tsoa-ra    kho-ng, re  ee    koa - na Ta -
|   :   |    : .s. | d   :— .t.    | ll.  :— .d
        Tsoa - ra   khong,  re     ee
|   :   |    : .f  | m   :— .d     | lf   :— .d
|   :   |    : .t₂ | d.  :— .d.    | lf.  :— .l.

s.  :—  |    :l .r | l .l :s .m ,r | ld  :r .l.
ung,        Tsoa-ra  kho-ng, re ee   koa - na Ta -
s.  :— .m. |m, : .s. | d :t, .t. | ll.  :l, .f.
koo    Ta  ung, Tsoa - ra  ko - to,  re  ee koa-
m   :— .d  |ld      :  .r  | m  :r .r | lf  :r .d
            Re ee    koa
d   :— .s. |m.  :r. .t₂ | d.  :— .s. | ll.  :f, .l.

s.  :— .s  |    :l, .l, .l, | s.  :— .m. | l— :l, .l, .l,
ung,
m.  :— .s. |s.  :f, .f, .f, | m,  :— .d. | l— :r, .r, .r,
na      Ta  ung, Ha Mole - tsa  -  ne,    Ha Mo - le -
d   :— .m  |m    :r .r .r | m  :— .s | l— :f .f .f
na      Ta  ung, Ha Mole - tsa  -      ne,   Ha Mo - le -
d   :— .s. |m.  :t₂ .t₂ .t₂ | d.  :— .s. | lm. :t₂ .t₂ .t₂

s.  :— .m. |l— . :m .r | m .m :m .r | ld  :l. .m.
m.  :— .d. |l— . :s. .s. | d .d :t. .t. | ll.  :r. .r.
tsa  -  ne;    Re e'o   bo - na ha ho po - loa ma -
m   :— .m  |l— . :s .f | m .m :s .m | lf  :f .d
tsa  -  ne;          ma -
d.  :— .s. |m,  :t₂ .t₂ | d. .d. :m. .s. | ll. :f. .f.

m. .s. :— |l— . :r | m  :— .r |lm .r .d :r .d .l.
m. .m. :— |l— . :t. | d  :— .t. |ld .t. .l. :l. .f. .f.
be - le,     Ba    she    ma - nyana ba tsoe - re li -
d .m :— |l— . :f | m  :— .m |ls .m .m r .f .d
be  -  le,                     li
d. :— .s. |m,  :r. | d.  :— .m. |ld. .m. .s. :f. .f. .l.

s.  :— .m. |l— . :r | d .m :— .r |ld .s. .d :l. .f. .l.
m.  :— .m. |l— . :s. | d .d :— .t. |ll. .s. .l. :f. .f. .f.
ko  -  to,     Ba    se - tla - ka ba bi - le ba i - kon-
m   :— .d |l— . :f | m .m :— .s. |ld .t. .f :r .r .r
ko  -  to,
d. :— .s. |m,  :t₂ | d. .d. :— .s | ll .m. .f. :l. .l. .l.
```

253

```
|s.      :—    |        ||r    :—    .d  |m    :—
                          He,     u ea  kae,
|m.      :—    |  |s. .m.|l.   :—   |s.   :—
ka.               Ha  u ea koo      kae,      ha u ea
|m       :—    |  |m .d |f    :—   |m    :—
|d       :—    |  ||s. .m.|r.  :—   |d.   :s. .m.
```

```
|r      :—   .d ,l. |s.   :— .   |r    :—   .s |m    :—
he,             u ea kae,           He,     u ea  kae,
|l.     :—    |s.      :s. .m.|l.  :—   |s.   :—
koo           kae,   Ha  u ea koo     kae,
|f      :—    |m    :m .d |f   :—   |m    :—
                                              ha u ea
|r.     :—    |d.   :s. .m.|r.   :—   |d.   :s. .m.
```

```
|r  :—.d ,l. |s. :—   .    |r ,r ,r :d ,d ,l. |s. ,m. .— :—
he,     u ea kae,            U ea kae, u se na   koto?
|l. :—  |s. :—   .          |l. ,l. :t. .t. |d    .d :s.
koo        kae,              U se na le  ko - to tjee,
|f  :—  |m :—   .           |f ,f :l ,l |s  .s  :m
                  U se na le  ko  -   to,     U se na le
|r. :—  |d. :m. ,m. .ma. ,ma.|r.    :—   |d.   :m. ,m. .ma. ,ma.
```

```
|l. ,l. ,l. :d ,d ,l. |s. ,m. .— :—   |l. ,l. ,l. :s. ,l. ,l. |s. ,s. .— :— .
Mona ho jakoa ka  koto;                 Eue, ho ja-koa ka ko-to.
|l. ,l. :t. .t. |d    .d :s.           |l.    :—    |m.      :m. .s.
U se na le ko - to tjee,                 ko  -   to?     Mo - na
|f ,f :l ,l |s .s    :m                 |f     :—    |m
ko  -   to,     U se na le               ko  -   to?     Mo - na
|r. :—  |d. :m. ,m. .ma. ,ma.|r.        :—    |d.      :s. .m.
```

```
|l. ,r ,r :d ,d ,r |m      :—   .m |r ,r ,r :d ,d ,l. |s. ,m. .    :— .
Ta-u-ng,  ha Mole-tsa  -   ne,     Ro-na re tlile le    tsona.
|l. ,l. :s. .s. |d ,d  :ta. ,ta.   |l. ,l. :f. ,f. |m. .m. :s. .
Ta- ung,  ha Mo - le-tsa - na, Ro   -na re tli - le le  tso - na.
|f ,f :m .m |s .s :m .m             |f ,f :d .r |m. .m :d .
                                                         tso-na.
|r. ,r. :t₂ .t₂ |d. .d. :m. .d.    |f. ,f. :l. .t. |d        :s. .m.
```

```
|l.      :—    |s.   .d     :m ,d .m ,d |l.     :—    |s.            D.S.
Hom,            hom, hom,                 hom,           hom!
|f.      :—    |m.        :—            |f.     :—    |m.
Hom,            hom,                      hom,           hom!
|d       :—    |d       :—             |d      :—    |d
Hom,            hom, hom,                 hom,           hom!
|f.      :—    |d. .,m.     :s. ,m. .s. ,m.|f.   :—    |d.
```

254

Chabana sa Khomo

Key A♭ S.T.B.S.T.B.

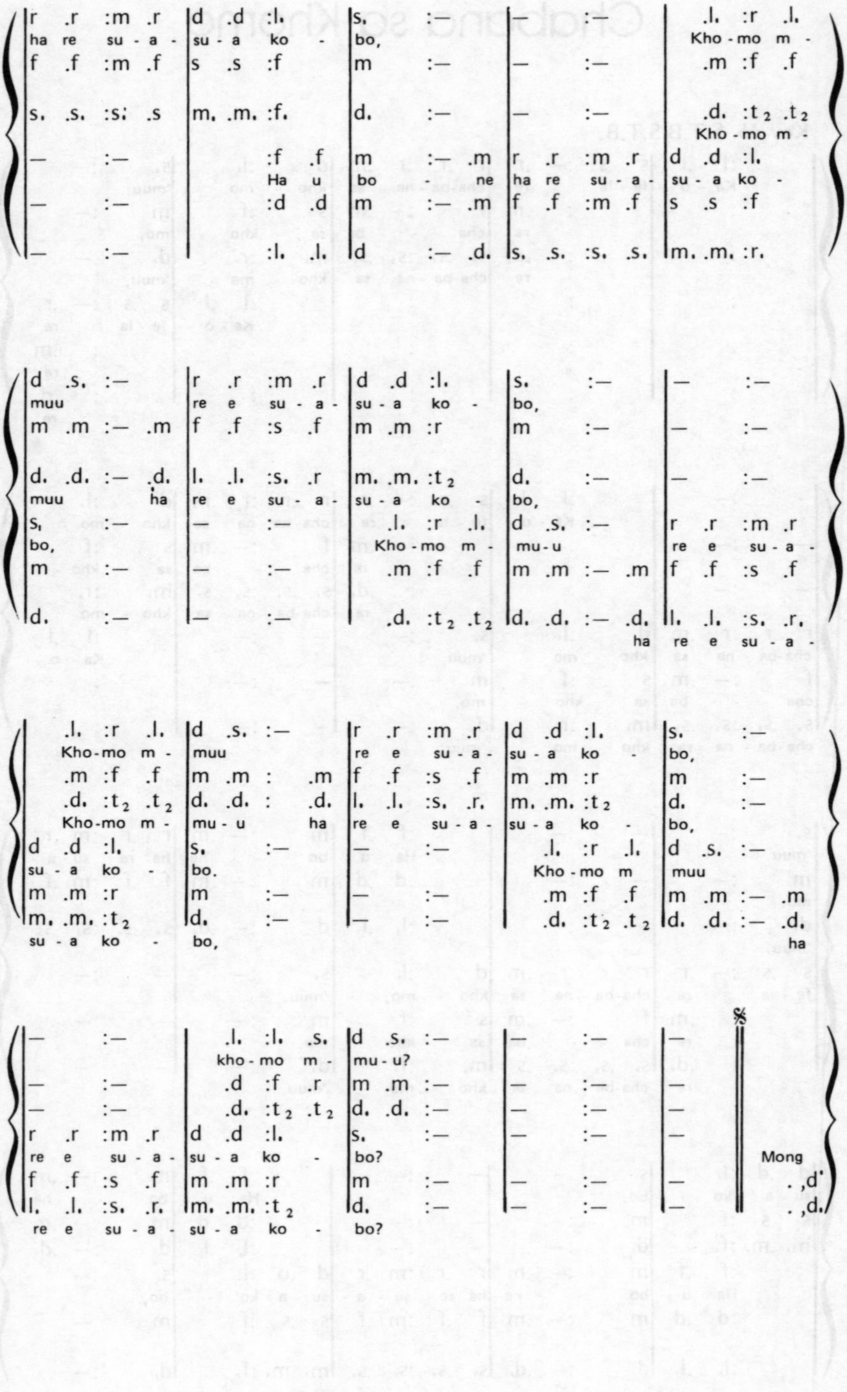
ha re su - a - su - a ko - bo,
Kho - mo m -
Kho - mo m -
Ha u bo ne ha re su - a su - a ko -
muu re e su - a - su - a ko - bo,
muu ha re e su - a - su - a ko bo,
bo, Kho - mo m - mu - u re e su - a
ha re e su - a -
Kho - mo m - muu re e su - a - su - a ko - bo,
Kho - mo m - mu - u ha re e su - a - su - a ko - bo,
su - a ko - bo. Kho - mo m muu
su - a ko - bo, ha
kho - mo m mu - u?
re e su - a - su - a ko - bo?
Mong
re e su - a - su - a ko - bo?

: . ,l.	r . ,l. :l. . ,l.	d . ,d . :l.	: . . ,l.	r . ,l. :l. . ,l.
	Mong 'a ko - bo bo -	hla - ja - na,		Mong 'a ko - bo bo -
s . ,m :m. . ,m	r : — . ,d	m : . ,d'	s . ,m :m. . ,m	r : . ,d
'a ko - bo bo - hla	ja - na,	Mong 'a ko - bo bo - hla	ja -
m . ,d. :d.	: . ,d.	m . ,d. :d.

|d . ,d . :l. | : || : — | : | :s . ,m . — |r .r :d .d |
|hla - ja - na, |
m :	:m	: —	:s . ,m . —	r .r :d .d
na, He,	h'a ntše	h'a	ntše ma - su - a - ko - bo;
: . ,l₂	m. :m.	:l. .	r. :d. ,d. . —	l₂ .l₂ :s₂ .s₂

l. : — .s.	l. :m.	: . ,s.	l. : — .s.	:m.
m, ho —	m, ho -	Ho — m, ho -	m.
f : —	m. : . ,d	m — :d	m. : —	:m.
hom,	hom,	Ho — m,	hom,	He,
r. : —	: . ,d. ,d. . —	l₂ .l₂ :s₂ .s₂	: . ,l₂

l. : — .s.	l. :m.	: . ,s.	l. : — .s.	:m.
m, ho —	m, ho -	Ho — m, ho -	m.
f : —	m. : . ,d	m — :d	m. : —	:m.
hom,	hom,	Ho — m,	hom,	He,
r. : —	: . ,d. ,d. . —	l₂ .l₂ :s₂ .s₂	: . ,l₂

l : —	:	: —	:s . ,m . —	r .r :d .d	:
l : —	:m.	h'a ntše ma - su - a - ko - bo,	H'a ntše
m. :m.	r. : —	:d. ,d. . —	l₂ .l₂ :s₂ .s₂	m. :m.

D.S.

l : —	:	: —	:s . ,m . —	r .r :d .d	— : —	— :
l : —	:m.	h'a ntše ma - su - a - ko - bo.	— : —	— :
r. : —	:d. ,d. . —	l₂ .l₂ :s₂ .s₂	— : —	— :

Appendix C

'HIGHBREAKS', played by Aaron Lebona, is a typical *marabi*. Describing such a musical hybrid in Western terms risks falsifying the African performer's own conception, and implying certain value judgements. Keeping this in mind, we can still see some of the ways in which tonality and part structure reflect traditional principles.

Blacking, writing of ocarina music among South African Venda,[1] introduced the term 'root progression'. He was referring to the short sequence of bass roots and the melody or melodies moving in relation to the tone centre in multipart structures in African music. Rycroft[2] used the concept of root progression as a substitute for 'chord sequence' because African polyphony does not have real chords or a fixed harmonic scheme. Kubik's observation that the 'concept of root progression is projected into tone and chord material of Western provenance' in African popular music applied to *marabi*.[3] Blacking notes that the distribution of the root progression in African music extends 'even in the Tonic-Subdominant-Dominant strumming that one hears on guitars and old pianos'. In addition, the combination of regularly moving roots and unresolved harmonic progressions gives the music 'that quality of perpetual motion, which is a prominent feature of much African music'.[4]

The transcription of 'Highbreaks' reveals a four bar root progression sequence, essentially I–IV–I4⁶–V⁷, with melodic phrases staggered in relation to it. This non-simultaneous entry of parts follows the structure of traditional vocal polyphony. It also appears in Nguni guitar and bow songs. Usually, the main melodic phrase appears to run from the second 8th note of measure 1 to the end of measure 2. It anticipates the harmony of subsidiary phrases following in measures 3 and 4 of the four-bar sequence, which are suggestive of additional parts with separate entry points. The phrase scheme for the first twenty measures is roughly AA" (repeat) BA" (repeat) CC'C'C". On page 262 we see the structure of 'Highbreaks' represented in a cyclical diagram,[5] in which the circle represents two repetitions of the four bar bass sequence.

In the right hand, short solo melodic figures occur at the top of a series of chords that move mainly in parallel motion. These chords are frequently 'irregular'. A typical Western listener might find them disconcerting, since they break the rules of standard harmonic practice, but not in any consistent way that might immediately indicate an alternative musical conception. While parallel motion does occur to some extent in Southern African traditional music, in 'Highbreaks' it may well be that the right-hand chord sequences derive largely from retaining a roughly consistent alignment of the fingers while moving the hand as a whole. The fixed recurrent root sequence, as in

Highbreaks

Leslie Ament and David Coplan

Aaron Lebona

'Highbreaks. . .' ad infinitum.

Highbreaks
(Transcription 2)

Circular transcription
after Rycroft

Recurrent 4-bar bass sequence

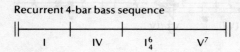

| I | IV | I$_4^6$ | V^7 |

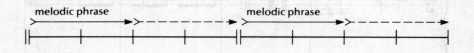

melodic phrase   melodic phrase

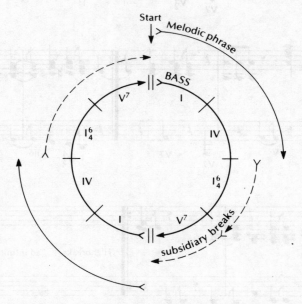

circle represents two repetitions of the 4-bar bass sequence

traditional bow music, limits the choice of melodic notes at any point apart from the prolonged dominant descant, which overrides other features. This variation provides a point of rest in relation to the root progression and staggering of phrases and it is used in both traditional Southern African music and Afro-American forms like jazz.[6] The rhythm has several complex and interesting features. The variety, syncopation, delayed beats, and other elements of early jazz are set to a traditional off-beat pattern and played on two tin shakers filled with pebbles.

Cadence to tonic, found in many melodic phrases in 'High-breaks', is not unusual in traditional bow or guitar songs; it is inevitable if they happen to end regularly at the same point in the bass sequence. Interestingly, cadential endings here (V^7–I) do not occur at the end of the bass sequence, which is on the dominant, but usually at the start of measure 3. In the sixth and seventh four bar sequences, where the melodic phrase is drawn out to cover four measures, cadence occurs in measure 1 of the next sequence. Both placements are anticipated, with syncopation, and provide tonic harmony.

Some variation results from phrase-shifting, and some melodic digressions may include short phrases from other songs assimilated from the player's musical environment. A difficulty in analysing the influences in 'Highbreaks' stems from the possible identity of Afro-American and black South African musical practices. A four-bar chord sequence, ending on the dominant, may reflect a segmentation of progressions commonly found in blues. The exact sequence I–IV–I4^6–V^7 does not occur in traditional South African music, though the two, four, or six bar recurrent root sequence is fundamental to it.

Notes

1 John Blacking, 'Problems of pitch, pattern, and harmony in the ocarina music of the Venda', *African Music*, II, 2, (1959), pp. 21–3.
2 D. K. Rycroft, 'Nguni vocal polyphony', *Journal of the International Folk Music Council*, xix (1967), p. 96.
3 G. Kubik, *The Kachamba Brothers Band*, Manchester, 1974, p. 24.
4 Blacking, 'Problems of pitch', p. 23.
5 D. K. Rycroft, personal communication, 1979.
6 Blacking, 'Problems of pitch', p. 23.

Glossary

abaphakathi (Zulu: 'middle one') In modern usage, people neither traditional nor mission-school educated; those not encompassed by pagan-traditional or Christian socio-cultural systems. Freely, rural or small town African lumpenproletarians.

African A native speaker of a Bantu language who is of reputedly complete African Negro ancestry; things of or pertaining to such people.

amahubo Traditional Zulu regimental anthems accompanied by slow, synchronised gestures and body movements.

amakumsha (Zulu: 'speakers of a foreign language') Implying trickster or turncoat. Used by traditional–rural Africans to identify African proletarians who are neither pagan nor Christian, but who affect European clothing and speech. See *abaphakathi*, 'dressed people', *oorlams*.

amalaita Organised Northern Sotho gangs who terrorised the streets on the outskirts of Johannesburg from shortly after the turn of the century to the Second World War. They also formed teams of competitive street fighters in urban African locations.

AmaRussia Name for urban criminal gangs of proletarian Basotho men that began as vigilante societies and developed into violent social predators. Suppressed by the police in Johannesburg in the 1950s.

Bantu 1) Group to which all Southern African Negro languages belong; 2) obsolete official name for African Negroes in South Africa, disliked by Africans on political and linguistic grounds.

bantustan Colloquial name for areas designated as autonomous homelands for Africans in South Africa. The assignment of citizenship of all Africans to one or another *bantustan*, and the corresponding cancellation of their South African citizenship, is a cornerstone of *apartheid* policy.

black A person both African and so-called Coloured, viewing these two groups as a single category; a thing of or pertaining to African and so-called Coloured people.

Black Consciousness A political movement with roots in the Congress

Youth Movement of the 1940s that uses pride in African cultural values and heritage as a philosophical basis for African political activity and unity. It became the ideological base of political resistance to apartheid among South African black students during the 1970s.

bombing The most traditionally-oriented form of Zulu-Swazi urban proletarian choral music (*ingoma ebusuku*), favoured by migrants and the least Westernised urbanites during the 1940s and '50s. Performances featured explosive choral yells compared by participants to the sound of bombs dropped by aircraft in the Second World War (seen in cinema newsreels).

Bushmen Aboriginal hunter-gatherers of Southern Africa, called San by the Khoi. See *Khoisan*.

cultural broker One who communicates between different sectors of a society; especially, one who mediates and transmits influences from one culture or subculture to another.

culture A broadly shared system of knowledge and its products; a value-oriented system of ideation and symbolic classification and its material and behavioural expression.

Coloured (so-called) An official and colloquial term for people of mixed European, Khoisan, East Indian, Indian, and African descent, or any combination of any two or more of these groups. The majority are of Euro-Khoisan descent, and have constituted a separate social entity since the early eighteenth century. Their native language is Afrikaans. Many Coloureds bitterly resent this term, and prefer to use 'so-called Coloureds'.

Coon Originally, late nineteenth and early twentieth-century American ragtime and blues songs caricaturing blacks in America. In South Africa, American-derived popular African ragtime songs and performers of the early twentieth century, popular with African students. Better known from the Coon Carnival, a New Year street parade in Cape Town of Coloured men's performance clubs in American minstrel costume and blackface, performing Afrikaans and American minstrel and jazz music.

dressed people A term used by English-speaking Africans for African proletarians without Western education who affected Western clothing, speech, and mannerisms to gain social advantage. See *abaphakathi*.

elite The highest stratum of African society in the colonial era; composed mostly of those educated at Christian mission schools, and before the 1950s, identified officially by an exemption certificate rather than by an ordinary pass.

Ethiopianism In South Africa, a separatist or independent African Christian movement based on an ideology of pan-African Christian unity and political and religious independence.

European In South Africa, an official and colloquial designation for people of reputedly complete Caucasian descent. Also, inhabitants of the continent of Europe, and things of or pertaining to European or white people, as in 'European music'. See *white*, *Western*.

famo 1)An urban dance and dance occasion in which Basotho women perform primarily for the entertainment of men, to the accompaniment of neo-traditional *focho* music or syncretic *marabi* music; 2) a form of Basotho proletarian women's song performed at *famo* dances and recounting the singer's life experiences.

focho (Sotho: 'disorder') A neo-traditional style of Basotho shebeen dance music performed with or without vocal accompaniment on the concertina or accordion, and drum. Occasionally accompanies *famo* dance and song.

formal sector Economic enterprises owned, controlled, and managed by the white government or authorised white private business and industry. Also, authorised businesses operated by blacks in a designated black area.

ghommaliedjie (Malay-Dutch: 'Drum-song') A South African picnic song sung in Afrikaans and accompanied by the *ghomma*, a Malay hand drum.

homeboys, homegirls A group of young men or women from the same rural area, residing in a distant town. They frequently form not only a social category, but also a tightly-knit network maintaining ties to the rural area among urban migrant workers.

Hottentot (German: *hotteren-totteren*, 'to stutter'; after the many click sounds in Khoi languages) Obsolete name for aboriginal cattle-herding Khoi (non-Bantu-speaking) peoples of South Africa.

ihubo Traditional song identified with a specific Zulu subclan or sib, performed at weddings and other occasions directly involving the subclan as a corporate group. Also, in Christian usage, a Zulu hymn.

indigenous 1) Anything deriving from Native African society or culture unaffected by outside influence, hence of local African origin; 2) in some cases, forms developed locally by Africans with some unconscious external influence. See *traditional*.

informal sector Unofficial, unauthorised, or illegal economic enterprises, especially those owned or run by blacks in South Africa.

ingoma (Zulu: 'dance, song') In urban areas, a form of dance and song in traditional idiom developed in Zulu male migrant workers in the mines, factories, and domestic service.

ingoma ebusuku (Zulu: 'night music') Any of a range of urban proletarian Zulu–Swazi forms of choral music patterned after African church choirs and combining Zulu–Swazi, European, Afrikaans, and black American performance elements in a syncretic blend. See *bombing*.

jive A term for American-influenced popular urban African dancing accompanied by American or African jazz; also, a term for African jazz, mbaqanga, or simanje-manje music. See *mbaqanga, simanje-manje*.

Khoisan The aboriginal, non-Bantu-speaking, non-Negro inhabitants of South Africa. Colloquially known as Hottentot (Khoi, pastoralist) and Bushman (San, hunter-gatherer).

kwela A form of urban African penny whistle music of the 1950s, syncretically composed of elements of traditional, *marabi* and American swing-jazz music.

lithoko Traditional Sesotho praise poetry.

location Obsolete official and colloquial designation for an authorised African residential area, commonly of two types: 1) government-built and administered suburban rental housing areas for urban workers; 2) a mission-owned or freehold African residential area. See *slum-yard, township*.

lower class The lowest stratum of non-traditional African society; unemployed or employed in the informal sector; lumpenproletarians whose urban status is not officially recognised.

makwaya African sacred or secular choral music developed by mission-educated Africans, combining European classical song and hymnody, American popular song and African traditional choral music.

marabi A pan-ethnic urban African proletarian style of music developed in Johannesburg during the 1920s and '30s. Also a term for the dance occasions where it was performed and for their patrons.

Malay A culturally and to some extent socially autonomous segment of the Coloured population originating in the Cape, descended from East Indian slaves brought to South Africa by the Dutch during the eighteenth century. More broadly, any Islamic Coloured person.

mangae Songs composed and sung by young Basotho boys at traditional initiation schools. Among adult men, performed as an expression of male camaraderie during competitive social events.

mazkanda (Zulu: from Afrikaans; *musikant*, 'musician') Neo-traditional instrumental music; that is, music in traditional idiom played on Western instruments.

mbaqanga (Zulu: 'African maize bread') Originally, the most widely distributed term for popular commercial African jazz in the 1950s that developed from *kwela* and blended African melody, *marabi*, and American jazz. In the 1960s, it came to be applied to a new style that combined urban neo-traditional music and *marabi* (not jazz) and was played on electric guitars, saxophones, violins, accordions, and drums. See *msakazo, simanje-manje*.

mbube See *ingoma ebusuku*.

Mfengu (AmaFengu) (Xhosa: 'destitute wanderers') Nguni refugees from Zulu expansion in the 1820s who settled among the Xhosa in the Eastern Cape and were among the Africans most eager to join Christian mission communities.

middle class The highest stratum of African society, composed of members of the professions, literate salaried employees, and independent businessmen who were educated at Christian mission schools. See *elite*.

migrant Person leaving a rural area to work in an industrial area, especially, an urban labourer who returns after a shorter or longer period, or habitually, to a home in the countryside. Things of or pertaining to such a person.

minstrels Originally, American stage variety troupes representing or caricaturing black American secular and religious popular performance culture. Among urban black South Africans up until the Second World War, song and dance companies presenting American popular song and dance, and approximations of American jazz songs sung in African languages.

modern Twentieth-century urban cultural forms in South Africa.

modernisation Consequences of African involvement in capitalist commercial, agricultural, and industrial labour or Western education in urban or rural areas. See *Westernization*.

msakazo (Zulu: 'broadcast') A term for popular commercial African jazz in the 1950s, used derogatorily by middle-class jazz musicians and listeners. See *mbaqanga*.

ndhlamu A Zulu dance in traditional idiom. Its leg movements have been likened to the sputtering of boiling water. First developed among rural peasants, it remains a favourite dance among Zulu male migrant workers.

ndunduma (Zulu: 'mine dumps') A form of urban Zulu vocal and instrumental *marabi* music. Also, Zulu proletarian concert-and-dance occasions where *ingoma ebusuku* and *ndunduma marabi* music were performed and used as an accompaniment for dancing.

neo-traditional An adjective describing any African expressive cultural form in traditional idiom modified by performance on Western instruments, urban conditions or changes in performance rules and occasions.

Nguni Originally, a language group encompassing the dialects of numerous clans in an area stretching from the Eastern Cape north to southern Mozambique and South Central Africa. In South Africa, the Zulu, Swazi and Xhosa-speaking peoples.

ninevites A paramilitary African criminal organization that resisted white oppression and terrorised the Witwatersrand between 1898 and 1927.

non-European Any person not of reputedly complete European Caucasian descent.

oorlams An Afrikaans term referring to clever, disingenuous Khoi and

Coloured people who had acquired enough knowledge of Western culture to exploit an intermediate position between whites and traditional blacks. Later, proletarian Coloureds and Africans Westernising through Afrikaans rather than English culture. See *abaphakathi, amakumsha, dressed people.*

performing arts Creative musical, dance, dramatic, and oral narrative-poetic skills realised in public performance. See *performance culture.*

performance culture The underlying system of knowledge and the material realisation of performance, as well as the relationships among performers, participants, styles, and occasions of performance. The complex of resources, perceptions, experiences, motivations, and behaviours of people involved in performance events. See *performing arts.*

petty bourgeoisie See *elite, middle class.*

popular Suited or intended for the general masses of people, thus generated and supported by the personal social and economic resources of the general population rather than by public institutional subsidy.

power The recognised ability to control the disposition of persons and things in the environment.

professional performer One for whom performance is the main supporting economic activity. As distinct from 'the professions'; law, medicine, teaching, the ministry, and clerical and administrative employment, professional performers need not be considered middle-class.

proletarian A person who has lost access to land, livestock, capital, or other material means of production, and is compelled to live either by selling his or her labour in the commercial economy, providing services to those who do, or by forms of social parasitism such as crime.

ramkie A small, three- or four-stringed plucked guitar developed by proletarian Cape Khoi after a model brought to S.A. by slaves from Malabar, on which were played blends of Khoi and Dutch folk melodies. In time, also adopted by rural Africans.

reinterpretation The ascription of old meanings to new elements, and the changes in the cultural significance of old forms brought about by new values. The cultural recombination of elements of structure and content present in experience according to their variable meaning in relation to changing systems of value.

sefela A type of melodic recitative poetry performed by Basotho migrant workers containing commentary on the experience of migrant labour.

shebeen An illegal private house of entertainment selling beer and liquor to black people.

simanje-manje A recent style of *mbaqanga* usually featuring a male lead singer and a four-member female chorus, performing blends of urban neo-traditional and *marabi* vocal music backed by Western instruments at stage shows and on records. It is directed specifically at urban workers, migrants and rural Africans.

slumyard An unauthorised urban African residential neighbourhood in an industrial, warehouse or abandoned white area on the fringes of a large town. Most Africans had been removed from such yards by 1939.

stokfel A working-class rotating credit association with entertainment, social and economic functions.

style A distinctive system of meaningful forms or method of treating characteristic elements, organised around the expressive purposes and outlook of its practitioners. Also, complexes of metaphoric symbols, forms and value orientations labelled and recognised by their participants and used to mark identity.

syncretism The blending of resources from different cultures in order to produce qualitatively new forms in adaptation to changing conditions.

tickey draai (Afrikaans, 'turn on a tickey' – a threepence) A Coloured-Afrikaans dance derived from Cape square dancing in which couples turn rapidly around in one spot. Also, a guitar style popular between 1880 and 1930, used to accompany this and other black dances in the Eastern Cape, Kimberley, and Johannesburg.

tonic solfa A simplified system for notating vocal music, using letters and punctuation marks rather than notes and staffs. It is based upon tonic-dominant-subdominant harmony and has been used since the mid-nineteenth century to teach music in African (and Afro-American) mission schools and churches.

township The current official term for urban residential areas where Africans are authorised to rent houses built by the government, subject to the Group Areas Act of 1950. Replaces the obsolete 'location' and does not apply to freehold or slumyard areas. Despite their names, Western Native Township was a location; Prospect Township a slumyard.

traditional Describes forms with no perceptible Western influence, or on occasion, forms perceived by Africans as entirely indigenous and African in origin.

tsaba-tsaba A working-class urban African dance, popular in the 1940s. Also a syncretic style of African urban music blending African melody and rhythm, American swing, and Latin American conga and rumba, used to accompany the *tsaba-tsaba* dance.

tsotsi A term for African street thugs or gangsters, current since the mid-1940s. A corruption of the American word 'zoot suit', it suggested a clever, street-wise petty criminal or hustler, flashily dressed in urban American fashion. Today it applies broadly to any young, potentially violent African urban criminal.

tsotsitaal (*flytaal*; *mensetaal*) The Afrikaans-based urban African proletarian dialect, spoken by all urban African proletarians up until the 1960s, but especially by young juvenile delinquents, some of whom spoke no other language.

tula n'divile A style of urban African proletarian music of the 1920s, blending Xhosa melodies and American ragtime and performed in shebeens, especially in Johannesburg's Western Native Township (a location).

umqhafi A type of urban proletarian Zulu street musician of the 1920s, influenced by American popular culture and participating in neither Christian nor traditional-pagan social systems. See *oorlams*, *abaphakathi*.

urban African A permanent resident of an urban area with no direct connection, or intention of returning, to any rural area.

urban (*performance*) **style** Any style developed in a city and in response to urban residence; being *of* the city and not merely *in* it.

Western Anything deriving from European or American society or culture, regardless of previous origins. Thus black American performance styles are part of Western influence on black South Africans.

white A person of reputedly complete European ancestry.

working class Unskilled or semi-skilled people or families of people ordinarily employed within the formal economic sector.

Zionism Separatist church movements that blend traditional African and Christian belief and ritual, producing new syncretic religious forms. Led by 'prophets', they aid cultural adaptation and revitalisation among African proletarians.

Index

274

275